To the Source
of the Yangtze

Map of China

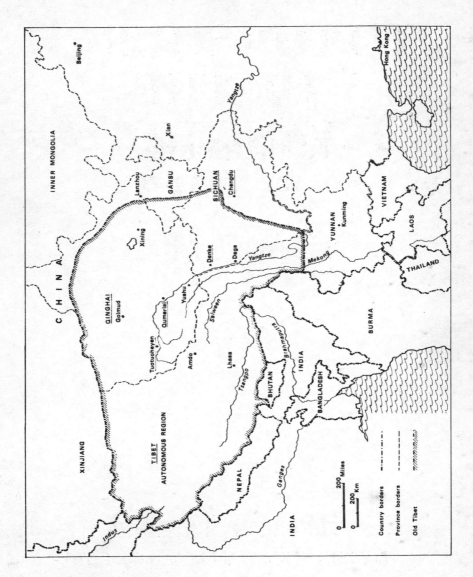

TO THE SOURCE OF THE YANGTZE

Dick Bell

Hodder & Stoughton
LONDON SYDNEY AUCKLAND TORONTO

Extracts from BRITAIN – CHINA used by
kind permission of the Great Britain–China Centre.

British Library Cataloguing in Publication Data
Bell, Dick
　　To the source of the Yangtze.
　　1. China. Expeditions
　　I. Title
　　915.10459
　　ISBN 0-340-53852-X
　　ISBN 0-340-53851-1 pbk

Published by Hodder and Stoughton,
a division of Hodder and Stoughton Ltd,
Mill Road, Dunton Green, Sevenoaks, Kent TN13 2YA
Editorial Office: 47 Bedford Square, London WC1B 3DP

Photoset by Chippendale Type Ltd, Otley, West Yorkshire.

Printed in Great Britain by Clays Ltd, St. Ives plc.

Eileen whom I chose out of
the whole world to be my wife

Joanna my beautiful daughter
who always brings me sunshine

Contents

Foreword

I am grateful for the opportunity to offer a few words of introduction to this fascinating book.

From the start I encouraged the team to go forward with the hovercraft expedition, even when doubts were being raised with regard to financial, political and practical considerations. Consequently, it is a great pleasure to me that the expedition has been such a tremendous success.

This book is both entertaining and informative and I greatly enjoyed reading of this "adventure with a purpose" from its conception to its conclusion. The combination of the adventure, coupled with the medical, humanitarian and Christian purposes make it a unique story.

I have visited China on many occasions and it is indeed a most remarkable country. To have explored so far into its heart, and to have reached the source of its most dangerous and difficult river, is a truly splendid achievement.

I pay tribute to all those who took part in the expedition, but particularly to Dick Bell for providing this excellent account whereby we may all share in the adventure.

The Rt Hon. Edward Heath MBE, MP
House of Commons
27 March 1991

Acknowledgments

My thanks to Mike Cole whose inspiration, tenacity, determination and perseverance made this expedition possible, and whose personal friendship and trust enabled me to share China with him; Nick Cole whose mastery with the pen beefed up my fat, flabby, fatuous text and made it couth, clear, comprehensive and gripping; Juliet Newport, my lovely editor, whose delightful personality, inspiring editing and appalling handwriting have been a constant encouragement to me; Bryony Todman, my second editor, sparring with whom over words, phrases and expressions has been delightful; Clare Meikle, whose determination, courage and grit in typing the text (along with Les and Carolyn Somers) amid the trauma of her illness and excruciating pain has been such an example to me, has made this a very costly book and often reduced me to tears; Barbara Pugsley whose amazing talents and commitment to me in collecting my £5000 contribution will keep me humble all my life; and to the expedition team, without whose friendship I would have been lost, without whose help I could have been killed, without whose prayer I would never have been the man I have become.

Dick Bell

To the Source
of the Yangtze

Introduction

I'm inviting you.

I invite you to climb a mountain with us. I want you to feel as we have felt; to anguish as we have hurt; to look upwards at an impossible task, and to tackle it, with us, just for the sheer fun and exhilaration of doing something no one else in the world has ever done before.

I want you to be with us where we've been:

- to enjoy a beautiful and rare part of our world
- to meet new people with cultures different from your own
- to enjoy the challenge of deprivation, disappointment and disaster
- to swing with us in the ebb and flow of unpredictable problems
- to know the thrill of achievement
- to feel the comfort and companionship of others who care
- and to love living on this good earth.

Shake off your shackles of routine and ordinariness and do something unconventional with us. You'll be different and, I hope, better after our adventure together.

Welcome aboard!

1

1

To Reach Beyond Tomorrow

Fish say, they have their stream and pond;
But is there anything beyond?
                                    (Rupert Brooke)

Ah, but a man's reach should exceed his grasp,
Or what's a heaven for?
                                    (Robert Browning)

'What next, Mike?' I asked.

It was an unfair question. We were sitting in a luxury hotel outside Lima in Peru. We were tired but happy. The team was around us drinking some foul local brew called Lemon Pisco. We were simply relaxing.

The date was November 1982. We had just completed a medical expedition to the weather side of the Andes, involving four six-seater *River Rover* hovercraft, 1000 kms of the river Amazon, hassle with inert bureaucracy and confrontation with bandits. We were now waiting to go to lunch with President Belaunde of Peru.

My question was loaded. I enjoy challenging people. With tongue in cheek I continued, 'I don't mean what's next for this afternoon. I mean, where's the next expedition going to?'

Mike shot me a look which said 'Dick, you've got a firm grasp of the non-essentials' and dismissed the thought in the abundance of that day's problems.

But I was persistent. I dragged him back from where his fertile, organised mind had refocused. Although the question had fun in it, coming at such an irrelevant time,

3

it also had purpose. I saw the vital necessity of renewing Mike's initiative and vision for leading expeditions, as soon as possible after the last one had been successfully accomplished. We had to move forward.

Mike was cautious. 'Well,' he said, 'we've had a suggestion from Zaire to take *River Rover* on to the Zambesi. We've seen the water hyacinth problem here in Peru. There are lots of places all over the tropics where water hyacinth is a thorough nuisance, because it grows so fast and clogs the waterways. And, really, a hovercraft is the only vehicle that can operate successfully in it, because it can fly over it. Let's wait and see.'

'But,' I continued, sensing something behind Mike's words, 'where would you really like to go? Where's your heart really longing to visit?'

'China.' Mike was sure, firm, resolute but low-key.

Mentally I gave the possibility 10 per cent. The doors to China had admittedly been opening up a crack since 1979, only three years before. That was when Deng Xiaoping had started the slow introduction to pragmatic westernisation. The Bamboo Curtain, I thought sceptically, could take another couple of decades to prise apart.

'Why China?'

'I've recently been reading the new reprint of Hudson Taylor's life. This story of a pioneer missionary who set up a mission in China against all odds never fails to thrill me. All the things those amazing missionaries fought and died for surely can't have been wasted? I'd like to see what they saw, go where they went. I believe we could open up China again. I want to follow, in however small a way, the footsteps of those great men. Maybe even penetrate areas they never reached.'

Hudson Taylor, I recalled, started the China Inland Mission at the end of the nineteenth century.

'Have you had any encouragement?' I asked.

'Yes indeed. In fact we were planning to get into China when we received an invitation to come here to Peru. I have already explored the possibility through Ted Heath, our patron. He went to see Mao Zedong a short while ago and raised the possibility of an expedition up the Yangtze.'

'Was that your first contact with the Chinese?'

'By no means,' Mike laughed. 'My first connection was when I got pulled up before the magistrate at Brighton! Didn't I tell you about it?'

My look exposed my ignorance.

'It was June 1980. Tim Longley and I had taken *River Rover* down to the High-Speed Craft Exhibition in Brighton. Two senior members of the Chinese delegation came and inspected it and took a tremendous interest in it – its simple technology and Renault engine. After asking a lot of searching questions, Mr Han Xi-Fu said, "This is an appropriate craft for our rivers." It was then that I first sensed a vision for China.'

'But what about the ticket?'

'A copper booked me for towing malpractice. Apparently in the UK the towing vehicle has to be heavier than the trailer and I was pulling *River Rover* in my Renault. We went to have them weighed and *River Rover* was heavier. When I explained to the magistrate that it was for the Third World he let me off with a fine. I was so thankful not to have my licence endorsed.'

That June exhibition in Brighton had been a turning point in Mike's imagination. So in the September of that year he put pen to paper and floated the idea of an expedition to the Upper Yangtze. He was a Squadron Leader and a Squadron Commander at the RAF officer training college at Cranwell. He wrote to the Deputy Director of Training in the Ministry of Defence, his ultimate boss:

The achievements of the 1978 Hovercraft Expedition to Nepal were a feature of the recent International Hovercraft and Hydrofoil Exhibition. A 6-man Chinese Government delegation, including the Head of Shipbuilding, visited the exhibition and carried out a full evaluation of the expedition and its craft. The possibility of a hovercraft expedition to China was discussed. Such a project would be certain to stimulate interest across the Western World. The idea was well

5

received by the Chinese and has now been referred to Beijing. The British have a long and romantic history of tussle with the Yangtze-Kiang river. The Chinese authorities have never before been so well disposed towards the introduction of 'Western' technology. The planning of such a project across cultural, engineering and political divides has the making of a most searching test of character as well as being coupled to a notable adventure of discovery. Some Chinese participation in the expedition is envisaged.

The aim is to attempt the first ever navigation of the Yangtze-Kiang river of the Republic of China from sea to source (3436 miles) using the unique character- istics of a specially designed lightweight hovercraft to penetrate previously unnavigable stretches. Two new hovercraft are now being developed and built specially to tackle the previously unnavigable stretches of the Yangtze-Kiang. The temperamental character- istics of the great rivers of China are at present a barrier to their use as a means of communication into inhospitable areas of the western frontierlands. The expedition will be using a newly designed craft, capi- talising on the Nepal experiment, to tackle one of the most challenging of the world's remaining river obstacles. The use of the fierce and complex river systems of the Republic of China as a means of regular communication remains one of the most formidable problems of exploration still to be solved. The hover- craft operation would be supported by Gemini craft and inflatable rafts.

But China was not to be in 1982. Instead the hovercraft expedition went up the Amazon in Peru, an extraordinary adventure which has been described in Peter Dixon's book *Amazon Task Force* and filmed on television.

A year after that project something unforeseen and devas- tating had cropped up. Dodnor Marine, the small Christian boat-building company on the Isle of Wight, declared itself bankrupt. It was a shame; it had built the beautiful *River*

6

Rover hovercraft; and now the last craft that had been built was to be auctioned off. No doubt some entrepreneur would buy it cheap, strip it and scrap it. It was a specialist craft. The whole of Mike's missionary and Third World vision suddenly hung on a very thin thread. Did God want this work to continue? Mike was uncertain. Yet in his heart he could not bear to see this precious craft, and craft's worth of spares, go to any old scrap merchant. He took an enormous step of faith. Flinging caution to the winds he went to see the branch manager of Williams and Glyn's Bank in Farnborough. This man had handled the Peru expedition's finances and those of the Nepal trip before it. He had been with Mike through their monetary traumas. Would he help?

He talked it over with Mike. 'Why don't you go to the auction, bid for it and get it cheap?'

'What, and let my Christian colleagues down?' Mike rejoined. 'No. I want to honour them as much as they have honoured us in the past. I don't believe in bleeding people when they are penniless. I would like to pay a fair price for the last craft and the spares.'

'What price?' asked Mr Collins.

'£23,000,' said Mike.

'Hmm, I see. And you want a loan for that amount?' Mr Collins put on his cautious bank manager's face.

'Yes please.'

'What do you offer as collateral?'

'Nothing,' said Mike. 'I don't have anything to offer but my word and my record. We've met all our bills for the last two expeditions and I will place my reputation, my faith and my word on this loan. We will pay it all back in due course.'

'Hmm,' breathed Mr Collins. Banks do not usually part with money on the basis of faith. 'OK. There will be the usual interest of course. I tell you what, I'll loan you a couple of thousand over the top for emergency use. Say £25,000? Will that be all right?'

It was. Mike drove at once to David Rivett, holder of the Dodnor Marine leftovers. David and his colleagues were

7

thrilled with this unexpected help with their problematic insolvency. It was more than they had dared hope for, and much more than an auction could have raised.

But Mike's faith had been previously stimulated. A month earlier he had received a cheque for £5000 out of the blue from a Sussex farmer, Peter Gunner. Ron Collard, an old RAF friend, had given a talk in Peter's church on the Missionary Aviation Fellowship and in passing had mentioned Mike's wish to mount a project to China. Driven by a burden throughout the meeting, Peter felt God calling him to give that year's farming profits to the expedition funds and earmark it 'for China'.

Mike was faced with a blunt choice: either return Peter's cheque or open an account for the China expedition. Peter's generosity and Williams and Glyn's spirit of cooperation tipped the scales of Mike's conviction. He came away with a *River Rover*, a trailer and a ton of extruded aluminium. Now he needed somewhere to house them.

He went for the best. The RAF gave him permission to store *River Rover* in a corner of a hangar belonging to, of all RAF units, the Queen's Flight at RAF Benson in Oxfordshire.

He also came away with a problem. He had to recover £20,000, which had already begun clocking up interest at 11 per cent per annum.

Between 1983 and 1987 he did it the hard way. The testing of his faith was supremely important. There is, was and will be no easy route to blessing. Mike spent his spare time in those four years driving thousands of miles up and down the UK and overseas, giving expedition lectures and selling Peter Dixon's *Amazon Task Force* to help raise money for the loan. He was able to pay off the interest, without touching the loan itself. It was a severe ordeal of faith and tenacity. Was he ever going to recover the money? Meanwhile he persisted in applying to China for permission to take his expedition in.

At that time he had no rationale for going – only that he felt God had called him to it. That was not sufficient: Mike had never embarked on adventure for adventure's sake.

There had always been the underlying motive of helping the poor, the destitute, the oppressed, the downtrodden: that is, adventure with a purpose. We had learnt from Julian Latham in Peru that poverty was not just having no clothes, no home, no food, no money and no possessions; the ultimate poverty was having no initiative, no power and no means of getting above it. Mike's Christian heart could not stop at doing nothing. Neither could it stop at raising money just for challenge. No, without a purpose to do something for the poor it would be raping their land to indulge in adventure.

A cause was suddenly presented to him. He had been meeting his old expedition team and other friends several times a year to share his vision for China. Throughout those years the humanitarian motive was missing. The Christian motive was there. All who met felt that what they were doing was right. But they had to go forward one step at a time.

Keith Richardson and his brother Mel had attended Mike's expedition meetings from the outset. Both had been fascinated with China for years. One day in August 1987 Keith was researching some papers at the Great Britain–China Centre in London, in his role as expedition secretary. An article in the centre's Spring 1987 *Newsletter* caught his eye:

Since 1982, shortly after it resumed its work in China following recognition of the People's Republic of China (PRC) by the United Nations, UNICEF's main activity has been to co-operate with the Chinese government in reaching the ambitious goal of 'immunisation for all by 2000'. UNICEF's work has been directed towards improving the vaccine stability and increasing the frequency of immunisation. In the past, immunisation was only carried out once a year. Vaccines were distributed from the national to local level in a relay. Vaccines need to be kept at specific temperatures to keep their potency. In areas without electricity, ingenious local solutions have often been adopted to keep the vaccines at suitably low temperatures. Among the Buyi people in Guizhou province a young doctor uses pumpkins to transport his vaccine after he has first brought it from town in a Thermos. He cuts a section in the pumpkin and scoops it out. The contents are then replaced by ice, vaccines packed in and the doctor has a safe vaccine carrier for three days enabling him to reach children in the remote mountain areas. In other parts of China the only way of establishing a cold chain has been to limit immunisation to the winter. With UNICEF's support thirty 'model counties' have now been set up in different parts of the country to take into account local cultural, environmental and economic variations. A successful immunisation programme relies on community involvement and appropriate personnel training.

The article hit him with force. Of course! The expedition could carry vaccines to the remote parts of China that UNICEF could not reach; not only that, but it could also carry out the inoculations. All it needed was a large medical team and some method of temperature control.

He brooded over the problem of pumpkins.

Meanwhile he telephoned UNICEF. The name of their agent in Beijing was Stephen Jarrett. The team's first reconnaissance to China was planned for September 1987; could they see him then and suggest the expedition's help in the UNICEF inoculation programme? They could. They did. Stephen Jarrett was thrilled. Bingo! The expedition could forge the missing link in UNICEF's cold chain, and the vaccine project could do the same for the expedition's *raison d'être*.

But pumpkins still bugged Keith. How do you keep vaccines cold for a protracted period? In the West we have refrigerators. But in China without an extensive electricity grid . . . ? What about alternative energy sources? Of course! What about solar-powered refrigerators? Keith rang Philips UK. They passed him on to a company representative in Belgium. Phoning him, Keith discovered from his secretary that he was already in Beijing talking to Stephen Jarrett of UNICEF. The timing was perfect. It seemed that UNICEF was already conducting a trial in Africa.

In the same newsletter of Spring 1987 another article had mentioned the twinning arrangements between various Chinese and UK cities. It was only of passing interest. Or was it? Keith read closer. There, tucked between the big cities, was Leicester. Leicester city was linking with Chongqing, and Leicestershire county with Sichuan Province. His brother Mel lived and worked in Loughborough in Leicestershire. So what? Dr Mel Richardson is a Senior Lecturer in Materials Engineering at Loughborough University and was already involved in the expedition. Was Sichuan important? Certainly. Sichuan was the province from which the expedition wanted to start. That part of the river Yangtze to which no boats can go because of severe rapids (and, by definition, ideal hovercraft country) forms the western boundary of Sichuan. If only they could join the twinning arrangements, then perhaps they could use the connection to accelerate or smooth their way in?

Keith had been in touch with Ken Warren, an American who had led a raft expedition down the Yangtze in 1986. He recommended that, when dealing with China, we should seek assistance from the China Sport Service Company (CSS) in preference to any other Chinese company. This company had a branch in Sichuan which had assisted him, and which was later to prove invaluable to our own expedition planning. Coincidental? None of us believed in coincidence any more.

Keith's persistent ferreting paid enormous dividends in other ways. Just before making the contact with UNICEF he had arranged for Mike and himself to meet Dr Peter Pattison, an Overseas Missionary Society (OMS) associate who had just returned from a medical tour of China. The consequence of their meeting was a letter of introduction to Peter Anderson, Executive Director of Friends of China (FOC) in Hong Kong. Peter is fluent in Mandarin, has led many teams into China, and knows the country intimately. He accompanied most of the reconnaissances, translated

11

the crucial negotiations that governed the formulation of the contract with Sichuan CSS, advised us, redirected us, and helped us in many other ways. He has that unique ability to turn up at the right place at the right time, even when not invited.

What of Keith's brother Mel? What dragged this highly qualified and important man into the team?

Away back, when he was a kid, Mel Richardson had belonged to a Crusaders' class at Winchmore Hill, North London. One of the leaders? Mike Cole. In 1984 Mel found himself a member of the Midlands Speaker Committee for Billy Graham's Mission England. He knew that Mike had recently been to Peru, so put his name forward as a possible speaker for five minutes to 39,000 people in Villa Park Football Stadium in Birmingham. Mike was selected. There he challenged thousands of young Christian men and women to get out into the Third World and transform it by the love of Christ with whatever skills and expertise they possessed. As Mike looked up he saw the Aston Villa motto in the stadium: 'Prepared'. God has already prepared us with abilities; are we now prepared to go?

Mel asked Mike that year, 1984, to speak at a special meeting at his church. A few days after Mike had left, Mel noticed what he had written in the visitors' book: 'Yangtze next stop – we need a plastics expert.'

Mel surrendered.

As he pondered over his new, unforeseen commitment, he realised that much of the work in which he was engaged in his laboratory could be ideally tested on the Yangtze. He was making inroads into glass fibre, carbon fibre and very strong, lightweight metals and composites. These could be used in the fans, decking, propeller ducts and insulation. Moreover special panels could be (and have been) put under both hovercraft to test their performance in the hazardous conditions of temperature extremes, rocks, waterproofing, and twisting loads. These could be monitored during the progress of the expedition, and could be pre-cracked to assess their reliability. It was a golden opportunity. And it was an opportunity that the Vice-Chancellor of Loughborough

University, Professor D. E. N. Davies, wholeheartedly endorsed. Enormous support was given also by Professor G. R. Wray, who unlocked contacts in Hong Kong and made many helpful suggestions.

But there was more immediate work: the expedition was a long way off. Mike asked Mel to share the task of finding sponsors. So he took up his pen and started writing; picked up his telephone and started phoning; took out his car and started travelling. He wrote over 900 letters, made thousands of phone calls, and travelled thousands of miles. Not much paid off: it was sheer hard grind, a thankless task with little return and even less encouragement. With the exception of our major sponsors, nearly all the money and equipment raised was from people giving small and often sacrificial amounts.

Mel attended the twinning meeting between Leicestershire and Sichuan in January 1989. There he was introduced to the Governor of Sichuan, Mr Zhang Haoruo, whose influence on smoothing the negotiations with Sichuan CSS and reducing the cost of the expedition was to prove crucial. Did we not have to hire interpreters and vehicles from CSS and ride their roads? The 2455 km road from Chengdu to Tibet was begun in 1950, soon after Mao Zedong had come to power. The highway was built to provide communications with the newly annexed Tibet and was divided into northern and southern routes. This was not only to ease the flow of traffic, but was also to keep it open in times of earthquake, landslip, ice or flood. It has been described as 'one of the world's highest, roughest, most dangerous and most beautiful roads'. This is the road we would have to travel to get our two hovercraft, plus equipment, to our first base camp high up in the Shaluli Shan mountains at 10,000 feet.

A team was growing. A small group had met four or five times a year since the Peru expedition to design a new hovercraft. Mike absorbed them into his team. Mel, Keith, Peter Gunner and their friends were invited to the meetings, which were now becoming more frequent. Word of mouth drew in others. Drs Bill Gould and David Langley of the Peru team were the first medics to be contacted.

They added their enthusiasm. About thirty people gathered regularly in the Aerodynamics Department of Queen Mary College, London to formulate plans.

The bank manager wrote to Mike. Mr Collins had left, the bank had been taken over by the Royal Bank of Scotland and the new manager, Mr Field, had brought with him a change of style. Although the loan was now under £10,000 he was worried: why had it not been fully paid off? Why was there no collateral? How much longer would Mike require it?

Mike's response was to write to Mr Field asking for the bank to make a donation towards the expedition. Head Office acquiesced and sent £250. But they were still concerned.

The rest of the team pressed Mike for a budget. It was wildly inaccurate in at least one area (what it would cost us to go on the Yangtze), but it came out at £241,330. For a start, every member of the team had to raise £5000. These were early days. The final budget figure was somewhere near £380,000. Just how was this money to be raised? We talked to God about it; after all, he had an endless supply, and an endless ability to move and motivate people. Psalm 50 tells us that God 'owns the cattle on a thousand hills' or, as U2, one of the world's leading pop groups, sings: 'The God I believe in ain't short of cash, mister.'

Mel went to the Plastics Exhibition 'Interplas' at the National Exhibition Centre at Birmingham in November 1987. It was his field, and the university had a stand there. During one of his tea breaks, and to get a bit of much-needed leg-stretching, he wandered over to the ICI Chemicals and Polymers pavilion and asked to see the senior publicity and public relations man. 'May as well go for the top,' he thought.

He was introduced to the Publicity Manager, Philip Champion, and the Group Publicity and Promotions Manager, David Dearden. Mel told them about China and the expedition; about its medical and scientific aims; about money. Their interest was sparked. Just a flicker, of course. A cautious response. But a light had been lit.

14

Much correspondence later, a presentation was arranged at Bowater House in London to senior ICI staff. Mel brought in Dr Bill Gould, our medical genius; Squadron Leader Mike Holdsworth, our newly-appointed accountant and financial wizard; Tony Burgess, our engineering expert; and Graham Gifford, the public relations ace from Griffon Hovercraft (one of whose craft we contemplated taking to China). Eventually ICI promised to sponsor the expedition; it was worth, in cash and kind, £50,000.

Have you ever had an encouraging and enthusiastic letter from a bank manager? After sending them the ICI cheque, Mike did. Well, almost. They have to couch their language in dispassionately professional terms. It was five years to the day since the £25,000 loan had been agreed.

ICI continued to support the project generously under the masterly direction of David Dearden. Two of their best young graduate engineers, Sam Brooks and Anne Hart, and their top apprentice for the year, Chris Fox, joined the expedition team. ICI supplied a multiplicity of equipment from its vast stores, as well as giving us the much-needed cash. Their finance paid for the *River Rover* with all its modifications, and we were delighted to put ICI's name on it.

We were taking two hovercraft with us, and were still short of money. The other one, the Griffon Hovercraft 2000 TDX, was to cost us £122,000 and this was a big hurdle to jump. How would this money come in? The story is one of those extraordinary ones that only seem to occur in fiction. God doesn't make fiction fact; he makes faith fact.

Mel Richardson had got his degree and PhD at Brunel University. In September 1988 some of his former colleagues decided to have a reunion in Abingdon. During the evening someone recalled that Mel was a Christian and used to invite them along to the Christian Union. Questions like 'Are you still a Christian?' and 'What are you doing now?' arose spontaneously. So Mel told them about the hovercraft expedition to the Yangtze. One of them pricked up his ears; it was just the sort of thing his firm in Brussels could benefit from. His name was Roger Carroll.

The firm he worked for? Neste International.

This company, unknown to most British people, is very well known in Scandinavia. Neste International is the Finnish State Oil Company (the word *Neste* is Finnish for 'liquid'). It was founded in 1948 and now consists of seven major sub-divisions, each financially independent under the main company. The sub-division for which Roger worked was Neste Chemicals. Manufacturing petrochemicals and polyolefins (a type of plastic), it was founded in 1980, turned over $1370 million in 1988, and is now the largest chemical company in Europe, operating between Finland and Lisbon. Scandinavian people, perhaps because of their Viking history, seem to be very interested in acts of adventure; they are keen to associate business with aid and do not see humanitarian projects as a waste of time or money. Roger knew this well. He also knew that China was welcoming western technology, and felt that his company could benefit from the huge Chinese market that was opening up.

Roger floated the idea to his company. It sank like a lead balloon. But he persisted, so they appointed Patrick Ellis – another Englishman – to look into the possibility and write a paper on it. He came to the public presentation sponsored by ICI on 15 November 1988 at Bowater House, and not only doubled his enthusiasm but declared himself a Christian. Yet still no one in his company responded to his plea for sponsorship. In the end, someone said, 'If you want to get anywhere with this, you'll have to talk with Jukka Viinanen' (he was the Executive Vice-President of Neste Chemicals). Patrick had no idea how to contact him.

At Christmas 1988 Patrick was on his way home and was sitting gloomily in Helsinki Airport. Because he is a member of the Finnair Club he was able to sit in the VIP lounge. He was alone. Helplessly, he decided to pray for an interview with Mr Viinanen.

The door opened and Mr Viinanen walked in! His aircraft had been delayed, and Patrick had fifteen precious minutes to tell him about the expedition and the need for £100,000. Mr Viinanen listened quietly, thanked Patrick, and then had to excuse himself; his aircraft was about to leave. As he reached the door, he turned and said, 'That sounds a good

16

idea. It's just the sort of thing Neste ought to do because of the humanitarian aspect. Send me a report.' Patrick sat back aghast. But very thrilled.

He spent a hectic Christmas trying to piece together a long, detailed paper for Mr Viinanen. It did not gel. In the end he decided to make it as simple and uncomplicated as possible, and sent it off.

Soon a telephone call came back from Mr Viinanen's secretary. 'The project's on; you have the money.' Patrick rang Mel.

Shortly afterwards Patrick received another telephone call, this time from Jukka Viinanen himself. 'The £100,000 needs support from other sections of the corporation. There are PR and other expenses that I do not think should come out of our sponsorship. Try Communications. Ring Atti Aho, Communications Vice-President. We need him on our side.'

Patrick was stuck. He had never met Mr Aho and did not feel comfortable about going direct to him. He mused on it for a few days. Then, one day, he was annoyed with himself that he had done nothing, and in his office, he simply asked God for his help. While he was praying a knock came at his door. The man there introduced himself.

'I'm Atti Aho. There are some things I want to discuss with you.'

Patrick swallowed his amazement at this second miracle as he made a cup of coffee for them both. Business matters over, Patrick introduced Mr Aho to the hovercraft expedition. He told of the Chemical involvement and sponsorship and suggested that Communications might like to fund all the PR, the specialist clothing, and medical equipment. Mr Aho was intrigued. He would call back.

He did. They would sponsor the expedition for £50,000. Patrick rang Mel. Again.

But all was not over. Nothing was on paper. All was by word of mouth and trust.

And then it happened. The next bombshell to hit the world, and particularly the expedition, was the shooting of thousands of students in Tiananmen Square on 4 June

17

1989. Up to that point we were glad to avoid political ties. Now they were unavoidable.

Neste International Corporation was worried. They did not want to be seen to be intricately involved with China post-Tiananmen Square. They expressed their fears. Mike asked if they were coming to London at any time and a date was set. Neste booked a room at the Sheraton Hotel near Heathrow, and Mike and Mel 'resold' the project to the chiefs of our major sponsor, stressing that the welfare of the children and the minority peoples of Tibet were our goal, and that this need had not been altered by the activities of their political masters.

The contract was signed, and we all breathed a sigh of relief.

'That day' is the way Chinese people talk about 4 June 1989. Neste's threatened retreat was not the only result of 'that day'. Mike's job became far more difficult and more political. He had to be diplomatic and wise in his answers, especially in Hong Kong, hyper-sensitive about the handover to China in 1997. Also, all open support from the British government dried up. The Overseas Development Administration had matched us pound for pound when we went to Peru. Now, despite letters to and from Lynda Chalker, Chris Patten and John Major at the Foreign Office, no financial aid could be forthcoming. But on the positive side, Chinese interest sharpened considerably – they wanted to be seen to be encouraging western involvement. Fax and telex communications took twenty-four hours now, having taken two or three weeks before.

Our task, above all things, was to help the poor and the children of 'Tibetan' China. Our humanitarian goal could not and should not be influenced by political pressure. We deliberately chose to go to a part of China and Tibet that was untouched by technology, unaffected by the gradually increasing standards of living experienced elsewhere in China, and not directly influenced by political happenings 1500 miles away. They were people in need, and that was our pressing burden and driving force.

Ted Heath was very encouraging. Mike wrote asking for

his astute and experienced view. 'I think you are right to go quietly forward and see how the events develop,' was his advice of 17 August 1989. We pressed on with our efforts for fund-raising and sponsorship.

Mike was beginning to be struck by the similarity between the expedition he had mounted to Peru in 1982 and this one. Eight years back the political crisis was with Argentina and the Falklands. Now, the political problem was how to be involved in China after Tiananmen Square. Then, the mountain of opposition that he had to climb by faith was huge; now, the mountain was just as great, and required just as much faith. Mike knew that when negatives and difficulties start to mount up, that is precisely where God's overruling power shows itself best. He became even more convinced that this project had divine approval.

Pam Phethean lives outside Nottingham and works for Marckom Publicity Group. She helped Roger Carroll and Mel in the process of gaining Neste's sponsorship. She held another important key.

'Is there anything else you want for your expedition, Mel?' she asked casually one day.

'Fuel!' came Mel's quick response.

'Hmm. Yes, of course. I'll see what I can do.' Pam had Exxon (Esso in Britain) on her books, and made contact at a very high level with them. The problem with standard issue fuel in China was that the diesel was dirty and the petroleum very low octane. The Renault 21 turbo engine we were putting into *River Rover* drank high octane leaded petrol – and nothing else. So we needed a good high-grade input from a reputable company. We got it from Exxon, who gave the task to the PARAMINS Division of Exxon Chemical Company. They promised to put down as much fuel as we could handle, in any location we specified in China, in any type of container we wished. Free!

We hastened delightedly to put their name in big bold letters on our hovercraft.

So far, we had as our three main sponsors three of the world's largest chemical companies: Neste Chemicals, ICI Chemicals, and Exxon Chemicals. They are competitors in

19

their particular field (chemicals and polymers), but were willing to be cooperators in our lifeline to the isolated under-privileged of remote western China.

Mike already owned *River Rover*. (Rather, the bank owned it; Mike was merely claiming possession.) But it was not ready to go to China. At least two things were lacking. First, the original Renault 20 engine could not cope with altitude. Secondly, the controls needed to be improved to tackle the mighty Yangtze, *River Rover*'s toughest challenge yet.

Take the engine first. Aviators will know that you cannot take a normally aspirated petrol engine up high without doing something about the density/temperature problem. Normally they screw superchargers on, and use variable pitch propellers. The decrease in power of an internal combustion engine is proportional to the decrease in air density with altitude. So we looked around for an air compressor or something similar. The Renault 20 engine had been specially chosen for the Peru vehicles because it was the only 2-litre engine with an aluminium block, and keeping weight to a minimum is all important in a hovercraft. So we turned naturally to Renault again, and discovered that their continued update had produced the computer-controlled, turbo-charged Renault 21. Mike had a go in the car, and concluded that its power and acceleration were Formula 2 standard. The R21 power/weight ratio was even better than that of the R20. We would go for it. Nigel Pool bought a Renault 21 car and said we could steal the engine from it while Renault were coming up with their gift engine.

Nigel Pool was Managing Director of Herbert Pool Ltd, a firm that specialises in hiring out high capacity electrical generators and other ancillary equipment. A quiet, retiring young man, delightful to talk to, Nigel's genius is organisation. And generosity. He loaned us premises at his site in Fleet, Hampshire, helped to pay for members of the team, and gave untold quantities of equipment and tools.

Then we had to find some people to work on *River Rover*. Tim Longley was the first obvious choice. He was its designer. He had been working in industry, but now we wanted him full-time on *River Rover*. He had been resisting this 'call' for many years, but now Nigel Pool offered to take him on full-time, pay him and give him a pension, and dragged him up from Gosport to Fleet.

Then there was Neil Smith. This whizz-kid had been a student of Dr Jan Wright's, studying aerodynamics at Queen's College, London during the Peru expedition. (Jan had been a member of the Peru expedition.) Neil did his thesis on hovercraft. He was reluctant to come out of a very good job in industry, but the lure of China probably tipped the balance in our favour. Neil is a computer buff, and wrote his own programme on the Computer Aid Design (CAD) software for skirt and hull design for hovercraft. The CAD software and accompanying computer had been loaned until the start of the expedition by Calcom. His aerodynamic background came to the fore as he considered the control limitations the *River Rover* had – the second of our problems with the craft. The upshot was that Tim and Neil considerably redesigned the elevon and rudder system in *River Rover*, making this unique (and patented) hovercraft control system almost as precise as a car on the road – or certainly as a boat in water. The elevons are, basically, plates positioned behind both fans that go up when either pedal is depressed. They make the craft bank and turn. When the control problems had been solved they started to look at the skirt. *River Rover* had a lot of trouble getting over hump (the displacement wave pushed up ahead of a hovercraft), especially in shallow water (see Appendix C). As Neil put *River Rover*'s skirt on his CAD, they discovered that there had been a simple mistake in the manufacture of that particular skirt. They modified it. That craft skips around the water now like a ballerina.

We had a third person. Steve Moody is a car and motor-spanner ace who used to run his own garage. He felt called into the expedition, left his job, and, together with his wife Rachel, moved down to Fleet. It was a great step of faith for them both. Their church in Bristol felt they should support them financially, so began giving sacrificially to maintain them on the team. To Steve we owed the wizardry of removing and installing the engines and the new fan and control system, and putting in all the electronic and other modifications necessary for this testing expedition. Mike has always made a ruling that he would not take any person with him on an expedition who had children under five. Steve's baby boy, Peter, was two. But his wife Rachel pleaded with Mike to let her husband go, although she was now expecting their second baby. Mike surrendered. Steve not only worked on the hovercraft beforehand, but worked on it throughout the traumas of China.

What of the second hovercraft, the Griffon 2000 TDX?

Griffon Hovercraft is a modest firm, designing and making small to medium size hovercraft – because they believe in them. They have had an enormous struggle persuading others that amphibious hovercraft have a place in this world that no other vehicle can fulfil, and have designed their craft cleverly. Each one is custom-built to suit the client, but using the same design. The hull can be built long or short, depending on the number of passengers or quantity of freight, and the appropriate power of diesel engine installed. It was a tried and tested design. Mike went down to 'have a go'. He found it easy to control. It could lift 22 passengers or 1 ton of freight, and was just what we needed to supplement the frisky lightweight of the *River Rover*. John Gifford, the Managing Director, was very patient and flexible as he came to sell his craft at our team meetings, and we went for it. At £122,000 it was another gamble of faith. We put down £5000 as a deposit and placed the order. The craft that would prove to be the workhorse of the expedition was eventually paid for by Neste International. We called it, in English and Chinese, *Neste Enterprise*, and it was handed over to us by Mr Thomas Franck of Neste Chemicals on 15 September 1989 at Hythe Marina. Sir Christopher Cockerell, the inventor of hovercraft, came for the ceremony. To accommodate the altitude problem, Deutz Engines of Germany supplied us with an 8 cylinder 2000 cc diesel, rather than the normal 6 cylinder 1500 cc. They gave us the engine free. And they paid £3000 towards the trials at RARDE. The Royal Armament Research and Development

Establishment at Chertsey is the only place in the UK with an altitude chamber big enough to accommodate hovercraft. We took both *River Rover* and the Griffon up to 4030 metres (13,097 ft) in the chamber. There was no problem with the Griffon. *River Rover* developed an air lock in the fuel lines, which we solved by pressurising the fuel tanks. The thrust that both craft produced at altitude was very encouraging.

Both vehicles were (only just) fit and ready for the expedition by January 1990. We eased them into three containers provided free of charge by Nigel Pool, who owns Northern Containers. Ben Line shipped them out to Hong Kong for us, which was terrific.

We had to design a new trailer for the Griffon. One of our reconnaissances to China had travelled the road to Denke, our first base camp. That road took in five mountain passes at over 15,000 feet, and was one-lorry wide, so that vehicles travelling south-east went in the mornings, and those travelling north-west went in the afternoons. There are no passing places. The new trailer had steerable, removable bogey wheels front and rear to enable it to get round the hairpin bends. Tony Burgess, Peter Gunner and Steve Moody decided to set the design width of the bogeys at 7 ft 6 in rather than 8 feet, the width used by the Chinese trucks. It was a shrewd move. At 7 ft 6 in the bogeys just fitted into the shipping container without requiring dismantling.

We had to have a number of reconnaissances into Hong Kong and China; five in all. The purposes were many.

We had to negotiate with Sichuan CSS (since renamed the Sichuan Mountaineering Association, SMA) for the main contract – what they would provide for us and what i would cost.

Drs Bill Gould and Rachel Pinniger had to liaise with UNICEF in Beijing, with Mr Zhou Xijie, Deputy Director of the Sichuan Provincial Health Bureau, and with the Epidemic Prevention Institute.

John Whatmore, ex-Director of Religious Broadcasting at Central TV, had to talk with Sichuan TV and Central China TV in Beijing about the television and media coverage for the expedition.

Dr Mel negotiated with Chengdu University of Science and Technology (CUST) and the Polymer Research Institute (PRI) about lectures, seminars, assignments and testing samples. Mel was thrilled when Professor Zhongren Lin approached him with a copy of a book in Chinese that was widely used in universities and colleges as a textbook. Mel looked at the title, *Polymer Engineering Composites*. It was his own book! Unknown to him, they had translated it into Chinese and were using it extensively.

We also needed to look at the river. The SMA guides took our engineers across this 'interesting' road, and opened our eyes to the appalling logistical task confronting us even to transport our expedition to Denke, which we selected as our first base camp. It was 1152 km of very testing, narrow, precipitous mountain road, punctuated by passes up to 16,000 and 17,000 feet, complete with mud, ice, snow and hairpin bends. At least they were able to choose Denke; the villagers seemed thrilled at the prospect of hosting such a unique expedition. It was, moreover, the only decent place from which an expedition such as ours could operate.

Lastly we had to negotiate with many people in Hong Kong, our lifeline to the West. ICI's Hong Kong boss, Lucas Wong, was very generous with office facilities, fax, telex, and photocopying. He gave us very shrewd counsel as we struggled to finalise the wording of the contracts.

What if either we or SMA felt unable to agree on the contract details? We very nearly did not. We used the five reconnaissances to clear as much of the contract negotiations as we could prior to our arrival in the republic. The Chinese style of bargaining is tentatively to agree on something, take discussions up to the last minute, and then slip in a further clause. They believed that, in the frustration of delaying tactics, we westerners would shrug our shoulders, sign the paper and run to catch the aircraft. But we had been briefed. They took our liaison team up to 1.30 a.m., knowing they had to leave at 6 a.m., and squeezed in a clause which said, 'You pay 15 per cent to the SMA for all money spent in China.' That would mean that, if we paid money to Sichuan TV (nothing whatever to do with

24

the SMA), we would have had to pay 15 per cent over the top. Our bill would instantly leap a further £30,000! No way! Our team said, 'No contract,' and walked out. Lucas Wong's wise advice when dealing with the People's Republic of China (PRC) had been 'Everything is negotiable before contract; once signed, nothing is negotiable'.

But we held two trump cards in all these trying negotiations. The first was that Mr Zhang Haoruo, the Governor of Sichuan Province, was on our side. He had been to Leicester on the Twinning Committee and had a good grasp of our humanitarian and aid motivations. At one point early on he had had to rebuke the SMA for their ludicrous money demands (nearly half a million pounds), and things became much more sensible thereafter. Nevertheless, the final cost of going to China was far more than we had bargained for or expected.

The second trump card was Australian. Dr Graham Zerk, an Australian missionary on the Fly Delta in Papua New Guinea, had asked Mike if we could take a hovercraft out there for their river. Mike went to reconnoitre it and found that it was absolutely ideal hovercraft country. They were itching to have us there, and soon. Yesterday, even. We told the SMA that if they were not going to play ball with us, and were going to procrastinate, then the whole show would be off. We would go to Papua New Guinea where they really wanted us.

Mike signed the Letter of Intent during the final 'recce' in early December 1989, just three short months before we were due to arrive. We had very nearly diverted to Papua New Guinea.

By this time our aims for the China expedition had altered. Nothing is fixed in this game and flexibility became a way of life. It kept us all humble too; most of our good ideas were filed in the waste-paper basket. Mike's original plan of travelling up the whole of the Yangtze, mooted to the RAF in 1980, had to be reassessed. It was decided to concentrate on the 800 miles of the headwaters, and to explore this area in support of the isolated Tibetan minority peoples. In the early years of this century the Royal Navy positioned squadrons of gunboats to patrol the lower 800 miles of the Yangtze. Now, in peace, with a very different motive, and at a different time in Sino–British relationships post-June 1989, we sought to tackle the headwaters of this great river for the first time in history, using appropriate British technology and Christian faith.

Tony Burgess has a sharp and precise mind. He is a well-qualified engineer with shrewd business acumen. He had been involved with the hovercraft expedition to Nepal in 1979. We sent him on as many of the 'recces' as we could (by this time he was working for us full time, so it was easier to insist on his going), because not even the Chinese could pull the wool over his eyes. He was too shrewd. As he drove up the roads to decide which location we should have for our base camps, he counted the kilometres, and copied the Chinese local maps. He noted the height and number of passes, measured the width of the road when it became narrow, and even wrote out for us a menu of edible and non-edible local Chinese dishes.

Plotting out the river from the best available maps, he worked out the exact position and height of every river confluence for the hovercraft operation, analysed the fuel requirements for both *Neste Enterprise* and *ICI River Rover*, and decided where we needed to put in fuel dumps. Then he calculated the number of vehicles required for the whole task, their location at any one time, their movements, the mileage for the vehicles between base camps 1, 2 and 3, and their cost to the expedition. I think we ought to rename him Spok – after the Star Trek Vulcan. I would hate to have to ask him to do it all again. Which, in hindsight, we did three times!

During Tony's research he discovered that the geographical location of the source of the Yangtze is in doubt. According to the RAF aviation maps we were looking at, there was another tributary that looked as long as the 'official' one. Perhaps – what a dream – we could pinpoint a new source, and declare the Yangtze to be the second longest river in the world?

We had done all we could. We had put together a team, an aim, the money, the hovercraft, and the organisation to go with it all. Now we needed to launch the expedition. At the Barbican in London on Friday, 16 February 1990 we gave a public presentation before Admiral of the Fleet, Lord Lewin, Lord Hunt, Roger Sims, MP, and other dignitaries. The main party left for Hong Kong four days later.

So we were ready. At least as much as we could be at that stage. The rest? The team was well suited to the rigours of change, and ready to tackle hard work, deprivation, diplomacy and disaster. What was more, we were a team. We had had a weekend in the YMCA training centre at Lakeside by Windermere. Tony Brindle, recently returned from Everest, jammed us through as much discomfort as he could, and declared that we were a remarkable set of men and women, well adjusted to tackling the demands and the unexpected obstacles ahead.

2

Real Success is Underneath

Orare est laborare, laborare est orare. (To pray is to work, to work is to pray.) (Anon. Ancient)

God has given us a series of breathtaking opportunities cleverly disguised as impossible situations. (Anon. Modern)

I was in Hong Kong reading a book. Not any old book. It had been pressed into my hands by at least three other members of the team. As usual I was 'a dollar short and a day late'. Others had, as it were, ploughed the ground before I had even hitched up my mule.

'It's very good,' Gwyn Davies-Scourfield told me. 'You really have to read it.'

'Where do I get it?' I enquired.

'Lots of book shops down town have it.'

'Any chance of seeing the relevant bits?' I asked.

'Sure.'

But before I had a chance to go and buy one Sarah Mather had lent me her copy. Sarah is the very attractive daughter of army parents. Her untamed heart drove her to orienteering, skiing and multiple outdoor pursuits.

The book was *Exploring the Yangtze, China's Longest River*. It had appeared in the UK shops about four days before I had left. I had been told about it then. Now it was here, and in my hands.

The author, How Man Wong, was a photographer for the *National Geographic Magazine*, and the book consisted of a myriad beautiful colour photographs of the area around China's longest river from its source to Yibin, 3496 km

28

downstream. I started to glance through it. South of Yushu, much of it was delightfully illustrated and an engaging adventure. But that was not my interest. What was there north of Yushu? I hurriedly read on. As I read, I became more and more excited.

How Man Wong revealed that the *first* time that anyone had definitely researched and found the source of the Yangtze was only as recently as 1976! Chinese historians in the Ming dynasty (1268–1644) had noted that the 'Great River' originated in northern Sichuan where the Min river, a large tributary of the Yangtze, began its flow. The famous sixteenth-century geographer Xu Xiake had learned that the Jinsha (another name for part of the Yangtze) could be considered to be the upper reaches of the Yangtze itself.

But in 1976 there was a Chinese scientific expedition, sponsored by the government, that set out to determine the source. Two years later, in 1978, further scientific research was carried out to confirm the earlier findings. They concluded that the Yangtze river started from a glacier coming off Mount Geladandong. The source position was 33 23'N, 90 56'E. The glacier, How Man Wong discovered from the Tibetan nomads, was called Jianggendirn – the Glacier of Wolves. He went there to see for himself, and produced detailed information for the likes of us. His mode of transport was a Toyota Landcruiser, yak and legs.

However, How Man Wong was not fully satisfied. So he went by Landcruiser and foot to another location, a spring on the side of a hill called Jari, at 32 42'N, 94 36'E. This was the source of the stream called Guangzhugou, which led into a river called the Dam Qu, which in its turn flowed into the Yangtze. It was some 348 km in a straight line east of the 'official' source. How Man Wong did some research into it, and estimated that this spring watered a tributary that was 60 km longer than the source itself. He then came to the startling conclusion that the Dam Qu is far more likely to be the source of the Yangtze than the stream from Geladandong's glacier.

I sat there mulling this over, a strange mixture of excitement and wonder enveloping me. What could we do?

29

Could we go to both sources? How could we measure distances accurately from a hovercraft? Were we here at just the right time to confirm or challenge either of the two source claims?

What I knew was this: there had been only six expeditions to the source of the Yangtze since 1976, and none before. No one, but no one, had gone *up* the river against the flow. We were going to be the first, the very first! What an incredible privilege. Excitement shivered through my body. I had never been first to do anything in my life before. This was unbelievably exciting. I had not quite realised before just how significant our expedition would be.

I shared it with Gwyn. He smiled. He'd read the book and been struck with the same thoughts. To have a *hover-craft*, a vehicle that could surmount the rapids, skim across shallows, laugh at sandbanks, sing sweetly over marsh and tundra – it was the only craft in the world that could actually travel upstream or down at will and not get bogged down or break its prop or demand an airfield. Ken Warren had led a raft expedition down from the source in 1986. A Chinese expedition had also done this the same year. A young Chinese student, Yao Maoshu, had rafted solo from the source, but had capsized below Yushu, and had died. It was a brave attempt. Ken Warren had lost a couple of his team on his expedition, and so had the Chinese rafters. As far as we knew they were the only ones to have travelled down the whole upper reaches of the river afloat. The Chinese expeditions of 1976 and 1978, as well as How Man Wong, had all used vehicles, animals and foot. Here we were: number seven, and maybe better equipped to do it all. We hoped we would never have to use our feet!

Mike mentioned in passing one day, 'If it's only a few kilometres from the source to Tuotuoheyan, and we run out of gasoline, we could hump the fuel ourselves.' 'Use yaks?' someone pleaded. How Man Wong had reckoned it to be 317 km! I reckoned 253; but it was still a long way.

Gwyn smiled again. He would not mind lugging fuel for many kilometres. He was our logistics leader, an army captain who had resigned from the Royal Green Jackets

30

just for the expedition. He was a calibre man; his father, a brigadier, was one of the few men in the Second World War to escape more than once from Colditz. Gwyn was the same breed. He had flown into Hong Kong with a team at the beginning of February. He put Duncan Hanton on to provisions, and Sarah Mather on to China travel and visas. First of all he looked into accommodation for the team. Lieutenant-Colonel Bruce Watson at HQ British Forces Hong Kong was a member of the Officers' Christian Union (OCU), as was Gwyn. He was prepared to stand as sponsor for our civilian team (albeit with strong service connections), and we were given functional and cheap accommodation in the Transit Block of Osborn barracks in Kowloon Tong. We were allowed to place our three 40 ft containers in the fire section yard at Osborn, and engineer both hovercrafts from there.

Gwyn's second contact, Major John Pentreath, was in the same regiment as Gwyn, so knew him well. Through him we were able to borrow our base camp equipment through army stores – tents, tables, chairs, latrines, shovels, stakes, lighting and so on. Sergeant Jim Mudie, from the tried and tested REME (Royal Electrical and Mechanical Engineers), was the only serving man in our expedition, so he had to sign for all the equipment we had borrowed. Good old Jim! Coming on this expedition could be quite a sacrifice if we sank a loo, a tent got eaten by a yak, or we burnt the chairs to keep us warm at −20°C.

Gwyn and his team had other important duties. They had to make sure the organisation for the press conference and public exhibition in Hong Kong from 1 to 3 March was slick. They also had to complete an inventory of equipment as cheaply as possible, because we had limited funds.

Lucas Wong, head of ICI (China), and his secretary Cathy Ng, continued to be as good as their word. They vacated an office and a telephone for us, where all our expedition activities were centralised. In charge of their office was Bondi Fung. How is it possible to have someone so efficient in such a helpful and gracious package? She not only seemed to run ICI (China), but most of Hong Kong as

31

well. Beautiful, brilliant Bondi: without her our lives would have been far less efficient and far more shabby.

Gwyn went to church in HMS *Tamar*. He met there the Chief of Police Radio Procurement, Stuart Read, who directed him straight to the firm with whom he dealt in Hong Kong, Waysun Communications Ltd. Gwyn made his way there, asking if they would like to sponsor us for three high frequency (H/F) radios for our expedition. No sir. Not interested. No amount of persuasion worked. Then Gwyn noticed a picture of a racing car with Waysun Communications' name on its side. Did they sponsor it? Yes.

'We have a sports engine in our *River Rover* hovercraft,' he said. 'It's a Renault 21 turbo, used for very high performance saloon-car racing. Are you interested in sponsoring us for that?'

The man's eyes lit up. He certainly was. He called in his publicity partner.

'What can you offer us in return?'

'We're going to put *ICI River Rover* on display in front of City Hall on Hong Kong Island from 1 to 3 March. You can have your name on it, and you can get as much publicity from it as you wish.'

It was done. They had loaned us three Icom IC-M700 H/F voice radio sets, one for each hovercraft and one for base camp; we particularly required them for emergencies. They are worth £3500. Waysun will listen out, they said, on frequency A1 throughout the expedition, just in case there is anything in Hong Kong that we need.

Now we had to put together our huge publicity exercise. When Mike Cole and John Whatmore came out, we had no definite VIP who could launch our exhibition. It so happens that the ADC to the general in charge of Hong Kong military is a Christian, and an OCU member. Gwyn talked to him. The ADC talked to his general. General Duffell was interested in helping, but his schedule was too tight and would not fit into ours. That was no problem to Mike. We would alter ours to fit the general's. And so it was done. The general was as delighted to honour us as we were to honour him.

32

Hong Kong defies description. The British jurisdiction covers the main areas and some other islands around it. To the north are the New Territories, which are on the mainland and border China. There is much building taking place there. On the southern tip of the mainland is Kowloon City. Much of the commerce takes place in this area, and the only sites left for accommodation are in the air. The same is true of Hong Kong Island, located 11 km south of Kowloon across Hong Kong Harbour. The island, like the mainland, is full of unclimbable mountains and high density sky-scrapers. Travel from the mainland to the island is achieved by ferries and tunnels – two for cars and two for tube trains. Cars on Hong Kong are deluxe, high powered, and bumper to bumper until 11 p.m. The train service (called MTR, Mass Transit Railway) is superb. Built in Birmingham ten years before, the trains were purpose built for Hong Kong and are wider gauge than UK railways. Food, drink and cigarettes are forbidden on the MTR. It is immaculately clean, and air-conditioned in hot weather. (I actually spotted a naughty, vagrant, sweet paper one very untidy day.) The airfield is on the mainland and sticks out from Kowloon City into the sea, the runway heading NW-SE. Pilots on the SE approach have to dodge around granite hills, fly their approach in a right-hand turn, and pass low over the city to land. Having aircraft pass by my earhole every ten minutes quite took me back to my piloting days.

Hong Kong Harbour is the busiest harbour in the world, with some 3500 ship movements a day, and shifting over 4 million containers a year. In Victoria Harbour the horde of boats ply up and down and diagonally across, the only rule being simply to miss each other. There is a channel for those going E-W, but not for those going across. Other than that, I think the only legislation was that speed was to be kept to a maximum of 15 knots. Riding *Neste Enterprise* in Victoria Harbour was quite uncomfortable, because the cross-wakes from all the boats made the sea a mess. As did many other things discarded into it.

City Hall is on the north side of Hong Kong Island. *ICI River Rover* was unpacked from its container, 'mantled' (as

33

opposed to dismantled) by the engineers, driven on its trailer at snail's pace across Kowloon City, through the tunnel, and put on display outside City Hall. It was in a strategic place; many people would pass that way, especially over the weekend. *Neste Enterprise* was unstuffed, mantled and trailered to the Royal Hong Kong Yacht Club, from where it put to sea in the harbour.

The first activity was on Friday, 1 March, at 2.30, when Mike, Rachel, Mel and John gave a press conference at the Yacht Club. This plush, luxurious, colonial edifice was 3 km east of City Hall. The club had generously lent us a slip-way for our hovercraft and a room for our conference.

During the press conference, a telex from Chengdu was stuffed into Mike's hand. He glanced at it briefly, and then had enormous difficulty controlling the expression on his face. The Chinese had cancelled the expedition: 'Refer to the Yangtze Expedition activity in China, and the contract/agreement signed between our parties; as it has not been approved by our senior management the contract is not effective yet. Therefore, please don't call up any press conference or other press release since it's not legal yet.'

It had come in Chinese. By the time John Whatmore had found someone to translate it, and had got it to Mike, the press conference had already started.

Mike fought an appalling battle inside: what it said was at variance with what God had told him many times. What was he going to say? Should he say anything? The press conference was now well under way. He determined to keep a tight-lipped silence.

After the conference the VIPs from Neste, ICI (China) and Exxon Chemical PARAMINS went with Mike Cole on *Neste Enterprise* to Queen's Pier outside City Hall. The press took the long way round by bus.

At 2.59 *Neste Enterprise* pulled up at Queen's Pier, Mike Cole got out and met General Duffell, and they both went into the City Hall for a presentation. The press was there in force. The Chinese have enormous difficulty understanding why the British pay money to buy hardship. There is no doubt that the expedition was becoming more and more expensive, and funds were getting increasingly meagre. This one was costing far more than any other expedition that Mike had led. But the press was impressed with our aims, our determination and our motivation.

Mike's faith was being thoroughly tested with the telex burning a hole in his pocket. 'Called for times like this' was a phrase that would not go out of his mind.

We brought children into the programme, because it was most important for Hong Kong to get the message that we were not simply zooming up the Yangtze for fun and a slice of adventure. Into our schedule had come the enormous task of inoculation and health care as our primary goal. So we brought children into the centre of the press conference, gave them gifts and took them for rides in *Neste Enterprise*. The first batch of children were eight- to ten-year-olds from the Hans Christian Anderson orphanage nearby. The second were teenagers from the Canossa School for the Deaf, who really appreciated their rides. They continually shouted silently at one another as their fingers and arms flashed out their interest, and their eyes glowed with excitement. This made it more than just a publicity event. We really enjoyed being with the children, and it was very satisfying to give priority and pleasure to those who would not normally receive it in that sort of context.

On Saturday and Sunday we laid on rides for our three major sponsors, their families and friends. The press was enthusiastic. We appeared in many newspapers, on three television programmes, and five radio networks, and were specially featured in three trade and commercial journals. On Monday we brought *Neste Enterprise* out of the water, lifted her sides, and took her back to Osborn Barracks to be dismantled and squeezed back into her container: ditto *ICI River Rover*. It had been a successful publicity event. Hong Kong knew all about our existence and what we were trying to do.

Someone approached us to try to arrange another press conference at Tuotuoheyan bridge, some time in May. Tuotuoheyan was only 200 miles from the source of the Yangtze and miles from anywhere else. Mike was delighted,

35

and agreed, but he knew it would never come off. He kindly pointed out to them that it might be any time within a three-week period, and that prior to that we had no idea where we would be or when. Moreover there was no way of communicating with us. If the press wished to stay at Tuotuoheyan, at 14,500 feet and −15°C, to wait for us, they were welcome.

On the day we were giving rides to our sponsors and friends I sat opposite a Chinese man at the Royal Hong Kong Yacht Club. Our lunch was courteously paid for by Exxon Chemical PARAMINS, and this man was clearly in the company. It turned out that he was the manager of PARAMINS Division. He was articulate, shrewd, experienced and delightful. Our conversation turned towards the People's Republic of China and I decided my best policy was to ask questions and express no opinions, being careful to maintain our non-political stand.

'Do you think that China has been affected by Tiananmen Square?' I asked.

'Of course,' Low Hee Teck replied. 'But only externally. Western firms are holding back from China, waiting to see which way she will go. They prefer to put their investments into more stable and secure markets.'

'And what about internally?'

'They are just as keen as they ever were to welcome western technology into China. I've been in many times, and I see no relaxation of zeal or enthusiasm towards what we have to offer.'

'What do you think was the problem with the tragedy of Tiananmen Square?'

Low Hee Teck mused for a moment. 'The real problem is that you can't change a system as big as 1 billion people overnight. You can't just stop a huge system like that and start again, as they are doing in Romania. For China, any system, however bad, is better than no system at all. Deng Xiaoping is a reformer, and has never changed his views. The real problem is that his no.1s have been too zealous, and have tried to change the system too fast. Neither the economy nor the system nor the people were able to stand

36

it. So they had to go. The man he has in at present used to be Mayor of Shanghai, and was in the forefront of the changes there. But he, too, realised that you cannot change China instantaneously, and is now bringing in his reforms more slowly.'

'But what about the students?' I asked.

'They wanted too much too fast,' Low Hee Teck replied. 'And Deng Xiaoping knew you couldn't do it. He had a revolution on his hands, and he had to put it down. He is continuing to do so because all they will do is cause unrest. It is the same with young people all the world over – they want to change every system they belong to because they only concentrate on its faults. But Deng is in favour of bringing in democracy. He has a professor on his central committee who is not a Communist and will not toe the party line. He is still there.'

'What do you think will happen?'

'That's the problem. Deng is now eighty-five years old. His no.1 has been given power, but has not had time to establish it for himself. If Deng survives the next five years, then the reforms will continue, and politics will steadily move to the right. If he dies, you may well find it veering hard left again. This uncertainty is what is holding western investment back. Someone remarked that China is waiting to see what is going to happen in Eastern Europe. When Russia or the satellite countries establish their new systems, we may well find China will adopt what these nations implement, and so change the easy way. But we'll have to wait and see.'

Low Hee Teck's assessment of China at this time was full of hope and discernment. I noted it carefully. Certainly their economy was growing very fast. The industrial growth in 1988 was 17.7 per cent. In 1989 they were aiming for a more sensible 7 to 8 per cent. I was looking forward to entering the country I had heard so much about.

We clearly had total co-operation for our expedition from people in Hong Kong. We fitted there, slotting naturally into the old British colonial social structure as well as into the vibrant dynamics of adventurous business. All was very positive. But all was very false. Discouragement and difficulty draped themselves over us from China.

We had received some hint of trouble before the brickbat message on the day of the press conference. From across the border the Sichuan Mountaineering Association had sent us a telex a few days previously: 'Without a full contract we cannot give you visas or a permit. There are many problems about fuel transportation, storage, security and cost. We require you to put off the start time of the expedition. After the contract signed we will decide when it begins.'

The Chinese were up to their old negotiating tricks again. The deal that Tony Burgess struck with them for the Letter of Intent, agreeing to £41,000 as the fee we should pay them, was arguably too generous to us. It was right and proper that we should pay for the hire of transport, guides and interpreters. But was it right to pay for the privilege of coming sacrificially and painfully to bring medicine to areas and people they themselves had done little for? The question arose: could not the Chinese have taken inoculations and vaccines supplied by UNICEF to the area we were going to? Of course they could. They had the technology, but the task was lower on their agenda. Now it seemed they wanted us to pay excessively for our own initiative and cooperation. It was a very odd way of working, and we struggled not to get exasperated but to continue to honour and respect them. At least, that is how we in Hong Kong saw it from a distance.

Mike telexed back: 'Confirm that Richardson, Gould, Burgess, Whatmore, Pinniger travel to Chengdu, CA 4303 arrive 15.10 hours Tuesday, 6 March.' We were to go forward, believing that we would find a way through. God's promise must stand.

We had two important cards in our hands. First, we were supplying all our own fuel through Exxon Chemical PARAMINS, who were also paying to transport it. This meant that the SMA did not have the fuel price as a bargaining lever. We were immensely grateful for that. Secondly there was a definite finishing time for our expedition. Mike had said, and meant, that we left at the end of June. If we had not achieved it by then, too bad. This meant that every day's delay the SMA placed on the start of the expedition entailed loss of money for them. We hoped this argument would work.

They had also sent another telex, this time from the medical division, insisting that Denke was not a good place to start our inoculation programme, or to put down our base camp. Instead, it should be at Dege. We did not yet know why they chose Dege and not Denke. Dege happened to be the administrative capital, and had, in time past, been a very important centre. Indeed to this day they are still printing the Buddhist Scriptures, the Ganjhur, in a monastery there. Some documents are irreplaceable and date back many centuries. The Dege Treasure House is the most important of only three Buddhist printing presses that are still working. When our 'recce' teams went there, however, the local major was particularly displeased to see us, did not welcome us, restricted our movements considerably, and insisted on our being accompanied by the security police. The armed police also looked on, and we were not allowed even to see the hospital. That was one reason why we had chosen Denke. Now they wanted us in Dege. Why? The rest of the telex implied another reason. The health authority in Dege could not support us financially, so, insisting that we start there, they also insisted that we pay 7000 yuan for doing so (there are approximately 10 yuan to the pound). We did not like their proposals at all. Dege was 15 km from the river, and although there was a tributary that flowed into the Yangtze we did not know if it was navigable by hovercraft. So, although our interpretation needed clarification face to face with the Chinese, we were having problems. There was more than a physical mountain to climb from here on. Our viewpoint at this time was limited. We trusted things would become clearer once we got personally involved in Chengdu.

On 6 March the five on the advance team arrived in Chengdu with the business visas Sarah had managed to negotiate for them. Mel and Tony were to do the complex negotiations with SMA. Bill and Rachel (whom we called

Ray) were to talk with the health authority, and complete preparations for the combined Chinese/English lectures taking place on 15 March. After that, Ray and Bill wanted to go to Lhasa in Tibet and Xining, capital of the Qinghai Province, to discuss medical affairs and clear our way into those two provinces. John Whatmore would complete his negotiations with Sichuan TV, help Mel and Tony, and then return on Friday. He would be replaced by Gwyn and Duncan, who were to sort out accommodation, storage and organisation in Chengdu. Duncan Hanton was a remarkable young man. He had been at school with Mike's son Nick, who had drawn him into the expedition. Mike longed for the vision to be shared with the next generation, and Duncan was superb material for expeditions such as these. He was a man of determination, enhanced by a delightful personality, good humour and a strong Christian faith. He was chosen by Mike to be our representative, along with Sarah, on the *Blue Peter* TV programme. He was a trialist for the UK rowing eight, and was strong, fit and single-minded.

Back in Hong Kong waiting for take-off, I looked out across the busy, thriving harbour and towards the hills of China, sticking sullenly out of the mists to the north. What lay before us across those mountains? We had met a fair few problems so far in preparation for blessing that land, but those, we were to discover, were merely a trivial introduction to what was to come.

3

The Beginning of Difficulty

Be happy while y'er livin',
For y'er a lang time deid.
(Scottish motto for
a house, 1901)

Multiplication is vexation,
Division is as bad;
The Rule of three doth puzzle me,
And Practice drives me mad.
(Elizabethan MS
dated 1570)

This was the first time I had been to Hong Kong. It
was Sunday, and most of us had taken advantage of the
churches that were to be found in Kowloon. Now I sat on
my bed looking at the beautiful sunset, and contemplated
the journey over the border the next day. I suppose we all
suffer some sort of apprehension in tackling something we
have never done before. I was feeling a strange mixture of
excitement and anticipation, as well as regret and anxiety.
The last two feelings came from a sense of deprivation
that was encroaching irrationally into my thinking. Hong
Kong is so sophisticated – like the England with which
I am familiar, but a bit more 'mega'. From here I could
write home, and even use a UK first class stamp, because
we had access to the British forces' postal service at the
army barracks. What was even more reassuring was that
we could pick up the phone and ring England in one
minute as if we were next door. But this slick contact with
family and friends was about to be severed. In China such

41

communication would be heavily curtailed, and we would be, truly, a long way away. I sat there, really missing my family. What if I was never to see them again? Each of the two previous rafting expeditions had had a fatal accident on the Yangtze, and somebody in the bar that evening expressed his fear that we, too, could have a death on ours. I rejected the idea, because God was in charge of us. But it was none the less an unpleasant thought.

I swallowed an impulse to sink fifty precious HK dollars into a phone card and make a panic phone call home. Instead, what I did was to write a long letter. So much cheaper. And a letter is sometimes so much better than a telephone call, because it can be read and re-read, and savoured again and again. A refrain from the old Negro spiritual went through my mind, 'Oh, darkies, how my heart grows weary, far from the old folks at home.'

I decided to get some comfort in the companionship of the team that God had so skilfully brought together. I noticed an interesting phenomenon: the married people I spoke to were all feeling like me – semi-reluctant to take the next step. The single people were as keen as mustard to get on with tomorrow's adventure. No holding back for them. I remembered it had been the same for me in my thirty-nine single years, and could now welcome the change from 'unattached' to 'belonging'. But it made adventures like this harder to undertake, and my commitment to it a far more serious business than in those single days.

Mike had told us to cut down our kit, because after Chengdu we would have to lug it around everywhere. I complied, but having packed what I considered to be the bare essentials into my 80 litre rucksack, I still found that I could hardly lift the beast. I staggered cotton-kneed to the taxi, deciding that at last the day had arrived when I began my 'get-fit-for-the-expedition' campaign. I wisely selected a T-shirt as attire, and the sun penetrated the 98 per cent humidity strangling my equilibrium at a mere 18°C. Local Chinese were in trousers and sweaters, and some even had coats on. It just had to be winter – depending on where you came from.

The Chinese express train for Guangzhou was all first class, with female attendants for every carriage, and the compartment covered in lace antimacassars. All seats had to be booked. Seats were in pairs, with plenty of western leg-room (Chinese people tend, as a race, to be much shorter than us), and were rotatable through 180°. An enterprising group of Chinese swivelled their seats around and drew out their pack of cards. Hilarious shouts and guffaws of laughter burst from them through the silky morning music throughout the journey. Not knowing any Chinese, I could not interpret this hilarity – whether it was 'Seven spades!' or 'You've trumped my ace!' or even 'Bingo'.

I had been quite surprised just how much space in Hong Kong was still unoccupied. Having been media-pumped that the colony was grossly over-populated and that there was not a square inch left even for a cockroach, we saw wooded hills and large untouched areas in the New Territories. There, many new buildings were being constructed as Hong Kong expanded north from the congested Kowloon/Island complex. China was trying to follow suit. Over the border was a special wired-off Economic Zone called Shenzhen, where the PRC was trying to create a buffer between the rich free-port and the more agricultural mainland.

Soon we were out into real China. The express mercifully and delightfully went tourist pace, and we were able to drink in the scenery. 'Discovery,' stated an Argos poster 'is seeing what everybody else has seen, and thinking what nobody else has thought!' The visibility was none too brilliant, and the sun blinked down from a bland, watery sky. I had expected more hills, but maybe I could not see them; or maybe I had not studied my physical geography map carefully enough.

Mike had said that I would be surprised at China's poverty. In fact I was delighted at the apparent lack of it. Hardly any visible land remained uncultivated. Maximum use had been made of all available space, and we saw pineapples, oranges, lemons, beans, cabbages, cauliflowers

43

and many other vegetables and fruit growing. We noted the careful control of water, cleverly channelled round most of the fields, as well as into the paddy fields. It was neatly laid out, beautifully cared for and abundantly varied, like a table laid out with tit-bits prior to a cocktail party. What surprised us was the lack of visible manpower. We could see a couple of people here and there hoeing or carrying water, but, apart from the towns, there were not many to be seen. We concluded that it was spring, and not much could be done agriculturally then. Certainly the alternative was not mechanical. We saw no tractors or farm machinery of any kind – only the occasional buffalo and load-bearing labourer. We saw for real what we had so often seen on film – lampshade straw hats, bundles of firewood or buckets of water carried in pairs across the shoulders like scales. The roads were mostly dirt, and the traffic light. One reasonably common mode of rural transport was the two-wheeled 4-stroke rotavator, towing a trailer on which the driver sat – clearly an ingenious and popular modification. I nicknamed it a 'peci-peci' after a boat in Peru with the same engine.

I was familiar with both tropical and Mediterranean cultures. In hot countries people tend to live outside; in cooler climates people tend to live inside. The design and care of houses and environment reflects this temperature necessity. China, I saw, was no different to any other hot country, and, as far as usage of the land was concerned, far more economical and thorough than the vast majority I have observed. Mud or mud-brick houses jostled with neat red-brick ones, dingy unkempt streets alternating with open, swept ones. There were very few dogs, but flocks of geese or ducks were often seen. It looked, and smelt, tropical. I loved it. If I could come round to loving the Chinese people, which I was rapidly doing, I would have no problem living in this kind of environment.

What we could see of their industry did not look so promising. By the side of the railway occasional smoke-belching chimneys stuck out of mounds of coal or stone dust, where filthy workers shovelled clouds of obscurity into the back of black-layered lorries, which coughed their way to who-knows-where, vomiting opaque billows over the side with every lurch and turn. The areas surrounding all such were finger-deep in the same grey or black coating.

We occasionally crossed rivers, many of which seemed to be treated as waste-disposal units. Some, I noted with glee, were ideal for hovercraft operations. We saw some wide, flat barges with very low free-board, supporting large barn-shaped coverings. We presumed they were for transporting coal.

On one of the reconnaissances Keith Richardson had given a lecture on town and country planning in the UK. In passing, he mentioned that leisure activities had to be planned into any new housing project. As we passed through Hong Kong to Guangzhou we slowly discovered what was missing from China that we were used to in the UK: recreational parks, football stadia, racing courses, wind-surfing, even make-shift volley-ball courts. We presumed that there is so much to work for that there is not much time for leisure activities. Perhaps it was partly the political ethic. Nevertheless the people seemed contented, unstressed and friendly. As we travelled round China in the ensuing months we saw that much of this was changing. Recreational facilities were growing, and China was preparing to host the Asian Games in the autumn of 1990. There were many smiling faces – particularly at us funny foreigners – but we felt they were laughing with us, not at us. I was certainly laughing at myself, with my red face, perspiring brow and 47 kilo rucksack. We wondered what the locals did with their meagre spare time. We could not help but notice the huge number of TV aerials that sprouted from the roof-tops. The Japanese electronics industry had taken a grip on the world's largest consumer market and got the Chinese investing their gradually increasing wealth into colour television. Two-thirds of the population (600-700 million) watch *News at 7* every evening.

It took two hours to get to Guangzhou. Customs clearance was hilarious and the officials delightful. When they asked me to put my overweight backpack through the X-ray machine, I had not quite got it off my back when the feeder started to pull it under the curtains. I started to go with it, leapt out of it in a hurry, and stood up laughing. This was priceless entertainment, and a sparkle in an otherwise drab routine. We filled out five forms, and showed our passports the same number of times.

Money-changing was a necessity, and our HK dollars went into FEC (Foreign Exchange Certificates). We sweated round to the Airport Bus Terminal, where we gratefully sat and sipped 7-Up. Street vendors were selling goat and antelope horns and what looked like eagles' claws. The bus ride to the airport took half an hour, and the driver wrestled with the traffic, the conductress with the tickets, and we with the micro-seats. But we eventually located the airport, crawling slowly through the sweaty gloom. We clambered last out of the vehicle and headed towards the terminal. It had cost us 3.20 yuan for all four of us – a mere 46 pence for half an hour's journey.

The airport was modern, but crowded. We discovered, almost too late, that we had to change our Hong Kong-issued tickets for CAAC (Civil Aviation Authority of China) tickets. We were fortunate to have Dr Arne Brantsaeter with us – it pays to go with the man who speaks the local lingo. Arne had spent two years studying in Beijing. I was sweating externally and internally about my 47 kilo bag. I suggested we pool our luggage, and prayed that my precious stock of FEC would not be seriously depleted by having to pay for 27 kilos of extra luggage. No problem. It slid on to the aeroplane without blinking. As we did. The Boeing 707 looked ancient, but we were told later by the Boeing representative that it was quite young – only fifteen years old.

The air journey to Chengdu soared over total cloud cover, unfortunately. We emerged out of the murk to see the same sort of fields as in Guangzhou, carefully cultivated and entirely utilised. The poor visibility limited our view, but the bright-yellow rape seed shone out like fireflies twinkling on a dark tropical night, brightening up our approach to land. I was struck again that there were no large fields

46

or estates such as there are in England or Europe – just little pocket-handkerchiefs like the neat, multi-patterned patchwork quilts of Devon, although smaller in size.

They had not finished building the new terminal at Chengdu when we arrived two hours later. It looked, from the activity going on, as if it could be another year before it was functional. After retrieving our luggage we were ushered on to the airport bus. This partly modern creation lurched and shook its way down the uneven highway at break-neck speed. I wondered idly if it would slow down at a road junction: it didn't. Instead the driver pulled out his lethal weapon, the horn. The first application of this howitzer made me leap in my seat. It had clout, this hooter. Chickens, cars, bicycles and pedestrians gave way to our fearsome advance. There was no logic and no lights on the crossroads. The vehicle with the loudest bell got priority, and that was ours. We careered onwards to our destination, approaching this city of 4 million from the south-west. Chengdu is not as prosperous as Guangzhou, and there are fewer vehicles. But it was not the occasional car or truck that one needed to watch out for. It was the bicycles. The place was black with them. No modern ones: all old, heavy, inch-thick tubing with rod-brakes and clanking chain guards. And bells: like the tinkling of thousands of goats on a Cypriot hillside, multiplied by twenty. A friendly newspaper in English (the *China Daily*) furnished me with the information that the bicycle output of China was more than that of any other country in 1989. It surpassed 36.7 million, or 34 per cent of the world's total bicycle output. Of these, they exported 2 million, and were the third-largest exporters in the world. The Chinese now own 300 million bicycles, or nearly one for every three people. I could believe that. We even spotted one man pushing his bicycle down a lonely Tibetan mountainside from his nomad tent. I was never able to master the Mandarin for bicycle – *zixingche*.

Having arrived in the city, we haggled with the bicycle rickshaws, and got our fare 'home' suitably reduced. Crammed on to a Chinese-size seat, kit and all, we carved our way hilariously through the plethora of home-bound cyclists to the gates of our new abode – the grounds of Uaxi, the West China University of Medical Science. We had been allocated the home of what we were told was the senior missionary of a bygone age. It was a luxury. We were pleased for many reasons to be living in the President's House.

The university campus was 47 hectares, the largest university in Chengdu. Stoutly built and spaciously laid out, the designers had insisted on traditional Chinese architecture in its construction. With curly-up roofs, ornate carvings above the doors, dragons and snakes entwined over the roof-ridges, they had added a lily lake, clock tower and ornate waterway for good measure. Most of those beautiful and massive buildings had been part of a university that was founded in 1921. But one, more ornate than the others, had been right where they wanted to build the Southern Avenue. So in the early 1950s they pulled it down, brick by brick, and rebuilt it by the lakeside. Pretty amazing. But the upkeep was not so impressive. Bare corridors, unswept staircases, unpainted walls, windowless doors all led now to class-rooms with *ad hoc* wooden furniture and teachers low on equipment.

When Mel, Bill, Tony, John and Rachel reached Chengdu on 6 March they went to see the Foreign Affairs Office. Chinese culture is divided up into work units. Each unit that deals with *waibin* (foreigners), such as SMA, has to have a Foreign Affairs Office (FAO) incorporated in its system. Foreigners mainly liaise with the unit FAO (Foreign Affairs Officer), who then talks to the unit, giving it clearance or restriction in its dealings. In each provincial capital there is a central FAO, and we were fortunate to be in Sichuan's capital, Chengdu. Fortunate too that a subsection of the central FAO dealt with twinning. So most of our arrangements were going through Zhao Shufen (Sophie), in charge of the twinning section. Her position gave her a lot of authority. And her total commitment to our expedition – its aims, motives and methods – meant that God had graciously given us yet another very important, intelligent and supportive lady to look after us. We believed that

48

she held the crucial link to obtaining permission to go on the river. What a beautiful blessing she was.

'Go back home,' Mr Zhao, SMA's FAO, said. 'Nothing is ready. We do not have permission. We cannot sign the contract. I told you to come back in February. Now you can come back in September.'

Pretty discouraging.

Mel started talking gently to him. They conversed for two hours, going through the whole process that had already taken a year and five 'recces'. It seemed as if the SMA had done absolutely nothing since the Letter of Intent and since we had paid them £2500 deposit.

As the conversation dragged to its close, Mel had a sudden thought. It was what Christian people would describe as a word of knowledge – special inspiration from God.

'What you mean is that you have a restriction from higher up,' he said.

'Who told you that?' Mr Zhao asked sharply.

'Oh, I just know,' he replied.

Mr Zhao's face changed as his emotions struggled with this unveiling of a closely guarded secret. He dismissed the meeting, and they arranged to meet the next day. Overnight, Mel made contact with a Chinese friend and came in with new information in the morning.

'Your restriction is really with the Beijing Sports Commission, isn't it?' he queried.

'Who told you that?' said the startled Mr Zhao again.

'We have our contacts too,' Mel replied.

Mr Zhao seemed relieved. 'Well, if you know that, it's fine. Yes, it is them. They think we should have involved them earlier. Because we didn't and they read the press reports from Hong Kong, they have told us to stop negotiating, and you are to go home.'

Discussions and objections dragged interminably on. But Mr Zhao let slip one day that, if Beijing was to grant permission, the expedition could be away within a few days. But mostly he refuted any possibility of it taking place, and repeated his demand for us to return home. In an unguarded moment, however, he added, 'We have much to learn from you about your heart and your spirit.'

Then the fuel arrived. A panic call came to the SMA that 28 tons of fuel had come in drums, and was lying in a dump on a railway station in Chengdu. The safety officials had inspected it, and demanded its removal within twenty-four hours, or the railway authority was for the high jump. The maximum fuel load allowed in any dump was 20 tons. The Station Master was distraught. It wasn't their fuel. The SMA was dismayed. Now they knew for certain we meant business and were going ahead. (Prayerfully, carefully, positively.) Moreover Britons kept turning up. Mike kept the team coming up to Chengdu in small packages on tourist visas. The Beijing Sports Commission was most upset that it had not been kept informed. The SMA was told to go up to Beijing to talk about it. We sweated for two days, deafened by silence, heavy in prayer.

Meanwhile I had set the engineers a problem. If we were going to ascertain the real source of the Yangtze, we would need the discrepancy in distances between Geladandong and Dam Qu. How Man Wong claimed those extra 60 km for the Dam Qu source. I had set to and measured the maps – aviation maps taken from satellite photographs. Measuring down from the confluence to the Tuotuohe and the Dam Qu, where the river began to be known as the Tongtianhe, I measured that the Geladandong source was some 15 km longer than the Dam Qu, even taking How Man Wong's source position. I measured it roughly with the dividers, also going round the wrinkles with my DIY pen-style map distancer. I just could not find anything near 60 km, much less give it to the Dam Qu. They both seemed to be much the same. Our task, therefore, to discover or confirm the real source of the Yangtze, became quite important, because we were the *only* people who were going to ride the river both ways. It would not be acceptable to go by vehicle, or count the intervening distances on a map.

But how could we measure distances accurately in a hovercraft? Hovercraft fly above the water surface and therefore nothing touches the water to give us speed measurement. On a lake or still water, speed, and therefore

50

distance, can be measured by a little propeller trailed behind. But on a river, current would violently disturb it. So, we would need to measure current flow. But in a rapid area, or on a bend, the flow speed varies enormously, so all measurements would be hopelessly inaccurate. Add to that the problem of wind, which would affect the craft's true speed substantially. So we would need to measure the wind velocity while the craft was stationary. We did that by installing an anemometer, giving the static wind speed and direction, on to the craft. If we moved the craft forward at 30 mph the anemometer would measure the craft speed plus or minus wind speed. We could subtract the two electronically. But the wind velocity we would subtract would only be the one we measured when we were stationary, and winds on rivers, scooting round hills and accelerating through the defiles are notoriously perverse. So there is no way that craft speed, and therefore craft distance, could be accurately measured. What we needed was to measure the speed at which the river banks were going past. We could not do that without some sort of radar. I gave the problem to Sam, Tony, Chris and Peter, while I went to take photographs of the local populace.

Drs Rachel and Bill were among the five disheartened group who were told to go home by the Foreign Affairs Office on 6 March. After that discouraging meeting, Mr Zhao Xijie, the FAO in charge of medical affairs, took them to one side.

'We cannot, of course, do anything with you,' he said. 'Because we have no permission and no contract signed by 16 March, we shall have to cancel the seminars.'

'That would be a great pity,' Rachel replied. 'How far have you gone in setting them up?'

'Oh, we have arranged the meetings, and told many eminent doctors and physicians throughout China.'

Ray and Bill were grateful to hear that. The scientific seminars which had been efficiently organised by an enthusiastic university had been cancelled already. (Sophie said she never knew why.) And the SMA had, it seemed, done nothing towards the expedition itself since the last

51

reconnaissance. At least the medical side seemed more promising.

'What about the vaccination programme?' Ray asked hopefully.

'We have been in touch with the district, the county, the townships and the villages. We have arranged for them to send their people to central towns, beginning with Dege. The immunisation will start with them.'

Ray and Bill were surprised and thrilled. 'What about Denke?'

'It is too small. We cannot centralise the work from there. It has to be in Dege, the county town.'

'What about the coldchain?'

'We have arranged that too,' Mr Zhao Xijie said. 'The vaccines will be ready in Ganze or Dege. We have arranged for three towns and one village to have the solar refrigerators installed. They have no reliable mains supply.'

'Which towns?'

'We have the names chosen by the local medical staff, but here we do not know the exact locations. We will find out when we get to Dege. We have Dr Fang with us in all our discussions, and he will come with you to Dege.' Mr Zhao was the medical FAO administrator, so the presence of Dr Fang was very good news.

Ray and Bill were impressed. In contrast to the SMA, the Chinese Medical Department had done a considerable amount of organisation in the intervening months. It was a pity that Dege was to be the centre of medical activity, for it was 15 km away from the river, and further south than we had hoped to start. Besides, one of our aims was to introduce the concept of a hover-doctor service, and working miles from the river would greatly reduce the possibility.

Mr Zhao paused. 'Did you get my letter in the UK?'

'Certainly.'

'I mentioned there that it will cost us 7000 yuan to send Dr Fang with you. Our problem is this: this part of the Expanded Programme of Immunisation (EPI) has not been allowed for in this year's medical budget. Included in it is the training of many doctors, and we have to pay their expenses. Could you help us to meet this expense?'

Ray and Bill were surprised. But the negotiations were so delicate at that time that they could not confront Mr Zhao with their real thoughts. They were non-committal. 'Perhaps we might be able to contribute something towards it,' they said. Truthfully they knew that we would probably have to pay it all. It is a different and interesting culture that asks a seller to pay for the goods he is selling. A western businessman wrote: 'You don't sell anything to the Chinese; they buy it off you.' Ray later discovered that the standard rate throughout China for a national to work with a foreigner was 50 yuan a day. So 7000 yuan was about right. Mr Zhao said they could provide oxygen and stretchers free, so there was a certain measure of collaboration, and Mr Zhao was becoming a good friend and sympathetic colleague.

When Ray had come on our May 1989 'recce' she had laid before the UNICEF authorities in Beijing our ten-point medical programme, asking if there was anything else we could tackle. They gave us two assignments: to get in touch with the High Altitude Medical Institute in Xining (capital of Qinghai Province), and to find out why tetanus did not seem to exist at altitude. These we would be glad to do.

Now, though, there was a problem. The SMA said that the Beijing section of their organisation had been badly hurt by some of the press reports that had come from Hong Kong. The media had apparently grossly over-emphasised our desire to test the waters of the Yangtze for purity. 'Pollution' the press had called it. A few years ago the BBC had made a TV documentary about the cleanliness of the Yangtze at Shanghai, and had not been very complimentary. Moreover pollution was a global media band-wagon, and the Chinese authorities wanted none of their rivers investigated, nor exposed to the eyes of the world.

Secondly the Hong Kong press had overstressed our aim to carry out a survey of diseases in the north-east area of Sichuan. As an area of 'minority' peoples (Tibetan), the press was going to be glad to receive statistics on whether the Chinese look after their minorities as well as their majority. This clearly had become too sensitive a task for us to undertake. So we revised our syllabus.

The majority of the inhabitants in Tibet, Qinghai and NW Sichuan are Tibetan, so these provinces are labelled 'Restricted' or closed areas. Mr Zhao offered to write up an agreement in English and Chinese on the medical pro-gramme, which he would return for signature the following day. Ray and Bill also rewrote the medical aims, leaving out the difficult areas, but added that we were:

> carrying sufficient equipment to be able to cope with most medical and surgical eventualities, and to ensure a safe water supply for the team. Other areas of interest include research into the occurrence of tetanus at high altitude, the problems of mountain sickness, and a study of incidence of physical disability as a follow-up of the subject covered in the Chengdu seminar.

They agreed these terms. But the contract could not be signed because the official permission for the whole ex-pedition was not yet granted. Now Ray and Bill needed to go to Xining, to talk through the medical programme in Qinghai and to address the problem of mountain sickness with the institute there. They were advised by the FAO to cancel their rail ticket only three hours before departure.

So they tried Lhasa, the ancient capital in the heart of Tibet. Bill had planned ahead. In October 1989 he had written to Drs Pei and Sui in Lhasa to see if he could do something for them on the expedition, quoting some work they had written up in a medical journal. Ray and Bill had other motives for pursuing this line of interest. Both had been working across the border of Tibet – Ray in Bhutan and Bill in Nepal – and had had frequent contact with Tibetan refugees for many years.

Bill was a remarkable man. He had been a missionary doctor and surgeon in Tansen Hospital in Nepal for many years, had received a medal from the King himself, and had been the initiator of all the hovercraft expeditions. His river, the Kali Gandaki, was the one on which the 1979 expedition began its 'adventures with a purpose'. Kind, wise and gentle, Bill's presence on all three expeditions was unique and irreplaceable.

Both were itching to go to Tibet. So they applied to fly there privately. This was difficult. Tibet was a restricted area, and both the Tibetan New Year and the Dalai Lama's birthday were celebrated in March. The only way to get in was as a tourist on a recognised tour. Providentially, the celebrations were over the day before they were free to go, and also there was a young Chinese American, Eric, who was awaiting a tour to Tibet. CAAC contacted him, Bill became the tour leader, and they went as a group of three, the minimum allowed. They received their tickets ten minutes before take-off. Their time in Tibet was mainly spent going round the tourist spots, closely accompanied by a lady security guide. The Tibetans themselves were delightful, warm, very friendly and generously welcoming. Both doctors were thrilled to be there at last. The security guide arranged for Dr Pei to come to the hotel (Dr Sui was on holiday). He was very pleased to see them, and explained that he had wished to come on the expedition himself, but Bill's last letter had taken three months to get to him, and he realised he could not apply in time. He invited them to his hospital. It turned out that the 'Institute' did not exist; Dr Pei was the consultant, and the main body of research was in Xining. But he did point out areas of altitude sickness – in particular, various biochemical levels in the blood – that needed to be researched. The best people to research would be the Chinese and Tibetan locals. But the authorities might not permit that without a qualified Chinese physician to do the work. So we would have to be content to use the team as guinea-pigs – which I, for one, was delighted to be; yet another adventure! Ray and Bill agreed to sell the expedition's blood-testing equipment to Dr Pei at the end of our adventures.

They returned to Chengdu in time for the medical seminars, though 16 March had long passed. Mr Zhao called Ray in and said, 'Even though we have no contract for the expedition, we have agreed that the seminars will take place. Are you sure that you have all the people coming?'

They were not sure. But they had, before going to Lhasa, communicated with all those eminent doctors to confirm their attendance and their travel arrangements. The most important lecturer was Professor Garth Hastings, a world authority on artificial limbs and a gracious Christian. He was supervising the establishment in Fuzhou in south-east China of a limb factory for UNIDO (United Nations Industrial Development Organisation). Mr Zhao was on tenterhooks. He had stepped out, he felt, with great risks to establish these seminars; he had invited many leading medical experts to attend and speak; his career could well be influenced by the success or otherwise of this huge three-day, twenty-lecture event.

Meanwhile Sam had been busy. Like excited schoolboys, he and Peter were discussing how they were going to measure speed, and therefore distance, accurately from a hovercraft. There was a possibility of using radar. But they were also considering using doppler – the principle that sound waves tighten up as speed increases, causing oncoming sound to be at a higher pitch than retreating sound. The effect is best experienced in the change of pitch of a railway locomotive horn as it screams past you on a train station. Using a 12 volt system, the same as that on the hovercraft, they started to design a little transmitter that could be pointed ahead of the craft, and a receiver that could pick up the change of pitch caused by speed. He had not actually designed an amplifier since the time he had fiddled around with a few transistors in the electronics club at Plymouth Comprehensive School. Peter Gunner had not done much better, but now, amazingly, they were buying silicon chips, transistors, capacitors and everything they needed in a local Chengdu shop. It was quite astonishing what was for sale in the shops. After days spent drawing and soldering dinky bits of kit on to a circuit board, they needed to test whether the transmitter was working. The frequency was ultra-sonic – above the hearing range of the human ear. How, then, could Sam test it?

It just so happened that there was a mangy ginger-and-white moggy that had taken up residence in the compound. It was blessed with a deep baritone voice, which it chose to exercise at a painful 6.15 most mornings. On test day it was sleeping peacefully behind a tree in the garden of the President's House. It spotted Sam's advance and ran at the application of ultra-sonics. Not being convinced whether the ginger tom was escaping from the fear of humanoids or from ultra-sonic overkill, Sam stalked him again, this time from the rear. At 20 metres he switched on the directional beam. The cat leapt in the air, pinned its ears to its back, and hot-footed it through the fence at breathtaking velocity. Aha! the device worked.

Now Peter and Sam set out to build an amplifier which would zap a coven of cats, a receiver to pick up the signal, and a comparator to detect the difference. Peter busied himself designing a little box in which the device could repose. Tony suggested we tried to involve the electronics section of the Science and Technology University. Some of the team had taken lecture sessions there in Monty Worthington's class. If the university could get involved, we could use their expertise, their oscilloscopes, and their name if a security man wondered what this electronic gadget was. Tony also suggested that we leave the device with the university on our departure, so that they could continue using it. Monty made the contact, establishing yet another cooperative project with these delightful people.

Rob Watson and I took seven days off while the politics, the medical task and the cat-scarer were developing. The delay in starting the expedition had enabled most of the team to go to look at some of the varied and extraordinary sights and sounds of China. Some went to Xian to see the terracotta soldiers; some climbed Emei mountain; some went to the giant panda reserve. Rob had spent the first four years of his life in Dali in Yunnan Province, and had heard that his old nanny Eva might yet be alive. This was his chance to see if his father's hospital was still there, and if Eva was still living in Kunming, capital of Yunnan. She was.

Yunnan Province is spoken of as the most beautiful and pleasant of China's provinces. I can vouch for both. The CAAC flight down (cheaper than a soft sleeper train fare) led us to glorious sunshine and clear skies, revealing rolling, russet-red hills and fertile valleys. We saw our lovely river Yangtze, and longed after it with anticipation.

It turned out that Kunming, set in a large open plain surrounded by hills, enjoyed almost permanent sunshine throughout the year. It was certainly good to get out of Chengdu's perennial overcast. Kunming is a pleasant city, as sophisticated as the larger Chengdu but boasting more traffic. Its hotels and buses were the same as the northern province's capital, and the people dressed in the same colourful and tasteful variety. One immediate difference was the presence of ponies, mostly drawing traps. We saw these, noticeable by their absence in Chengdu, everywhere we went in Yunnan.

The pleasant countryside was filled with the same intensive manual labour on the farms, and again we were impressed by the use of the land: hardly a wasted square centimetre. All the fields were the same allotment-size we had seen elsewhere, and often there was a bevy of people working on one plot together. This was particularly so in the rice fields or when buffaloes were ploughing a field. All manner of vegetables and cereal were being grown, and some barley had been harvested, even though the *xinghua* (apricot blossom) and *taohua* (peach blossom) decorated the colourful countryside with dancing splashes of white and pink. The rich red earth was a dormant promise of fertile abundance, and water was carefully piped or channelled into the appropriate fields. I reckoned that their detailed retention of all available water had been inherited through many generations, and established as a cultural and survival necessity.

In our six days in Yunnan we saw much of the countryside. We had two ten-hour bus journeys between Kunming, Xiaguan and Dali, and one train ride from morning to sunset back to Chengdu. Yunnan is a hilly province. Some mountain ranges (the highest pass at 2390 metres) and undulating foothills were interspersed by wide valleys, steep-sided gorges and narrow defiles. Tumbling rivers, sluggish streams and brown reservoirs enabled the much-needed water to be channelled and fed to the thirsty small-holdings. Even on our highest passes fair-dressed peasants were farming the land, and modestly dressed girls were cycling to somewhere important. The place was not opulent, but one could not help feeling that civilisation and culture had finally arrived at this most ancient of civilisations and cultures. I had expected to see people in 'Chairman Mao' suits, any colour as long as it was military green or naval blue; but I saw very few, and those were of the oldest generation. All the rest were in individually chosen western clothes, neatly turned out, tastefully matching. I was astonished and delighted. Advance towards modernisation was clearly progressing rapidly. An Australian businessman I met in the Green Lake Hotel said that in Beijing in 1980 he had had to make out a written application to get a taxi, and the quickest reply he received was one and a half days later. Now, taxis were plentiful even in this provincial capital and throughout lesser towns. He also said that he had noticed a radical change in Chinese society every year wherever he went.

We were glad to meet some tourists from Hong Kong in Kunming. In the light of the reunion in 1997, we felt it was good that people from Hong Kong were taking the opportunity to see at first hand the encouraging economic progress that China is making. China has probably as much to offer Hong Kong as Hong Kong has to offer China. And the West should be encouraged, as we were, by the rapidity of the changes going on in this vast country. The modernisation which we saw had come in only five short years; what will their progress be in the next seven?

The Chinese script is difficult to master. So the government introduced a romanised version of it called Pinyin in 1979. Pinyin is taught in all the schools and, from 1990, has become the major form of Chinese script taught in primary schools. Moreover English is compulsory in all secondary schools, and is introduced at primary level. But, as Professor Fang Lizhi would frequently point out:

> China spends less per capita on education than almost
> any country in the world. On top of that there was the
> Cultural Revolution, when a whole generation missed out
> on schooling. About a quarter of the population is illiterate
> (defined as knowing less than 500 Chinese characters) even
> according to official figures. Even in the Communist Party
> half the members have never had more than primary school
> education. (*Britain–China*, Spring 1990)

Professor Fang Lizhi is China's foremost dissident, now living in Cambridge, having taken refuge in the US Embassy after the Tiananmen Square massacre.

Most children greeted us *weibin* with 'Hello' and a giggle. The urban Chinese are keen to learn English. Mel's lecture in the University of Science and Technology was all in English, and he used technical jargon that baffled even me. The Chinese students not only received it, and mainly understood it, but had to do their homework on it in English. Every Thursday and Friday evenings in Chengdu, and also in Kunming, they had an 'English-speaking corner'. Anyone who wished could come to speak and hear English, and they love westerners to come along. We could talk on any subject we liked. I chose to probe into their knowledge of current affairs, to see if they were well-informed, or whether there was a restriction on information. They knew about the nuclear power station explosion at Chernobyl; a little about Mother Theresa (they knew she had won the Nobel Peace Prize); the Channel Tunnel; and even about the poll tax riots in Britain that had occurred since we left England. Remarkable.

I asked two girls when they had cut their plaits off and taken different hairstyles. In 1985. That year also girls generally started wearing make-up, but perfume, they said, was too expensive, and few wore it. The best of the available goods, clothes, gadgets, named products, were being advertised on the four commercial TV channels. Westernisation was advancing at an enormous rate. Most shops were well stocked, both in Chengdu and Kunming, with reasonably high-quality goods. Even British brand-name trainers and toys were on sale in a four-storey department store.

It is so easy to come new to any nation with a critical eye, and write about featureless corridors, dirty streets and cultural oddities. These were still there. But my sight and experience of China was giving me enormous encouragement. As a people the Chinese are industrious, visionary and determined. They have dignity, bearing and pride, both in themselves and their country. Rural Chinese are certainly not lazy, but city people are more laid-back. They sometimes get emotional. There is no disparity between the sexes. They are longing to go forward. This bodes well for the future. The Chinese, when freed into capitalism, are its masters. If Japan, Taiwan, Hong Kong and Singapore have done so well in such a short time, what will China do, and how long will it take them, with their 1100 million people pushing behind the plough?

Rob and I sat on the bus returning from Dali to Kunming. The ten-hour outgoing journey had been difficult, sitting in the rear seat with our luggage on our laps. The return, we determined, was going to be better. The bus was bigger, and rode the bumpy tarred-by-hand roads better. Nevertheless it shook, rattled and rolled. A pinkish-golden sun vibrated the cool, crystal dawn awake, the bus repeating the performance at a different decibel-level to the people who lived within 500 metres of the road. We were able to see better this time, drinking in the multi-coloured fields, the rich red earth, and the rugged, ravined ranges of hills over and through which the road wound precipitously. The traffic was fairly heavy, increasing in numbers of bicycles, peci-pecis, pony-traps and pedestrians, all in the middle of the road, as we drew towards and away from towns. Many people pushed hand-carts heavily laden with debris, paper, vegetables or ready-made furniture. The quantity, quality and size of the vegetables surprised us; pumpkin-sized cabbages, cartloads of legumes, and double-hanging baskets of onions made their way to and from the street markets in each town. For all their lack of agricultural machinery, food was prolifically available and beautifully harvested. The presentation of it in the town restaurants was not quite so attractive. I felt that a good pail of water and mop on the marble or concrete floors would have helped; but I suppose that as long as the local populace continues to spit out their pips, bones and unpalatable food on it, blow their noses on it, throw their paper, cans and scrap peel on it, there is likely to be a reluctance to clean it up on any regular basis.

Towns, especially the major ones, were diversified by red-brick or concrete buildings, displaying western tiled or flat roofs. But most of the villages and the lesser towns were still using red mud-brick accommodation, with the famous, and beautiful, Chinese curly-up roofs, all covered with the same half-round tiles, locally fired in huge, smoking brick kilns. It took me a while to discover why the Chinese tip their roofs up at the corners; it did not seem to me to be logical, and I would have thought that making them straight would have been an easier and more economic form of construction. Apparently it is to stop evil spirits settling on their homes.

Electricity was everywhere. There must be some hydro-electric sources, but the few power stations we spotted were coal-fired. Their provision of a safe and reliable electricity supply was one reason for my confidence in this country. Huge modern pylons took the lines straight over the mountain ranges, and the wires occasionally spanned ravines 1 km wide. One even stretched right over the river Yangtze. We mused together about how they got the pylons up the near-vertical hillsides. The lack of heavy plant machinery fired our imaginations with the thought of hundreds of scurrying Chinese, each with a hard wicker hat, pulling or carrying the parts up by hand. It could well have been so.

The journey to Kunming taught me that vehicle drivers in China have considerable prestige and esteem. Ours was a tall, athletic young man, with a high-collared, open-neck shirt, smart fawn flared trousers, and *High Chaparral* cowboy boots. He strutted around the bus, issuing orders like Napoleon. The same authoritative rhetoric was given to

62

the drivers of other vehicles on the road, of which he was without doubt King Elvis. He drove at enormous speed over the uneven road, breaking every traffic rule known to man and justifying his misdemeanours with blasts from the klaxon. Amazingly, oncoming traffic on the legitimate side of the road gave way meekly; as did the heaving, sweating, overladen lorries we raced past on hairpin bends and blind corners up the cliff-edge mountain passes. Only once did Elvis give way: faced by a ten-wheeled Mitsubishi carrying 5 tons of pig-iron, our virtuoso reluctantly surrendered. On one stop he had spotted my expedition sunglasses, so when the sun came out he asked if he could borrow them. I was glad to oblige; after all, who would cross a bus driver and perhaps provoke a savage increase in driving skills? Elvis waved nonchalantly and proudly at the passing opposition, enjoying the kudos of deep black, yellow-tinted, azure-rimmed snow glasses. He soon tired of them when the sun went behind a cloud; it must have been like driving at night for him.

His ticket collector had got on the bus late, dragged from his bed, I suspect, at the last moment. This man was a diffident, nervous, under-confident, cockerel-pecked slave. Stopping to relieve ourselves at one appalling public toilet, Elvis noticed that oil had splashed the back of the bus from beneath the engine. The ticket collector was called, rebuked, and ordered under the vehicle. He hardly had time to don his oil-stained overalls. Instructions poured from Elvis, responded to by meek mumblings emerging from underneath. Elvis went reluctantly to fetch an adjustable spanner, delicately held between the fingertips, and flung it carelessly in the direction of an oily hand, accompanied by much haranguing and noisy objection. The drama between these two men was as entertaining as a pantomime.

We were hoping that our speed over the roads would result in an early arrival. Not so. It merely meant longer and more frequent stops in between. The final stop was in an unnamed, but reasonably large town. I assumed it was a loo stop, but searched in vain for the hieroglyphics that register 'Men'. We sauntered round and looked at the sights, and then returned to the bus, where we discovered the reason for our stop: one of the rear pair of seats had become disengaged from its base, and Elvis had stopped by the blacksmith's to get it welded.

In Kunming and Chengdu, both capital cities, we saw something we had not seen from the train – leisure activity provisions. The medical campus in Chengdu in which we were staying had a football pitch, gymnasium, volley-ball pitches, and gymnastic equipment. Kunming had parks and a beautiful lake with pagodas, and was used by many as a place for relaxation. Moreover the teenagers would go round in groups, giggling and poking fun at each other, just as they do in other countries. It seemed to me that here at least the internal policies of the Chinese government were bearing good fruit at grass-roots level; the standard of living was rising, individuality was being set free to express itself, private enterprise was developing, and many of the people appeared to be living contented and happy lives. In commerce or government business, though, shop assistants were incredibly reluctant to sell us goods – almost as if they did not want to or did not care. Requests for service became guilty intrusions into their privacy. It was in remarkable contrast to the keen selling of private-enterprise shop assistants.

By this time, expedition affairs at a political level were becoming tense. After the initial rebuff through Mr Zhao of the SMA, Tony and Mel awaited the return of the Chengdu delegation from Beijing. It seemed that the Beijing Sports Commission (BSC) was digging its heels in; and the SMA faced more and more obstacles that hindered the signing of a mutual contract. Yet more delays. Yet more frustrating meetings. We were already having to take a fortnight out of the planned river operations at Base 2. We prayed that there would be no more, but we did not hold out much hope. Eventually things ground to a halt. Mike was in Hong Kong, keeping in touch with us daily in Chengdu. He faxed Ted Heath, and asked for his help. He in turn wrote a letter to the Chinese Ambassador in London on our behalf. Roger

Sims asked a Parliamentary Question, enquiring if the British government was aware of the British expedition. It was. Samuel Jones, Chief Executive of Leicestershire City Council, telexed Zhang Haoruo, Governor of Sichuan, asking him to give us as much help as possible, using the twinning network. All this political and diplomatic activity did not seem able to clear the blockages. If we were not careful, the time that the expedition would have on the river would be seriously curtailed, and we were watching many years' careful planning disappearing into nothing. I had worked out with Gwyn and Tony the least important on-river weeks we could axe: the two weeks at Base 2; one week at Base 1; one more week at Base 1; one week at Base 3. If we had to cut all this, we would be left with just two weeks on river for the whole expedition. God forbid. But if it had to come to that, we would cut Base 1 as well as Base 2, amalgamate what was left and go for the source. We prayed we would never have to be in that position.

Then we saw the extraordinary hand of God at work for us. Back in 1987 the Chinese Academy of Sciences (CAS) had come in on the expedition, and the senior professor from Shanghai had given his overall approval. This contact was not pursued as the SMA avenue opened up in the following years. During one of the recces in 1989, the Sichuan CAS heard about the expedition and contacted Sophie, saying that it was just the sort of thing they should be participating in. Sophie was pleased, but had replied that all negotiations were being channelled through the SMA. Unknown to her or us, the Sichuan CAS, in submitting their budget to Beijing for 1990, had placed our expedition at the top of their list. Thus in January 1990 all the top officials in Beijing had given their seal of approval to the CAS budget, and it included our enterprise. So just as our approval through SMA encountered monumental difficulties, another avenue opened up, and we leapt towards it with delight. We dropped the SMA for good, and realigned the expedition as a scientific project. All obvious hindrances in Chengdu vanished at once. A two-man team from the CAS went up to Beijing to talk to what seemed the last hurdle, the People's

65

Liberation Army (PLA). Mike also went up to Beijing to be on hand to sign the contract or to help in the discussions. What a break-through! And what terrific, 'coincidental', planning ahead. That was not all. Xie Jinkang, the head of Sichuan CAS, had been on the 1986 Chinese expedition to the source of the Yangtze, and knew the area.

But more darkness lay in front of us.

4

A Foggy Pathway Through Many Mazes

> There is a tide in the affairs of men,
> Which, taken at the flood, leads on to fortune;
> Omitted, all the voyage of their life
> Is bound in shallows and in miseries.
> On such a full sea are we now afloat,
> And we must take the current when it serves,
> Or lose our ventures.
> (Shakespeare, *Julius Caesar*)

The date for the medical seminars in Chengdu was approaching fast. Mr Zhao's apprehension increased, as did the work the doctors put into their preparation. Mr Zhao had requested that the team submit their lectures at least three days in advance to be translated into Chinese for interpretation. In addition to our UK medical team, there were a number of other eminent speakers. Dr Arne Brantsaeter from Norway spoke English, Swedish, Danish and Chinese as well as his native Norwegian; he became a most useful team member. Ton Schreuders was a Dutch physiotherapist at a leprosy hospital in Thailand. Mr Padman Ratnesar, consultant surgeon, and Professor Garth Hastings were from the UK. In addition we had three representatives from NAPS, Dr Krag (solar fridges), Mr Lehtonen (Asia representative) and Dr Bo Bentzen (solar-powered dentistry). They were a distinguished group of experts, giving most important information to the Chinese doctors who attended. Our own doctors in turn learned some interesting facts about Sichuan from the Chinese lecturers. The province is about

67

the size of France, with a population of 105,897,000, of which 88.7 per cent is counted in the rural areas. Sichuan is divided into 21 districts, 211 counties, 8687 townships and 76,374 villages. There are four levels of doctors in China: a university-trained doctor, taking six or seven years to qualify; a college-trained doctor, taking three or four years (both of these are on a par in terms of qualifications, job and wage prospects, but the university doctor may go on to specialise); a technical college doctor, taking two or three years; a village (or barefoot) doctor, who has no official training and gets his knowledge from reading books. Medical specialisation when qualified is chosen for individuals by the state, and is according to the prevailing needs, although it seems that the individual's preference is sometimes taken into account. The ratio of doctors to patients in Sichuan (presumably from the first two categories) is 1:1250 overall; in rural areas it is 1:4000. In the UK at present it is 1:550.

The three days of lectures were well attended and enthusiastically received. The quality of the seminars, both in presentation and content, was highly appreciated, and Mr Zhao received much honour from all the delegates for arranging such a magnificent programme. He expressed his thanks to the medical team by giving them a banquet on the final evening. The consequences of this conference, together with the accord generated by such cooperation, were likely to continue for some years.

The first spin-off cropped up the following week. Ray, a paediatrician in the Third World, had a special interest in children under seven and their mothers, and she had spent many years in Bhutan training young people as health workers. Ray is a delightful, shrewd, unthreatening lady, whose fire for the missionary task has been tempered by many years' work in the Far East to a strong blend of faith and patience. The woman in charge of all the Sichuan mother and child health work attended their lectures and invited Ray and Bill to a model unit in Chengdu, which was in excellent condition and very well run. She asked if more lectures or teaching along the same lines could be given, and if a proposal could be written up for future cooperation together. Who knows how that contact might develop?

The second came through Ton Schreuders. He and Bill were invited to the Sichuan Institute of Dermatology in Chengdu. The doctors had heard Ton's lecture, and were so pleased with it that they gave him a very warm reception and were glad to share their own experiences. In particular they were struck by Ton's statement, 'You must never separate the surgeon from the physiotherapist in leprosy work', for in China physiotherapy does not play a major part in the surgical treatment of leprosy deformities.

'Yes, we now see that you're right. We did the surgery, but many of our operations failed. Would you like to come down south and see the leprosy work we have done there?'

Dr Hu Lufang broke in. He was the leprosy expert in Sichuan. 'I'm afraid there's no question of that. We don't have permission from Beijing and it would be quite impossible to get it in time.'

'But,' Ton had a sudden thought, 'surely I'm part of the expedition, and the permission has already been granted?'

'Of course,' Mr Zhao brightened up. 'I'd forgotten that. Of course we can let you go. How long have you got in China? We could arrange lectures. How would you like to visit some of our other leprosaria in Sichuan? How much longer do you expect to remain in Thailand? Do you like China? Would you be prepared to come and work here?'

Questions and enthusiasm tumbled from him. Within a minute he had virtually offered Ton, and Bill if he wished, *carte blanche* to work anywhere in Sichuan they chose, for an indefinite length of time. (Bill had had many years of hands-on experience of leprosy surgery in Nepal.) We were starting to see the gracious hand of God bringing unexpected blessings out of our expedition. Ton had a month available in China, and because there were few leprosy patients in the north-west where the expedition was going, he was prepared to spend those weeks in the places where his expertise would be most valuable.

Meanwhile the struggles at the top to get permission to go on the river continued unabated.

The task of negotiating with the Chinese proved exceedingly difficult. We had not anticipated it would take as long as it did – just week after interminable week. The greatest number of pre-expedition visits that Mike had made to any other country was two to Peru. This time he and five others travelled five times to China, and seemed to achieve much. But once we were there for real, we discovered we had far from finished our bureaucratic work; it was as though we had not even begun. The real problem we found was that the Chinese do not see things with the same honesty that we do. That is not to call them dishonest – it is to try to recognise that they have a very different set of priorities and values. In the West we are achievement-and-efficiency orientated. Time matters. In China they seem to be person-orientated and time is infinitely available. The Chinese spend months getting to know a person before asking him what he came for. The effects of this cultural disposition have been compounded by bureaucracy and Communism, which, because it is a rigid and fairly dictatorial system, insists that, above all, good relations with one's boss are the paramount consideration in any situation. If the director says 'No', then the subordinate can quite legitimately tell the customer what he likes, provided he does not actually let himself or his boss down. Because each unit has a system and a Foreign Affairs Office, and each section has a tier of superior units above it, the bureaucracy becomes immense. No one will make a decision at any level until their next superior has agreed. So no decision can be made until everyone has had a go, everyone agrees, and no one has an objection. It takes weeks. Nor will they plan ahead. If the final decision has not been given, nothing can be permitted to happen in between to ease things when that decision comes. Add to this the cultural insistence on not losing face – which makes it very difficult for a Chinese man to apologise, admit he is wrong or change his decision – and you are left with a towering bargaining system that is very tedious, very frustrating and very difficult to handle. Above all, the customer must not lose his cool – that would be a great insult to the Chinese man.

70

So, when our team of five had sat down in front of Mr Zhao of the SMA on 6 March, he first of all said that they must go home. He cited at least seven reasons why the Chinese were unhappy about the expedition, and so started an interminable series of negotiation meetings trying to put all the objections straight: in fact going over ground that had been adequately covered and agreed before. When the team dealt with one of the objections – such as a survey of the Yangtze water purity – and returned, they discovered that this was no longer a problem; but another difficulty had arisen. The next day the team found a third difficulty was hindering the signing of the contract. This went on for a month. Every time we came back they had moved the goal-posts. In the book *Gunboats on the Great River* a story is told about the steamship *Kuling* in 1887:

> She reached Ichang and was stuck there for the better part of two years during protracted, and in the end fruitless, negotiations with obscurantist Chinese mandarins who put forward a series of most ridiculous objections to the ship's passage to Chungking. 'The monkeys,' they said, 'would throw stones from the high cliffs, making it unsafe to proceed' or 'Emperor Yu never intended steamers to enter the gorges; had he wished it, he would have invented them then.' Finally the Chinese Government, with bland duplicity, bought the ship and promptly sold it at a considerable profit to the China Steam Navigation Co. who operated it successfully on the Ichang–Hankow run for a number of years.

As a comparison, consider this illustration of playing a game of badminton. First of all, you spend a day deciding the rules. You come back the following day with a racket and shuttlecock and dressed in shorts, and discover that, in fact, the game was not badminton after all, but bridge. You shrug your shoulders, and use the rest of the day to agree new rules. Returning the next day with your pack of cards, your opponents are surprised you brought it, for they were actually planning to go roller-skating.

We were required to pay for each item that was agreed.

Everybody wanted us to pay money for everything. We were forced to pay the customs men £64 for 'services rendered' – the administrative cost of our walking into their office. Gwyn had suspected that the containers had arrived in Chengdu railway station, so a bunch of us went to see. We tried two stations before we found the right one, which was fortunately empty during the lunch hour. Strolling in, we found them, and then returned to the customs to ask that the three containers be cleared for transportation to the medical university grounds. What containers? Our discovery had thrown them completely. Gwyn had to go in half a dozen times to ask, each time registering a 'No', and on each occasion clocking up money we had to pay merely for going in.

Thus nothing was actually done, and we went from game to game, at an enormous cost to our pockets and man hours, and still did not unearth what the real blockage was. In Mr Zhao's case it was the fact that between our Letter of Intent in December and our negotiations in March, he had done nothing at all, even though we left him £2500 deposit in good faith. With the transfer of sponsorship to the CAS, Mr Zhao of the SMA lost our contract and a lot of money for his company. And the young men in the SMA were very disappointed: one of them had turned down a trip to the American Rockies in order to come with us on the river. The real hold-up was that his bosses at the Beijing Sports Commission were disgruntled that the expedition was there in China without their prior knowledge or approval. In fact the first the BSC heard about it was from the international noises we made in Hong Kong. God had given Mel insight into the root of the problem, so we insisted that the SMA's FAO started to negotiate with the BSC. That took days. But, we supposed, once the BSC boss had said 'No', then it could not be rescinded without loss of face. We realised that the 'no through road' signs were beginning to go up along the BSC avenue. The rigid system meant it was impossible for the SMA to take the initiative on anything without approval from higher authority, or they would lose face if it turned out to be wrong or was reversed. Fortunately other units' FAOs were prepared to stick their necks out, and progress was made through both the scientific and medical departments.

As God had providentially planned, the scientific avenue opened up before us, and Mike hastened to Beijing to monitor the Sichuan CAS team's negotiations with Beijing's CAS team, led by Professor Yang Li. Since Beijing CAS fortuitously already knew about it, and had given approval to the expedition, there were no other initial hold-ups.

However Mike felt that enough of our precious time had already been wasted. Quite a few team members had resigned from their jobs in the UK to come on the expedition, some had sold their businesses, others had left theirs in inexperienced hands, and all had given personal savings to come. So Mike now introduced as much top-level input as he could, hoping to move the bureaucracy from above. Norman Willimot was a First Secretary to the British Council at the embassy in Beijing. He had helped early in 1989 and, as a Christian, was keen to help again. His fluent *Putonghua* (Mandarin) and knowledge of Chinese culture meant we avoided more unnecessary pitfalls.

Mr Padman Ratnesar also devoted his confident charm to try to tease out the knots of our tangled situation. Padman is a Sri Lankan-born British citizen, a consultant with Bromley Health Authority specialising in ear, nose and throat medicine, and also has a profound concern for the underprivileged. He had been involved with Mike in some of his South American adventures, and was now intimately embroiled with him in Beijing. Padman, in time past, had been involved in a rehabilitation centre for deaf children in Beijing. Ted Heath and Roger Sims, MPs, were also involved in its support, Mr Heath having given all the proceeds of a concert towards the building of an extension to the centre. The Chairman of the China Disabled Person's Federation was no less than Deng Pufang, son of China's Chairman. Pufang had been crippled when he was thrown out of a window during the Cultural Revolution, and was now confined to a wheelchair. Pufang was a personal friend of Padman's, but was unfortunately ill at the moment. Yet his second in command, Liu Jing, was glad to welcome Padman, who shared the plight of the expedition and asked him to put in a good word for us.

As another extraordinary providence, Padman discovered that the Sri Lankan Ambassador in Beijing was an old school and university friend of his; they had known one another since they were eleven. Mike, Padman, Arne and Norman Willimot went to dinner at the Sri Lankan Embassy, where the Ambassador said he would do all he could for the expedition through diplomatic channels. While he was there, Padman asked if he could telephone Mrs S. W. R. D. Bandaranayake – who was related to his wife – a previous Prime Minister of Sri Lanka and a good friend of China. She was delighted to fax the Chinese Premier Li Peng on our behalf.

The Sichuan CAS returned to Mike, having spoken with Professor Yang Li of the Beijing CAS. Everyone they spoke to supported the expedition wholeheartedly, except one group: the People's Liberation Army. Could we give them details of the expedition so that Beijing CAS could brief the PLA? We certainly could. Perhaps we were getting close to the original blockage that no one had ever bothered to mention to us?

Three days went by.

The Sichuan CAS called Mike back in. 'There is no objection to the expedition from the PLA in Beijing or anyone else. The only blockage is with the Sichuan PLA in Chengdu.' So we were back again with our local PLA Commander, and the three trudged back from Beijing to Chengdu, grateful to Norman for his help.

Arne Brantsaeter had gone up to Beijing with the other two, only because there had been problems within the team. Two who had joined the team just prior to the medical seminars were representatives of NAPS (Neste Advanced Power Systems), a very small subsidiary of Neste. Matte Lehtonen and Dr Nils Krag were giving papers on the solar-powered fridges that were to be taken up the river. After the seminars they asked to see Bill and Ray, and then dealt out to them a severe critique on how badly the medical

74

side of the expedition had been handled. The conversation was taped. This was quite a shock to all of us. The following day they repeated the criticisms, Matte claiming to represent Neste, our major sponsors, and saying that UNICEF knew nothing of our activities or our expedition, that they were not associated with it, and that they had a letter from headquarters in Geneva to say as much. They videoed this interview. Bill refused to answer the accusations, and sent for Mel, who answered the questions, showing written evidence that UNICEF in Beijing knew exactly what we were doing, and were fully informed, fully briefed and fully supportive. Matte was not satisfied, and went to Mr Zhao Xijie, to whom we were forced to say that neither Matte nor Nils spoke for the expedition. Moreover the letter they showed us from UNICEF Geneva had been written early in March, and Arne asked to see it. Nils did not know that Arne could read Danish. There, at the bottom, was a note in Danish to Nils, saying, 'Please get in touch with the leader of the expedition immediately.'

'You accuse me of inefficiency, Nils,' said Arne. 'Why did you not show us this letter? It is at least four weeks old.'

Matte and Nils decided to go to Beijing to talk to UNICEF there. Mike said that Arne, knowing so many languages, should go too, to monitor what Matte and Nils were doing. Mike let them know that despite their Neste connections, they were neither in control nor in command of this expedition: their place was a minor one in the medical team, and as such they were to work under the direction of the medical leaders. Eventually it appeared that their behaviour was the result of a misunderstanding; Nils wanted to use the expedition in order to sell solar fridges, and he did not see our aim as contributing to that. When they all visited UNICEF together in Beijing, UNICEF said they were quite happy with the expedition, knew all about it, but had to tell Matte and Nils that they could see no way they could support or assist the sale of any solar fridges in the foreseeable future. Such commercial goals were not to be part of our expedition.

While the negotiations were continually involved in trying to get permits, the rest of the team had little to do. So we 'discovered' Chengdu and rooted around for interesting aspects of Chinese culture. I was fascinated by Chinese moral attitudes.

Sex is a well-tried and trusted method of reproduction, and China, with its immense population of 1200 million, has positively proved that; but it has therefore been forced to face and tackle the problem of birth control. Stamping on all moral, ethical and other considerations, China focused her attention purely on numbers. She needed to do something: 1 in every 5 people on the planet is Chinese; 1 in every 45 resides in Sichuan. Chairman Mao at one point recommended large families, so that the earth could be filled with Chinese. But the bad agriculture techniques accompanied by disastrous drought, flooding and pest infestations in the 1960s brought a dramatic reversal of that policy; all of a sudden Mao Zedong realised that China was unable to feed and support the ever-expanding number of hungry mouths, and that, economically, it would be crippling to have to import foodstuffs and pay the populace. So China addressed the problem of overpopulation, and introduced the most radical and most efficient of birth control policies and education of any nation in the world. Despite earlier attempts, the 1972 birth control mandate was by far the most effective, and we discovered considerable knowledge of its recommendations and considerable adherence to its policies wherever we enquired.

Girls are not allowed to marry before the age of twenty, and men before twenty-two. Marriage is a civil ceremony in law, and is a huge social occasion. We found no evidence of any Christian or religious ceremony overtly practised in China, but, no doubt in the coastal zones where Christianity is strongest, many marriages will have been contracted in churches. The state does not like couples to have children before the age of twenty-five, but the real control is done in the *danwei* (work unit) to which every adult Chinese belongs. Because the *danwei* does not wish to have too many women off work at any one time, control of pregnancy

76

is strictly governed by them, and children are only permitted in order. One lady per unit is detailed to go round to all the other women every month to check whether they have had their period. All children conceived out of turn are automatically aborted, as are all of those conceived out of wedlock. The main methods of contraception are the pill and the IUCD of which the family planning clinics recommended ten different shapes. Every *danwei* has its own Family Planning Training Centre. Officially, there are no back-street abortions, for abortion does not appear to have the unhappy cultural overtones that it does in the West.

Families are limited to one child only. There are certain minor exceptions to this rule; if, for example, there have been two previous generations on both husband's and wife's sides that have had only one child, then the couple are permitted two. Minority peoples are allowed two. All third children are to be aborted. If a couple have a malformed child, they are sometimes permitted a second, as the first generally does not live long. A family history of genetic malformation precludes the birth of a second child. We discovered, however, that many of these rules are ignored in rural areas because of the difficulty of implementing them.

Even though the authorities heavily restrict the number of children per family, we discovered that they also care about infertility. If a family cannot have a child, they can visit the Infertility Advisory Unit. Among other ways of helping a wife to conceive, artificial insemination is practised in this unit. Even using a donor is not frowned upon.

Families mostly remain together throughout their lives, and the incidence of separation and divorce is rare. However, quite a number of instances of husbands and wives living in different locations were found, where the state required one to be in one area and the other in another. If husband and wife, for instance, belong to different *danwei*, then they live separately for most of the year.

That the family planning policy is bearing fruit is shown in their statistics. In 1952 the number of children per 1000 was 30.6; and this had reduced to 13.5 by 1988. In the 1950s the average marrying age for women was 19.35, while in the

77

1980s it had risen to 22.57. Again in the 1950s the average number of children per family was 5.4, and in the 1980s it was down to 1.41. Between 1970 and 1988 the policy reduced the population increase by 200 million. Pretty effective. Unfortunately for the planners, better medicine has lengthened the lives of older people, and this has compounded the population problem. Planning is very difficult – Chengdu will have 1.2 million adults entering childbearing age in the last decade of the century and they want to keep its population below 9.85 million by the year 2000. Old fashioned ideas, they say, like 'The more children, the happier, are counter-productive, and people need to be re-educated to think differently. By and large, they are, but it is a slow process.

Westerners take a radically different approach to birth control, feeling that governmental dictates of China's sort would restrict individual freedom. Western birth control is by personal choice, taking a rational and mature view of our own and the world's situations. About a quarter of the Chinese population is illiterate, and Jasper Becker has pointed out that:

> there can be no population control without coercion since only when a country's education and wealth reaches a certain level will ordinary people stop wanting lots of children on their own accord. And that means a China with too many people will always be poor. There will never be enough money to go round to spend on education, roads, houses, hospitals, foreign travel and the good things in life, except of course for the élite. ('The Last Empire', *Britain–China*, May 1990)

Rob and I were invited to a girls' dormitory in the Medical University. The room was about three metres square, with whitewashed walls and an abysmally patched ceiling (a cat, they said, had fallen through it). Pictures of a western *Vogue* model in red flowing silk on an evening beach blended with postcards and Chinese jokes – all typical of a student's bedroom. High-rise beds with very hard bases were covered with sheets, quilts and pretty, embroidered pillows, and circumnavigated by thick mosquito nets. Each of the four girls had a dark brown, flat desk with a small cupboard attached on the right side – standard issue. Books on medicine and anatomy were stacked neatly on each top. I wondered where they kept their clothes and Jenny pointed to a suitcase, jammed between her chair and Amy's bed. I could not help noticing that Jane's top bunk was in need of serious carpentry.

'What do you think of marriage?' I asked Rosalind, continuing my investigations into Chinese ways.

'It's important,' she replied.

'Do many people live together without being married?'

'Very few,' Amy broke in. She was short and round and wore glasses. 'There have been one or two on the campus, but they were expelled immediately.'

'Are there many pregnancies, say, on this campus?' I persisted.

'Oh no!' Amy replied, shocked. 'There's nothing like that here in China. It is really looked down on in our society.'

'Do any schoolgirls get pregnant?'

'Very few,' Jane interjected. Jane was slim and wore an iron-grey trouser-skirt and three jumpers. 'Maybe some very young teenagers. I suppose the youngest I've known of was seventeen.'

I was more than interested. Clearly sexual morality in China was of a higher standard than in the UK.

'What would they do if they did get pregnant?' I asked.

'There is so much shame attached to it that they would probably go out into the country and get the pregnancy terminated.'

'You mean back-street abortions?'

'Yes. There are a number of women in the countryside who specialise in that sort of thing. Or, they might go to another city.'

'And what about divorce?'

'It is hard in China to get a divorce. But the number is increasing slowly. Divorce is looked down upon here. If you want to get on in China, you have to have a good

79

political stance and have a good private life. People who are divorced never get on.'

'And,' here Jenny's turn came, 'your life follows you wherever you go.'

'What do you mean?'

'Everything you have done is recorded, and the records go from *danwei* to *danwei*. So if you've done something wrong, you can never shake off its stigma.' Jenny was petite, with typical Chinese-girl slimness, short hair, glasses, bright eyes and a radiant, magnetic smile that lit up her face like a beacon.

'Do you have arranged marriages in China?'

All the girls giggled. 'Some take their boyfriends home as soon as they meet them. Others are a bit shyer. But if your parents believe in arranged marriages, all we do is go to them and ask for an introduction to our boyfriend. They then "arrange" it for us.' Clearly the young person's way of stamping on tradition and altering the culture.

'Is there much prostitution or homosexuality?'

'No,' Jane said. 'I suppose there are some prostitutes if you go down to the Black Cat restaurant not far from the Jin Jiang, that's the place you can see them. In fact the police have a purge on the Jin Jiang Hotel itself every now and then.'

'Homosexuals?'

'Our society thinks that they're disgusting,' said Amy. 'But many foreigners think there are lots here, because both girls and fellows hold hands or hug one another. It is not considered wrong or unusual here at all. And it's certainly not homosexuality.'

Rob said, 'My girls often hold hands with their girl friends, and in the UK no one thinks anything of it. But men never hold hands in our country.'

'We even have men dancing together,' Rosalind laughed. 'I don't suppose you do that in England?'

We shook our heads. 'Certainly not. Girls, yes. Men, no.'

'Things have changed such a lot here,' said bright-eyed Jenny. 'Six years ago everyone who wore jeans was thought to be terrible.' I smiled. She was sitting on her minuscule stool in a pair of faded jeans, with a couple of butterfly patches on them. 'There was a media campaign against them. Newspapers carried articles against them, and the TV viewed them as . . . ' Her English was good, but she could not think of the right word.

'Trendy?' I suggested.

'No, no,' Rosalind came in again. Her collarless shirt had been washed in brown water and was as wrinkled as my self-washed T-shirt. 'Quite the opposite. Disgusting. Scandalous. Shameful.'

Peter, another Chengdu student, came in. He enquired in a very loud voice what we were doing, and, because his 'Chinglish' was too slow for all he wanted to get out, he used a mixture of *Putonghua* and *Yinggua* (English), getting everything translated. The conversation turned to the expedition.

'I do not believe this expedition will succeed,' Peter rather angrily concluded after many enquiries. 'It is too dangerous.'

I assured him that our hovercraft were man enough for the river, and pointed out that the Tiger Leaping Gorge, which he claimed would destroy them, was 1500 km south of our operating area. To find such cynicism and defeatism in a young man surprised me.

The raised voice brought responses from next door. Two voices – male and female – asked a question, and they seemed to be remarkably loud. I prodded the wall. It gave in. It was merely a piece of mosquito netting draped over the gap.

Jenny laughed. 'Our room was too big. So we cut it down. They are coming in.'

Agnes and Ugly Boy joined us. (Yes, they really called him that!) Agnes was sharp-minded and articulate, with grey, discordant teeth. Ugly Boy – well, I was so embarrassed and unhappy to call such a delightful young man by that name that I hardly addressed him all evening.

'Are you subjected to much political indoctrination?' I loaded and fired another bullet. I confess that I am still

81

somewhat confused by their answer. They had three lectures a week in secondary school on 'Marxist economics and capitalist stupidities'. But these classes generally turned into discussions on moral and social ethics instead. Here in the university they had one three-hour lecture on Communism per week, but none of the girls seemed perturbed by any of them. Another girl, on another occasion, was particularly scathing about these lectures and did not believe a word of them: boring, irrelevant, unnecessary and fatuous were the words she used. I found another quote from Jasper Becker's article, 'The Last Empire', in *Britain–China*, Spring 1990:

> The trouble for the diehards in Moscow or Beijing is that – as we have seen in Eastern Europe – the masses given the chance to vote are so fed up with socialism that they want nothing better than to throw out the Communist parties immediately, even though they do not necessarily want to abandon the welfare state . . . China's party has less than 50 million members, so less than 4% of the population controls the rest.

'What comes over the camp loudspeaker at 6.30 a.m.?' I asked.

'That's the international news.'

I confess I had thought it to be political rhetoric. It was a great disadvantage not to have any decent knowledge of the written or spoken language. And my pidgin Chinese was not getting any better.

'What are the notices on the board at the front gate?'

'Oh, they are just advertising coming events,' chimed in Agnes.

Again, I was surprised, and glad, to see that there was very little oppression in terms of political and social 'education'. I had expected there to be far more than there was, especially in the university. The authorities generally seemed to allow students – and those outside the campus – far more freedom to think and choose than had been permitted to their predecessors.

above *Neste Enterprise* in the busiest waterway in the world,
Victoria Harbour, Hong Kong.

above Duncan Hanton answers questions at the Hong Kong waterfront.

above Some of China's 360 million bicycles going all ways round a roundabout in Chengdu.

above Dr Arne Brantsaeter compares the Mandarin and English scripts of the contract, assisted by Sam Brooks.

above The expedition team awaits the advance to the river at the President's House at Chengdu University of Medical Science.

above On our way to the river at last! We were impressed by the Chinese genius for land recovery.

inset above One of our many new friends practises his English.

Inset above A journey is made possible by our innovative engineers.

above The first pass outside Kanding brought us into the crisp air of 4,000 m and exposed the snow-capped mountains many kilometres away.

above Sophie - Zhou Shufen - from Chengdu Foreign Affairs Office.
She was a great encouragement as we tackled bureaucratic problems.

Our conversation drifted through issues such as who paid their fees at university (parents or state for food and books, depending on income); unions (set up to encourage workers to work harder and to organise social parties); lawyers (loser pays all); and policemen (you can bargain with them if you get fined). The girls offered us tea. Rob had the big ex-coffee jar, and I the small one. The tea was pale; I guess the leaves had been washed through a few times, as with most Chinese tea.

Rob and I declared stumps drawn at 10 p.m. The lights in the whole block would all be centrally extinguished at 11 p.m. The girls accompanied us out into the silken night (doesn't Chengdu ever get any wind?) and we parted, after a most enjoyable evening, at their classroom, where Rosalind had left some books.

During our explorations, the negotiators had been getting more and more bogged down in muddy confrontations. Getting permission for this expedition to go into the restricted area of Sichuan and Qinghai was the most appalling of experiences. It was like trying to fight a giant octopus in an opaque sea without breathing apparatus, where you can't see, you don't know which sticky tentacle to deal with first, and you are gasping for breath just to survive. Norman Willimot said that if God had not been on our side and fighting for us, the expedition would have been more than a failure – it would probably never even have entered China. He should know, he had been dealing with Chinese cultural methods for years.

The most positive negotiations had been those between John Whatmore and Sichuan TV concerning media coverage of the expedition. In the preceding year, John had been trying to interest UK TV companies in sending a crew with us. None of these responded, and in retrospect we could detect the overruling hand of God in this. The real problem lay in the way the world press presented the events of Tiananmen Square. The TV reports that came out of Beijing in the summer of 1989 did almost irreparable damage to China and its image in the world. The consequence was a total clamp-down on all foreign TV reporting – particularly in the closed areas. This restriction on foreign TV was further tightened as a result of a clandestine operation by Granada TV, who sent a team disguised as tourists and filmed some of the students trying to escape from China: it was broadcast in *World in Action* in the autumn of 1989. The Chinese took considerable objection to this programme.

The aftermath of these incidents meant that it would have been virtually impossible to get a British TV crew in officially on any pretext whatever. Moreover, those we planned to have would have cost the expedition £120,000, and a considerable proportion of that would have been lost as they sat back kicking their heels with us in Chengdu awaiting permission to move. So John fell back to setting up a contract with the Sichuan TV company. This was a shrewd move, as it meant that it was a Chinese eye looking through the viewfinder on all expedition film. The contract enabled Sichuan TV to have a duplicate copy of all film taken, which they could edit any way they wished. But John, who was to direct all the shooting, would retain international copyrights. John cleverly side-stepped a financial deal by arranging a straight swop; Sichuan TV would film the expedition in return for the Chinese crew spending a few weeks in the UK in 1991, as our guests, filming some negotiable subject. The contract for the TV rights was made out, confirmed, worked, and eventually signed as soon as formal permission for the expedition was given.

The medical contract underwent a covert initiation, where nothing could be agreed until permission had been granted, but the seminars were permitted to go ahead. The EPI programme, which had been the cornerstone of the medical work, and indeed the humanitarian reason for the whole expedition, flowed sweetly throughout most of the protracted negotiations. Then, for no reason that we could ever fully uncover, it hit a rapid. Rather, a waterfall. Ray, Bill and Arne were invited to a meeting with the Chinese medical negotiators (except Mr Zhao Xijie, who was away for two days), just as the permits were imminent.

They simply said, 'We cannot now carry out the EPI programme. The Tibetans are a backward race, there are not many of them there, and they would be unable to handle solar fridges or continue the programme after you have left.'

This was shattering news. If it was true, then the doctors' main task would revert to looking after the team, and the rationale that had caused Neste to sponsor us and the trust of many hundreds of people who had invested in us, were blown to smithereens. As usual, trying to get to the root reason was like trying to nail jelly to a tree. Had we not come to care for the backward, the oppressed, the forgotten?

When Zhao Xijie returned it became difficult to arrange a meeting with him. Eventually Padman cornered him to talk about a rehabilitation centre for the deaf, and Ray, who was with him, was able to say we were prepared to compromise on the location of the solar fridges: two in Chengdu for training and relocation, two in Dege, and two on the hovercraft. But Ray was adamant that Neste had given us, not Nils Krag, the responsibility for determining the location of these devices, and, if we were unhappy with what the Chinese were planning to do with them, we would pack every single one of them in the containers and return them to the UK. This was startling news to Mr Zhao, and five meetings later he agreed to our terms about the fridges.

The leprosy spin-off developed beautifully. Ton Schreuders was a really superlative ambassador for the Leprosy Mission to send. He was a good communicator, listener, encourager, and stimulator, and his quiet, but strong Christian commitment gave him a genuine love for leprosy patients, a consuming interest in the subject of leprosy and an undoubted professional competence. The outstanding contribution that Ton made to the Chinese knowledge of leprosy was that disabilities could be prevented, a concept totally new to them. When they complained that it would cost money, Ton pointed out that it only needed soap, water, vaseline, oil, bandages and simple dressings even made out of old sheets and shirts. Ton's second contribution was to introduce to the Chinese the necessity for physiotherapy. Without it, reconstruction surgery would be a failure. Dr Hu, the director of the Sichuan Institute of

Dermatology, planned to issue a formal invitation to the Leprosy Mission to send out one or more people to the four leprosaria in the Province for a two to three month period of advice. He recommended that Ton should head it.

On Easter Saturday, 14 April, Ton flew down to Kunming, on Dr Hu's invitation, to visit leprosaria in Yunnan Province before returning home to Thailand. It seemed as if God was opening a door in China for the Leprosy Mission after many years in which they had not seen even a crack of opportunity.

But to our dismay it seemed as if God was closing the medical door on the expedition itself. Having tried to cancel the EPI programme altogether, and reluctantly put it on again, Mr Zhao Xijie came back to us and said that, because it was too difficult to organise a good EPI programme in the mountainous Dege district, we were only able to carry it out at Dege itself. That would take only one day. Ray and Bill were appalled. One day? For a whole year now we had been promised three weeks of EPI inoculations, covering the whole of the river area of north-west Sichuan. Bill was all for cancelling the project entirely, and taking the NAPS solar fridges home. Ray was more philosophical, accepting the proposal, but she insisted the Chinese increase the one day's inoculations to five days' teaching, instruction and health care. It was a grave disappointment. We had brought enough syringes to inoculate 250,000 children and adults, based on the promises given in 1989. What were we to do with them?

We wondered whether Nils Krag had something to do with the curtailment. Or was it the Chinese? Or was it genuinely impossible to organise an efficient programme in the mountains? If the latter, why did they tell us only three days before the permit was granted, and five weeks after negotiations had begun? The medical programme had been severed to one thin strand. We hoped that God was lining up for us something much greater, for which the curtailment was a necessity.

On Wednesday, 18 April, after the trauma of getting hold of the main permit to go on the river, the medical contract was signed. The only difference between that and the original of 6 March was that all reference to the medical seminars was erased, because they had already taken place.

There had been nothing on the scientific side for a while, but suddenly things shot into action. The scientific seminars, so well planned, had been zapped by the BSC via the sponsoring unit, the SMA. But when the CAS initiative was revealed, the scientific side, and with it the training emphasis, rose sharply. Suddenly the scientific aspects of the expedition became the core rationale for all we did. A contract was drawn up, and the CAS progressed through all negotiations with the PLA, both in Sichuan and Beijing. At one stage there was a flaming row (not in our presence) between Mr Xie Jinkang of the CAS and Mr Zhao of the SMA. After that Mr Zhao of the SMA became repentant, more human, more smiling and less obstructive.

We got verbal clearance to go to the river at 4 p.m. on Saturday, 14 April – not time enough to open our containers nor to do anything constructive that day. But at least we had the clearance. It was Easter Saturday. We awaited resurrection dynamite from the next day onwards. We did not exactly get it. On Easter Monday Mike went down to the FAO demanding that Customs open the containers. He got a guarded response, which prompted him to quote that a member of the British Parliament, Roger Sims, the Chinese ambassador to Britain, Mrs Bandaranyike of Sri Lanka and even Li Peng, the Chinese Prime Minister, were all saying that approval had been given. Why could not the FAO give Customs an order to open the containers? It was phenomenally difficult to instil any sense of urgency into the Chinese authorities. They only moved when Mike threatened to ring Beijing himself.

The next negotiating area was logistics. We had to pay the Chinese for transport. This came in two parts – equipment and fuel. We were having to pay for the equipment convoys, and Exxon Chemical PARAMINS were, thankfully, paying for both the fuel and its transportation, although we had to arrange it.

The equipment trucks were originally being negotiated

through the SMA. Now of course we had to begin again through the CAS, though they could at least hire the same lorries, and, like the SMA, had a few of their own to throw into the pool. Speaking for the CAS was Mr Xie Jinkang, head of the Chengdu Division of Mountain Disaster (that is, earthquakes) and Environmental Research Institute. He was as sharp as a tin-tack, as were all his supporting entourage. Fencing for us were Tony Burgess, Sam Brooks and Arne Brantsaeter (ace interpreter), an equally acute negotiating team. Without a doubt the Chinese were out to get as much money from us as possible. We were also out to get as much from them as we could, for a fair and reasonable price, and we had to be as relentless as they were.

Monday, 9 April started by clearing the ground. The CAS helpfully accepted the original parameters negotiated by the SMA as stated in the Letter of Intent. Under discussion came the type and number of vehicles, the distances to be covered (with the let-out clause that if any day's mileage exceeded 100 km we must pay an exorbitant 3.8 yuan extra per kilometre), the type and number of accompanying Chinese, their accommodation and food (they don't like living in tents and they don't like western food), and the length of time we would be in the field. Most Chinese refused to travel in the hovercraft. They were deeply fearful of the Yangtze. How they planned to get 900 km to the source was a mystery; as was how they would survive at −15°C to −20°C without warm clothing. We had got spare Neste kit for only five extra people. The Chinese piled more and more people on to us; they seemed to think this was to be a 'jolly' where they could just trot up to 15,500 feet for two months without serious training or preparation. The cut and thrust of bargaining was conducted in a charming, cooperative and knowledgeable way. Mr Xie Jinkang, who preferred to sit or squat on the floor, initially took no notes or committed anything to paper. But he missed nothing. Sam accelerated his own caffeine intake to addictive proportions during those endless days of confinement.

Towards the end of these traumatic bargaining negotiations the FAO put on a banquet for us. It was a little premature since the permit was not yet in evidence, but it was Mike's birthday, 10 April, and they decided to celebrate it with Chinese food, which Mike only endures with grace. Hosting the evening was Mr Chen Linzhang, deputy director of Sichuan FAO; an important man. In his speech Mike started off by quoting from a birthday letter he had received from his teacher daughter, Carolyn. In the burden of those unbelievably difficult negotiations, where disappointment, frustration and incomprehension were battering us hourly, Carolyn's letter to her dad was a tonic of inexpressible delight. I quote part of it with permission:

> As you read this letter you'll be sitting in a tent by the river; it might be hot, it might be cold. Pressures will be all around you, team members being awkward, political hassles, beautiful smiling faces of Chinese children, the sound of roaring water, towering mountain peaks, ice-blue glaciers, cultures, traditions, bright reds and oranges of the local people – toothless grins, bright eyes and God's mission within your heart. Challenges all around you, and you wonder if you can keep going. It's your Birthday today and, even as your child I hope I'm a blessing within your life – a creation because of love. As you think back over the last years of your life – you've learned so much and done so much – each building up to this moment – maybe; or is there even greater ahead? A man so stubborn and single-minded for God – a Father I'm very proud of. To those to whom much is given, much is required, and no one could ever doubt that you have ever given less than 100 per cent to God.
>
> Conquer this Mountain, Dad, and come back safely to us.

Starting with his daughter's first sentence, Mike publicly expressed his disappointment at not yet being by the banks of the Yangtze. Throughout the evening he took the opportunity to ask this important man why we yet had no permit, why the Customs officials would not open the container doors, why was there such a hold-up? Mr Chen was stung into asking the same questions to his subordinates. They, in their turn, were able to tell him that they were doing all they could, but the delay was in Beijing. And, truth to tell, the Sichuan FAO were the most cooperative and helpful team of negotiators we had – all batting furiously for us. Especially Sophie – Zhou Shufen – who was three months pregnant and had to cope with morning sickness and mounting stress together.

Tuesday, 10th – Mike's birthday. Saturday, 14th – verbal permission. Monday, 16th Mike went down to the FAO and was ruthlessly adamant with them: if other world capitals had confirmation that the permit was granted, why didn't we? It was hurriedly faxed through that afternoon after a heated telephone conversation from the FAO to Beijing. At 9.30 p.m. on Tuesday, 17th the container doors were opened. At last we could take out *Neste Enterprise* and *ICI River Rover* and do the essential engineering work on them.

Still outstanding was the sponsoring contract with the CAS for equipment transport. The transportation of the fuel had been initiated privately with Dr Hu Shiyan of the Chengdu Aircraft Corporation, in the early days with the SMA. Dr Hu was faithful to all his promises (and spotlessly punctual for all appointments) and, as a test run, had transported the three containers from the Eastern Railway Station to the medical campus. China is not yet fully geared to handle containers. The railway had lifting cranes, but there were no trucks available specifically designed for containers. The Chengdu Aircraft Corporation (CAC) brought in some lorries. The container was gently lowered on to the first, which started to tilt backwards alarmingly under the weight – grossly and comically inadequate.

We recorded all the excitement on video. Gwyn, who was arranging the fuel contract and had been rushing around for three days trying to make Chinese officials move, threatened the CAC with the loss of the major fuel transportation contract if they did not come up with better lorries. They did. Within two hours. Three huge articulated lorries (not container trucks) appeared and, at a financial loss to the CAC, trundled the boxes to the campus, three days and six hours later than advertised. The crane they arranged was a 16 tonne mobile crane, inadequate for lifting 15 tonnes of container. Containers need a crane on both ends. But, with bland engineering ignorance, the Chinese put a split wire strap round the container bellies, jacked them off the 'artics' and lowered them to the ground. Our three ICI team members turned pale, covered their eyes and walked away, after expressing their distress at this practice. But for the fact that all three containers were new, they would have buckled and folded in the middle. But God sometimes favours the ignorant, and always favours the faithful; the three containers only suffered bent bottoms, and the three ICI employees suffered expanded experiences. The CAC, in spite of their malpractice, but blessed by their initiative, got our contract. We knew, too, that they were likely to give us a good deal, because Dr Hu wanted to publish a book in the West, and Mel was navigating that through for him with his own publishers. The contract we wrote with the CAC was fair to both sides, and we faxed the amounts to Exxon Chemical PARAMINS for their approval and ultimate payment. There we encountered another stumbling block: Exxon's calculations of the budget were short by 75 per cent, despite starting with the same figures as we had. They wanted more quotes from other transport companies. But they soon realised that there was no point in doing this in China, because all the agents you can find belong to the government. We sent Andrew Sneller down to Hong Kong to sort it out.

Andrew is a chartered surveyor who came late into the expedition, and brought with him a wealth of business acumen and financial expertise. He is a lined, wise old buzzard, equipped with half-moon glasses on a chain and a delightful sense of humour. He soon became Mike's adjutant, and before long was carrying the purse. He was ideal for the job – as tight as a rusted lock-nut for twisting money out of. We nicknamed him 'Renminbi' (the local Chinese currency), which soon changed to 'RenminA' in deference to his name. His visit to Hong Kong had a dual purpose: he also went down to collect a loan from our UK bank, an overdraft of

£33,000. They promised us up to £60,000 if we needed it. It was of interest to discover that capitalist banks take twelve days to transfer money from the UK to Hong Kong, but just two hours to transfer an overdraft for the same amount to the same place, cash in hand. Perhaps our western ways are no less devious than the Chinese practices that were frustrating us!

Andrew came back with our loan, £20,000 up front from Exxon Chemical PARAMINS and the promise of full payment from Managing Director Low Hee Tek. The negotiations for the equipment contract with the CAS went into overdrive, every meeting hitting a new peak of covert tension. The mollifying factor was that the Chinese syndicate consisted of delightful and affable people. All meetings started and ended on friendly terms. In between it was all sweat and gore.

To each new meeting the CAS brought new proposals for charging us more money. We fought each one (some of which were quite ludicrous), stressing the humanitarian aspects of our expedition and the fact that many of our resources derived from sacrificial gifts from hundreds of individual supporters in the UK. We told them about our £33,000 loan, and that we were paying mega-interest on it every day. We convinced them to such a degree that they began to question whether we were actually financially viable. (Of course we weren't; not all works of God are, on paper.) We discovered that the Chinese are not 'British' in their bargaining techniques. If we give a little, we expect the other side to concede something too. Not the Chinese. They accepted every concession and asked for more, because to give in was a sign of weakness, not decency. Mr Xie Jinkang asked for a recalculation, so we did it all on the blackboard; it came to less than the original. For the first time, we noticed that he got rattled. Very unusual for the inscrutable Chinese. They rewrote the contract; they added more people (all of whom we were asked to pay for); they changed the bus; lorry drivers are more important than guides and need more money; guides need more money than lorry drivers because their jobs are more dangerous; they thought of everything they could to jack up the cost. In the end it became clear that they were not going to sign for any less than 350,000 yuan, regardless of accountability. Preferably 400,000 yuan. We discovered this when our figures arrived at 330,000 and Xie Jinkang said, 'You've forgotten the extra 20,000 yuan.'

'What 20,000?'

'The tax.'

'What tax?'

'The special tax for going to the river.' He was struggling for a good description.

'But we've already paid that.'

'No, no. This is an internal tax.'

'Let us see it in writing.' He could not comply. Instead he came up with five suggested descriptions, before finally fixing on the 'Special Programme fee'.

Mr Xie Jinkang was definitely showing signs of strain. It became more evident on Thursday night (they went on negotiating until 10.30 p.m. most evenings) when Mike came in and got very angry. He had made that Thursday a final decision night for the expedition to go ahead or be cancelled.

'If your own Prime Minister Mr Li Peng says the expedition is going to the river, why are you holding us up? We have been willing to sign every day for ten days now.' Nevertheless that night we gave a lot of money away.

The contract wording was kneaded, rolled out, massacred, massaged and recut from Wednesday onwards. But we added the concession that, despite a contract agreement of 350,000 yuan, they would only get 250,000 up front, leaving 150,000 yuan to be under Sophie's more neutral control from the FAO. They were determined to get their 400,000 or bust. Mr Xie Jinkang very nearly bust. He was definitely under buckle load. He was pacing the floor and perspiring. Sharp man that he was, he could not handle the pressure. Plans were put into action for a huge send off outside City Hall in front of the Governor of Sichuan on the Saturday. Xie Jinkang was being pressurised from the political branch of government to get the contract signed fast – or else; and being pressurised from the financial branch of government to bleed us of 400,000 yuan – or else. He was torn between the two. He knew he could not justify the cost, but he had to. And he could not rely on the normal Chinese fall-back for whittling foreigners into submission – time. He disappeared on Friday, precisely because he was required to negotiate and to sign. We found him, long after the appointed time, hiding in the gate-keeper's house on the campus. Everyone else in the FAO had been waiting. Mr Xie Jinkang was approaching breakdown. I don't suppose the fact that he himself had been ordered by his boss to accompany the expedition on the river helped to stabilise his equilibrium!

Neither was he obvious at the City Hall on Saturday for the big send off with the forty-strong children's band, the red banner (proclaiming friendship and cooperation), the two immaculate hovercraft (*ICI River Rover* having been pushed down the main road by eight team members), the loudspeakers, the large crowd, a line of seated senior Party officials in posh suits and making polite speeches. It was indeed a glorious day; for the first time since arriving in Chengdu we had clear, unobscured, hot sunshine, white, fleecy clouds, delicate filigreed cirri and blue sky. Mike, at the beginning of his speech, raised his hands to heaven and said that his God had blessed us with such a good day. (It was not translated that way into Chinese, but at least it was there in English, and recorded on TV.) The Governor of Sichuan, all smiles, came round to meet the team, looked at the two hovercraft, inspected the NAPS solar-fridges, and was given three cheers by the team. Perhaps now we could go and leap on to our river? Well, no. Not until the contract was finalised and signed.

We sighed. The negotiators went back to the negotiating table on Monday, 23 April. The engineers went back to engineering the hovercraft, which, in the delays, were fast approaching perfection. The pray-ers went back to praying. Many of us had never before prayed so long and so frequently and so sacrificially in our lives. This was a vertical mountain we were climbing, and conquering one cliff face only revealed another beyond. Please, couldn't we go and tackle the river or snow or rapids or frost-bite or

altitude – the things we all relished? Maybe one day . . . ?
Half the available expedition time had now been spent
negotiating to do the expedition.

The resilience of the team started to shine through. The
heavy work was being done behind closed doors by the
four negotiators, shredding the contract paper, and then
sticking it together again. Those team members needed
all the encouragement they could get, and the rest of us
eagerly listened to their frustrations and their triumphs,
taking as much steam out of their systems as we could, and
building up their tenacity, patience and peace. Meanwhile
the rest of us found things to do. Some discovered Chengdu.
Some photographed Chengdu. Some shopped in Chengdu.
We contacted the campus students and challenged them to
volleyball or soccer. We established some deep friendships
with the young Chinese people at this time. It was extraordinary how we were able to settle down and endure with
an almost supernatural patience the interminable delays that
came our way every day. We just felt we would win the
battle, and we hung on with grit to see it through.

A few days before the official send-off, on Wednesday,
18th, the day the medical contract was signed, we discovered why this signing had been so protracted and had
caused so much hassle. We also found out why the Chinese
doctors' friendship had cooled off.

Nils Krag had returned from his activities in Beijing
to rejoin the team and start preparing the solar fridges.
He was friendly and cooperative and the change in his
attitude was remarkable, as revolutionary as a Christian
conversion experience. We hoped that the earlier clashes
and misunderstandings were water under the bridge.

Mike was walking through the Jin Jiang Hotel that
Wednesday night, when the Chinese girl assistant waved
at him and said, 'Here is the fax for the hovercraft team.'
Mike glanced at it, and saw it was from Matte Lehtonen
(still in Beijing) to Nils. Mike read on, in growing disbelief.
It was addressed to Neste authorities in Helsinki, copied to
Nils. In it the expedition was accused of inefficiency, irres-
ponsibility, incompetence, ignorance, disinterest, duplicity,

95

sloppy planning, misrepresentation and ineptitude. It was full of lies and half-truths. Nils was asked to remain with the team, and to record on camera and video all the other 'incompetences' that took place on the expedition, clearly as a plant to spy on us. We were accused of causing all the delay in getting the expedition on to the river, and the doctors were blamed for the curtailment of the medical programme. God had placed in our hands the major document that spelled out why the Chinese medical team had become unfriendly; Matte and Nils had been plotting behind our backs to scupper the whole expedition and in particular to torpedo the medical programme. We thought we had sorted out all this nonsense. No longer was their behaviour a mere misunderstanding: it became clear that it was a deliberate attempt, on a long-term basis, to kill the whole expedition.

At that time of heavy negotiations, we needed this as much as a hole in the head. We could find no rational or sensible reason why paid NAPS personnel should try and destroy a project in which Neste were the main sponsors. Were we not supposed to be on the same side? What were their motives? We could envisage no sound business reason why they should stab their supporters in the back.

Mike did not delay. He photocopied the fax and sent it direct to Mike Holdsworth, our UK liaison officer, for onward transmission to Neste Chemicals headquarters in Brussels. He formally requested permission to sack both Matte and Nils from the team. He received permission to do so, and acted on it two days later. Neste initiated a top-level meeting in Brussels on Tuesday, 24 April attended by the Vice-President of Neste Chemicals. Dr Padman Ratnesar and Dr Bill Gould were about to return to the UK, so we sent them home early to attend the meeting with Mike Holdsworth, and confront the Neste officials with the facts. Bill and Rachel typed out a paper answering the criticism of the medical programme, while John did the same for their indictment of the press relations and overall aims of the expedition.

At that meeting the Neste authorities, having Matte's

reports in their hands, confronted Bill and Padman. They, of course, having no previous inkling that these reports were being sent regularly to Helsinki, had not seen occasion to send any reports themselves. Now, however, quietly and confidently, they presented Neste with the facts, detail by detail. The executives grew more silent as the truths emerged, accompanied by documentary evidence. At the end they thanked Bill and Padman for their work and their efforts in coming to Brussels, and went into private conference together.

The results were threefold. First, they totally upheld Mike's decision to ask both Matte and Nils to have nothing further to do with the expedition. Second, they immediately recalled Matte to Europe for further training. Third, they recalled Nils to Europe for medical examination.

Mr Xie Jinkang had assured us that the negotiations to finalise the contract would be completed 'very shortly' after the written permit was received. That permit had come in on Monday, 16 April. Our expectations rose as the negotiators went back to the table. But they were pared down as the days slipped past and endless talk on endless details continued well into the night. The CAS bowled fast and furiously; we padded up or dodged the bouncers. They argued for the cost to be paid in US dollars instead of PRC FEC. That took a whole day to sort out. (We won that!) We were to provide cold weather equipment for the guides, or pay them 700 yuan to buy their own. The guides (which they insisted must come) were to be paid 37 yuan a day, plus 30 yuan for food and accommodation. A guide's normal pay is 60 yuan a month. 'On the road' expenses while travelling were to be 45 yuan a day, over and above the other. There were students on the campus who were itching to come at no cost to us; but no, they were not explorers. The CAS 'explorers' preferred to live in hotels! And we would pay 10 per cent extra as a service charge for every place we stopped at on our road journey. They even wanted us to pay them if we guarded our own trucks overnight while travelling! They left no stone unturned whereby they could find an excuse for us to pay more. There was no doubt that we came

97

out of every meeting kicking and screaming. Outwardly, of course, we were calm. Mel, ever dispassionate, at one stage started to unbutton his shirt and throw it on the floor. Perhaps they might accept it as down payment? The others restrained him.

We knew we were being taken for a ride at every point, but we knew that if we wanted to get to the river, we would have to capitulate on all but the most ludicrous of suggestions. They held the trump card: they had got something we wanted, and we would have to pay their price for it if we were going to get it. Mr Xie Jinkang went doggedly on, making gold from every grain of sand he could find until he was reasonably contented that we had agreed to pay the price 'the mandarins' had arbitrarily set as the cost of the expedition. Until that point, he would not sign. And he was perfectly happy to keep us in Chengdu as long as we liked until we had met all his estimates. Any tactic or lie was justified in this negotiating syndrome (I don't think they did a course on it – it just came naturally and culturally to them). Ten times we wrote out the contract (the final text of which is reproduced in Appendix H), laboriously translated by Arne well into the night, and twice Mike shook hands on it, only to have them bring up some new point in the morning which entailed the scrapping of most of what had previously been done. In all this, our four negotiators, Tony, Mel, Sam and Arne, coped tenaciously. Much credit must go to Arne, the interpreter. It became difficult to believe that English was not his native tongue.

As the realities of the contract were being finalised, and the stupidities were batted out of the grounds (sometimes three or four times for each absurdity), they raised the fact that there was a 15 per cent government tax on top of the whole cost of the expedition. We raced down to the FAO to check: yes, it was true. Why did they not tell us before? It never occurred to them. We managed to avoid 5 per cent of it on the grounds of the friendship link. But 10 per cent was with us to stay.

Mr Xie Jinkang was ready to sign the contract at 3 p.m. on Wednesday, 25 April, eight weary days of labour after the permit was received. Was this birth natural, Caesarean section, forceps, induced, epidural, or even next week? We gathered in a conference room in the Jin Jiang hotel. At the entrance to that very hotel students had been shot in the troubles of June 1989. They put little flags on the table. The two TV crews were there. So was the FAO. We waited, and 3 p.m. came and went. At five we rang up. Where was Mr Xie Jinkang? They were printing out the Chinese version of the agreement. At 8 p.m. Dr Hu from the CAC came in to sign the fuel contract, precisely on time. Sophie and Mr Luo from the FAO stayed – a magnanimous gesture on their part. Mike sent the team to the restaurant: we had planned a farewell dinner for Arne, who was leaving for Norway the following day. At 9 p.m. Mike got up exasperated. He said he was going back to the President's House; Xie Jinkang could come there when he was ready.

At that very moment, Mr Xie Jinkang walked in. We were beyond believing it would ever happen. At 9.15 p.m. the main contract was signed, Arne having checked it was word perfect. At 9.20 p.m. the fuel contract was signed.

It was so very, very good to get home that night.

I think there was only one unlikeable Chinese person we met in all our many meetings with these remarkable people. As individuals they are pleasant, friendly, delightful and companionable. I cannot stress how glad we have all been to have visited China. But China is not full of paradoxes; it is full of contradictions. In the negotiations themselves, both with the SMA and the CAS, we found they resorted to every subterfuge that could be envisaged, smiling all the time. They certainly had a firm grasp of the essential, and that essential was money. They drove unswervingly towards getting as much as possible from us. To be fair, their goal was one-sixth of that paid by the American Raft Expedition of 1986. They knew the British were poorer. They hold a totally different interpretation of 'friendship' and 'cooperation' to us. They were unmoved by pressure of time, undeviated by any financial constrictions, unaltered by other objectives – even from their own Prime Minister. The quite extraordinary thing, and the biggest contradiction,

99

was that these attitudes, morals and ways came out of the nicest of people. It was very difficult to handle.

Arne got very angry with them at one time and said, 'If you treat westerners this way, you'll never get agreements with any of them. You're digging your own grave.'

'We know,' was their only answer.

Why do they treat westerners in this way? They do, of course, have a history of being trodden on and massacred by outsiders. They have suffered from many internal conflicts and civil wars (as in the war of liberation and the Cultural Revolution), and have benefited from appalling attempts at colonisation, not least by the British. A perfect example of imperialist aggression stood in Shanghai Park, put up on the gate in 1885. It read 'No admittance to dogs and Chinese'. But how much of the frustration we were encountering derived from hereditary factors and how much from the political system? An inkling was given by a senior executive to one of our team members.

'The real problem with China,' he said, 'is the problem of the two bowls; the iron bowl and the big pot.'

'Oh?'

'The iron bowl is your own. If you drop it, it does not break. The policy in China is that there is to be no unemployment – everybody must have a job, and everybody will have much the same wage. You can't get the sack; you can't get promoted; if you do a good job, it makes no difference; if you do a bad job, or are lazy, that also makes no difference. Your bowl will never break.'

'Doesn't that restrict initiative?'

'That's the trouble. There is no incentive to do anything worthwhile in our lives. And time is unimportant.'

'And the pot?'

'That's the government's large provision pot. If you are in trouble, the state will bail you out. If you're a bit short, the government will provide. It kills all motivation. We don't bother to take out insurance for anything here in China – the government will recover all our losses.'

'But that is not totally true. We've seen many people with lots of initiative and lots of motivation.'

100

'True. But they have their own businesses. Private enter-prise is recovering the Chinese tradition for hard work.'

The illustration was a good one. The Marxist philosophy was that the state should be the great provider and great empathiser; should be God.

I was beginning to see what a grip the system had over these people. There are still a few Chinese around who remember the liberation. But the rest have been brought up 'in the system' and have difficulty knowing any other. People seemed imperilled by believing their country's own propaganda that they were free. The bureaucracy is part of the Socialist effort to provide jobs – just add another tier in the line. No wonder things take months to accomplish, and all decisions come only from the very top. I guess our advice to anyone else attempting to do what we have done (or to bring western technology into China) is to make sure they start their negotiations with the Chinese Ambassador in whatever country, and get permission through him before ever setting foot in China itself and working with those at the bottom of the pyramid.

One of the most extraordinary contradictions we saw occurred when China's top pop star came to Chengdu. Not that that was a significant event in itself, although my eyebrows went up at the thought of such western decadence being present in this culture. I was delighted that Chengdu was only one city in his tour of many cities in China, and that the motivation was to raise money for the Asiad – the Asian Olympic Games being held soon in Beijing. The thing that surprised me was what the authorities had allowed him to sing; they were protest songs against the system and sarcastic parodies of the Mao years. A Chinese who attended the concert commented: 'His songs reflect young people's grievances against our social sys-tem, our government and society. His songs are bold and unconstrained. People who feel politically and socially depressed like his songs. In Beijing, he's the only one who's popular among young people.' Some of us went to the concert, and others listened to the tapes. We could not make out the words, of course, but the music was good;

101

some of it was excellent and professionally presented.

'Tell me about law in China,' I asked Kevin, a young American who was passing through Chengdu. He was going round universities and colleges in China teaching international company law. The question was explosive.

'There is no law in China. There is no basis for it.'

'What do you mean?'

'Law – external, arbitrary, natural law – assumes an external, governing authority, higher than and beyond national governments and rulers. It assumes a higher morality than man himself – that in the universe there are many things which are intrinsically right and wrong. Objective standards or morality, in contrast to subjective standards, assume objective accountability. That assumes objective purpose. That assumes objective design. That assumes a God who thinks and is and creates.'

'So? That's what I believe.'

'Certainly. But the Chinese don't. Their life philosophy goes much further back than Communism. It is rooted in Daoism, where God is impersonal. When Daoism – and, from it, Buddhism – asks a man to deny himself, it means essentially to empty himself to nothing; to have flat brain waves. Christian meditation is to fill one's mind with God. Daoist meditation is to fill one's mind with nothing. Daoist and Buddhist *perfection* is to be absolutely empty. For example, Christ told us to "go and do good to all men"; it is a positive command. Confucius said, "If you do not want others to harm you, do not harm them." You see, Confucianism is neutral, negative or passive.'

'But how does that affect law?' I said.

'Western society is a conscience society. If you are alone and tempted, you feel guilty and don't do the wrong thing. In China it is a shame culture: you must not do anything that brings disgrace on your society or unit. If a Chinese man is alone and steals, that's neither right nor wrong because there is no objective morality. If he's *caught*, that's bad. Law in China is a cultural, communal concept. It's based on *guanxi* – who you know. The old feudal system that governed China for centuries before liberation was that individuals gave their allegiance to the mandarin, who in turn protected them and provided for them. Peasants had *guanxi* with the mandarin. With *guanxi*, all law became a code between a mandarin and the dependent peasants under him; it was relationships, not law, that protected. No one was an individual under this system. And you can see that this is still very strong in China. The Chinese look after the Chinese first. The word "China" means "middle kingdom", and is, to them, the only kingdom of significance anywhere in the world. That is why no foreign company to my knowledge has ever made a profit in China.'

'How has Communism affected these centuries of Chinese cultural thought?'

'Hardly at all. Communism is an impersonal, atheistic, anti-individual philosophy. It and Daoism, Confucianism or Buddhism were tailor-made for each other. Moreover Communism is an authoritarian, political system, no different from the mandarin except for size. China now is a *guanxi* society on a national, rather than a local scale. To the Chinese, Communism is only another dynasty, and their ancient culture blends admirably with it. Once they even used to say grace to Chairman Mao before eating food.'

'What do you think of private enterprise? After all, it's fundamental to company law, and gradually entering China.'

'Western objective law is something the Chinese have asked me to teach, because without it no industry in China can communicate or do business with the West. But they do not know what they are asking me to do. I have to explain to them the fundamental principles which govern all western dealings – that there is an external, objective morality above considerations of the society or personal convenience. This opens their understanding – as it must – to the possibility of the Christian God. It is absolute dynamite here in China. It is a concept that contains seeds that could change this society's lifestyle from inside out.'

Not that all was negative in China. In a meditative moment I pondered what destructive elements there were in Britain that were seemingly absent here: violence, anger,

103

sexual lust, rebellion, envy, rejection. We found none of these attitudes in China. By and large the streets of China were safe and friendly to walk in, and we often came across single women and children sauntering alone at night – a thing rare in Britain today. What we did find there was hopelessness; there is a kind of grey, inevitable futility about their attitudes – almost a death. Some people there are without sparkle, without life, without vision, without a belief in the possible. But one delightful act of generosity came when the Chinese invited us to a private performance of ethnic dancing, given by a dance school. It was a joy to see, and a pleasure to receive such a gift.

Bureaucracy had vied with the physical hardship of tackling the Yangtze as the greatest obstacle in our expedition. Ten years of preparation and five previous visits to China had achieved nothing. For six weeks we were held captive in Chengdu.

Some students laughed at us for ever believing that we would get our permission to go to the 'closed areas of China'. The force for change is amongst the young, but it disappears like a stream into desert sand. One said: 'I think my future will be unhappy. The truth about our leaders is that they have no education and no retirement except death. It's an old man's country. The government is frightened of too much western influence. I do not think it will ever change.'

The very large statue of Mao Zedong towers over the people of Chengdu, but his friendly wave is no longer returned. All over China statues of the Great Helmsman have been thrown to the ground. The rules are that the last Emperor must be removed under the hours of darkness or he stays. It is all a matter of saving face. In the UK we put up statues to men when they are dead. In China they put them up while people are alive, and remove them when they die. Whether Mao's statue remains or not, his policies and actions have deeply affected a fifth of mankind, and were still influencing our permission to go to the river. Nevertheless our trials were nothing to those of Old Hundred Names

– the average Chinese – who battles year in and year out with requests to indifferent officials.

The public reception 'For our hovercraft friends from Britain', with handshakes from the Governor of Sichuan, bands, warm speeches and TV presentation, ignored the frustrating negotiations and the fact that they had held us up for six weeks. Indeed, at the time, the contract was still being fought over. In faith we had grasped the promise of the river and we were not disappointed. At last we were given the priceless permits, and could advance to the river. A mighty rushing door to Tibetan China opened up to us.

We heard that, a short while before, a French expedition had come to Sichuan, and had left without achieving anything. It was a total failure. We were grateful, in all this mess, to have emerged at last with clearance to go and do what we came for. Maybe, with the twinning link, we had *guanxi* with the Province of Sichuan? Or maybe, through Ted Heath and Padman Ratnesar, we had *guanxi* with the highest authorities in Beijing? Or maybe, simply, we had *guanxi* with God.

5

A Breath of Fresh Chinese Air

A wise man will make more opportunities than he finds.
(Francis Bacon)

It was an inauspicious start. Ray and Dee and the team heading for Dege were ready to go at 7.30 a.m. on Friday, and all the rest of us were out by the containers to see them go.

So was Mr Xie Jinkang. As they got (late) into the Landcruiser to go, one other Chinese got in with them. The only possible explanation for this extra helper was that, sneakily, they would get another 1000 yuan off us. That was totally unacceptable.

Unfortunately the person who wanted to go with the medics was Melanie Hu, Dr Hu's daughter. She was very sympathetic towards us, could speak perfect English, and we would have been delighted to have her with us. But Mr Wang was the CAS guide for this journey, and he was the sort of adviser we could have done without. We suggested that he swop with Melanie. But no sir; Mr Xie would not hear of that. An hour's heated and protracted discussion later we agreed to take Melanie, but at her own cost. We flatly refused to pay for her, so in the end Mr Xie gave in.

Sunday was the planned day of departure for the main party. We expected hassle. We got it. We even formed a small committee ahead of time to deal with it.

The convoy was seven vehicles long, and we were praying for seven drivers. Our guide was Mr Zhou, a diplomat from the FAO. He was a delightful man and, because he had spent some time in Madrid, he could speak Spanish. I

106

found it quite miraculous, for it enabled me to speak to him regularly, having polished up my schoolboy Spanish in Peru. Madam Zhou, no relative of Mr Zhou, was the senior CAS person. With her was Lili, the nineteen-year-old flighty and verbose interpreter. Lastly there was Mr Cheng, the policeman, instantly nicknamed Plod. He was an amiable and courteous gentleman.

Even though there had been lengthy negotiations for some five weeks, and numbers agreed, they arrived with two extra people (for whom we were required to pay); an engineer and a driver. We pointed out that we had superb engineers on our team, and carried more engineering repair equipment than anyone could possibly find on the road to Denke. We refused to take any more people both on the grounds of necessity and expense. The discussions went on for two hours, with us maintaining a solid refusal. The team was tremendously supportive and sent Anne over to say we were right behind the negotiators and would be prepared to wait all day rather than pay more. Mr Zhou of the FAO was getting far more embarrassed than we were by the delay, and put pressure on Mr Xie. He came back with an offer to charge just for one, with the other free. In answer we made a compromise offer to pay an additional 1000 yuan, and the second man free. This offer they accepted. But we insisted that he sign an agreement that there be no more additions to the contract.

Andrew, heading the negotiating team, had discovered that, in dealing with the Chinese, we had to establish an uncompromising refusal for a minimum of two hours. After that, they would come up with a compromise.

Based on these twin experiences, the third party that left talked to Mr Xie two or three days ahead of departure and were able to leave without any hassle whatever.

An interesting incident occurred at the first of these discussions. One of the 'inserted' Chinese people got into one of the trucks as John Whatmore was filming it. Mike spotted the fellow and went over and pulled him out. This interfered with TV continuity and John rushed in to remove Mike because he was spoiling the film. This was an interesting

107

clash of priorities, and Mike, after a private discussion with John, got his way. The main objects of the expedition had to take priority over television.

The main party left Chengdu at 9.40 a.m. on Sunday, 28 April, two hours and ten minutes late. But not as late as the date; our original plan was to leave on 2 April.

We drove through Chengdu by-pass and out along the road to the south-west. We were unsure at that point which route we would be travelling. We hoped for the short, four-day run, using the middle route over an awkward pass. But when Mr Zhou said that we would spend the first night at Ya'an, we suspected they wanted as many days 'on the road' as possible; it would certainly boost their income and deplete our budget. There was no way we could get any of the Chinese to change their minds. So to Ya'an we headed.

The road, for the first hour or so, travelled through Chengdu's gloomy drizzle. We were now used to it. The country gradually became more rural, as did the villages and the people. We passed blocks of shops selling anything and everything; people using the main road as a pedestrian and cycle precinct; an old man tying a huge cardboard box to his bicycle pannier; pool tables under awnings in the street; little, unattended stalls, with a base of plaited bamboo; numerous ladies selling rows of cigarettes (there is no age restriction in China for the consumption of alcohol or tobacco); men selling sugar cane, and teenage girls chewing, sucking and spitting it out; shoe-heelers with hand-cranked sewing machines sewing five or more patches on to a pair of trainers; pots or woks or pick-and-shovel ends displayed on the street; food being sold, also by the roadside, and getting splashed or dusted by the passing traffic – all so typically Chinese. We passed an overladen Dong Feng coal lorry which had folded in two under its load.

And people. People in blue and grey-green; ladies in pretty colours and always in slacks; people, all young or early middle-age, for there seem to be few Chinese who are old; people who stare continually at everything and par- ticularly at passing *weibin*: people, people, people. Humans

108

are the largest economic asset of China. Inquisitive, shy, plain-living Chinese carrying babies, hugging each other, just living; some busy, most with lots of spare time; China is a godsend for those intrigued by people. It is government policy for everyone to have a job, however small. The street sweepers transferred dust from one side of the road to the other with their branch brooms, and then swept it back again. I wandered into a pet shop during one prolonged stop, and discovered it to be a butcher's!

Within an hour, and across a wide river of clean running water, we started climbing hills. They were only little ones, but I had not realised how flat and monotonous the Chengdu part of Sichuan is nor just how much we had missed 'up and down'. How lovely to have a view blotted out by a skyline silhouetted by trees and little huts, instead of the inevitable disappearance into grey mist. Even the allotments in this market garden of China started to be ranged at different levels – and that not because they were paddy fields but because houses were built and fields were planted on the sides of undulations. The fields were on ledges and shelves to save space.

It was very different from Yunnan, where the hills were huge and the distance vast. Here there were country villages with dusty, untidy streets and brown-orange brick buildings with low-slung roofs and curly-up roof noses. These were close-knit farming communities. The copious eucalyptus trees lining the road were now accompanied by others in the countryside, forming little woods with bamboo clumps and poplars. The rape, which, when we first arrived, splashed the countryside with yellow, was now bowing over in the weight of seed, had lost its bloom, and was being scythed and ranged out neatly to dry. The odd field of barley was ripe here, but mostly it, and the wheat, were still green. We seemed to be travelling through one of those Ming hand-scroll paintings.

Passing through one market town we saw an abundance of vegetables; huge lettuces, new potatoes and the most enormous set of radishes I had ever seen. They were some 15 cm long and as thick as a camera telephoto-lens. We

109

stopped briefly in Pujian County; the roadside toilet was utterly filthy and disreputable. But there we discovered that one of the tyres on the Griffon trailer had a slow puncture. It took half an hour to change the wheel.

It was so lovely to see trees – as well as the eucalyptus the countryside was speckled with skinny beeches, hedgehoggish firs and bushy maples. There were copses dotted across the landscape and even some sizeable woods; and fir trees poked out from the middle of the orange groves.

As we moved south-west the landscape became 'tighter'. The villages and towns consequently became more compact, with houses hemmed in by barns, ducks and paddy fields.

In the farming towns we passed through, the narrow, winding streets were crammed with ancient, tacked-together buildings covered with filth and antiquity. People sat outside drinking their Sunday afternoon cups of jasmine tea, and soaking up the drizzle and the effluent of heaving, honking lorries, gradually accumulating a personalised dust and age. The buildings in these towns were nearly all timber, their levels meandering up and down like contours on a map, with huge, overhanging, gutterless roofs covering the streets like umbrellas, and allowing the drips to plonk on to cyclists, pedestrians and cars that passed beneath.

We laboured through perhaps a dozen such villages, slowly climbing the ever-increasing hills until we could see panoramas of valleys with networks of rivulets and the endless pocket-handkerchief fields climbing up the wooded hillsides. Some, with the variety of green that beautified the trees, could well have been Surrey or Kent in England's garden landscape.

Through the light misty grey-blue of the distance, the rugged outline of high, purple mountains etched their presence, and slowly began to leer a dominance over the cringing countryside. We were gradually coming into the foothills of Sichuan's western Daxue Shan mountain range. Straining up one hill revealed a quilted pattern of fields across the other side of the valley, the gaps in the wheat looking

110

as if a giant had raked it with a monstrous comb. Over the brow the valley with Ya'an in it stretched into the shrouded distance, watered by a huge river snaking slinkily down the bottom, and surrounded by towering peaks. These fell into the distance like a line of camels, their humps standing alongside each other, craggy, curved and unique. Quite beautiful.

Ya'an was a compressed city, straddling the river with three bridges. We could have bought as many wares as we wanted there as in Chengdu, but it would have taken us only a couple of hours to do it, rather than a day. We were ushered into a first-class hotel, and started to negotiate the prices. Mike and the majority of the team had already accepted first-class rooms, and were busy taking showers, when Tony Burgess pointed out that all expensive accommodation would add to the bill. It was 12 yuan a night for en suite rooms. We argued with Madam Zhou about it, and plumped for second-class rooms at 7 yuan a night. Had we but known it, it was the last time we would have the opportunity to sleep in anything approaching posh until we hit Lanzhou at the end of June. Silly us. The rooms slept six persons, and the beds were planked and solid. Funniest of all was the washroom, which had six filthy basins and only two serviceable taps. Loos were outside, through the rain, down the next block, and stinking. It was our first taste of sleeping by grace without complaint. Neither did we complain about the disco that attacked all and sundry just across the courtyard, entertaining droves of giggling girls and swaggering young beaux until midnight.

We set off next day at 9.30 a.m. after dawdling. The road led us upwards into the mountains, twisting through green, wet foliage, round hairpin bends and inside tight gorges. The Chinese way of agriculture was insisted upon in the bottoms of the valleys, but was curtailed on the slopes as the rocky outcrops and sheer incline made terracing too difficult. The luxury of it struck us all, as we saw road-sides gaudily painted with orchids and other wild flowers and grasses, trees overhanging the edges and buffaloes helping the farmers to sweat out their manual labour in

111

the rice fields and the dank atmosphere. Up we went into the mountains: green, grey, cloud-topped, dark, dangerous, intriguing, adventurous. What tales did they hold of countless farmers, peasants, politicians, policemen who dug the slopes, planted the paddy fields and harvested the barley in their childhood and teenage years, learning the value of hard manual labour from dawn to dusk? Huge mountains, carved in cliffs, crags, crevices and ravines; dominant and overbearing, yet friendly, fascinating and secure – the everlasting hills. This stage of the journey was damped down by overcast weather, reminding us of many pictures we had seen of China – misty and dripping; little houses or villages huddled together on a hillside living mysteriously in the intrigue of the disappearing mountain tops.

Round each corner appeared a new combination of granite forms misting into the distance, lightening in colour as their memory faded, covered with a tapestry of green, layered by terraces which disappeared into the skyline. Gorgeous valleys focused the hills into clear rocky rivers, freshly fed from the soaking clouds, and gathered by the crevices and waterfalls into the sparkling white of tumbling rapids and life-giving water. They looked good for a bathe. The tops of the three passes (2155 m, 1013 m, 2255 m) spread out new landscapes of superlative views, a veritable tourist's paradise.

The top of the highest and last pass was shrouded in cloud and road works. Men and women were remaking the side of the road, concealing the surface with pebbles and boulders and peci-pecis, while they skilfully created dry stone walls to halt the threatening landslides.

Just 60 m or so down the other side the cloud bottomed out and the vista that confronted us was bathed in the late afternoon sunshine. Reds, browns and fawns were picked out in the vast panorama by the rays, and on many of the western slopes the light spring-green of the apricot and other fruit trees was backlighted on the hillside. As we drove down the hill the evening sun reflected on the polythene 'weed restrainers' through which the Chinese planted the maize seedlings. They were in strips in between the rows

112

of potatoes. The sight of whole hillsides and their intervening valleys shimmering in refracted polythene, looking
like mountainsides of scintillating water, was extraordinary.
And this immense market garden, spreading in terraces and
slopes right up to the peaks of the mountains, was so *neat*
and so very tidy.

There were more road works. It was one reason why the
routes to Denke (ours was the long, pretty way via the
south) were so difficult to predetermine. A landslide of a
few weeks back had resulted in extensive road works and
the rent-a-road-worker gang with their picks and shovels
had homed in. Their aim seemed to be to lower the road
level. Covered in mud and sticky slime, our bus bounced
and slithered slowly on the remaining rubble, passing the
queue of trucks which had been stopped by our in-house
policeman. The bus, leading the convoy of seven, struggled
to the end of the hold-up, followed well by the *River Rover*
lorry. But the Griffon trailer . . . We shouted for our bus
driver to stop and squelched hurriedly back to see what the
panic was all about.

The vehicle had stopped. The rear wheel of the trailer
had slewed right off the edge of the road, and was dangling
in the air, the axle tilting down alarmingly; another 10 cm
and it would have toppled over, certainly tipping *Neste
Enterprise* and its huge tow-lorry right over the edge. That
would have ended our expedition. What would Peter and
Steve do about it? It was fortunate that the tow-lorry had
stopped exactly when it did. They put rocks under the axle
to save it collapsing further. They pulled out the jacks and,
very carefully, hitched up the 'down' side of the trailer from
the rear. Slowly it went up, watched by 100 instant locals
and road workers, gluing 200 eyes to the point of disaster.
What a day for them! We pushed them back in case the
plan failed to work and they were crushed by the rolling,
descending hovercraft. As the overhanging tyre lifted clear
of the surface we held our breath, and the angle tilted
towards the hill, the safe wheel slipped and the whole tail
end moved one-third of a metre into safety. A gasp of
wonder came spontaneously from the crowd, apt approval

113

of a job well done. Peter and Steve put the jacks back in their racks, unlocked the back wheels, and Peter steered the craft slowly, laboriously and shakily over the rocky roughage of road works. The trailer had proved itself.

We stopped at a town at the bottom of the valley at about 6.30 p.m. to bed down. Shafts of evening sunlight searchlighted through keyholes in the clouds, picking out fields of green and brown and rich red earth. The town was called Han Yuan and, because the conflict between us and the Chinese had abated, they selected good rooms for us. Same sort of price – 8 yuan a night – but rooms for two, and an electric fan, needed because it was very hot and humid. The washroom at the end of the floor was communal, and the toilet duplicated for a bathroom. All-over wash or shower was by basin or pouring a bucket of water over oneself. The hot water was collected by servant girls, who giggled away as we washed and showered. Mel used his empty basin after the shower to preserve his modesty in their presence; they had no intention of leaving. It was good to unstick in the sweltering evening heat, even if I had to get back into my thermal clothes. (Leader had said go as light as possible, and wear thermals for the journey.) Supper was much better than the previous night, where all food had been penetrated by curry and ginger. This evening the food was very edible for westerners, eaten as a royal Chinese feast with white table-cloths and gold-coloured napkins. Some of the Chinese bought bottles of rice whisky, which was lethal and foul and instantly inebriating. In their merry mood they tried desperately to get some of us to join them. Jim did a bit. Mike poured his glass down his front – a well-proven method of pretending to drink without actually swallowing anything. The rest of us simply refused.

Breakfast was geared for 7.30, with lift-off at 8.00 a.m. The latter was delayed by 30 minutes as we refuelled the lorries from the fuel trucks. In the West we colour our diesel fuel so we don't mistake it for petrol. In China they colour the petrol. We panicked because we thought we had put petrol in the diesel lorry, and were very nearly caught out.

114

The beautiful mountains towered above us as we headed south along the floor of our valley. This we knew would lead to what looked on the map like a large river. So it was. We turned west along the northern shores of the river Dadu, which was a gorgeous hovercraft river. Wide and shallow, it had banks of fine grey sand, tongues of shingle, and boulders jutting out or forming in its heart. Lots of shallow rapids gurgled and tumbled in it, down which no boat could go, but up which a hovercraft could fly with ease.

The river and scenery were all the more beautiful because the day, unlike the previous one, was bright, sunny and warm. We all felt that we were on holiday – no different from an expensive coach trip to some luxurious tourist spot, except that it was probably much better.

The towns and villages were all the better in that they were unspoilt by tourist trappings, Coca-Cola cans and western throwaway rubbish. It was untouched rural China, where *we* were the objects of hilarity and surprise rather than the locals. We loved it. I suppose the only pollution came from the klaxon of our bus, which obliterated the peace of those quiet communities with the vanguard of western decadence. The driver, though, was good and safe.

Many farms were edged by fruit trees – orange, lemon, walnut, apricot, almond, banana – and fig trees, now in fruit, lined the road.

They were harvesting the ripening wheat along the rich, fertile valley, some 100 km long. Surprising, because the crop was far from ripe at the top of the hill 100 km back. Harvesting was all by hand and sickle, and many people were working on the fields and carrying the straw in large bundles on their backs to some central depot. A real community effort. Some wheat was being 'plucked' – pulling the grain off the top and leaving the stalks in the ground.

Early in the journey huge caverns appeared by the side of the road, from which manganese was being mined. It was difficult to credit that in the last fifty years this peaceful valley had been the scene of many bloody and fearsome battles between Mao and Chiang Kai-Shek – the battle between the Communists (mostly peasants) and

115

the Nationalists (mostly wealthy landowners). The Chinese now refer to this time as the 'Liberation of 1949'. Hard to believe among what looked like a happy and contented rural population.

This led me to meditate on Chairman Mao. I realised that his power was the rifle, and he had slaughtered millions of his own countrymen. Nevertheless he must have been an enormous personality and a military genius to unite such a vast country. He removed decadent and oppressive systems and united this whole nation under one administration. He had fire in his belly and he communicated that blaze to the most populated nation on earth. As we sped through this magnificent valley, just a microscopic part of Sichuan, just one of thirty provinces of China, where man himself is dwarfed by its grandeur, my admiration went out to the one significant personality who had made such an enormous impact.

We passed the town of Shimian, then headed north, the road still hugging the river Dadu. The mountainsides gradually came in on us, and steepened to 70°-80° to the vertical. We were looking at the forested tops through the central skylight of the bus. The river, having lost its lazy, summery flow, and restricted by the hillside, started to boil and burst on the bends.

The hovercraft drivers watched with interest, trying to work out how we would tackle each rapid, while I tried to give the rest of the team some idea of how big a wave height the hovercraft could conquer. *Neste Enterprise* was an unknown for, although Rob and I had travelled in some pretty heavy swells in the Solent, there was no telling how she would tackle rapids, or large waves on an incline.

Rapids, for hovercraft, come in various forms. There's the delightful, where it is sheer joy to bumble up and down them. There's the intriguing, where, if you choose your path carefully, there is no problem. There's the exciting, where you know it is not dangerous, but you have got to fight all the way up and all the way down. Then there's the adventurous, where you know that it is not possible without the grace of God on your side. Lastly, there's the impossible, where all but I would walk in the other direction and start contemplating emigration.

The gorge produced rapids ranging from the intriguing to the adventurous, and three we categorised as impossible. Some exciting ones were so long and complex, and climbed such a protracted gradient that I seriously doubted if even Griffon could get up. We prayed that the upper reaches of the Chang Jiang did not contain any of these.

The road climbed up to 1500 m (5000 ft) to service a village up there, which produced the end of the short cut we could have taken over the very difficult pass. Some American friends said later that a landslide had completely blocked that road on the Sunday, the day we set off. Once again we felt protected by a providential God. Looking down, we could see the water in the river speckled with white, and the paddy fields and houses looking like Lilliput below us. Our slow descent brought us to Luding, a scene of one of the bloodiest battles of the liberation. A large stone monument on the other side of the river stood guard over a bronze statue of frightening significance to commemorate this victory. Here Chiang Kai-Shek, leader of the Nationalist Kuomintang, was finally defeated by Mao's numerically superior army, and he fled to Taiwan, from where he led a rival government in exile.

We stopped just by the famous suspension bridge. Communist guerrillas had crossed this bridge, picked off by the thousand until sheer weight of numbers enabled them to establish a foothold on the western bank and so defeat the Kuomintang. The bridge itself was supported by four very heavy chains, disappearing into pagoda-style toll houses at each end. The slats that covered lighter chains forming the floor of the bridge were primitive, and one could easily put a foot through the gaps. It was five people's width and swayed precariously. Great fun! The mighty, muddy waters of the Dadu swirled and hissed 15 m beneath.

We soon turned off the Dadu and made our way up even tighter mountain walls to Kanding, which we reached at 7.30 p.m. It was May day holiday, and the square was full of Tibetans in holiday mood. From then on we were in Old

117

Tibet – that area, now carved up into five different Chinese provinces, that had been Tibet before 1950. All the locals we met beyond Kanding were ethnic Tibetans. Such long-despised minority races occupy semi-autonomous regions along all the frontier lands. The minorities are only 7 per cent of the Chinese population, but occupy 50 per cent of the total land area.

The variety of clothing these Tibetans wore was striking; gold coats, cowboy stetsons, multi-shaped topees and other headgear, browns, maroons and greens. The ladies were in red with aprons splashed horizontally with multicoloured stripes and red and black braid plaited in their dark hair. Adults and children alike stood and stared, delighted to smile and laugh back at us. The circus had come to town. Foreigners are not normally allowed in this closed area, so it was a great privilege to be there, and East and West stared and giggled at each other. Dressed as we were in khaki, and being dirty, sticky westerners, I felt a bit like occidental effluent in an oriental extravagance.

We were surprised and delighted that many, if not all, the foreign teachers in Chengdu had gone (in fact, been sent) on a trip here to Kanding over the May Day holiday. So we were not the only westerners there, and it was good to see so many friends again so soon. The hotel was adequate – at least the beds were soft – but the toilets were small, inadequate and bracketed the main door of the hotel, giving newcomers a 'different' aromatic welcome to the establishment. None of us could get a wash down from our sticky journey. But at least the temperature was cooler at 2600 m (8,530 ft).

The journey on day four started from 2600 m and churned up to the highest pass so far, at 4300 m (14,104 ft). The sun was shining gloriously, and it was fresh and delightful on the journey. As we moved higher the first sight of beautiful snow-capped mountains poked like white-gloved fingers above the green-topped hills. It was enervating to get up into clear atmosphere; some mountain tops must have been up to 100 km away. The road to the top was tarred, but from the summit onwards it was dirty, dusty and uneven. We levelled off at about 2800 m and travelled along a Tibetan alti-plano. The valley floor was broad, almost like a plain between the hills, with short brown grass grazed by yak, sheep, goats and the occasional pig.

Beside the stream appeared Tibetan houses. I was surprised. I suppose out of my ignorance I thought all Tibetans were nomadic. But here were large, stone walled, double-storey buildings, about four or five windows wide, flat-roofed and very substantial. The windows looked small and dull, but on closer examination each was beautifully decorated, mainly in reds and yellows. The homes appeared on their own initially, just dark grey, with no garden or premises. Soon clumps of these houses appeared, well spread out and distinctly separated from one another. The style of architecture was all the same, but different from anything else we had seen in China.

Further down the road the Tibetans started to move from livestock to arable farming. But here there were no little market garden plots as in the rest of China. We now saw hectares of planted savannah, and the wheat or barley was just starting to poke its tiny green shoots above the ground. To our astonishment the seedlings were in straight lines ending in semi-circles. Could it be that the farming up here, in this apparently primitive area, was mechanised? Sure enough, it was. In an extensive farmyard we spotted a tractor through the narrow entrance. Most of the farming from then on was mechanically assisted. So different from China, where all agriculture was manual.

Some smaller fields had Tibetan prayer ties in them – little sticks with white cloth on them sticking up like Michaelmas daisies. Elsewhere the prayer flags became more prevalent. Some were grey, fluttering in the breeze, and almost every home had one on or near it, and some had little shrines. In places, mainly out on the hillsides or on lonely stretches by rivers, more sophisticated 'tents' of prayer flags, in red and grey, appeared. At one spot a large prayer-flag tent contained a dozen men; the tent was some 8-10 m high. We saw very few prayer wheels; half a dozen or so in a shrine in a village, or three or four wind-vane types on the roof of one house.

119

Wherever we stopped a group of Tibetans of all ages would materialise from nowhere and investigate our convoy. All were initially shy at having their photos taken, but some really enjoyed it when they found it was not painful. Some, particularly teenage girls, posed like sophisticated western models.

I am particularly sensitive about the pollution of the camera. In Peru in 1982 our team found a delightful Campa village, took photos, and then spread the word. Day after day for three or more weeks people trotted up the hill to photograph the people. It was not long before the Chief refused any more access to cameras, and then decided to charge handsomely for each photo. I realised what an intrusion into people's privacy and dignity the camera can be, particularly when it is wielded by unempathetic, gawping, selfish, here-today-and-gone-tomorrow tourists. There were many occasions in China when, longing to have a particular photo of an interesting personality, I refrained from it at their request or refusal. One little family, Grandma, Mum, two teenage girls and a filthy dirty, snotty little boy blessed us particularly. Simple, hard-working and friendly, they chatted to us and laughed with us and were fascinated by these strange white-skinned people. Their tanned faces and weather-beaten hands were almost maroon in colour. I do not suppose they had washed for years – maybe never. Grubby Boy poked the sweet we had given him in and out of his mouth with the most revolting set of little fingers I have seen. He must be a walking antibody. And quite adorable.

I felt sorry for these people as we sped past them in the bus. The day was dry and we covered everything within 20 m, including ourselves, with dust. Pedestrians, cyclists (yes, even here), horseback riders, peci-pecis, the odd yak and the occasional tractor formed the modes of transport. And we covered them all with filthy grit all day long.

The houses changed their shape and style from the large square types we had seen at the start of this part of our journey, and the villages became more communal and sophisticated. From then on the houses were generally lower, single storey with high, small decorated windows, flat roof to catch the rain, a courtyard and a tower (a loo?) in the corner of the courtyard. A novel ladder, consisting of notches cut into a pole, was used to get on to the roof. Where the local area had stone, that was used for the outside walls. Where no stone was available mud exterior walls, often painted white, created insulation against the cold. We saw some houses under construction and were surprised to see that the whole frame was thick, tongue-and-groove wood that was beautifully decorated. These houses were spacious, warm and very strong. Seeing some landslides, we presumed that this whole area was subject to earthquakes; hence the strength of the houses. The villages were built more compactly together than the first ones we had seen, many homes butting on to others, and little paths between them forming the streets. We also saw many caves in the hillsides and were told that there are some 30 million cave dwellers in China. Some we saw were unoccupied and we assumed that they served as shelter for men and animals in winter.

The sunny day gradually clouded over, threatening the imminence of a weather system. As dusk came on we reached a town called Danfu, lying at 2895 m (9500 ft) on a wide, flat plain inside round green hills. It was late. Peter and Steve had a casual look around *Neste Enterprise* and its trailer to see how it had fared on the rough road.

It was bad.

Three of the main leaf-springs had become misaligned. A few more kilometres and we could have had a nasty situation. The stand at the rear, from which Peter steered the trailer, was broken in a number of places and the weld that held it on to the main chassis had fractured on both sides. The worst damage was to the rear of the hovercraft itself, which was starting to split where the feet attached to the body, because the lips of the metal housing in which they sat had been bouncing on the hull. This was a sealed section, and the cracks in the aluminium hull were to present us with an unsolved, though not critical problem for the rest of the expedition.

121

All the damage was initiated by the driver who, with the most powerful motor in the convoy, raced over the rough roads, even though he had been told to slow down many times. It caused the engineers to work on until 10.30 p.m., all of us with headaches from altitude sickness. We loosened the U-bolts, took off the wheels and banged the springs straight. We removed the rear platform and put it on the tow-truck. Peter mended the trailer hydraulics, which had come adrift and trailed on the road for a few kilometres. And we jacked up the hovercraft the following morning and put padding in the steel cups holding the feet.

It had rained overnight and was snowing when we woke up. All yesterday's green hills were now mantled in white. It was decidedly cooler and, we hoped, would be less dusty on the road. We were not able to leave before 10.30 a.m.

A few kilometres outside Danfu we crossed a large river, floating with logs, which had appeared from nowhere to accompany our journey. The bus had no difficulty negotiating the bridge over this river, and, because the corner to it was quite narrow, we waited over the other side for *Neste Enterprise* to get through. Rob, John and I went down to the river's edge to take photos of both hovercraft crossing the river and to see the nifty log-directing device which straddled the river on hawsers.

Some local Chinese emerged from a cave on the other side of the river, started shouting and running towards the bridge. We ignored them and took the odd photo, particularly of the log-device. The *ICI River Rover* truck started to move through and the official on the gate waved his red flag, shouted vociferously, ran to the driver, opened the cab door, dragged him out, and they started fisticuffs on the bridge. By now the Chinese on the far bank – a dozen or so – had reached the bridge, still shouting, and started to run over. Anne, who had gone on to the bridge, watched with horror as two soldiers pulled out their high calibre rifles and pointed them at Rob, John and me, who were innocently taking photos, dressed in military-green Neste gear. Soon the Chinese caught up with us and were shouting and gesticulating in a very ugly way. We pocketed

122

our cameras, shook hands with them as affably as we could, and went slowly back to the bus. It seemed that they were very sensitive about people photographing bridges, and we three came within a hair's breadth of being shot. What excitement.

One of the things we were starting to realise was that we were privileged to be travelling across China. Hardly any of the local inhabitants ever left their district throughout their lives. We had seen more in four days than they had ever seen, or would see. Local administrations and sensitivities changed; it was so easy to forget this as we sped through them.

Much of the journey on that day passed through barren valleys, up above the tree-line at 2800 m, where rock, shale or short brown grass covered the round-topped hills, becoming greener as the snow melted. This lasted until we reached the pass at 3800 m (12,464 ft). It was a slow and steady climb that brought an emerging vista of craggy, serrated mountain peaks behind our round-capped hills. Both the near and far tops were covered in snow and it was Alpine in its beauty. Large lakes reflected the blue sky and the fleecy cirrus, which had slowly replaced the high dull overcast.

We stopped at the top to throw snowballs and look northwest, where other grand peaks were steadily being engulfed by a heavy snowstorm. We wrote 'Hovercraft Expedition 1990' in the snow. It was good to be children again and to gallop around breathlessly in the rarefied atmosphere.

We plunged into the snowstorm as we descended rapidly to Ganzi, an administrative centre and Buddhist monastery in a fertile valley. Here there were vast areas of mechanised cultivation and the spring was so far behind that, for many hectares, no green shoots were emerging from the rich brown earth.

The government hostel was opposite the TV and radio station. TV was sucked in by satellite, and the radio loudspeakers broadcast international news in Chinese at 7.30 a.m., just when all the local Tibetan populace were walking swiftly round inside their Buddhist temple spinning the numerous

123

prayer wheels. The Chinese have brought electricity – through many hydro-electric schemes – TV, building improvements and general civilisation to the Tibetans, which is good. Of course, one can control a whole nation, and unite it, through TV. And they are teaching their minorities the common Mandarin tongue, not the least through public radio broadcasts. At least it did not go on all day. And the Chinese are clearly helping the Tibetans with their agriculture; no one could possibly afford a tractor in these remote communities. So the colonisation of Tibet extends the old country's integration into mainland China. But the one thing that China will probably never accomplish is to deny the Tibetans their religion, or to rid them of it. The Chinese had not counted on the tenacious faith of the Tibetans and they found it hard to believe that such a dark, grinning people who never washed could be so passionate. The religion of Communism is slowly dying and more religions are taking root in China, even in the cities. We Christians had hope for these Buddhists; once someone can acknowledge the possibility of the supernatural, they are available to find the Son of God and become sons themselves. The people in this world most to be pitied and prayed for are materialists; they have an uphill struggle opening their minds to the possibility of a life beyond earth and its bounty.

The evening's snow on the hills, soon fading out and revealing a glorious moonlit night, closed the passes in the mountains. The road to Dege, where the TV team needed to join up with Rachel and Colin, was reported to be submerged under 2 feet of snow. There was no pass on our road between Ganzi and Manigangge, only 95 km away, so the way there was clear. The pass beyond Manigangge leading to Denke, our base camp, was reported closed.

But Manigangge was at 4000 m (13,120 ft), in a basin, and the medical worry was that, if anyone got altitude sickness (for which the only cure is to go downhill), they had to go up before going down. Should we stay at Ganzi and wait for the passes to clear, or go to Manigangge and risk losing a team member through sickness? The altitude can kill, as it did to one Australian on an earlier expedition.

Mike had been aware for some while, particularly on this journey, that only six of the team had expedition exposure or experience, and he was determined to intensify our resolution by increasing our hardship. We needed toughening up. So he decided we must press on to Manigangge. The closer we were to the difficulties, the sooner we could overcome them. We must force march. This was the fifth day of what should, in other vehicles, be only a four-day drive, and we were inevitably going to take six days.

The mountains sparkled in the pink dawn, creating a magic fairyland backdrop to the still, cold morning. We set off at 10.30, going north up the valley on another clear sunny day. We prayed as we sped along the dusty road that the passes would be open and that we would be able to get to the river by Saturday.

The mountains on either side were a rugged, forbidding enormity, only softened and beautified by a liberal sprinkling of God's icing sugar, and stretching into the distant, crystal blue horizon. The journey itself was uneventful and covered a long tundra plain with few people and many yaks.

Manigangge was a hamlet in the midst of a vast wilderness, with snow puddles on the green-and-white capped mountains surrounding it at a fair distance. The Tibetans wore a variety of clothing, many layers of which were tough maroon coats with lamb's fur edges. The women were in dresses, and a few wore trousers. A mother with a sleeping child on her back had a headband of turquoise on a red cloth, and her hair had turquoise beads intertwined. Some had large necklaces of huge amber or turquoise beads, most had earrings, and the pigtails were interwoven with red or scarlet wool. One lady was spinning black wool on a spiky six-pronged wooden cross, which she spun as she untwined the rough fleece in her hand. Some men and women wore trilbies, and many wore the Tibetan gaucho wide-brimmed hat. One lady's long plaited hair had been unchanged for ages, and her crown contained nearly fifty narrow plaits, some of them with five or six strands. They all came to watch me writing, and they reeked extravagantly, and happily.

125

The weather forecast (an unscientific local estimation) for the pass to Dege (where the TV team wanted to go) and to Denke (where we wanted to go) was all gloom and doom, so the main team decided to stay the night at Manigangge. Because we had arrived early there was time to do a side trip – as if we had not eaten enough solid dust already!

But the trip proved to be a treat and many went on it. Half an hour down the Dege road there was a unique lake with pale green, turquoise water. Some mineral was being washed down from the mountains and discolouring the water in this remarkable and beautiful way. Half-covered with ice, with the steep and majestic snow-covered peaks surrounding it, the lake was a peaceful, idyllic magic land that left us utterly speechless. No words could describe its wonder and we marvelled at such a place. The pine trees that guarded its privacy curved gracefully above its mirror surface. High peaks of crystalline white reflected right round its perimeter, tingeing the image with turquoise, broken only by the opacity of the half-covering of ice and two Vs carved out by a pair of migrating bar-headed geese. I doubt if there is anywhere else on earth that would compare with the delightful combination of glory, tranquillity and exquisite elegance of this place. Its name was Lú Long Hú – Green Dragon Lake. Of course we took photos, loads of them. It was better than any picture postcard we had ever seen of any Alpine wonderland. We were all very breathless at 3700 m (12,140 ft), but were more than glad we had made the effort.

Back in Manigangge John Whatmore spotted a couple of lorries that had come over the 5000 m pass from Dege, and pushed his reluctant TV crew to get into their Toyota Landcruiser, and give it a go. Beautiful Sarah, as Mike called her, went with them to take part in the TV filming. They never came back, so we presumed they made it. All things here were guesswork because there was no communication outside these remote villages. By now Gwyn and the last four would have left Chengdu with nine fuel lorries. We wondered whether he would tackle the short, difficult pass

126

that we had circumnavigated. Ray, Fiona, Duncan, Dee and Colin were in Dege. There was no news of them. And we were here. Stuck.

This was our planning situation: Ray's medical programme in Dege was expected to last only five days. John had now gone down to video them, particularly for *Blue Peter*, since the deadline for programme inclusion was looming. *Blue Peter* had broadcast some of our trials on the river Dart in Devon prior to our departure from the UK, and it was important both to them and to us that a follow up was completed before the 1990 series was over at the end of June. We needed to get to Denke this day – Saturday – so that we could unpack on Sunday after a short morning service, engineer the hovercraft on Monday, and go down to Dege by hovercraft on Tuesday to marry in with the TV programme. It was exceedingly tight. John Whatmore and his team were due to return by road from Dege to Denke on Monday, giving us news of Ray and her team.

But now we could not leave Manigangge for Denke. No one had travelled that road for three days, and five lorries and the local bus were stuck with us. All the drivers were in fear.

We refused to allow fear to govern anything we did. We prayed, and we felt that God wanted us to go forward. This was one situation of many we encountered in which every indication and opinion militated against what we felt God was saying yes to. Those of us who believed in God started to pray that all the others, and particularly the Chinese, would come into faith. That morning no one stirred (except the restless sleepers) before eight and the breakfast in the government hostel was scheduled for 9.30. None of our drivers would move, and they would not even refuel the lorries. Rob and I together, and others separately, went away to pray for them, and we asked God to produce a sign to them by eleven that we could go over the pass. It was time for a showdown and for stepping out in faith. Today was Saturday, day 7 of an epic journey.

At 11.15 a jeep came in. There was much talk. The result was that the local bus embarked its passengers, some lorries started up, and they went up the hill. Prayer was answered: at least the Chinese were reacting positively. Giles, our Chinese speaker, accused our drivers of lack of courage, and shamed them into setting off. We would give it a go. A number of tanker lorries passed us, which was a blessing to come.

The road from Manigangge was initially dry and dusty and passed through the same beautiful white-edged valley that had brought us in. The scenery otherwise was fairly normal, and what we had been used to for a whole day. It lulled us into a false sense of security. We did not know what was to befall us, and in many senses it was good to be cushioned by ignorance.

The bus ground in first gear up the hill towards the pass. As we climbed from 3800 m upwards the view became more extensive. Again we were blessed by a bright sunny day, and the snow-capped peaks jutting out into the azure sky sparkled their welcome and invited our admiration. But mountains can also be dangerous, and difficult. This was the dreaded Hai Zhi pass.

We spotted the lorries that had passed us earlier stationary at the top of the hill. Our hearts sank within us. There was clearly something wrong on the down-sun side of the pass. The side we were struggling up was perfectly clear. Surely there wasn't much of a problem? There most certainly was. We stopped behind truck no. 20 and walked to the top to have a look.

It was not easy. Our altimeters read a height of 4550 m (about 15,000 ft). None of us had been up to that altitude before in China, and none of us was acclimatised. Some had even felt a bit rough at Manigangge.

We trudged, puffing, past the fuel lorries to the brow to survey the scene. What a mess!

About 1 km of snaking roadway was covered in 6 ft deep drifts of snow. Below that, another kilometre looked pretty rough, with the road churned up, slush, snow and ice intermingled with the skid marks of trucks that had tried.

One lorry driver, seeing the endless blocked road, had taken the initiative and gone straight downhill, trying to cut off the hairpin and the lesser-gradient road. The gradient he had chosen had made it possible to drive downhill, but impossible to go back up. Needless to say, he had gone down without chains and had got stuck in a 4 ft bank of snow, and his passengers were digging the lorry out and pushing it furiously. I felt sorry for him; he had shown great spirit.

Meanwhile a bevy of forty Chinese and Tibetans were already hard at work clearing the road from the top. They had taken away the snow to the hairpin, and had just started round the corner. Mike ordered us to get the picks and shovels we had brought, and go and help. All of our expedition team went to help, but of the Chinese who had come with us only Lili, the nineteen-year-old interpreter, volunteered to cooperate. Tang and Wang, our two young scientists, and a TV man were suffering from altitude sickness and were definitely pale and unwell. Bridget was not too good either, and Tony had to pack up half-way through the enterprise.

We joined in with the forty or so Chinese who were labouring, and, with us, there were sixty-four working on the road. We were organised by a Chinese man in a peaked cap, and we covered about 20 m at a time. Most of us worked in threes, so that when the shoveller got tired he would hand over, and no spade would be left idle. Eventually though, we found it as well to do what the Chinese were doing. Some would start in the middle of the 20 m, but most would be at the back. They would work at the wall of snow like maniacs and hand over to someone behind when they were puffed, and then go to the back of the queue to recover.

For our team it was the most unwise and foolhardy thing we could have done. We were not acclimatised, and to do hard manual labour at 15,000 ft invited all sorts of medical repercussions. We broke all the rules, and Bridget was agitated. She was the only medic left to accompany the team on the road. Ray was in Dege, and the replacement doctors were in Chengdu, about to come out with Gwyn and the fuel lorries. Although suffering from altitude sickness

129

herself and feeling very unwell, she was magnificent in the way she looked after us. She carried a 'Norwegian' container of water down the hill for us to drink, knowing that the one thing everyone needs above all at altitude is water, water, water. She tended Tony and Wang in the bus sympathetically; Wang, especially, needed a lot of comfort as he had never been ill to this extent before and was a very frightened man.

Despite breaking the rules, we set to with whatever capacity we had to shovel, dig or manhandle lumps of packed or frozen snow off the road. The bright sun soon thawed out where we had reached the earth surface, and a Chinese jeep started to come down the ruts behind us.

It was hard and exhausting work. The brilliant sun scorched our faces and we all suffered considerable sunburn, amplified by the reflection from the silver snow. We had started working with the Chinese at 2.00 p.m. Five and a half hours later, after we had cleared 800 m of roadway, the jeep drove through to a loud cheer from the whole company of clagg-clearers.

We were exhausted, but exhilarated. The need had been for perseverance, tenacity and a total dependence on one another. That self-same spirit that Tony Brindle had so commended and seen in us on our training weekend in November 1989 was still there. Now it was for real, and not just an exercise to assess what calibre of people God had called together for this momentous adventure.

The 'lorry with initiative' was really struggling. He had chains but had not put them on. The more he revved his engine the more the wheels spun and dug down into the snow. One elderly Tibetan went in front of him with a stick, so that he could ascertain the depth of snow ahead. He then marked out a route for the lorry to take. Unfortunately, on one of the skids, the lorry slid downhill (like a hovercraft does) and plunged into another 4 ft snowdrift. It was lying at an alarming angle. But the Tibetans carried on shovelling the snow out, moving the lorry forward half a meter, and then digging it out again.

Another lorry followed it down, and got into the same

difficulty. It was followed by, of all things, the local Manigangge to Denke bus, also without chains. The bus fared no better but at least it had a bus-load of locals to drag and push it down the slope.

The first of the stationary lorries, with chains, hammered and skidded down the main road. It pushed the snow-banks back and slushed out the track, digging violent grooves in the now muddy earth. At 7.45 p.m. it was still daylight – the whole of China is on Beijing time, and in west China we were at least two hours adrift of daylight synchronisation.

Then ten lorries came down, making the pass more and more negotiable. Included in them were Giles and two fuel trucks. We told him to go on. The next three trucks down stopped to tow out our three short-cutters. That took an extra hour.

Then our bus came down and was fine. The tow-truck with *Neste Enterprise* came next. We had had trouble with that driver before, and his policy in tackling icy roads was to go at it like a maniac. Certainly he had little care for the hovercraft trailer. He stopped on the hairpin as the trailer would not go round. Peter unbolted the rear axle, coupled up the hydraulics, and gradually steered the rear end round the corner. That operation went well.

But now, totally oblivious of Peter and the trailer behind, he set off down the second part of the snow-dug road at 20 mph. Peter, who had to walk behind because the trailer stand had been broken by this driver's folly, could not slide and run over the rutted road fast enough, and steer at the same time. The wheel flew out of his hand, spun round, and the rear trailer wheels spun into a position 90° to the direction of travel. Everyone by the roadside was shouting at the driver, who refused to stop.

Eventually Steve stood in the road in front of him, so he had to stop. He was so uninterested in what had happened that he only got out of his cab half an hour later to see what all the fuss was about! With the rear wheels at 90° to the road, the trailer could easily have rotated about them and toppled over the hillside. Mercifully, it didn't. But the hydraulics were now useless. The ram had ripped out of

131

its housing at both ends and we had no way of turning the wheels back and locking them into fore-and-aft.

Together with Jim and Neil, Peter and Steve decided to try to jack up the rear of the trailer, the wheels of which had now jammed in the snow, and see if they could turn them round. They failed. Instead they bent the jack shaft. Eventually they decided to attach a canvas strop to one edge of the bogey and to the front of the *ICI River Rover* lorry, which had stopped on the hill behind them. The lorry drove slowly backwards, and, very carefully, the bogey rotated back to normal, all the while creating a possibility of its rocking over the edge.

The *ICI River Rover* lorry, having momentum, unfortunately dragged the bogey past the normal. This stripped the hydraulic pipes from the broken ram, creating more damage. That took about an hour to mend. Eventually *Neste Enterprise* was able to set off again at 8.30 p.m. It was dusk and the sun had just dropped down over the horizon. It was also getting cooler.

At the start of the day the Chinese had asked Mike to sign a form taking responsibility for the safety of the convoy. It was just as well he did, for the Chinese would never have given us authority to start down the pass.

So off went the driver, again much too fast. I had gone down to the bus, which was 2 km down the road and lower, because I was getting cold. I saw the tow truck and hovercraft disappear from sight round a second bend on the hill. We waited. And waited. There was no sign of it.

Meanwhile, as if we did not have enough trouble, Wang was being violently sick out of one of the bus windows. His condition, due to the altitude, was becoming critical. I blew my whistle to those at the top, and shouted for as many of the bus passengers as possible to come down, as we had problems.

'What about Plod?' shouted Sam. I consulted Lili, then shouted back: 'Send him down, and everyone else.'

They came. But still we waited.

Where the 'initiative' bus and two lorries had come down

the hill there were some very deep ruts on the downhill side of the road. The tow-lorry driver was told to avoid the rutted side of the road, but did not. The trailer skidded into the ruts. He tried to correct it by going into the hill, but got the tow-lorry stuck. The trailer was again only centimetres from the edge, on a slush-bound road, with a very steep snow slope dropping away to disaster.

Peter and Steve now tried to slide the trailer tail back on to the road, just as they had successfully done at the road works a few days earlier. But this time they were not able to position it quite correctly, and they could only use the one serviceable jack that was left. It, in its turn, could not stand the strain and bent beyond further use.

We waited. Mike went up to see what the delay was. Eventually Sam and Kevin, being the fittest, also went up with a series of code flashes on their torches to tell us if all was well, or if they needed help. It was now quite dark. Fortunately a waning moon provided grey-silver light to give some poor visibility.

What were we to do? We were stuck on a snow-bound hill at 15,000 feet in the dusk, unable to move, worn out, with seriously ill men aboard, and a queue of lorries on both sides of the tow-truck waiting to tackle the pass.

Steve, with the tow-lorry, suddenly thought: there was a Chinese lorry with chains just there – could he not tow us out, using our strop? Steve asked. He was glad to help. After a further half an hour the jam was cleared. Time: 9.30 p.m.

One final hurdle confronted us. There was one more hairpin. Believe it or not, the trailer could not get round it, now that the rear-wheel steering had died. It stuck on the corner. Here total commendation must be given to Peter Gunner. He is not a qualified engineer – he is a Sussex farmer. But his ingenuity and initiative is quite extraordinary, and his practicality had made him irreplaceable on this expedition, and particularly on this journey. It was for this that he had come. Tony Burgess and he designed the trailer together. So far all their careful, pragmatic and prayerful foresight had enabled all the facilities they had built into it to be used. All but one. Now it was the turn of that last invention to come into use, and Peter thought of it.

They had designed a towing arm that was usable at either end. The rear bogey wheels were stuck in the fore-and-aft position because the steering mechanism had been severed. If they could only put the tow arm into the rear bogey, and use the tow hook on the front of *ICI River Rover*'s lorry, would it not be possible for *River Rover*'s lorry to push the rear end of the trailer round the bend, skidding it if necessary?

They tried it. It was all they could do. The tow-lorry pulled forward gently, and the push lorry shoved the tail end round. Very sparingly, they managed to push the trailer end off the edge of the slippery road, and on to the straighter part. What a relief!

And then, of all the dunderhead things, the tow-lorry driver continued to drive forward. He dragged both the trailer and the *River Rover* lorry down the road, the latter driver screaming his head off and standing on his klaxon, struggling to keep his vehicle on the road. He even put one hand outside to open his cab door and jump for it if his lorry was forced over the edge. It was terrifying.

At that point we nearly lost both *Neste Enterprise* and *ICI River Rover* for the umpteenth time. It was, but for the grace of God, the end of our expedition. Steve rushed in front and forced the driver to stop, who also got a thorough earful from the driver of the rear truck. Well deserved. From then on, Steve walked at a slow pace in front of the tow-lorry to stop any more stupidities.

Kevin and Sam signalled to us in the bus that all was well, but still Mr Zhou would not allow it to go downhill to alleviate the altitude sickness. The tow-lorry at long last came round the bend and into sight. When it reached the bus Steve let out a great big shout of 'Alleluia'. It was 11.15 p.m.

Slowly the convoy went down the hill. Where were we to stay the night? We did not know. All we knew was that we were safe, on our way again, and that we had been through the Knacker's Yard. But we had won!

The nearest town was Denke, and that was about 95 km away, four hours at our pace. Bridget and her patients were glad to be going downhill.

About 1000 feet down the hill we stopped at a Mountain Workers' place. The twenty-one workers who lived there had come up to help unstick *Neste Enterprise* at about 11.00 p.m. They had shovels over their shoulders and looked a bit like the Seven Dwarfs. Mr Zhou decided to stop there for a break. It was as well that he did; Giles was there waiting for us with the two fuel lorries. He had been waiting four hours. It was so very good to see him; we had been wondering if he had pressed on to Denke.

Madam Zhou went hysterical. I guess it was the tension of the hour, the pressure of the adventure, the altitude and the lateness of the night which all combined to loose off a torrent of angry abuse. Then it rose in pitch. Then she burst into tears. From what we all gathered (because it came out in Chinese), it seemed that she had been very worried about Giles and his two fuel lorries. Giles particularly. She was the senior CAS member and was responsible not for fuel or lorries but for the *weibin*, including Giles. She should not be allowing any *weibin* to go out into a minorities' area without being chaperoned. She slaughtered Giles verbally for going off. Poor Giles; he was just carrying out Mike's instructions. Then Lili laid into him, and Mr Zhou followed suit. And because he could understand Chinese, he collected the total weight of the broadside. He came in to where we were all sitting, slumped despondently on to a stool and said, 'I resign.' We encouraged him in his moment of despair.

We were in a tiny, poky room, fogged out with smoke from the yak-dung fire, where the team were drying their socks out and thawing their frozen fingers. One of the workers had boiled a huge pot of water and we pulled out some tea-bags from the compo rations.

It was late: midnight. We just had to trust the Chinese to find us a bed for the night. That was what the contract said and we knew they were glad to get decent accommodation for themselves. But soon Mr Zhou appeared through the gloom, silhouetted in the door by the moonlight.

135

'We stay here tonight,' he told me in Spanish.

'Where do we sleep?' I asked.

'Here.'

'In this tiny room?' I asked. 'We cannot get sixteen people in here.'

'There is nothing else,' he said. 'You might like to stay in the bus.'

I passed this information on to the rest. There was not one murmur of complaint. We were so tired and exhausted we were glad to have any decision. Three stayed in the room; two of them froze during the night, failing to relight the yak-dung. I decided to sleep under the stars, in the yard with wolf-hound and lorries, and with Chinese going to the toilet all night. I blew up my comfortable sleeping mat and got in. I rated relaxation that night at no more than 20 per cent. The others did not fare much better in the bus. They were woken three times by the driver starting the engine to keep it from freezing, and a lorry driver repeating the same exercise twice. With the roar of the engines and wolf-hound barking madly and senselessly round the area, sleep was grimly elusive. Too much exertion at too high an altitude too soon had given us all rotten headaches. The cure was to go downhill; failing that, drink plenty of water. Needless to say, the water froze in our water bottles overnight!

We woke fitfully to a bright, sharp and very chilly morning. A few of us tried to replenish our water bottles in the crystal clear mountain stream. The freezing water solidified in the water filter before it had emptied into the bottle. All of us were sore. Only two attempted to wash in the stream. I was one. I vowed I would never try to be macho again!

We were keen to get off as soon as possible. We had a way to go to reach our destination – Denke.

The lorries gradually shook themselves awake and got into some sort of line. *ICI River Rover* lorry, parked directly behind the bus, tried to get out by going forward. It scraped the rear of the bus, bending *ICI River Rover*'s port fan guard. The driver did not hear our shouts, and carried on. Thus he smashed the rear left-hand window of the bus. The

136

shouts penetrated. But it meant that we in the bus were forced to travel the dusty road from then on with a gaping hole in the back, engorging more and more suffocating sand.

It was 9.30 a.m. on Sunday, 6 May, day 8, that we left the workmen's hut, on our way to Denke. The road passed through a desert wasteland, inside the rolling hills. Few animals and few trees greeted our advance. There were not many Tibetan buildings either, and those we saw were shoddily made of mud, very poor in comparison with others we had seen. The dust accelerated our desire to reach our destination. We strained to see the Yangtze, that huge river which we had come to do battle with, but were denied any glimpse for hours.

There were hold-ups. We went from the main road on to the Denke road and it was not long before we came across a bridge that was decidedly dodgy. Would *Neste Enterprise* get over on its trailer? We all got out and examined it and expressed our varied opinions. Mr Zhou was not prepared to commit himself. He asked Mike if he would take responsibility for the safety of the hovercraft. Of course Mike would.

Mr Zhou sidled up to me and said tiredly, '*Hay muchos problemas con nosotros cada día*.' (There are many problems with us every day.)

'Yes,' I replied. Then added. 'It is normal in expeditions. What we are here for is to overcome them.'

I thought afterwards that we were forging our way onwards to attempt something unique in the history of the world. That sort of thing is never likely to be easy. But we were there to provide solutions. Only insoluble problems bothered us and, in the end, we encountered almost none of those.

At about 5 p.m. we saw the Yangtze. We stopped to take photos. Our hearts rose within us. It looked what it is; formidable and powerful, and one of the mightiest rivers in the world. Only a few more kilometres. A whole hour and two more unserviceable and contentious bridges later we entered Denke. We were exhausted but thrilled.

We had travelled 1145 km (712 miles). It had taken eight days at an average of 20 km per hour. The distance covered

137

was almost the same as that which we were planning to tackle on the great river itself. We prayed that the river journey would not be such an epic as its dusty predecessor. But we doubted it: this river has killed.

6

A Rapid too Far

Courage is the thing. All goes if courage goes. (J. M. Barrie)

I don't want to be a might-have-been. (J. M. Barrie)

It very nearly killed me. And because it nearly killed me, it nearly killed us; I was driving. It was that rapid below Denke towards the end of our time there.

Denke is a small town 'down by the riverside'. The Tibetans and some Chinese call it Dukon. In 1978 the name of the area was officially titled Lo Xie – which is spelt as two words but pronounced as one, Lohshi. I shall call it Denke. It is a two-horse town, because it had another street off the main street at right angles to it. The reception we had there was warm, friendly and helpful. The mayor gave the whole town two days off when we arrived, so we set up camp to a vast audience.

When we arrived we went straight to the government hostel, where we were greeted by Colin, four days out of Dege and frustrated by being restricted in everything he did by uncomprehending and anxious town officials. It was a joy to the rest of us to see Colin and Anne meet in a huge marital hug. They could not help it, having been separated for some while, but were nevertheless embarrassed at showing affection for each other in front of a team who were split up from those they loved. Colin and Anne were sensitive to others; it was hard being the only married couple on an expedition, but they had thought it through beforehand and had determined not to allow their marriage to come before the expedition. Perhaps their Territorial Army experience helped? In fact they were delighted with the amount of time they were able to be together, and found that it was good to have each other so that they could unburden themselves. Colin's quiet, Scottish ways, his wise appraisals, his immediate willingness and his great strength made him an invaluable team member. Anne's technical skills, her delight in getting dirty, and her humble disposition added depth and quality to the engineering team. We found their unselfishness and helpfulness of great benefit, and they endeared themselves quickly to the rest of the team.

The senior FAO officer of the county and the senior county official travelled 300 km to welcome us. After supper they and Mr Zhou took Mike out to a site we could use for our camp, not far from town. Mike sent the jeep back for Kevin, Colin, Peter and me, so that we could pitch in our opinions too. The location had three disadvantages; it was some 30 metres from the river, many rocks would need removing, and there was no fresh stream handy. The Yangtze itself was muddy-brown.

Mike decided to send us four early the following morning ahead of the main party; Peter thought there was a better place about 2 km out that he, Tony and Ray had reconnoitred in May 1989. We looked. It was certainly better. The 'runway' to the river required only 10 m of rock clearance, and above it was all sand. There was a mountain stream passing very close. And there was an adjacent area cordoned off by stones. We felt that the stones provided a natural fence against intruding and inquisitive Tibetans, but I was concerned because the area was something similar to a prayer quadrangle. A prayer flag fluttered on a pole outside. And, extraordinarily, practically every stone had Tibetan scriptures carved into it. Apparently, if your carved stone got blown on by the wind, or your prayer flags flew, then you gained house-points in heaven – or, rather, Nirvanah, the state of Eternal Nothingness. I was bothered because I am aware that demon spirits can inhabit 'things', and it could mean continual pin-pricks, hassle and hindrances that pioneers like us could well do without. Nothing, of course, that prayer could not handle, if it was necessary to be there. It was. We set up camp in the square and put the fuel dumps and hovercraft near the water. It was good to become more vigilant in prayer. I went back to tell the main party our decision, using a Tibetan horse as transport. I was the first, but by no means the last, to use this kind of vehicle.

We spent a hectic day putting up tents – food, medical, stores, engineering and scientific. At 7.30 p.m. an additional seventeen personal mushrooms went up with different degrees of success and speed – our first attempt at doing our own. These were followed the next day by latrines, wash enclosure, garbage pit and soakaway.

The time at Denke, Base 1, was to be a shake-down period. The medical team were doing their project at Dege, and our whole task involved the engineering and assessment of the hovercraft. Peripherally, it was important to do three other things with the hovercraft; first, to see if *Neste Enterprise* could get up river to Base 2; second, to try and hover all the way down to Dege and back; third, to do a miles-per-gallon check on *ICI River Rover*. Mike thought that this would take two or three weeks.

Meanwhile the medical team, separated from us, was struggling with the hassles that had now become an expectation of our expedition. Their journey to Dege, having only a stores truck (Colin) and a Landcruiser (Ray, Dee, Fiona, Duncan and guides), had taken three days. Chola, the high pass between Manigangge and Dege, presented them with almost the same adventure as we had – lorries sliding to the edge, getting stuck in snow, being towed out, Fiona and Colin digging people out, and Duncan having altitude sickness. The pass was at 4917 (16,200 ft), the highest we went bar the source itself. They nearly lost a lorry.

They found Dege to be a two-street county capital, straddling an apology for a river. Poor people on the river's edge had mud-walled huts on stilts, but others' houses were more substantial. The town, population 4900, nestled in a basin, but behind the outside rows the hills rose steeply,

141

confining any rebuilding and stopping the town from expanding. The dominant feature was the Buddhist monastery, set 100 metres back along a side valley, accompanied by its usual accoutrements of priests' and novices' dwellings. The printing press, into which our team went without consulting the official guides, was fascinating. The texts were carved in reverse on blocks of wood. One priest brushed on ink, a second slapped a sheet of paper on and brushed it, and then took it off. There were thirty-two pairs of priests working. A lad regularly came round to collect the printed sheets and distribute them elsewhere. Buddhist scriptures were flowing out of this printing press by the thousand.

The monastery itself was being refurbished, with wooden carvings being repainted, and statues, recovered from hiding during the Cultural Revolution, being restored. They mainly depicted gurus in various holy postures. There were also magnificent paintings and murals on cloth, again of gurus and lamas.

The Cultural Revolution was one of the worst things to hit China; even worse than being invaded. I presume Mao Zedong just could not live without a revolution of some kind, forgetting that progress can only be made in a nation at peace. Was there nothing inside those young people, all dressed up in their finery as Red Guards, to tell them that they were doing wrong? It is a compelling idea – standing society on its head, putting children in charge, tormenting parents, declaring ten years' holiday, settling old scores. But it does not take ten seconds to realise that such a society then becomes brutish and backward. It took China ten years to realise it. At the time the revolution was declared 95 per cent good, and 5 per cent bad. Those figures have now been revised: the revolution was 95 per cent bad and 5 per cent good. What percentage was good for the 15 million who died?

The first two days of the medical team's visit were the May Day holiday. On the Wednesday a reception and inauguration ceremony was given, overseen by the Party Leader and the lady Deputy Magistrate. The medical staff attended from the Mother and Child Health Unit, the hospital, the

142

Epidemic Prevention Station and those in charge of the EPI (Expanded Programme of Immunisation) at Ganzi and Kanding. Ray donated the two solar fridges and 10,000 needles and syringes to the EPI station. The contract had reduced their immunisation task to one day, but they were able to see, and help inoculate, 150 children in two sessions. One of these was videoed by John for the *Blue Peter* sequence and the other for our own expedition film. The latter was shown on local TV.

The six days they spent in Dege were most rewarding. Ray lectured on the EPI programme, Duncan spoke on solar power, and Fiona on the fridges. The UNICEF and China policy for solar fridges was that they should remain in towns and not in villages. The proper use for them would be in a mobile capacity, so Ray suggested adapting them both for a jeep and a yak.

Within twenty-four hours the local people produced a frame for the jeep, on which the panel could rest. They tried it out on the road, and it worked excellently. They then put the fridge on a yak; after all, it worked with camels in the desert so it should work on a yak in Tibet. It did. The fridge was on one side, the batteries on the other, and the panel rode on top. A little redesign of a yak saddle was required, but otherwise it worked very well. Thus mobile solar fridges can complete the cold chain, allowing local medics to carry the EPI programme to remote villages in north-west Sichuan. The local EPI programme started in 1971, and the Chinese claimed 80 per cent coverage. But because the team were on TV once, and local radio twice, the interest in this free facility was extensively renewed. Ray offered the local health authority any one of eight lectures they could give. They said 'Yes'. So they gave all eight to between seventeen and twenty-five people, mainly on basic health care and prevention of disease in children. The week ended with the team being invited to a show by the local Tibetan Dance Group. Our team were dressed up in Tibetan costumes and taught cultural dances, to the immense enjoyment and great hilarity of the townspeople. Duncan said it was one of the best evenings

143

he had had in his life, and certainly the best in China.

But there were the normal problems. The team found themselves immensely restricted in their movements. They were not allowed into either the Tibetan or western hospitals, and Fiona was not allowed to visit the animal husbandry official; all these things were 'not in the contract'. One afternoon three of them wandered down the road towards the Yangtze, hitching a lift on a passing tractor, just to enjoy the countryside. They were caught by Mr Wang, puffing unfitly on a bicycle stolen from an unfortunate peasant, who demanded they return to town immediately. One wondered what on earth the Chinese had to hide. The hotel in which they stayed was fairly insalubrious. There was a communal wash place, and the toilets hung over a 3 m drop into the river. Not so the Tibetan house into which they were invited. The animals lived downstairs but the people occupied remarkably clean quarters upstairs. The rear wall was the rock hill and another wall was covered in slate. Beautifully worked and painted wood-carvings adorned the windows, and a wood fire warmed the home. The man of the house had built it himself and it was a tribute to his skills.

The medical team left Dege by road, and both they and the TV team arrived at Denke together, followed almost immediately on the same day by Gwyn and the last team members (Dr David Langley, Stan Baldock, Tony Shewell, Andrew Sneller, Dr David Johnson) and nine lorry-loads of fuel. All on Tuesday, 8 May. It was terrific to have the whole team together at last.

ICI River Rover was the first to come off its truck. We assembled Peter's A-frame and winched the craft off. Neil had expected it to go straight on to the water; all the engineering work that was necessary had been completed during the protracted negotiations in Chengdu. But it was not to be so. The dent in the port fan duct guard, caused by the thump at the workman's hut below the Hai Zhi pass, had to be knocked out. And Neil discovered that Sam's scientific data-logger box, screwed to the buoyancy chamber at the front, had split the bulkhead through vibration on the bumpy road. That had to be repaired.

144

It was ready the following day. There was no opportunity for a test run; all the township was there for the inaugural sortie, as were the Mayor and dignitaries. Speeches were made, a ribbon was cut by the Mayor, and Mike powered out into the Yangtze, covering the onlookers with dust and spray. Mike wanted the first two sorties on the mighty Yangtze river to be manned by those who had been on previous expeditions. So on the first ride Jim and I accompanied him. On the second Tony Burgess and David Langley came with me. We felt it prudent at that stage to have crews of just three people. On the second sortie, when all was going well, I got out of the driver's seat and let David take over. Almost immediately afterwards a strong wind blew up and the craft went out of control. It was not possible to stop it hitting the rocks on the side of the river. I brought the craft gingerly back to the 'runway' (laboriously cleared by the whole team the previous evening), where we examined the damage. The rear end was severely bent and Neil, whose baby she was, was decidedly upset that so much damage had been done on her first day on the water. What was more, he had to mend it. It was entirely my fault, and I humbly apologised. I had forgotten that the early days of river work is always a high risk period.

Neste Enterprise needed a lot of work prior to going on the water. The cracks in the buoyancy chambers, near the feet, caused by the bad driving on rough roads, had to be inspected, drilled and sealed. We replaced all the plastic shackles that held the fingers to the skirt shift hawsers with the stainless steel ones David had brought from the UK. Then the sides had to be lowered, and the duct, propellors and control surfaces 'mantled' before she would be ready. It took us two days. Finally we were able to take the bogies off to lower the trailer frame on to the sand.

Meanwhile Peter had been working on repairing the trailer. He wanted to go home to his farm, since his contribution to the expedition had been to see the craft safely over the hills on the trailer. Now he was determined to repair it prior to his leaving, so that the hydraulic steering would be operational again for the return road journey in two

145

months time. We lowered the engine end, using the shorter, subsidiary jacks because both the originals had been bent on the Hai Zhi pass. We immediately encountered a problem. The front end bogies had been moved to their innermost position to minimise the damage on the road. Now that one end was down, the other bogey's pivot point, in the centre of the trailer, raised the jacking end to an unreachable height. Two railway sleepers were insufficient. We dreamed up all sorts of means of raising the jacks, none of which was safe or sensible. Reluctantly in the end we were forced to cut the sleepers into eight blocks (with a cheap, bendy saw) and stack them on top of one another to enable the jacks, on their limits, to release the bogies. This method was very unsafe. Twice the precarious stacks of blocks wobbled, the craft lurched, one of us shouted 'Run!' and the jacks crashed to the ground. The safety feature that stopped the hovercraft from overturning when the jacks collapsed was in the form of tubular supports which we pegged higher as the jacks raised the trailer end. They saved the whole craft from tipping over and dying. But it worked eventually. We were concerned for our own safety, but far more for the horde of Tibetans who crowded closer and closer to see what was going on. We just could not push them back.

Having got the lady on to the ground, our next task was to hover her off the trailer. Previously we had hovered on and off backwards. But the trailer was wrongly positioned (the front end pointing downhill) and we had to hover off sideways. That presented repeated problems in the form of wires, metal bits, and skirt fingers getting caught up in protrusions on the trailer bed.

It took us one and a half hours to take *Neste Enterprise* off the trailer bed, something that should normally take ten minutes. This exercise involved Colin and Chris going underneath while she was in the hover to free what was tangled. Very dangerous and very risky, but regrettably necessary. We had hoped to fly her that evening, but it was too late by the time she was ready. She flew well the following day, preceded by another set of speeches and, this time, with Ray cutting a medical ribbon.

above Our first view of the mighty Yangtze, 12 kms outside Base Camp 1 at Denke.

above The inhabitants of Denke were given two days' holiday to watch the hovercraft launch into action.

left The Mayor of Denke cuts the "ribbon" and *ICI River Rover* becomes the first hovercraft to fly on the top third of the Yangtze.

below left We had to clear 20 m of large rocks from the river side to provide a runway for our hovercraft.

below Dr Ray Pinniger inoculates a child at Dege.

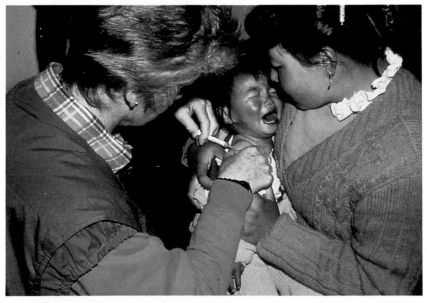

above Children at Denke Primary School put on a show of traditional dancing for us.

above How good to see! Two Tibetan men rode for two days through a storm to be fitted with free spectacles.

above Mr Zen Jinchuo, our Mr Plod from Denke.

above This Tibetan girl was intensely curious about the ways of her new friends.

above *Neste Enterprise* negotiates turbulent rapids above Denke.

left *Neste Enterprise* immobilised after crashing south of Denke. We had permanent Tibetan friends wherever we stopped.

right Sunday worship by the river, later broadcast on Chinese television.

above The narrow pony tracks on the precipitous mountainsides were the only way to reach essential spare parts for our marooned craft.

Pressure to complete the filming of the *Blue Peter* sequence was high, as Peter Gunner was due to leave Denke for home the next day and he would take the film with him. So the rest of the morning was spent walking Sarah and Duncan on and off in various locations. But we had a problem which we were forced to live with: the fuel transfer pump was inoperative because the 'full' ballcock was stuck in the UP position. This meant the craft was trimmed tail-heavy causing all the hover air to escape out of the front. That made hovering very difficult, and, worse, it was captured on film; but we made it. Returning at lunchtime, Chris and Sam went through the wiring diagram and fixed the vagrant pump. She was fit for another sortie in the afternoon, and went well. Encouraging.

ICI River Rover did not fare so well. Neil had mended the dent in the back end and taken it out for a test run, where he discovered an engine fault – it was coughing and occasionally losing power. Mike decided he would fly it with the problem, because of the pressure to get all the filming done, and went down river with Peter and Sarah. It was a mistake to go down the river; he should have gone up. It was a mistake to take *ICI River Rover* with a misfiring engine. The little craft all but packed up just below the bridge. The engine rpm was varying between 2500 and 4300 with the throttle at maximum. Mike dumped her on the rocks on the Tibetan bank. Peter, in the back, remembered that the fuel tanks were pressurised, and that by a hand-pump in the rear seat. He pumped. But the engine only responded intermittently and they wondered if they could get back up river. Very slowly, in fits and starts, and mostly below hump (see Appendix C), *ICI River Rover* struggled up the hill, up what felt like rapids but were only burbles, and strained painfully back to base with Peter pumping like fury, Mike battling like fury, and Sarah praying like fury.

These first two days of hovercraft shake-down had come close to disaster. More was to come.

We needed to see how far *Neste Enterprise* could get up river. Our aim was to try to take her up past Yushu to Base 2 at Qumerlai. Saturday, the following day, was to be the attempt. It was somewhat early in our plans, but time was short and we had to force march our activities. Mr Xie Jinkang had been in the tent the previous day (our Chinese guides only appeared occasionally and none came on the hovercraft), and warned us of the location of two areas of bad rapids, one on each side of Yushu. He drew up another note, asking Mike to sign, stating that Mike took full responsibility for the safety of both craft on this treacherous river.

The guides were never to venture on to the river. We had the Yangtze to ourselves, and complete freedom to do as we chose without the restraints that the Chinese carried with them.

But we took off fully warned.

I drove, and promptly banged the tail end of *Neste Enterprise* on the rocks that edged our widened runway, ripping a hole in her starboard hull and fracturing the hull end of one of the struts. It was the first of many such 'boings'. The hole in the buoyancy chamber was not reparable, but would be fine, provided the craft was not actually sitting in water and ingesting it.

The river to the north-west bifurcated and we had trouble locating a decent pathway; this water pattern was to be normal all the way up the river from Qumerlai to the source, according to the map. After about 6 km the sides closed in and the hills narrowed to ear-defender distance. The single flow was easier to navigate, but we anticipated some rough rapids as a consequence. Moreover there were few places to land if we had engine trouble, or if we wanted to stop. It reminded me of my early flying days, when we had to be on a constant lookout for fields into which we could force-land if the prop stopped. So we went cautiously. Some good rapids came our way and *Neste Enterprise* sailed over them as if they were not there. She rode the rough water excellently. The gorge narrowed and the river twisted; at one point we were heading due south and the special provision of an on-board compass was a real boon. We drove on for some 43 km.

We rounded the bend and saw heavy white water ahead. I slowed down. The waves were on the far side of the river, and a stream of them came right across. It was impossible to see where the river was coming from, for it was obscured by a bank of cliff. I eased over to the right to determine the best path up. It seemed that, if we were to cut across the heavy water about half-way up, we would get into smoother water beyond. But the subsequent sharp left-hand turn was a problem: *Neste Enterprise* needs a fair amount of width in a river to turn because of its control system (it uses yaw and skid via the rudders as its main turning device) and it did not look as if we had the room. The craft rotates beautifully below hump, but then she does not move forward. We needed forward speed to continue up whatever gradient confronted us (if there was one) round the left-hand bend.

I explained to Rob what I was planning to do and we crossed the initial white water at about the right place. The smooth water beyond fell over at quite a gradient and, because the white water had dissipated our speed, *Neste Enterprise* struggled to surmount the brow of the liquid hill. I was glad to see, dead ahead, a sandy bank to which we could escape if it was necessary.

We climbed over the hill, just over hump, and *Neste Enterprise* started to accelerate as we went left round the solid promontory. Confronting us was another huge rapid, with a sharp right turn. We were instantly committed. It is in these blind situations that one has to think very fast and take the best decision one can under the circumstances. It is not always right, and hindsight is invariably better. As someone so aptly put it in another context, 'The one thing all parents should ensure is that they have their second child first.'

To the right of this really bad flow, and hugging the rocks on the bend, the water looked easier. I went for it. Our forward speed was not very fast: this helped to get over the roughage but did not give us sufficient momentum to climb the incline, particularly with a hard turn involved. Half-way up and after the bend, *Neste Enterprise* gave up. She stabilised on the hill. Very, very difficult. To the left was treacherous water; to the right were perilous rocks. And that hovercraft is a long one. There was certainly no room to turn round. But at least the craft was stable,

149

allowing us to look round and make decisions and call 'rapidly' on God.

Eventually (three minutes or so) I decided to reverse backwards down the river, pointing up it, and trying desperately to keep out of the damaging water and off the bruising rocks. I got her half-way down, and then felt there was enough room to swing her by pivoting on her base, and allow the nose to inch past the rocks. We 'boinged', but very lightly. We moved into the smooth water half-way up, and gratefully sought the refuge of the sandbank.

We had failed.

But I never accept one failure as defeat. I would have another go. At least the sandbank allowed us to disgorge a few passengers (those loving photography and drama) to lighten the weight.

We lifted off again and I moved as far backwards down the smooth water as possible, to get a run at it. She went over hump quickly and we were able to hit the rough with enough speed to wangle our way up. Just. Relieved, we pulled in to the side to engorge our passengers again. I then handed over to Rob for the smooth bit beyond.

The river twisted more and more, and narrowed even further. The depth of water ensured that the rocks were well submerged, and there were no rapids to speak of. It was just difficult getting round the corners, bearing in mind *Neste*'s turning circle. Rob did well. He was a cautious driver.

We rounded a bend. There, some 50 m ahead of us, was a rock. Right in the middle of the river. Not a little rock, with water lapping over its top; it stood some 10-15 m high, and the water gnashed and gulped down either side in the narrow gorge, restricting the gaps enormously.

Rob throttled back. The water to the right was least heavy; but the gap was too narrow for *Neste Enterprise* to go through with any degree of success. The left-hand side was wider, but the water was heavy, with wave heights of up to a metre. *Neste Enterprise* could cope with that, as there were only about five or six waves. Once those had been covered, the main flow was smooth. But what if she didn't? There was no gentle water round the rock to guarantee success. If she stuck part-way, there was granite either side and no other escape route. Rob was trying to maintain *Neste Enterprise* in a 'heave-to' condition in the middle of the river, below hump, not an easy thing to do, while I chewed over the situation.

'No,' I decided, 'we go back.'

We had come to see how far up river we could get, and I was disappointed that we had only travelled about 45 km. But I saw that there was no point in jeopardising the craft, and there were those reported bad rapids further up. It was a difficult decision, because it committed the whole expedition to moving from Base 1 to Base 2 by road. Despite the problems of taking both hovercraft by road, it was clearly the sensible, if disappointing, option.

Rob gratefully turned the craft. He had been anxious about hitting the back end against a rock, as spray cut visibility to nothing.

Now it was his turn to get down 'the' rapid. He discussed it briefly with me, and opted to go down backwards rather than forwards, feeling he had greater control that way. Neither option was ideal. The problem with going down backwards is that, despite the two excellent lorry-size rear-view mirrors that were specially installed, you go down blind. The problem with going down forwards is that control is initiated from the rear (unlike a car) so the back end swings out before the craft goes where it is required to go. So the rear could easily get caught in the heavy water and get swept down river.

At the top of the rapid, Rob swung the craft round and went tentatively down backwards. He was certainly on tenderhooks, as it was the first decent rapid he had ever tackled. He came down slowly, and was doing well. But he decided to go forwards half-way down and turned too early. The craft nudged into the rocks on the corner. He extricated himself from them with difficulty and got on to the smooth water. Just getting over hump in time, he burst through the cross-current rapid and sailed gladly into the river beyond.

About 50 m down there was a nifty sidewater cul-de-sac.

151

We drove in, parked the lady and got off for a late but delightful lunch.

Rob went for a walk. He had been very tense coming down the rapid and needed to get rid of some pent-up energy. It had been his first. He had not quite got it right, although I wasn't bothered about that. After all, I have made a mess of more rapids than I care to remember and, as long as one emerges without too much damage to the craft, who cares? Rob did. I was not actually aware that he was as worried as he was, but I now knew that we had time on our hands. The pressure to go as high as we could was off, and we had plenty of time to return home. I had a suggestion:

'How about staying here for an hour or so, and using this rapid as a training exercise?'

The thought filled him with horror. He had been glad to emerge in one piece and the thought of putting his head in the lion's mouth again was far from pleasant. But I knew that if a driver can tackle a difficult rapid as many times as would take away his fear, then his confidence curve would take a mega-leap.

I had often had to do this with my students in my flying instructor days; after a cup of coffee, put them straight back in the aeroplane and do the frightening exercise again. Rob did not like it, but he did it.

We took the photographic gang to their vantage point, and then Rob and I went up and down the rapid five or so times. The more you see it, the more familiar each wave and each rock becomes. The more you fly up and down it, the easier it becomes. Both of us were happy, relaxed and confident when we eventually picked up the photographers who had, in their turn, picked up a few Tibetan horsemen amongst their photographs. Rob drove home.

Meanwhile Neil and Jim and Steve were tackling *ICI River Rover*. Her fuel problem was one 'up with which we could not put'. They drained both tanks. Steve dismantled the fuel pump and found it filled with Explosafe bits. Explosafe is a special alloy that looks like strands of silver paper, that was stuffed into the fuel tanks to stop

152

them exploding when the petrol level was low. This material was clearly disintegrating. They decided to install another fuel filter between the tanks and the pump to supplement the filter between the pump and the engine. Then they filtered the petrol from the drums into jerrycans, and discovered that it was filthy. It also did not 'feel' like the 98 octane we had ordered, but we had no way of checking. From then on we filtered all the petrol twice. It worked; *ICI River Rover*'s engine suffered no further fluctuation problems.

We had sadly to bid farewell to three of our company, and temporarily to five more. It was time for Peter Gunner to return home to his farm. Tony Burgess was involved with the organisation of Friends of China and was committed to seeing a group into China in the summer. His input had been invaluable. Chris Fox, the ICI apprentice, felt he had to return home for personal reasons; his contribution to the electric and electronics side had been significant. We were disappointed that they felt they ought to return to other activities, and were sadder for their departure. We missed all three.

Five ace administrators took to the road, and went north to be a vanguard for Base 2. Andrew led the negotiations and took Mr Xie Jinkang and our two CAS lads, Wang and Tang. They went to Yushu to get permits to enter Qinghai. Colin and Kevin went up to recce, select and establish Base 2. Giles accompanied them to translate and David Johnson went as in-house medic. Kevin Mentzel, a former sapper captain and now a curate in Maidstone, had shown his personal qualities in his ability to persuade his bishop to release him for the expedition. Wiry and tenacious, Kevin was responsible for the devotional programme and rations. His store-keeping was meticulous with one exception – bourbon biscuits. We had a mountain of bourbons and Rev Kev rationed them so well that we ended up with a marginally lesser mountain, but now diesel flavoured! His ability to control so many Christians from so many denominations without conflict in the daily devotional time was shrewd, gracious and generous, and led to a lovely atmosphere throughout the team.

153

Andrew was able to return, with Xie Jinkang, the following Saturday, complete with Base 2 details, appalling road details, and permits 'yet to be produced'.

The next day was Sunday. A blessed half-day of rest. We held a Christian open-air worship and communion in the morning to encourage our faith and fortitude. This was videoed. Extraordinarily, part of it was shown later in the year on Chinese National TV, without comment, with the expedition film. We claim a world first *Songs of Praise* in China.

Sunday afternoon was PR day. The Chinese had in the last twelve months built a suspension bridge across the river to the Tibetan side. It was probably a 'plan ahead' bridge because there were no approach roads to it from either side; only footpaths. It was interesting, like some bridges we had seen in Yunnan, in that one vertical support for the bridge was the cliff, the hawsers disappearing into holes in the rock. But it was excellent for photography. *Neste Enterprise* (Rob) and *ICI River Rover* (me) went up and down the river six times in different formations for TV and still photographers to have a field day. Afterwards *ICI River Rover* went to do some driver training. This was the only hazard-free day we had at Base 1 with either hovercraft.

Monday was to be another PR day. John wanted some TV of hovercraft on difficult rapids, so Mike decided to send both north to 'the' rapid, so the celluloid and magnetic-tape men could have a field day. (John got the drama he was really looking for, but not on that day.)

The journey up was uneventful, apart from *ICI River Rover*. Neil and I were in her, and she developed a vibration at high rpm that concerned Neil. It soon disappeared, and the engine ran sweetly. But, prior to one rapid, a really heavy vibration appeared at a much lower rpm. We met at lunch-time in the cul-de-sac we had selected a couple of days earlier, just below the dramatic rapid. We discussed the vibration. The original plan had been to deposit the TV crew on the bank and take each craft up separately. But the vibration was too severe to ignore. There were insufficient facilities to examine the engine 'out in the sticks', so we decided to return *ICI River Rover* home and investigate the problem there. To hammer her up and down a rapid with a known engine defect would have been imprudent. We needed her to get to the source next month.

Neste Enterprise stayed behind and shot the rapids four times. The craft performed beautifully.

Neil and I in *ICI River Rover* left the sunny lunch area just one minute too soon. We went down the main river, in the tail end of the rapid, trying to get over hump. No sooner had we cleared it into calmer water than I noticed sudden ripples of wind on the surface. There on the hillside facing us an instant heavy wind was sweeping sand off the pony track into a howling dust storm. *Neste Enterprise* was delayed by this storm as well.

I had noticed this phenomenon on the Yangtze at Base 1. In the afternoons, and totally without warning, strong winds would blow up from nowhere. One day at camp they came from all four quadrants in turn, lasting some 20-30 minutes, and with a gap of an hour in between. Occasionally in the heat of the afternoon dust-devils would suddenly arise. I was familiar with these from my childhood days in Kenya. Local hot spots would create instant low-pressure areas and a swirl of dust, like a mini-tornado, would whirl upwards and suck our hats off. But a 15-20 mph wind from off the mountainside? Down or up river I could understand, and at the entrance of a valley. But from bare-faced rock?

Within a minute the wind had caught us. Not a little wind either. It mostly measured out at 25 mph, and regularly gusted to 40. Now wind and hovercraft are a lethal combination, because the craft is very 'slippery' on its cushion of air. *ICI River Rover*'s wind limit is 15 mph. This squall was behind us, which was a mercy, and it raced us down the river almost uncontrollably. I managed to stay near the centre of the river as we were buffeted along. It was exceedingly difficult and I often had to throttle back into the high vibration area. Neil had not seen anything like it before, and I am not sure that I had. We turned a corner and found ourselves downwind of the dust storm, right in its path. Dust storm it was. The visibility went down to 5 metres, then to one. We could barely see the water in front of the craft, and both banks were totally invisible. It was a complete 'white-out'. The only thing we knew for certain was that we were upright. I cannot recall how long we were whipped along in this situation. Every now and then it cleared a little as the sand blast swirled around the rocks, enabling us to get a momentary glimpse of the shore. There were many times when the craft heeled over, and either I sat on Neil's lap to right her, or he sat on mine. We wished we had brought a third person with us, as we had done on the way up.

The battle must have gone on some ten minutes. It felt to both of us like an eternity. We dared not go to a shore until we were sure the wind would blow us on to it. At last we found one. I turned the craft round into the teeth of the gale and manoeuvred carefully to the side. Neil leaped out into the sandstorm with the anchor and tied the craft to a rock. He then leaped inside again, covered in sand, and we closed the canopy and shut down the engine. There was nothing to do but sit out the storm. Inevitably some Tibetans came to watch, in the form of two children, who covered the side of their faces with their peaked caps from the mobile sandpaper.

The storm raged for an hour, covering everything with sand and whipping the dust horizontally across the top of the rocks. After that the hills clouded over, and it began to sleet. It fell as snow on the hills. We had some drinking water, some boiled sweets, and our sleeping bags. We could sit it out for the night if we had to, but certainly preferred not to.

We both had half an hour's sleep, and were woken by voices outside. The storm was still raging and the windows had now fogged over. Clearing them we saw that our two children had gone off to root out the family, and we now had a dozen fascinated Tibetans staring inquisitively at us. We bid them a cheery wave, and that was all we could do.

One and a half hours after it had begun, the storm abated. We gave it ten more minutes, because we would be catching it up going down river. We started *ICI River Rover* and shooed the Tibetans away before they got covered with

156

spray. Neil turned the craft round and we set off home without further incident. The camp, when we returned, had been devastated by the storm and, once the remaining team had battened down, settled down to pray 'for those in peril on the sea'.

Steve and Neil examined *ICI River Rover* in the quiet aftermath of the storm. Two of the four bars that held the lift fan in place had fractured and a third was cracked. The blades had scored the fan housing in four places. Clearly, this was what was causing the vibration. Neil kicked himself that he had not noticed it before. Just how long it had been going on he was not certain. The fan hub wobbled dangerously in its housing. Had the third strut broken, *ICI River Rover* would have been irreparably damaged, maybe for ever: it was that close.

Hovercraft were not the only consideration at Base 1. They seemed important because they provided the *modus operandi* of all we needed to do there. But people matter more than things, and we were forced to remind ourselves that we were Christian people and there was no possibility of our ignoring others in need. How could we turn a blind eye to disease or deprivation? We had no commitment to any medical or rehabilitation work from any of the three base camps. Only Dege had been 'in the contract'. But it became more and more impossible to turn away from the need which we saw all around us.

Throughout our stay Tibetan people of all ages hung over our wall and watched our every move. The local council had helpfully provided Mr Zen Jinchuo, a 'Mr Plod' policeman, to shoo Tibetans out of our compound and generally look after us. He was Tibetan, and quickly warmed to the expedition team. There were many times when his uniform and his local culture were in conflict with each other; but we were proud that his activities erred on the compassionate side.

Mike and 'Denke Plod' were always first up. Plod loved cleaning our porridge dixie for his morning exercise. Mike would cook the breakfast on a wood fire outside the mess tent rather than attempt to light our temperamental petrol stove, which went through a few explosion tantrums.

Wood was hard to come by right on the tree line at 3125 m (10,250 ft), but we bought some from the local Tibetans, which turned out to be sandalwood, and produced a beautiful aromatic smell every morning. A galley of Tibetans watched. An enchanting child, wrapped in her yak skin cloak, her bare feet cracked and dirty, stared and smiled at us with a wide-grinning face and cheeks of a bruised peach colour. She sat and watched as Mike made breakfast, her eyes exploring every move. He opened a tin of compo rations. She held out her hand for the empty tin, so he put some sweets in the bottom and handed it over. To her and all the Tibetans, everything we did was a source of wonder, and their insatiable curiosity was rarely satisfied.

We noticed an elderly man rotating his prayer wheel (we think it was the only prayer wheel available, and handed round for those who felt inclined), standing among our audience, whose glasses were split in the middle and badly tied with string. We invited him in. As it happened we carried with us a few boxes of cast-off spectacles, some of which were generously given by Mr A. Fremlin-Bailey on behalf of the British and Overseas Optical Missions International; Mike brought the rest from his South American Mission, EUSA (since renamed Latin Link). We made out an eye chart of numbers, and tried various spectacles on him. Eventually we found a pair that suited him perfectly. He was thrilled. The word went round like wildfire, just as healings must have done in Jesus' day.

Mr Plod himself was one of the next, with a stomach ache. He was cured. From then on he brought in quite a number, fairly secretly, to be treated. They were delighted to be helped too. One day he brought in an elderly woman. Stan sat her down to give her an eye test and recognised that she had a cataract in her left eye and an infection in the other. He called Bridget. She said she was blind in the left eye, and that the doctor should see her. Bridget recognised other symptoms, so she went off to find Ray and David. At that point Madam Zhou, whom Stan had not yet met, screamed petulantly at him in Chinese. He was taken aback and tried to explain that the old lady was waiting for

158

the doctor. Madam Zhou screamed even louder, caught his jersey, and violently pulled him away. She then pulled the woman from the chair, screamed at her, and drove her away. At that point Lili came up and provided translation. Madam Zhou said the lady had an infectious disease that was incurable. She said that it was not in the contract for us to treat medical cases outside Dege. She said that we were not permitted to treat anyone, and our pleas of curing her from blindness or other diseases fell on deaf ears.

By this time John Whatmore and David had joined in. Madam Zhou insisted that the lady was not to be seen by us, and got John to guarantee it. She was to go and see the local doctor only. Mr Plod was very embarrassed by all this outrage and disappeared quietly. Stan was furious. David, from Bridget's description, thought her problem could either be a venereal disease or leprosy. Leprosy did not exist in this area, the Chinese said: except the three people the doctors definitely diagnosed. We were told that, from now on, we were not to treat Tibetans.

In contrast, Lili was taken ill late at night and Dr David was summoned from his bed at camp to Denke village to treat her for stomach cramps. To the Chinese, the Tibetans seemed savage and unpredictable and not worthy of western medicine. This was where Communism and compassion polarised at opposite ends of the spectrum. And it made us very sad. John, trying to understand their perspective, suggested that our medicine and our success might escalate very fast, denigrating the local medical service, and embarrass the Party because the local hospital was poorly staffed and inadequately equipped. What a shame that we were not allowed to do things together.

Madam Zhou did not put off Mr Plod. When she had left he invited more people in. We were able to heal them all. The difficult ones were those who needed glasses. Every day Tibetans would circle their eyes, stick their thumbs up and say 'OK, OK' or '*Cato, Cato, Cato*' (Tibetan for thank you). We could not set up an eye clinic and it hurt us to have to turn most of them away. Our intention was to leave a load of glasses at the local hospital just prior to leaving along with a lot of other medical supplies. But the doctor, whom we invited, did not come to our farewell dinner. So he did not get any of the supplies he so desperately needed.

We did treat two elderly Tibetans who stood outside in the rain one night. Mr Plod explained to us that they had ridden for several days from the Tibetan side of the river to get glasses. How could we possibly turn them away, regardless of what the rules and regulations said? We brought them into the tent under cover, and were as delighted as they were that we could find sets of glasses for them – as well as for a persistent local lady. We had difficulty persuading one of the men that a multi-coloured pair of curled-up frames without lenses was less efficient than a plainer pair that enabled him to read!

But one night Mr Plod brought in a Tibetan dad and mum. Dee met them, and the man showed her a sheepskin rug under his coat. She thought he was trying to sell it to her, and said no. But he persisted and opened it up, despite her protestations, to reveal a tiny baby tucked close to his chest to keep it warm. It was very ill. Dee called David and Ray. They tenderly took the child and examined it. It had acute pneumonia and was dying. Ray slipped out and told the rest of us to pray. They gave it the appropriate medicine; if the parents had come a day earlier they could have saved its life. But it was too late. The baby's heart stopped beating. Between them they gave it artificial respiration three times. Three times its heart stopped and started again. Ray said that the baby had reached the point where she would walk out and prepare the relatives for a funeral.

'But,' she added, 'I've never before been in a situation where twelve people were praying for a child.'

There was nothing more either doctor could do. The father put the baby back into its sheepskin next to his side, and gently blew over it. Ray did not know whether this was instinctive, knowledgeable or whether the man was a shepherd. The only scientific reasoning she could think of was that blowing over the child increased the carbon dioxide overpressure, which could stimulate its breathing. To their amazement and joy the baby started breathing, and its spasmodic breath settled down. God had intervened in an impossible situation and brought life. The couple gratefully left. Rob was out by the side of the river praying and he was prompted to go and pray for these two and their baby. This he did, and they disappeared, more than appreciative, into the dark of the night and the beginning of the rain.

Of the many instances of opportunity that we were given on this expedition, the two of the old woman and the child stand out in contrast, and demonstrate Madam Zhou's and our diametrically opposed attitudes. Her thinking was gauged by a culture of fear, darkness, regulations, anxiety and death. We were coming from a place of freedom, peace, wholeness, compassion and life. We had come to bring life into death, light into darkness, help into need. And that aspect of our expedition was, to us, more important even than achieving our goal of getting to the source of the Yangtze. Our fulfilment would be complete if we could handle and achieve both.

Mike told Madam Zhou that if we were not able to treat dying children then she had better kick us out of China immediately. She relented. But guardedly allowed us to treat emergencies only. From then on we interpreted 'emergency' very widely.

We nearly lost all towards the end of our fortnight at Base 1. *ICI River Rover* was having her cushion fan repaired, and that would take until 11 a.m. *Neste Enterprise* was ready for her next foray. Mike was keen to see if she could travel the 70 km to Dege down river and back. *ICI River Rover* would follow when she was serviceable.

The aim had been to leave at 9 a.m. on Tuesday, 15 June. Water in the back end delayed our departure until 9.30. I was driving. We roared gladly under the bridge and on down to a new adventure.

Going down river in a hovercraft is far from easy. The craft are so low in the water that we can barely assess a rapid before we are on top of it, and the water invariably falls away from sight down the incline. This section of our beautiful Chiang Jiang, apart from the 100 metres around the bridge, was utterly new to all of us.

161

I took it cautiously. I went far slower in *Neste Enterprise* than I would have done in *ICI River Rover*; the latter, with her evelons, has got a very effective braking system and her shorter length would enable her to rotate quickly in emergency. So, in the larger, less manoeuvrable craft, we went slowly to assess thoroughly each unknown that the river could throw at us.

About 2 km down we came to a sharp left-hand turn, with a huge buttress of rock sticking out, and white water beyond. We slowed, turned, and pulled into the side to view it before tackling it. It was a heavy climb up the buttress, but it was well worth it; the river round the corner was wide and navigable, and the white water could definitely be by-passed by the far bank. It pays to be cautious. One could break the craft by a bit of carelessness or bravado. I have broken aeroplanes in time past that way, but I did not intend to jeopardise our expedition by a bit of foolhardiness. I knew God had given me skill and experience to get out of most river difficulties, but I was not out to seek them for their own sake.

Some parts of the river were wide and open, and the white water was no trouble for that craft. She really did ride heavy water well. Other parts of the river twisted and turned sharply, and the hills pulled in to 70°, towering above the craft. Slow – cautious – careful; every new corner was a certain difficulty and a potential disaster.

About 26 km down the river the smooth water turned a sharp corner left. I slowed down even further. As the craft went tentatively round the corner the water looked smooth and inconsequential. We went further round. And further. It was a very sharp bend.

Suddenly, without any warning whatever, we were on top of it. Although we were coasting just over hump, there was no way of stopping or turning. We were committed. What opened up before me was a very heavy rapid to the right, with a dozen mountainous waves. To the left were a series of deep troughs which clearly contained rocky centres, and which could easily dissipate the cushion and thump the craft on the rocks.

162

I called to the other eleven people on board, 'Hold tight! This could be a bumpy ride.'

I chose the smooth water right in the centre. As we came towards it, I saw to my horror that it was a smooth flow over a huge rock, and that beyond it was a lethal cavernous hole. I pushed max skirt-shift to the right, and jammed the rudder hard over, to get as far away from the cavern's edge as I could. *Neste Enterprise* responded sluggishly because we were so slow. Then I jammed on left skirt-shift to level her off, left rudder to swing the tail to the right and avoid the rock, and we plunged into the boiling pot.

What actually happened in the next ten seconds remains a mystery to me. The bow plunged down into two mountainous waves in succession, and the brown, silt-laden water swept right over the canopy, completely obliterating my view. I was aware of the craft banking steeply to the left (presumably into the cavern) and of a 'boing' amidships. I had often been in the 'no visibility' situation before and knew two things: first, that hovercraft are made to float like boats and that there was no way we could either tip over or sink. For that reason I had no need to panic. Second, that the air cushion was the thing that was absolutely necessary to fend us off rocks and to keep the craft in its design mode. So, regardless of anything else, I had thrown on full power just before we dived into the appalling waters.

Rob and Anne, in the back section, thought we were going over, and could not push open the canvas top. They got down on their backs and literally kicked it open. John Whatmore's Chinese cameraman had the right-hand door up and open and was filming it all. He survived the first water overflow and was completely drenched, with his camera, by the second. As soon as he could get on his feet in the cabin he started filming again from inside. It was brave of him. Many others inside were quite frightened. Meanwhile the craft emerged from its sheep-dip, and I could see again. She responded very sluggishly to the controls and I realised very quickly that we had lost the cushion pressure altogether, and were operating like a boat, being carried downstream fast. We were over to the left of the river and heading for a rock that was sticking appallingly and threateningly out of the, by now, less turbulent waters. I struggled with everything I knew to pull her away from that rock, but was unable to do so.

Within three metres of it, I called out, 'Okay, guys. We're going to hit a rock in front of us, and there's nothing I can do about it.'

We hit. I had managed to get some starboard bank on and had slewed the back end round to the left to try not to hit head on with the front fuel tank. She crunched on the front left decking, where the front two struts held it to the hull. It was an ominous and heart-rending thump, and I saw the front decking crumble and twist upwards.

I had by that time full left rudder on, to swing the tail end to the right into the open river, and applied full power. Mercifully the crippled lady came round and we gained a modicum of control. We searched quickly for a landing spot. There was only one friendly patch of sand on the Tibetan side and I started to manoeuvre towards it. I glanced in the rear-view mirrors. The one on my side had been shut against the side of the craft by the waters that flooded over and I called for someone behind me to open my window and put it back in position. The starboard side was fine, and there appeared to be nothing wrong that way. But when I saw the port side, I immediately knew the cause of my difficulty: there was a huge gaping hole in the skirt just opposite the cushion fan. It stretched from the top all the way down to the fingers. We had no hover capability at all.

We struggled to our steep but welcome sandbank and I managed to get her nose on it. I closed the engine down to idle, and we got out to assess the damage and lick our wounds. The damage was extensive but not insurmountable. We dragged four broken struts out of the port underside, some severely bent, and others with the attachment points fractured.

It was indeed a rapid too far, and we were in big trouble.

Rob felt that our next task was to bring the craft further up the bank, because the rear end was very much awash and we were sensitive that we had previously holed a couple of buoyancy tanks there.

Meanwhile Sam suggested that a 'get help' party leave immediately. 'Those who make the suggestion get the job', so Sam and Anne set off by foot, on the Tibetan side, to go back up river. Uppermost in their and our minds was the fact that *ICI River Rover* was not far behind, and she had to be warned to keep away from that rapid.

We got on the ropes to pull the crippled lady up. But she would not budge. We were able to move her tail end further in, but she was not far enough along the sandbank and the rear butted against a large overhang of rock.

So we set to to clear the runway. We shovelled sand for some two hours, to give *Neste Enterprise* a reasonable gradient to climb up again, and still she barely shifted. It then became obvious that, without a hover cushion, no one was going to lift or move 4.6 tonnes of aluminium. And of course, we were stuck on the wrong side of the river, unable to get across to the Sichuan side where our base camp was situated.

Mike climbed up the steep slope beside us to see if there was a way out and told us that, were we to get lift-off, there was a gentle rapid down which we could hover, and what looked like a reasonable spot to park on the Sichuan side.

So the primary task was to mend the skirt. David raided the medical box and picked out as many sutures (medical sewing kits) as he could find – four. He started to mend the skirt as he would sew up skin after a surgical operation. It was fascinating. He finished all the gut and then gave it a little test. It pulled apart. It was a shame; all that work for nothing. Then someone suggested plastic shackles. David cut holes in the skirt edge and John threaded the shackles through, then screwed them up. The resultant picture was not aesthetic but it worked.

Meanwhile Rob had repaired the front as much as he could by putting rags and sticks in the hole produced by the dent. One of the front struts had fractured on a weld, so we put a stick inside it to try and give it rigidity, and screwed it in place again.

It was 5.30 p.m. by the time everything was complete; we had been there since about 10.30 a.m. We prayed that the crippled Hover-Queen would fly. She did. She was heavily waterlogged at the back and we sat 'on skirt' for a while to push out as much water weight as possible. It looked fine.

The paramount thing was to transport the majority of the team to the Sichuan side of the river. The plan was to release as many people as possible to return – somehow – to Base 1. They would send out Jim and Neil to effect an expert repair on *Neste*. It was not possible that she could be collected by road and transported on her trailer; there were no available roads anywhere near the river. We were irrevocably committed to getting her as serviceable as possible, and going back up the rapid that had zapped us.

I turned her round in the river and we set off to bumble down the burble, and try to find a runway to land on. I glanced in my mirror. To my horror, the centre of the port decking was bent upwards and arched like a Tibetan hill. I did not know what the cause was, but it was certainly wrong. I did not mention it to anyone – there was no need to panic folk again.

But sure enough, as we went down the burble, the pressure thumps under the cushion caused by waves fractured the plastic bolts we had just put in. The repair to the skirt held together beautifully. But instantly we lost cushion pressure again and sank into the rocks and roughage of the rapid. We were reduced to semi-submerged boat once more. Beyond the burble the water was delectable – peaceful, calm, smooth and welcome. At the end of that, and to the left, was a tiny sandy beach – a runway to which we could head in our new distress. We took the current and sailed down smoothly. I misjudged the turn-in because there was a back-current at our beach. We fended off a couple of offending rocks and plonked on to the beach. We tied the nose to a rock, and the gang got out to haul the rear end on to the haven, where I was able to cut the engine and sink on to the sand. At least we were safe, and on the Sichuan side of our beloved Chiang Jiang. She can bite, this river, and she had bitten us hard.

166

Sam and Anne had set off up river. Their progress was initially baulked by a cliff, across which they could not pass. So they climbed up and, trying to go forward, found themselves going sideways across a scree that had been a recent landslide. There were no handholds all the way down and it was dangerous. They lost their footholds a couple of times and almost fell headlong. It was about 50 m to the rocks beneath. Anne said she felt the presence of God with her that day in a way she had never sensed before. David and Mel stopped working on *Neste Enterprise* to pray for them.

They eventually scrambled over the scree and were able to make their way down to the river's edge, where they hopped from rock to rock, as they had learned to do as kids. They saw a patch of sand past a couple of hill-end promontories; it took them 2.10 hours to get to it. *ICI River Rover* zoomed round the corner. They waved and gesticulated, and Steve, Neil and Dee came alongside in the princess. They explained what had happened to *Neste Enterprise* and said *ICI River Rover* must not go down that rapid.

To put two more people on board would have overloaded *ICI River Rover*, so they gave some petrol to local Tibetans, and threw two jerrycans worth away. Anne got into the craft, and Dee and Sam began their walk, on the Tibetan side, towards Denke. The horsepath took them to a village. They were welcomed by the head man, who led them through the village, with all the villagers following on behind. At the far end they were able to communicate with a deaf Tibetan, explaining that they were on the hovercraft. This man knew where it was on the river, identifying its location by gesticulation. The deaf man and most of the village took them to where *ICI River Rover* was now parked. That journey took them about three-quarters of an hour. Again wind had curtailed the princess's progress and they had to wait a further hour for it to die down. They had dropped Anne on the Sichuan side, and she had walked alone for one and a half hours to get back to Denke.

When the wind died down a bit Steve, Neil, Sam and Dee

167

had two attempts to ride up the rapid in front of them, but failed. They then felt that the only way to get up was to fly lighter, so Steve and Sam, the heaviest two, got out. Neil and Dee, by God's grace, managed to get *ICI River Rover* over that rapid and then, because the wind was swirling and strengthening, stopped again on the Sichuan side. It took Steve and Sam three-quarters of an hour to reach them. Dee guardedly told us months later that she had been terrified to go in the hovercraft up and down rapids. She bit her lip, and was determined never to show it. None of us suspected. She was the wife of the General Secretary of a missionary society, the RBMU (Regions Beyond Missionary Union), and she and her husband Geoff had sacrificed enormously for her to come with us. We were so glad they did: Dee proved to be excellent value throughout the expedition in a multitude of different ways. She was so willing to try her hand at anything.

The next thing that happened was that the rest of the TV crew, who had not been in *Neste Enterprise*, rushed up in their Landcruiser. Anne had walked and jogged to Base 1 and, before she had time to organise anything the TV crew had rushed off. They came without petrol or provisions, and *ICI River Rover* used a jerry-can of their fuel to fill up their empty vehicle. Not long afterwards Anne, Tony and Jim and lots of Chinese guides arrived. The next rapid for *ICI River Rover* was too rough for her to climb. So they attached a rope to the front and all the new arrivals, Steve, Sam and loads of Tibetans, dragged the princess round the bend. She only just made it. From then on it was plain sailing and she sped back to Base 1 at Denke.

Anne, Sam, Tony and Jim continued on in the Landcruiser to find *Neste Enterprise*. More and more they realised that the road was leading them away from the river. After a while they stopped and reassessed. They reckoned they had got as near to the spot where *Neste Enterprise* foundered as Anne could remember. So Anne and Tony got out, stacked up with food and water, and set off to walk to the hovercraft. It was 7.30 p.m. They went through the Tibetan village on the Sichuan side, which we later discovered was called Ren

Ko Xi, and then to the place where Anne had left the craft. It was gone. Her heart failed within her. All this effort, and where was the craft? Tony's practical mind worked out that the craft could only have gone down river. They started walking, and some of the villagers pointed south. Coming to the top of the hill they saw *Neste Enterprise*, with both doors closed, sitting snugly on her sandbank. They ran down. There was no one there! David and I, in command of the craft, had wandered 50 metres down river to pray as the evening sun sprinkled the snow-capped hilltops with gold and pink. We saw the doors opening and ran to see who was raiding the craft. We met on the pony track with much rejoicing. Tony and Anne had walked for two hours. We brewed up and spent a glorious evening together under a crystal clear starlit night, in immense peace, and then slept in the hovercraft under the constellations and satellites winging their silent way across the heavens.

Anne's contribution to that day was enormous. Gladly sacrificial, she had walked some 20 km over seven or so hours, to get help for a crippled hovercraft and bring help to two lonely team members. Meanwhile eight team members had left *Neste Enterprise* at 5.30 p.m. to try and get back to Base 1. Rob tells the story.

*   *   *

Dick and David stood by the craft and the rest of us set off for the local village, about a kilometre away. We didn't know how we were going to get back 25 km but someone suggested hiring Tibetan horses; we went to investigate the possibility. We were duly escorted by all the local Tibetans who had spent the day watching us, and were taken to what appeared to be the village headman's hut. It looked the best house, and was a two-storey wattle and mud walled building with a timber top. Other local houses were single-storey dwellings. This house had a walled courtyard with an area covered in for the animals and a further open area with a telegraph-size pole. This pole had grooves cut into it to make steps to get to the upper level. This required a certain

169

nimbleness to climb (which was evident in the locals, but not in us), and we were kindly shown into the guest room and allowed to wander to the other parts of the house.

For a wattle and mud impacted house with flat roof and wooden support beams and mud floors, it was spotlessly clean, and sheepskins were put out on the floor for us to sit on. In this room was a wooden single four-poster bed with mosquito net and all the blankets neatly folded. The room was large, like all the rest. So was the kitchen. The spaciousness was far greater than any city dwellers' flats made of modern materials, and it had a view which would be the envy of thousands. The kitchen stove was of baked mud construction where wood was used to start the fire and yak dung to maintain it.

The kettle was on when we arrived and within a short time we were offered yak tea, which we found quite acceptable to our western palate. All the kitchen utensils were in place and it looked one of the tidiest kitchens I had seen. The only part that I would wish to improve would be the flue: there wasn't one. But if you haven't the materials on hand to make an efficient one, their design of a hole in the roof and a section over the hole to keep the rain out, was satisfactory. Clothes were hanging in another store room over a long pole and in the corner the yak dung was drying out through a vent in the roof above it.

We were treated like honoured guests, with what seemed to be the whole of the village present, while the eight horses we asked for were being rounded up. Their houses have stood the test of time and are cheap to build using the materials close at hand. The practical construction incorporated flat roofs for drying out farm produce, and verandas to sit out on or sleep on. They felt very much like a home, a place to be proud of.

One by one the horses arrived, adorned with pretty beads, coloured bands and picturesque decorations. The saddle holders were intricately designed as were the stirrups. The tails were plaited and intertwined with a coloured ribbon, and each mane was differently attired. Their horses are a lifeline, and highly valued. We were not asked if we were horse riders, but they didn't take the risk of letting us loose on them, for each horse was led by one of the village lads.

We left at 7.15 p.m. with hearty farewells, many thumbs up and some laughter: perhaps it was the way we were sitting in the saddles, for most of us were novices at horse riding.

Soon each of us was very glad to have a personal guide, because the tracks became steeper and narrower, and it wasn't long before we were skirting round the side of a mountain. The path at times was only wide enough for one horse and horseman to get through, and at the best it was wide enough for two horses to pass each other. To our left was a precipice with the great river Yangtze swirling some 300 m below, and sheer cliffs above, reaching up to the snow-capped Alpine-type mountains on the other side. The view was dramatic and quite frightening.

To add to our nervousness was the fact that the worn part of the path was on the precipitous side, and these horses would invariably hold to the outside edge of the path. This was against all our sense of safety, for one misplaced footstep would surely mean a tumble and certain death. I felt we were all leaning in towards the cliff and working out our plan of escape. Mel was wondering what would happen if the horse had a heart attack, and was hoping he could discern the symptoms before it happened! This thought was occasioned by the sight, in the gloom, of a horse carcass just down from the pathway. Our guides obviously took all this as normal and occasionally looked at us, perhaps to see if we were all right, but on one of these passes I remember they were urging the horses on with a very emphatic word that sounded like 'Chi', and the horse began to speed up, much to our alarm. We responded in English, which of course they couldn't understand, but our faces said everything and all they could do was laugh! I sometimes wondered at their sense of humour, but perhaps we laugh at near disasters without realising it.

As time went by our guides began to trust several of us and allowed us to guide our own horses, which was fine until we came to an even higher precipitous mountain track.

171

We just had to trust the horse implicitly. (The following evening, when others of the team returned along the same route, there were only two guides for six horses and ten of the team. This meant four horses with two people on each which added to the apprehension.) We found out later that the horses were trained to walk to the outside of the path, for when they carried their packs on either side of the saddle, if the load hit the side of the mountain this could unbalance them and cause them to fall over the precipice.

The journey was longer than we realised, and for us non-horse riders it was good to get off and walk when we went down steep slopes. It was our knees that ached, as much as our backsides, and our first few steps to get the circulation going must have made us look like bow-legged cowboys.

The scenery continued to be awe-inspiring, and in each of the seven villages we passed through we aroused great interest, and a ready response to our greetings. The Tibetans laughed predictably at our difficulties. What a privilege to travel in this way, with these hardy and most admirable people.

The sun set, and we continued on in the dark under a clear, starry sky, which just gave sufficient light to see the horse and rider ahead. The horses were sure-footed even in the dark; we wondered how they knew where to place not only their front feet but their back feet in this rocky terrain, without being able to see. Fortunately there were no more precipitous paths.

We arrived at Base 1 four hours later at 11.15 p.m. Our guides, however, indicated that they would be returning home. After our weary journey we felt relieved, tired and saddle-sore, yet these lads seemed to think nothing of going back in the dark, even after walking with us all evening. One could only admire their toughness. No wonder they have survived in this rough terrain without all our mod cons. They are a great people and we had the privilege of being with them for a brief time.

*   *   *

172

Back on the northern shore of the beautiful Chiang Jiang, Anne, Tony and I rested well overnight in the hovercraft, followed by a lazy morning. The sun did not hit the craft until 10.10, and the temperature rose with it from −6°C to 20°C. The first person to arrive was John who had been driven by his TV crew in their Landcruiser. It was thrilling to see him. Gradually most of the rest of the team came down the rocky donkey track and, last of all, Jim and Neil and Mike. They had taken a different route from the rest, but it was their input for which we had been waiting. Everyone had walked between two and four hours, carrying heavy equipment with which to mend *Neste Enterprise*.

Jim set to with his characteristic thoroughness to tidy up the front. He sawed off the end of the hinge that had buckled, and bolted some angled aluminium over the gap and over the buckle in the fibre glass.

Neil attacked the middle where the decking had lifted. The centre strut had come adrift from the side body; in fact the fibre glass, where the strut was bolted on to it, was completely gone. Then, to our disappointment, the rechargeable drill packed up. We had drained the battery completely, drilling mainly through steel angle. We could not complete the job. But Neil had a way of 'bodging' it. He squeezed some wire rope through the gap between the two deckings and put a large bolt in to hold it there. We also had to 'bodge' the strut in the front that had sheered, without having the facility of bolting it together.

When all was ready we packed up the craft, untied the ropes, and lifted off into the calm water. The rest of the team had left to get back before dusk, leaving Rob, Jim, Neil and I on the craft. I glanced again in my rear-view mirror as soon as we reached the water. The port deck was arched once more like that ancient Tibetan mountain. I knew she would not take a rapid of any description. I called Jim and Neil to look at it and, regretfully, decided to take her back again to our little beach.

'We can't do anything with it,' Jim said as we clambered out. 'That's it.'

'But I'm not sure why it bends up like that: the other side

173

didn't when we lost a strut,' I said, puzzled. 'Besides, we haven't lost another strut that side.'

'I'm afraid we have,' Neil came in. 'While I was underneath I noticed that the next one forward of the join was also detached from the decking. And it bends upwards because the fibre glass is cracked underneath along most of the front deck.'

I went underneath to look. At last it became clear. The decking, normally rigid, is easily able to maintain its shape with one strut gone. But, when it is cracked, and with a missing strut, the only strength it has is from nylon bolts holding the top of the skirt. They are by no means strong enough for that, and we had two struts gone.

'There's nothing more we can do,' Jim said again. 'We've got to give it a go and try to get home.' I knew he wanted to get back. Both he and Neil were desperately tired. But I had to be firm.

'We will have to wait until tomorrow,' I said. 'The others will be back with the recharged drill, and we can fix the strut to the deck then. It's plain suicide tackling that rapid with a broken and unsafe craft.'

All four of us were disappointed at this. Jim and Neil went straight to bed; it was 7.30 p.m. Rob and I stayed up a bit later, and we only managed to sleep fitfully in *Neste Enterprise* that night.

At noon the following day Jeremy and Tony came in with two drills, the second of which we could work from the craft's 12 volt battery. The strut was fixed and we hovered at full power on a tether to determine whether the deck was secure. It was. Well done, our two intrepid engineers!

Rob's diary records how we got home.

* * *

The time came for the final trial of the craft to see if the repairs were sufficient to withstand the rigours that lay ahead in order to get back to the base camp. The alternative was miles of unknown rapids downstream in the hope of finding a spot where the craft could be recovered by road, and one felt that that option must be used only as a last resort, because we knew of no road by the river until Dege.

We set off, with Dick knowing full well what lay ahead, for he had had the front-line view on the way down. Besides, he was determined that no rapid would defeat him.

The first rapid looked quite long and normal, and was the one we had to go up before tackling the big one. To our amazement the craft would not make it, which didn't help our confidence. We had to fall back down into the calm water below. There was a side flow with an even gradient, but it was very narrow and had several rocks sticking out. Dick drove the craft up it carefully; the craft rode over the small rocks and skilfully missed the big ones. That was good, and one could sense the audience which had gathered on the cliff top from the local village were pleased to see the craft succeed, but were positioning themselves for the spectacle of the next dangerous one. This scene no doubt would be the talk and story of the river for years to come.

As we approached the rapid it was narrower than I realised; it was rough. There were dangerous rocks and it was fast flowing and had deep troughs. In other words, it looked impossible.

To the left was the turbulence – the hidden rocks, which became visible with the variable flow; to the right there was a smoother narrow patch with a tall rock bordering our passage, but ahead of that path was a broiler, a rock with a smooth flow over it where the water beneath it becomes a permanent wave. Initially Dick went for the smoother path and managed to get the craft bow over the flow of the rock, but then we could get no further. *Neste Enterprise* stabilised on the gradient. We would edge ahead and then drop back, and it would seem that the air cushion was being dissipated in the huge trough underneath us; so there would be a sinkage of the craft giving more resistance fore and aft, thus inhibiting movement.

Dick eased back so as to go astern and have another run at this obstacle, having to keep critical control with a rock to the right and fast, turbulent flow to the left. He decided

175

to run up slightly more to the left, that is, closer to the turbulence but further away from the broiler. This didn't succeed after two attempts, and we were there with six of us in the craft anxiously praying and urging the craft through for at least ten minutes.

Dick's concentration was intense and his control was marvellous, but in spite of that we were not getting through. Jim suggested that we should lighten the load so that there would be only two in the craft, to see if that would make sufficient difference. Dick agreed and had to turn, taking the bow into the mountainous flow to swing through 180° quickly. Once in the flow at least six waves came over the bow and over the windscreen, knocking the wing mirror into the side, but air cushion and direction were kept and Dick was able to come to a smooth section and drop off four of the crew. Only I remained with Dick, and once again we set off, I praying audibly for success and Dick agreeing out loud.

We went for the same passage as before, and on the first attempt rode over this bad patch almost with the stern hanging over the edge but still inching forward. Dick was verbally urging the craft along, and slowly, very reluctantly, *Neste Enterprise* nosed forward. However, a few metres ahead was another small rise which we had to tackle. Did the craft have sufficient momentum to surmount it? We struggled and prayed, and we just edged over. Ahead of that was a rock with smooth water flowing over it, bordered with other, steeper rocks, making it very narrow. To the left the turbulence remained. To get over the rock flow ahead required a run to get us over hump, but there was no room for that and effectively I felt trapped.

Dick had surveyed the rapid earlier at a high vantage point and quickly spotted a passage to the right which was smooth, with less flow, but very narrow. To me it looked like a dead end because at our level in the craft we could not see the exit because of the boulders and rocks. At least it would be a respite place where we could regather our thoughts and nerve, and give Dick a rest from what was very concentrated control. If a movie could have been taken of his face during this period it would have provided quite a picture!

This route was indeed the way of escape, for as we rounded it on hover at slow speed the exit became visible. In spite of going very slowly the sideways movement of the turn caused the craft to nudge a rock on our starboard side, and I immediately thought, 'More damage'. Fortunately it was just a nudge and we squirmed and squeezed out, the rocky edges missing the craft by inches either side. At this moment we were at right angles to the main flow, with the turbulence and hazards with which we were all too familiar very close to the left. To the right was the smooth flow. Dick took her out, turned, and left behind the impossible rapid – the rapid which had tested both craft and driver to their limits, which had nearly killed our expedition altogether, and tested the practicality of our faith to the extreme. There was no doubt that, but for God's grace and enabling, we would never have got through.

*   *   *

We picked up the rest of the crew, who had walked round.

But the problems had not ended. Further on towards home the rear fuel transfer pump failed, which meant that we could not transfer fuel backwards. This was the dangerous one, because the engine fed from the rear tank. There were another two rapids, up which Neil had been unable to take *ICI River Rover*, and which he briefed us about as we continued our journey. It was not wise to try and tackle any of those seemingly difficult ones with the possibility of engine failure. The only solution was to park *Neste Enterprise* nose up on a sandbank, let the rear end sit in the water, and let gravity do the job of transferring fuel from nose to tail. This we did twice.

Rob was driving, and he had to tackle the rapids with only two people on board because of the difficulty in getting the craft trimmed. That day there wasn't the wind that *ICI River Rover* had when she struggled to get up. We passed, with ease, the rapids that had caused so much trouble to the princess and motored serenely back to Base 1, greeted with great joy and relief by the rest of the team, who had asked God for our return that day.

ICI River Rover was a temperamental thoroughbred. On the very day that *Neste Enterprise* returned, she developed clutch slip. We did not know why, as the clutch had only done the equivalent of five days' town driving. The engineers took her off the water and ran her up. There seemed nothing wrong. So Neil, Jim, Fiona and Anne took her out on to the water the following morning. Sure enough, the clutch slipped again, giving 5000 rpm for the same fan speed. The previous maximum had been 4200 rpm. That was not all. Jim noticed a fountain of spray coming from the engine. A leak had developed in one of the water coolant hoses, and the coolant was pumping dry by the minute. They were 7 km away, and out of radio contact. All they could do was fill up the radiator, drive for ten minutes, plonk on a beach, wait for half an hour to cool down, refill, and start the exercise all over again. When they reached a reasonable place, Anne got out to walk back and let the rest of us know that they would make it home. She was growing used to volunteering for such activities!

But the rest of us were getting anxious. The evening was drawing in, they had been away four hours or more, and there had been no sign of *ICI River Rover*. Mike decided that we would take *Neste Enterprise* out to look for her. No sooner was she on the water than we spotted Anne walking back. We picked her up and she explained that *ICI River Rover* was coming down the left bank of the river. So we went up that side (there was a huge trifurcation of the river just above base camp), and failed to see her. She had come down the other side! We received a radio call to say that the crippled craft had arrived at base, so *Neste Enterprise* returned home.

The coolant leak was easy to fix. But the clutch required the engine to come out and the fan transmission system to be disconnected. It could take four days. And we did not have four days left at Denke.

178

We had shaken down on a most challenging stretch of the river. We had tested the hovercraft to the limits.

Despite warnings from the Chinese that the Tibetans would be hostile, we could find nothing but a friendly welcome from all of them, coupled with an intense curiosity. During our hectic fortnight there, they had become our friends. When *Neste Enterprise* was crippled down river, the team remaining at base camp paid a visit to the local primary school. It was Rob's idea, although he was unable to be there. It was a delightful occasion: we taught the children some Christian choruses, and the children did some ethnic dancing for us. We left these cheerful, smiling people with heavy hearts.

Late on the last evening we expressed our gratitude by taking two large boxes of gift blankets for the poor of our local hill-top village, Wen Tuo. We were benevolently taken there by Mr Plod, who, *officially*, had no knowledge we were doing it!

So ended our time at Base Camp 1. It had been filled with difficulty, near disaster and renewed challenge. It had also left us a legacy of further engineering work in an ever-shrivelling time capsule.

There were more troubles ahead. But the team's resilience had been sharpened. We were determined that nothing would deter us from seeking our goal, and equally that nothing would destroy our integrity, buoyancy or our claim to victory. We had come to China to achieve – to do something that no one else in the world had ever done, and we had set our wills to surmount, with God's grace, every hindrance and obstacle that stood in the way of that achievement.

7

Trouble Every Day

Beware that you do not lose the substance by grasping at the shadow. (Aesop)

Farewell to our Denke Tibetan friends was painful.

We were left with a minimal amount of time. This was how the future weekly plan looked to us as we prepared to depart from Base 1:

Friday, 18 May	*ICI River Rover* with four days engineering required.
Sunday, 20 May	Leave for Qumerlai by road; allow up to a week, but plan (and hope) for three days.
Sunday, 27 May	Settle in at Qumerlai, Base Camp 2 – two days operations establishing fuel dumps.
Sunday, 3 June	Operations establishing fuel dumps and trying for Tuotuoheyan, Base Camp 3.
Sunday, 11 June	Trying for the source and return.
Wednesday, 13 June	Last day for seven team members to leave river to reach UK in time for their employers' deadlines.

That left two and a half weeks only to establish Bases 2 and 3, and sub-camps A and B, and get to the source. Which source – Geladandong or Dam Qu? We hoped for both. But the Dam Qu was looking ominously difficult.

180

Mike felt it imperative that we establish two sub-camps along the 373 km of river to Tuotuoheyan. That would entail, ideally, a sub-camp every 117 km. We looked at the map. Nothing is perfect in this world, and those distances would land us in what looked like swamps. So we picked two places on the map that looked more suitable and stuck a pin in each. We needed at least two people per camp, plus tents and logistic support, and various drums of fuel for hovercraft supply. We estimated that it would take at least three days to set up the two sub-camps (the map at Appendix A shows where they were eventually established and the distances involved). It was vital that we sent a lorry with fuel to Tuotuoheyan by road, otherwise the whole logistic support would have to be accomplished by *Neste Enterprise*, and would take somewhere near ten days. That in itself was half the time available. But it would take a fuel lorry between six and ten days to get the fuel by road to Tuotuoheyan and set up Base 3. Mike was unhappy to release a truck nearly 2000 km by road from Base 2 until we had all arrived there, because plans might change. But every day's delay was crucial to the success of the project. It was a planning dilemma, a logistic nightmare, and was very much dependent on spare days available. So the sooner we left Base 1 and got to Base 2, the better.

Andrew had come back to say that the road to Xuxue was fine, but there had been some rock falls in the first 100 km to the T-junction. The drivers instantly descended into a quagmire of negatives. One driver flatly refused in any circumstance to move, even though his boss told him to go. Mike spent two dismal hours on Sunday evening trying without success to persuade him.

We packed up camp anyway, except our personal tents, the mess tent and the latrine – in case we were able to leave quickly.

Gwyn and Andrew went into the town the following morning. The drivers should have been with us at eight; they were still in bed at 8.30 when Gwyn found them. I do not know what our two said to the Chinese drivers, but at 10.30 Gwyn came in to say that we were off. It was a triumph of grace over fear, and we packed up camp elated. Not that we really wanted to leave Denke and the little village of Wen Tuo on the hill above us. Even in that brief fortnight we had grown accustomed to the place, and grown to love the people.

Mike had rearranged the convoy so that the hovercraft went on their own, and the slower bus and some stores lorries followed behind. That day we were so keen to leave that the hovercraft team left straight away. The remainder of the convoy packed and left two hours later. The first day's journey was the longest – 158 km. We were unaware that it would be so far and the fact that we left late aggravated the situation.

The drivers were about 30 per cent justified in their concern about the road. There had been some heavy rock-falls on the mountainside in the 100 km from Denke to the main junction. We had to move a number of boulders off the road, but the *Neste Enterprise* trailer negotiated them all without difficulty. On the way in we had stopped at the half-broken bridges, but now we hardly slowed for them – once bitten, twice bold.

A Tibetan family invited us into their tent for lunch. It was an instructive experience. This family with three children had only just arrived on site, and they shared the pasture area with four other families. These people were rich. They owned a winter home in a village, and here they were grazing 600 head of yak (valued at about 700 yuan a head) and twelve horses (valued at 1000 yuan a head). It seemed that the Chinese authorities had given up trying to control their capitalist lusts. Looking at the number of yaks on the hills led us to believe that all four of the families were equally provisioned with livestock. The tent was divided into three sections, the central one being the kitchen/living area. The yak-dung fire was made of mud brick, and the smoke went through a hole in the top, which could be opened to all four points of the compass to provide the best ventilation.

The rest of the journey was normal; there were no outstanding geographical features, and we drove mostly down

182

valleys with round-topped hills on either side, clambering up to only one pass at 4300 m (14,104 ft).

The wildlife throughout our journeys in China had been sparse. We saw very few birds in the Han section of Sichuan, and no flocks whatever. It seemed that in the 1960s, at the time of harvest failure, Mao Zedong had ordered everybody to stop work at 5 p.m. every day, and to chase the birds away, particularly the seed-eaters. They were kept flying until exhausted, when the people simply picked them up and killed them. Apart from the odd crow or bird of prey, there are still few wild birds in cultivated China.

In Tibet it was different. I did see some flocks of birds (four in all) and these were seed-eaters – buntings or finches. Other birds were eagles, vultures, migrant geese (in lay), a cormorant, a heron, many hoopoes, pied and yellow wagtails, a couple of sandpipers, snow buntings, some forms of shrike, sparrows, crows, ravens, a bustard and numerous buzzards. But the altitude precluded large quantities of any birds, and many of the smaller ones were scratching the snow for food. Mid-May was spring, so we saw many pairs of birds and many nesting. The swallows, swifts and martins had migrated from the west or south by then.

The vultures could spot a death from miles, and those we saw were wheeling above a carcass or sitting scoffing some tasty corpse. The Tibetans sometimes present their human dead to the birds, and we could never tell whether the vulture food was biped or quadruped.

We had wondered earlier what there could be for eagles to eat, but we soon saw. On the road from Denke we spotted quite a number of animals that looked like otters with longer legs. Vet Fiona identified them as marmots. They lived in holes on the side of the hills and foraged for food. Further up the road we were astonished to see numerous rodents scurrying around, popping their heads in and out of holes in the ground. In places these herbivores could be seen running down well-worn tracks. The fields seemed to be alive with them. They looked like guinea-pigs except that their ears were longer and they were tailless. Also they were no bigger than hamsters. Fiona identified them as conies, sometimes known as hyrax or rock-rabbit.

A few hares were seen and the occasional herd of rare white-lipped deer, as small as roe deer (British roe deer, I was told, originally came from China). There was no other wildlife that we saw, either in Tibetan Sichuan, Qinghai or China. Most of the hills were covered with the woolly yak, what we thought was a yak–cow derivative, which I called 'yakkle', but Fiona assured me they were real domesticated yaks. (I thought yaks were bigger and the wild yak is, apparently). They ran with their tails in the air and with a lot more energy than a cow. There were many flocks of sheep and goats, supervised by unschooled and sometimes dormant children.

One of the things we noticed was that the Tibetan populated areas were 'doggy'. Every village and town had its midnight howlers who set one another off in discordant cacophonies, from bass wolfhound to yelping puppy. I think the Tibetans breed dogs to activate only at night, and especially to disturb the sleep of vagrant foreigners. The Chinese breed dogs to eat. (Why there are so few dogs in the rest of China is possibly because the populace is not permitted to keep them in urban accommodation.)

The journey seemed interminable. Every small habitation of houses evoked the question, 'Xuxue?'

'Meiyou' (No), would come the reply again and again. As evening drew on, the snow level came down to road level – either that or the road went up. The wide plain with lowish hills accompanying the telegraph poles and highway in unison accrued an increasing whiteness as the sun sank lower towards the horizon. The precipitation, which had earlier fallen as snow on the hilltops, fell first as drizzle, then as rain, then as sleet, and finally as snow again. There were light flurries in the wind as we eventually approached Xuxue. The government accommodation there looked attractive from the outside. It was decorated in Tibetan style, with gaily-coloured window surrounds and an ornate wooden doorway. And the accommodation was indeed sound. The Chinese provide two very heavy duvets on, in or under which to sleep, a hard pillow, a face towel, and, if one is privileged, a washing bowl per person. Generally the latter had to be shared.

Chinese toilets consist of a rectangular hole over which one squats. I confess that this aspect of expedition life was the hardship I was least able to handle. And the toilets stank. I guess the most hygienic were outside, where the sun and rain caused a natural redistribution of both stench and proceeds (it is hard to think of a nice word for effluent). The trouble with an open air loo is that it is cold, windy, often raining or snowing, and communal. The worst open-air one we found was at Xiwu, the next town down the road, and it consisted of five bendy pole-planks with rounded tops, set too wide apart over a 1 ft drop. Of course in the snow or rain it was exceedingly slippery, and a number of us nearly fell in. That one was not only communal but unisex. By the river itself loos were simply a hole in the sand.

We had a palaver finding a suitable lock-up for *Neste Enterprise*, and had to lift five or so low flying electric wires to turn her round in the streets. The driver never really mastered the art of reversing the trailer. We eventually deposited her in the police compound, where all the other vehicles in the convoy huddled round her for the night. The police compound also sported a captive vulture, which they were very sensitive about our photographing. They even brandished a rifle at John when he flourished his camera.

Xuxue was quite a metropolis. Someone said there was coal in the area. Many of the buildings were constructed of brick or block, and there were rows of terraced houses for the workers. It was the first place we had seen for some time that actually had a pavement by the side of the road.

That night it snowed; good, solid, crusty snow. It lay 2-4 inches thick as we walked to breakfast next morning, and crunched satisfyingly under our feet. Typically British, we started to throw snowballs, while the hills disappeared and merged into the white of the snow and the grey of the sky. The Chinese thought we were childish, the Tibetans that we were stupid, but we laughed, unembarrassed at being ourselves.

185

If we had trouble getting the drivers to get on the road at the prospect of hypothetical landslides, what price their travelling on real snow? None whatever. They threw a wobbly, en masse. Yet another opportunity for prayer. Mr Zhou decided we would have an early lunch and then look at the road prospects. During the morning the snow stopped, the sky semi-cleared and a watery sun started a melting process – just what we had prayed for.

Meanwhile Steve, examining *Neste Enterprise*, discovered one of the brake connection rods on the trailer was free. He examined it. There were at least three interlocking devices that would preclude it coming free on its own. It had definitely been undone by human activity. The brake problem did not in any way deter us. But the cause was disturbing. Earlier the previous day, Sunday, we had prayed for safety on the road. The Chinese had overheard it, and one driver's reaction was that he would pray for an accident on the road. Maybe the dislocation of the brake had something to do with it? But our God is Lord of all things and nothing can deter his hand. We were all safe. And the person who had disconnected the brake had grossly underestimated our tenacity and determination.

The snow melted off the streets in beautiful clouds of steam, covering everything and everybody with wisps of ethereal mist. As we had prayed, the drivers acquiesced and we set off up the road after lunch. It was only a short distance to our next stop, Xiwu, which stood at the junction of the main Xining to Lhasa road. It was only about 80 km away.

The journey was far from easy. The snow had blanketed both the road and the local countryside with white, and the slush was barely melting. Only a few vehicles had passed that way before us, causing us to be the ice-breakers for others behind. Snow covered the hills, the plain in between, and merged with the light grey sky. It was very bright and painful to the eyes.

Some three hours out we ground up a pass, which registered on our altimeters at 4400 m (14,432 ft). The road was getting rougher and rougher, and we had to slow down considerably to enable the lorries to negotiate the holes safely. Tang, dynamic driver of one of the stores trucks, decided to pick a route round the edge of a huge hole. His rear wheels slipped down the incline at the side of the road, and his truck ended up banked at 30° and stuck. We all got out to look. Tang's relationship with the team was a delightfully progressive one. Duncan records the sort of incident that endeared him to us all:

> After going over a severe bump Tang stopped, pulled off the radiator cap (which produced a geyser-like effect) and proceeded to empty the tobacco from three cigarettes into the radiator and then refill it with water from a nearby puddle. The holes were plugged and we carried on. After watching him negotiate hairpin bends while trying to light a cigarette, I calculated that it was probably less of a health risk to light his cigarette for him than to have us tumble off a cliff with a truck half-loaded with petrol, and a half-lit fag! From then on we were firm friends. He's a bit of a rogue (he likes the disgusting rice wine), but his heart is in the right place. Of all the drivers, he's the only one I really respect, and he's always prepared to work hard and give things a go. The other drivers are more concerned to try their hardest to make life as easy as they can for themselves.

The expert at getting Tang's lorry out was Anne. Her Territorial Army experience of manoeuvring vehicles enabled her to brief everyone on exactly what to do. But none of the Chinese drivers wanted to listen, and Lili, doing the translating, had a lot of difficulty persuading them what to do. She failed. They made a pathetic attempt at obeying, using another tow lorry, but did not really try. By that time there were some four or five of our team making suggestions, all the Chinese drivers adding their contributions, much shouting, and nothing actually being achieved. We gave it another try. But Tang's lorry only went deeper into the mud, and its tilt angle became more alarming.

We decided that the best and safest policy would be to unload all the heavy stuff from the vehicle before trying

187

again, since it was top-heavy. So we set to. It was snowing. It was muddy. It was cold at 4400 m. There was only the expedition team working, with Tang the one Chinese to help. But we got it all off within the hour.

We then unhooked Big Mac, the tow lorry, from the *Neste Enterprise* trailer, and drove her round to tow. She was too light and too powerful, and her wheels merely skidded. So they put the first stores lorry that had tried to pull Tang out in front of Big Mac, and together the pair of them pulled Tang's beleaguered truck out of its predicament.

Then we repacked it. That took a further hour of jovial Britons enjoying hardship. Of greatest hilarity was the sight of Mike sneaking off carrying a box of compo rations from the stores lorry. Everybody stopped and laughed and pointed at him and shouted, 'We'll tell Kevin' or 'We'll tell Tony'. The saga behind that was that both Kevin and Tony, our provisions men, had tried to get us to eat Chinese food while on the road. Mike and a few others really do not enjoy Chinese food and prefer army composite rations.

This team that God had picked was quite unusual. Sam was remarking that he had sat in on interviews at ICI where staff had worked for two years to put together a special team for a particular purpose. And there were personality differences and difficulties even after such careful planning. But our team 'just happened'. Some of the members had been associated for a long time, and some came in at the last minute. Many applied, not all could come, but in a remarkable way the spread of talents was amazing. Everyone had something essential to contribute. Only one was missing: Marq Gorton had an ulcer, and was unable to join us. He was the fluent Tibetan speaker.

It was also significant how well the team blended together. There was a buoyant sense of expectation that was immensely encouraging. There was sympathy for folk in trouble, and a great desire to support others who were low or sick. There was empathy across the team for all in their positions of excellence. Above all, there was very little criticism of any other team member. I could not help but compare this group with the team on the last hovercraft expedition to Peru in 1982, where there had been a number of critics. People felt less free to say they were tired, that they needed a break, or that they could not crack a job. There, some people were martyrs, grimly working on with tight lips until they dropped. There was little freedom to keep oneself physically on top, with breaks if he were tired and needed sleep, without feeling that someone else disapproved. But this team was so utterly different. People were gracious, kind, helpful and generous. We could feel free to be entirely ourselves, to express how we felt, even to be childish or stupid if the mood took us. One of the things that was lacking was the macho spirit of 'we're on expedition, so we've all got to appear to be tough guys'. People were just themselves, and it made this expedition infinitely enjoyable and thoroughly good fun. What was more, we got the job done. Beyond doubt all of us would put the reason down to our Christianity, which had already broken down our selfishness and defensiveness. We were encouraged by having a time of Bible reading and prayer together every morning, and a time of prayer every evening. Most would say how much other people's Christian walk had changed their own, and how much more they had come to appreciate constant prayer. The strengthening that we gave each other on this unique expedition was beyond compare and defied description.

Mike too was different. He had turned fifty-five during our four months in China. His increased age had slowed him down, and he was not so driving as he had been in Peru. There were times in Peru when he would listen to no arguments; his mind was made up. But in China he welcomed as much input as he could get. His decisions were still positive and wise and everyone acknowledged his leadership. But it was noticeable that he spent a lot of each day alone with God. I observed that his prayer life had increased considerably and his spirituality was far more evident than it had been in Peru. His dynamic leadership was delightfully low-profile, and he encouraged us all, and gave us opportunity.

189

The weather backed off fractionally as we prayed our way over the pass. The snow had fallen on both sides of the mountain, but the sun was more effective on the further side. Nevertheless the road could never be described as good. We crawled slowly down and round the hairpins, and eventually emerged on a bridge at the bottom of a valley in heavy drizzle. This was Xiwu, a one-street town with a Buddhist temple and seminary on the main road.

We waited patiently by the bridge for a while in the rain, watched intently by Tibetans outside getting wet. Shy, giggling girls would drop their eyes, run away and come back to look again. Men in decorated headgear would stare and stare and eventually melt with a grin, sometimes encouraged by a 'Ni hao' (Hello). Laughing boys would raise their eyebrows up and down cheekily and unsuccessfully try to wink back. They could have stayed there all day. So might we, waiting for Mr Xie to arrange accommodation and food for us. Our convoy was quite a shock for any system with forty-four people pouncing on them as the sun was setting. The first to get accommodated were the vehicles, of course. The Chinese drivers and guides went into some couth accommodation on the other side of the road. It was just as well that the rest of us were prepared to rough it, and were determined to enjoy it.

Our accommodation problem revealed another difficulty. There was no room for us initially because many other lorry drivers were sleeping there. Why? Because the road to Qumerlai was closed. Andrew had warned us: they were doing road works for the first 70 km. The road was now even less navigable because the rain and snow of the previous two days had wiped out what was left of serviceable surface.

We were eventually given dormitory accommodation with a yak-dung stove in the centre, and were distributed indiscriminately around the compound. The rooms reminded me very much of western attempts at illustrating the stable in which Jesus was said to have been born. Mud walls, rickety poles and wooden beams held up a cardboard ceiling, which leaked on Rob throughout the night. The staff – one middle-aged Tibetan lady – provided the thick

190

Tibetan duvets that we had grown used to, which were very warm. The straw-filled pillows were comfortable, provided they were not stuffed too full. The yak-dung stove presented us with a challenge. Mike felt that he had already gained his boy scout 'yak-dung fire' badge at Xuxue. We discovered that the larger lumps burned best, and that the stoves had to be refuelled at least every five minutes or the fire would go out. The room service lady came in just after we had selected our beds, poured some liquid into the top of the stove, lit a piece of dung, and in a few minutes the fire was roaring away with a cherry-red chimney. (For readers who are fascinated, the dried yak-dung does not smell. I slept with my head by the pile all night.) Without the liquid, which was some kind of oil, it was exceedingly difficult to light. We brewed up soup and Mike cooked a stew. We really enjoyed the poverty of the place – the earth floor, the simple bedding, the rudimentary fire. More than all we appreciated each other's company and humour.

What we did have a lot of difficulty appreciating was the road. The arterial highway from the capital of Qinghai Province to the capital of Tibet was, as we had discovered, being repaired. We had had, in our travels so far, plenty of negatives from the drivers, nearly all on phantom, hypothetical problems. Now, when there was a real problem, we got it worse. They dug their heels in. No way were they going to travel on that road, not for a fortnight anyway.

Typically, and rightly, Mike was not satisfied with reports. He wanted to see for himself. The following day he went in a Landcruiser to assess the difficulty. He came back: it really was as bad as everybody had said. The chances of the *Neste Enterprise* trailer getting through even the first 10 km that he had seen was, in his view, no more than 20 per cent. The chances of heavy damage, even total loss, were extremely high. He returned very quiet.

What alternative was there? We could not put the hovercraft into the Yangtze there although it was only 12 km away: we did not have the available fuel and there was a tricky rapid just north of where we were. And, if the hovercraft got through to Qumerlai, what of the rest of

191

us, and the stores? How long would we have to wait for the road to be open?

'Three weeks,' said the drivers.

'Surely there must be another alternative?' Mike asked.

The drivers shrugged their shoulders. They were not very interested.

'Are there no other roads?' Mike persisted.

'There's a track on the western side of the river,' said Mr Zhou. 'But we don't know what it's like. You'd have to go to Yushu to find out.'

Yushu was 50 km away to the west, in the wrong direction. But it did contain a spark of hope. The main road was, in Mike's opinion, far too risky.

'All right,' he said, 'we will go to Yushu tomorrow, contact the police and officials there, and investigate the road to the west.'

Mr Xie and Mr Zhou agreed to that, and we settled down for the night. At least it was better to do something than to sit in Xiwu, not a particularly salubrious village, for a fortnight. Besides, we didn't have a fortnight to spare; we didn't even have days.

But we did have fun. It happened that the day Mike went out investigating road works was the annual village Buddhist festival. We were woken regularly in the middle of the night by large explosions, the banging of a gong, and the drone of a deep bass horn played on one note.

We investigated. Up the hill was the Buddhist temple, and people were winding their way to it on different pathways like ants returning to their nest. We joined the ants, and tucked ourselves covertly among the Tibetan crowd, who were all dressed in their festival best. We were, however, spotted. A man with enormous muscles and a shaved head, looking like a combination of Yul Brynner and the Incredible Hulk, suddenly stopped punishing the gong, ran down the steps, strode across the display area, and pulled the team out. We felt that this could be the Buddhist revenge for infiltrating infidel Christians. But no. He grabbed an arm, indicated that all other arms should follow, and marched up the steep stone stairway to seat us in the place of honour in front of the temple entrance. He then strode back to thump his gong, which was taller than he was. Soon goodies appeared in front of us: sweets of various kinds and diverse other delicacies.

We had arrived late on day 2, the last but one day, of the festival. Most of the dancers were male. The costumes were brilliant, with carefully interwoven greens, reds, golds, silvers and bronzes. They were multi-layered, and the participants must have been very hot. The head-dresses were as colourful and elaborate as the costumes. We were unsure what the dramas represented, but one was a fairly hideous representation of hell, with grotesque masks, embroidered skulls, knives and bowls. It was bright and vivid, and the dance steps looked complex but monotonous. There were two enormous collapsible horns, which droned continuously on two notes. The rhythm was provided by Yul Brynner on the gong, and his similarly enormous bald-headed brother on the cymbals. It was not musically inspiring.

Other dances were entertaining: two dancers wore stag heads and it looked like a mating dance, a hunting scene or a deer fight. Another looked like a royal procession. Communication in Tibetan was too difficult to ascertain the full significance of any of them. We were able to photograph these dances, on still and video, as much as we chose.

On the following day we clambered into our convoy and went casually to Yushu. It was casual because the road works extended all the way there. It was good to cross the bridge over the Yangtze, some 70 km north of Denke. By the bridge was a memorial to Yao Maoshu, the young Chinese rafter who died on a rapid in 1985 near there, when his raft, *Descendant of the Dragon* broke up. There was also a monument to the 1986 Chinese expedition, and Mr Xie Jinkang's name was there as a participant. We were not allowed to photograph the bridge, as usual. It must have been made of gold, although it looked remarkably like concrete. John took out his polaroid camera and took a deliberate shot of the bridge, which he gave with a flourish to Mr Plod, who, after a brief furrowed brow, smiled widely.

Yushu was the capital town of one of the six autonomous

193

regions in Qinghai. The smallest of these six regions is larger in area than the United Kingdom. Yushu was certainly a sophisticated, though smallish, town. It was far more Chinese than Tibetan, with a government supermarket, cinema, post office and shops like those we saw in Chengdu. Many of the mud-walled buildings were being or had been pulled down, allowing for rebuilding in brick and prefabricated concrete. We stopped outside the town centre, and instantly attracted a huge crowd of locals, who simply stood and stared at us, refusing to move even for vehicles. Soon, however, we drove across the town square, up a rickety hill, through a tight gate and into an enclosed courtyard. That was the bus and lorry bed. Our beds were back across the same rickety road, down some enormous steps and up to the fourth floor of a supermarket store. Beyond doubt everyone was puffed by the time they reached their bedrooms, a fact that brought great encouragement to geriatrics like me. Perhaps it was the altitude, at 3658 m (12,000 ft). We bedded down in adjoining dormitories of four. The recently painted white distemper on the walls gave a fresh, appealing initial impression, and left a white, unappealing impression on our jackets after we leaned against them. The duvet covers, of pastel green, and pillow cases of pastel pink matched the curtains of pastel blue, and were being arranged as we struggled in with our back-packs. We threw the duvets on the beds and lay down exhausted. Some three minutes later a young man appeared with an aerosol and sprayed perfume on our beds and, for those who had removed their boots, on their socks. A very nice touch! And the first time we had actively encountered perfume in China. I idly wondered if our feet smelt: one grows impervious to feet after three weeks.

The washrooms were at the end of the corridor, the gents down a floor. Water was turned off between 9 p.m. and 8 a.m., handwashing thereafter being from a tap from a huge barrel, the surplus of which gradually accrued on the floor overnight. I accidentally wandered, dopily, into the ladies' loo one night at 3 a.m. and found the floor awash 6 inches. No loo could be flushed until 8 a.m. At least they had flushing loos there, but they were the standard squatting

194

type. Basins came at one per room of four. Hot water was available on the third floor, as was, of all things, a washing machine. Duncan and Co. captured and commandeered this device; but Duncan left much of his washing behind for our use when he left early for Tuotuoheyan.

They invited us into the reception room and plied us with Chinese tea while we decided what we could do. We had the local authorities in, and they said that there was a road up to Z'do but from Z'do there was no road down to the river. The bridge that was shown on Chinese maps no longer existed. Mike was not satisfied. He wanted to go and see. He figured that if there was a road to the river from Z'do, and the road to Z'do was reasonable, we could take *Neste Enterprise* there, put her down off the trailer, and use her as a bus to transport the engineering equipment either across the river or up to Qumerlai. Qumerlai was only 78 km up river. The remainder of the convoy would go the awful route. Z'do was 190 km away from Yushu. Mike wanted us to set off straight away, so we would not lose half a day. But it was impossible to move the Chinese that fast: they said 9 a.m. next day and, of course, a night at Z'do, making it a two-day round trip. These were precious days we could ill afford. But there was nothing better we could do.

Neil suggested that the engineers change the clutch in *ICI River Rover* to buy time. Mike agreed. They set up half the 'A' frame by attaching it to a building one side and a stores lorry the other, had the engine and transmission out, and the clutch removed, changed and replaced within the two days. It was a magnificent effort. The cause of the clutch slip was, they thought, the weakening of the springs when we engaged the clutch after closing the engine down. It had been in the engaged position throughout the four month sea and rail journey to Hong Kong and Chengdu. We revised our clutch procedure. They also discovered that the nylon fan pulleys had worn on both fans, so they replaced them with aluminium alloy pulleys. Fiona, in the absence of suitable veterinary work, took up engineering with Neil and Jim. It was a happy and effective

195

partnership. Fiona was a very hard worker, learned well. Moreover she never raised any objection to getting filthy.

She did, however, have some opportunity at Yushu to visit the animal husbandry clinic. Vets there do not have much status, and the clinics are short-staffed and overworked. It was such a shame that there was so little veterinary work for Fiona. The senior animal husbandry man at Yushu included Qumerlai in his parish, and would often be out from home for a week or fortnight on his visits. He travelled by horse or yak (did no one ever tell him about hovercraft?). The Tibetans take much pride and considerable interest in their animals, particularly the yak. In an idle hour one day in the coach my puerile mind started to muse on the usefulness of the yak, and I lightly pieced together a bit of doggerel concerning this beast, upon which Tibetan survival is totally dependent:

> The Yak is a lovely woolly cow,
> Her wool is used to knit and sew (oops!);
> She keeps folk warm with clothes and coats
> Providing skins for floating boats.
> Her hide is used to make black tents
> Which cover locals with odd scents.
> Her milk is thick with cream and food;
> Yak butter, in tea, they say is good.
> Her fat brings warmth to cold Tibet
> To it they owe a massive debt;
> For Buddhist monks burn up the fat
> In their religious ziggurat.
> While drivers grease their wheels with it
> Some sculptors use it in their kit;
> And Ma Tibet completes the scene
> For with it cooks her butterbean.
> Yak dung, when dry, is used for fuel
> And heats the cream and meat for gruel.
> Her beef is sweet, they often eat
> Both horns and tail, and where they meet.
> The yak is fleet of hoof and foot –
> She skips and dances with each boot.
> She gambols round with flying fur,
> And sticks her tail up in the air.

196

She's used to ploughing stony ground,
And safely carries goods around.
Tibetans ride upon her back;
Her foothold's sure on mountain track.
Her horn's an aphrodisiac,
That incredible, wonderful, useful, amazing
    Tibetan Yak.

The following day Mike, Sean and myself plus a Yushu policeman and the Chinese tow-lorry driver squashed into a Landcruiser to travel the 190 km to Z'do. The valley north-west out of Yushu sported a little used but recently renovated road which, after a number of potholes, turned out to be very good by Chinese standards. Certainly it was one along which *Neste* and trailer could pass unthreatened. I followed its path carefully on our half-million scale aviation map. It tied up with it nicely until Red Mud Mountain, some 55 km up the valley, where the Chinese engineers had preferred to wiggle their U-bends up the side of the hill. I redrew the map. The snow at the top had obscured the road, and vehicles had chosen any of a dozen routes to cross the stream there. Each pathway had its tortuous bit that would present the trailer with a problem. But it was not insurmountable. We went on. A long beautiful plain led us to Qiang-nan, a minuscule metropolis of twenty houses 30 km further on. The river there was very hovercraftable, I noticed. Round the bend and up a side valley, the road started climbing towards the snow, which had fallen in the last few days. I was not sure where the snow-line was, as the dull overcast had refused to let the sun melt off the surplus. Mike and I grew quieter and more watchful as the Landcruiser wound its way to the top of the pass. Great pits, ruts and potholes started to appear where earlier vehicles had got stuck and churned up the surface to make headway. We slipped gear into 4-wheel drive. Stopped at the top was a lorry full of sad-faced Tibetans. Slowly labouring up ahead of us was a jeep, with not quite so many of the same kind. We were now driving through ruts of snow, through which there was

197

no sign of earth. The landscape at the top was beautiful. But that was the only plus point. Two vehicles had definitely gone through ahead of us: we could see their tracks. Of the road there was no sign. The tow-lorry driver was the first to chicken out; he had shaken his head half-way up the hill. Now all the other Chinese except Sean went sad-faced too. We could see where the road eventually ended up, crossing a hill in the snow some 5 km away. But we were unable to decipher exactly how to join it to our present location. Mike and I persuaded the driver to try to find a way through. He gamely did until the vehicle cranked at an alarming angle and started to skid down an incline that, from the snow, had looked flat, using the 4-wheel drive in toboggan mode. Without speaking both Mike and I decided that, even if we managed to get through in a Landcruiser, the convoy could not go until the snow had melted. We sadly and grimly agreed to turn back. The driver encouraged us all to push the Landcruiser out of its predicament. We had got half-way to Z'do, and I recorded 102 km on the map.

Now we had no choice. We would have to take the vehicles through the appalling roadworks beyond Xiwu. Perhaps they were better than the lorry drivers had described.

Jim, Steve, Neil and Fiona had not yet completed the clutch change on *ICI River Rover*, and Sam, Anne and Rob had not yet finished patching up *Neste Enterprise*. We had discovered to our dismay that one of the welds that attached the front fuel tank to its housing had split. As the tank was, we believed, an integral part of the structure, there was no satisfactory repair that could be done except to reweld it. We hunted through Yushu and eventually unearthed the only man who could weld aluminium. He came to look.

'Yes, I can do that,' he said, after a lot of chin stroking, 'but it is difficult.'

'How can we help?' we asked, preparing ourselves for acts of violent initiative.

'Aluminium liquifies under heat and runs. You would have to turn the craft upside down so that the weld does not fall out on to the ground before it cools.'

We had been tensed up to do practically anything. But to

198

turn a 5 tonne hovercraft upside down was a little more than our facilities and even our initiative allowed. Regretfully, it was so for all the other dozen aluminium repairs that were needed, so we were unable to use him and he trudged his way home sadly. He had heard of the expedition through television news and had been very keen to help.

So we put a patch on it, using pop rivets and a diesel-resistant sealer. It sealed beautifully to start with, but the next few days' road travel caused it to weep for the rest of the expedition.

The time at Yushu was not wasted. Mel and Stan Baldock, our sixty-nine-year-old artist, like ET, phoned home. It was a very painful and lengthy procedure. Others bought Tibetan hand-made carpets. We bought, from an open-air shoe repairer, a hand-cranked sewing machine with which to patch up the torn skirt fingers. He was delighted with his 250 yuan (£32), to which we screwed him down; it was more than three months' shoe-repair income. We sampled the local cinema, relishing a Taiwanese 'hoo-dun-it', suitably blood-thirsty, violent and hilarious. As funny was the carpet of sunflower-seed shells that lay half an inch thick on the floor after the one and a half hours' performance. Local in-house entertainment was provided by young men flicking lighted fag-ends randomly around the dark, smoky auditorium.

Why had we been diverted to Yushu and held for three days? Mike had been impatient to go forward, but could not. On the third day a Tibetan approached him and stuffed a piece of paper into his pocket. It said he loved 'Jusus'. Soon we were contacted by some other Tibetan Christians, who asked for Bibles. We were able to give them loving encouragement and to pray for them. Now we knew why we had come out of our way to this civic centre. It was so heart-warming to know that, hundreds of miles away from any known Christian activity, God had still got his people.

Late one evening this man and his family sought us out in our hostel rooms. We had to play cat-and-mouse with Madam Zhou who kept coming in wanting to borrow things as an excuse for finding out what was going on. The man could speak broken English, which he had picked up from radio broadcasts and a dictionary. He felt he could write better than he could speak, so he wrote the following out as his introduction. For obvious reasons, I have left out his name:

> When did you go to Yushu?
> When will you go to
> How do you do?
> I'm Tibetan.
> My name is . . .
> I'm nice to see you.
> Are you American or English?
> Where do you come from?
> I have heard of you had a Book
> that is a New testament.
> please. Give me one
> I Belief God. And Jusus.
> I thank For the present.
> Bey. Good luck!
> On 26th May 1990 . . .

Now we were committed to going from Yushu to Qumerlai, Base 2, the hard way. There was no alternative, except perhaps to wait a fortnight for the workmen to finish punishing the road. A fortnight was about all we had left for the expedition, so that solution was untenable.

We had a pow-wow. The repairs on *Neste Enterprise* could be wrapped up quickly and she would be ready to road-it by the next day, Sunday. *ICI River Rover* was further behind. We felt we could not delay the expedition for one lorry, and she could follow on later, when the repairs were completed. If we were to get to the source, then there was a huge logistical problem with fuel: we had to dispatch one full truck to Tuotuoheyan Base 3, as soon as possible. We were unsure how long it would take to get there, but if it took more than a week the chances were that it would be too late. So Mike sent Tony Shewell and Duncan off that day to Base 2 in a stores truck, to cheer up the three awaiting our presence there, tell them we were on our way, and to prepare the fuel lorry for immediate despatch to Tuotuoheyan.

Mr Xie Jingkang decided he needed to go to Xining and Lanzhou (capitals of Qinghai and Gansu provinces respectively) in order to get permits to enable us to travel to Tuotuoheyan and beyond. He would take the red Landcruiser. Was there anything he could do for us there? Yes there was. He could take Stan Baldock back to Lanzhou, so he could return home to Cornwall.

Stan was an extraordinary man. A retired RAF Wing Commander, and a Christian, he had taken up painting as a pastime, and was very good. Mike had commissioned him to do a painting of *River Rover* after the Nepal expedition in 1979. Now he had asked Stan to do two paintings of this expedition for our two major sponsors. He was the most ancient of our expedition members but his heart and outlook were still nineteen. His joviality encouraged us, his willingness lightened our load (particularly in the kitchen) and his enthusiasm stimulated us. But there was no doubt that the altitude was getting to him, as was anxiety to contact his wife at home. We were way behind schedule, and Stan knew, as did most of us, that wives at home tend to think that no news is bad news. But there were a number of things he could do for us back in the UK, not the least of which was to contact families and tell them we were all alive and still bright-eyed and bushy-tailed. We had been out of contact with the West since we left Chengdu.

The other thing he could do was to try to find out what had happened to our videos. John Whatmore had been able to contact Hong Kong and discovered that all our precious video tapes which had gone with Tony, Peter and Chris had been waylaid in Chengdu by Customs. It was a bombshell to us. The *Blue Peter* tapes, for which we had made so much effort, now seemed lost for ever, as the time available to show them was all but up. We wondered if the authorities were concerned about some of the contents, and wanted to erase portions. Communications were so bad that we were very much in the dark as to how, when and why the videos had been removed. Stan could get more clues for us, and

201

try to recover them. So his task in returning home was very important. He was reluctant at first to accept it; he wanted to come further in and further up. But in the end he went with grace.

Jim, Neil, Steve and Fee slipped their engineering into overdrive on *ICI River Rover* and had her finished and ready for the road prior to our time of departure on Sunday – a brilliant job.

Meanwhile, Ray, David and the medics had sauntered up to the local hospital to see if they could help in any way. It was an interesting visit. The senior doctor was delighted, and told them the situation. In line with all the hospitals we had encountered in the Tibetan minorities area of China, they were short of expertise, equipment and supplies. The doctor here at Yushu was an exception in that he was well qualified. But there was not much professionalism in his colleagues, nor was he able to update himself with new techniques and medicines from Chengdu.

He showed Ray and David a young Tibetan man who had a problem with his pancreas, and asked their opinion. It happened that we had carried with us the medical equipment necessary for a correct diagnosis and they offered to use it to substantiate his assessment. To our amazement he simply said that it was time to go home, and thanked them for their visit. To be sure, neither we nor the Chinese had the equipment to treat the case, even if we had the correct diagnosis, and the lad really needed proper hospital treatment. It was not available. The alternative was certain death. Such situations were very hard for us to handle as every solution we could think of needed, from the Chinese authorities, a new understanding, better facilities, an injection of funds and revised politics. It tore at our hearts to walk out and leave a man in the prime of his life, dying of something that we knew our western medicine would cure with ease.

Sunday dawned drizzly, with hovering wisps of cloud on the surrounding peaks and shiny, glistening tarmac on the early-morning deserted streets. We prayed the rain away, knowing that heavy road-works would be considerably aggravated by sogginess. It stopped at 10 a.m., and the sun peeked through an hour later. We left at 9.30 a.m. Mr Zhou said we had 100 km to go to Qingshuihe, and the following day 150 km to Qumerlai. Could we do it all in one day?

The Christians among us felt deprived at not being able to have a time of worship – however fabricated – on Sunday. So we in the bus attacked our portable songbooks and sang hymns and choruses for an hour and a half. It was good fun. The greatest barrier to overcome was the jogging of the bus on the corrugated road, making our voices warble wildly, as if we were being given physiotherapy on the back by a beefy Russian mama. Some could not handle it initially. Others were convulsed with laughter at the bizarre noises coming from those persevering. The road works between Yushu and Xiwu over the Yangtze forced the bus to stop regularly, enabling us to realign the broken fragments of musical keys that had long since been shattered and give concerts of Christian songs to the bewildered Tibetan road workers, who happened to be lounging inactively on their shovels. It was not coincidence that on entering Xiwu again, with its heavy Buddhist enclave, we were able to sing and pray 'Drop Your still dews of quietness till all our strivings cease. Take from our souls the strain and stress and let our ordered lives confess the beauty of Your peace.' They needed God's peace. And from then on we needed it too. In front of us was 70 km of road works. One or two (Mike, John, Andrew) knew what we were in for. We had already experienced Hamlet's 'slings and arrows of outrageous fortune', and now had no alternative but 'to take arms against a sea of troubles'.

Chinese road works are different from anything one could imagine anywhere else in the world. In other countries the road would have been closed and another route recommended. Here, of course, there were no other routes. We had done our best to find them. It had been decided (from Beijing?) to 'do' that road. Their aim seemed to be to raise it up by some 1 to 2 metres (maybe to poke it above winter snows and floods) and to build proper culverts and bridges to enable flood waters to pass by without destroying the

203

highway. Very commendable. Their method of doing it was unbelievable. They drafted in around 10,000 road workers, two bulldozers, one road roller, shovels, picks, peci-pecis and tents. These workers were to distribute themselves over the 70 km of road and rebuild it all at the same time. We were not to encounter one bad patch and the rest was free: we were to encounter a bad patch nearly every kilometre. For light entertainment John and I counted the road works on that 70 km stretch. There were sixty-one. Some of them were at least a kilometre long.

As if that was not enough, no provision had been made for passing traffic. Most of the way there was no road at all on which a truck could go, and all vehicles had to find their own way across the uneven and unprepared turf by the side of the road. Getting off the road into the adjoining countryside down the raised banks was exciting enough for the trucks and bus. But for the *Neste Enterprise* road trailer it was one continuous daytime nightmare. Peter Gunner had been able to fix the rear-wheel steering on the trailer, and this was used nearly every kilometre. Without it, it would have been totally impossible. At one road work on a hillside, where they were building a bridge, the provision made for passing trucks was a small area cut out of the uphill slope. It was about the length of the truck and trailer combined, and quite impassable. Thirty or so of the road workers stopped what they were doing and took half an hour to carve away more hillside to enable the trailer wheels to pass within centimetres of the edge. At another site Steve had to run and shout to the driver to move forward; the rear wheel of the trailer was visibly sinking into the collapsing road with a metre drop below. Further on, as the trailer was taking a detour off the road over a rivulet, the tow lorry skidded and lost traction altogether. We had to unhitch it from the trailer, put a long wire hawser on it, so that it could get traction on a better bit of turf, and drag it out from there. Once every five minutes or so we all had to pile out of the bus and other convoy vehicles to manhandle a lorry or the trailer through the mud, over the rocks or across the wiry yak grass filled with potholes or humps. I glanced up from my seat in the

204

bus at one point to look at the trailer climbing back on to the road ahead of us. I wish I hadn't. As it went slowly forward I saw it tip over at some 30°, both uphill wheels spinning in the air. My heart went into my mouth: was it going to roll down the hill? Fortunately it righted itself. But I decided from then on just to pray and not look. Mike was particularly concerned for the safety of all the vehicles and fasted and prayed all day. The burden rested on him like a brain-hammering headache: we could have lost everything at least two dozen times on that road. 'This is bloody battle,' was his description of that day, and he was not swearing.

It took us nine hours to do the 70 km, averaging some 8 kph. It was a very heavy day. But for those who had eyes to see, all was not bad. The early morning rain had passed, giving us a muddy road, of course, but also ranging cloud along the hilltops. The snow-clad Tibetan hills were delicately crowned with a filigree veil of cloud, daintily adorning and draping their crests. Wide, luxurious, diversely coloured valleys spread out by the roadside, encapsulated in purple mountain excellence, and set off by sparkling white streams, gambolling down the slopes to the Yangtze. Hills gave way to plains; miles of wide open veldt, held in on the distant horizon by blue-green grazing hillocks, and freckled with thousands of minute grazing black yaks. For those who enjoy space and distance, this was glorious freedom. Ranks of hills fell in and retreated, with their deep azure ravines and sunlit slopes, mossy tufted grass varying in shade from dark brown to light green and yellow, and the gradually emerging blue sky allowing the warmth and sparkle of the sun to enliven the glory. An early afternoon shower produced a rainbow in front of a closer hillside. For some reason that I have yet to discover, we only saw the top segment of the rainbow. Every other rainbow I recall seeing, regardless of the time of day or latitude of the earth, has been a large semicircle. But this one was small, just the top eighth. Curious.

But for the road, it would have been a fabulous journey through some of China's most attractive countryside. We counted 70 km on the odometer, relieved when it was all

205

over that nothing had broken. We only had another 50 km to go to get to our resting-place for the night. Our destination of Qingshuihe meant 'Green Water river'. God gave us a beautiful sunset on the way there – the first decent one we had seen – and we felt that he was crowning our day's agony with his blessing of peace.

Qingshuihe was a tinpot little village, its main excuse for existing being the army staging post that was there. I never found any river, much less a green one. We arrived at 10.30 p.m. and it was dark. The crystal-clear stars twinkled out of a black night sky that was unobscured by fossil-fuel effluent murk.

We stopped outside the 'restaurant'. Mr Xie went off to find accommodation for us all, and we were ushered aimlessly into the feeding house. The owners, judging from their skull-caps, were Muslims. A wood and yak-dung fire stove was cooking food in four woks and belching out its smog into the room. Candlelight was dimmer through the smoke but it looked and smelt homely and cheery, in a stenchy, Tibetan way. We ducked through the arched doorway and sat down at the tables, which were clean enough. Round the walls were pictures of beautiful Chinese ladies, fully clothed, of course. I guess it was the nearest these folk could come to pin-ups. Incarcerated among them was an ancient picture of Chairman Mao and entourage.

Food was the inevitable bowl of lentils, vegetables and 'things' swimming in soup, reddened by chilli, all to be eaten with chopsticks. Most of us by now had mastered the art of chasing little incomprehensibles around bowls using chopsticks, but those who had not soon pulled out their dusty expedition spoons, gave them a cursory wipe, and tucked in. The Tibetans tucked in too – into the room, that is. In ones and twos they came, not to eat, but to look. They squeezed round the gaps in between the thirty-five or so of us, until there was hardly enough room to breathe, gradually producing a serious lack of consumable air. In their wide-brimmed stetsons, knee-length boots, maroon coats, dark red-brown faces and sunny smiles, they watched everything we did with the utmost scrutiny and amazement.

From outside, window space was at a premium. Five or six (mostly female) faces would be jammed to the glass, all trying to soak in as much matter as possible for the stories that would be told to generations to come of the white-faced, big-nosed foreigners who rolled up one night in their village.

It took a long time to eat. But it gave Mr Xie enough time to fail to find reasonable accommodation. The inevitable happened – the Chinese would get the better rooms, and the *Lao wai* anything else. We wandered to a few locations but eventually ended up at the soldiers' barracks on the edge of the village. It was pretty late by the time we unloaded the rucksacks and sleeping bags from the top of the bus. I managed to catch sight of four bedraggled soldiers, half-dressed, staggering out of what was their permanent quarters, trailing clothing behind them. I thought it was nice of them to vacate their beds for us. But no. They had been ordered out. And it was for the Chinese, not us.

We were shown into another room, in another block next door, just by the satellite dish. The only creditable thing was that they had cleaned it for us. There was a body-length board, on legs, around three walls of the room. It seemed to be padded. In the centre was a sorry-looking stove that I cursorily dated late Ming dynasty and had long ceased to fulfil its design function.

'We sleep on that?' I queried, pointing to the board.

'Yes,' said Mr Zhou. He looked apologetic.

'All of us?' I was persistent.

'Yes.'

'¿Las señoritas también?'

'Sí.'

Ah well. It was the first experience I had had of unisex accommodation. I passed the message to the ladies and was embarrassed for them. They took it in good part, and the following morning Ray muttered that she was going to write a book entitled 'Men I have slept with'. We threw our sleeping mats and bedding on to the boards and were asleep by midnight. Funnily enough it was remarkably comfortable.

We got up at 6.30. Mr Xie, Stan and others had to leave in the Landcruiser by 7.30 for Lanzhou. They were planning to do 700 km that day, and we wished them all the best. We were sorry to see Stan go. Actually there was such unity on the team that we were sorry to see anyone go.

The barracks had a toilet but no water. So we set off for the restaurant unshaven, dishevelled, greasy-faced and furry-toothed. There, fortunately, we were able to prise water from the proprietor and repair the night-time damage.

We left at 10.00 a.m. for Qumerlai, the last lap of our second, extraordinary eight-day road journey. We arrived at 5 p.m. There were no hassles on the road, no breakdowns, no hold-ups: only beautiful landscapes and zebra-striped hills. It was wonderful.

Qumerlai was a large town, set in a flat plain surrounded by hills. It was the end of the road, a cul-de-sac, and, as such, was a surprisingly large and well-organised township. It was neatly set out, with streets at right angles and high walls around the compounds. The town seemed to consist mostly of these compounds with a few independent tents dotted haphazardly round the outside. The Yangtze was nowhere to be seen.

We allowed the Chinese to get off to find their hostel. They were planning to stay in the town throughout the time at Base 2, and expected to come down to the camp only at spasmodic intervals. The rest of us set off to find our camp.

It was 6 kms away. The road was ancient and covered with what felt like desert sand, as the bus swooshed and swayed its way across it. A large 700 m (2000 ft) hill stood between Qumerlai and the river and the track took us to the south of it, past the abattoir, through a tight valley and out on to the riverside. The camp was stretched out by the water's edge, on a flat bank standing 1.5 m above the water. It was good to see Giles, Kevin, David, Colin and Duncan again. We had missed them. And they had done an excellent job on setting up the tents. Tang's lorry, with all the fuel on it, had broken down, but had managed to reach Qumerlai. We were now stuck with which truck to send to Tuotuoheyan and when.

We had taken eight tortuous days to travel a mere 761 km from Denke. The day was Monday, the date 28 May. We had surmounted countless obstacles on the way. We had dug trenches, heaved vehicles, removed rocks and rubble, got stuck in snow, and winched lorries out of deep mud from the torn terrain; it had been sheer physical effort by all the team. We were already behind in our new, squeezed schedule by four precious days. We struggled to believe we would ever reach Tuotuoheyan, much less the source, in the available time, with all the unknowns that lay before us.

8

To the Source of the Yangtze

'Tis not in mortals to command success,
But we'll do more, Sempronius; we'll deserve it.
(Joseph Addison)

The team members who had been living at the Qumerlai base camp told us of horrendous weather changes – dust storms, snow, ice, heavy winds and bright, hot sun. Our first day was typical. A sharp frost in the night took the temperature down to −7°C, and this remained until the sunshine touched the camp at 9.30 a.m. Camp was on the down-sun side of the hill in the mornings, so when the sun actually came it brought the temperature immediately into the 30°C to 40°C range. One moment we were in our winter woollies; the next in shorts and T-shirts (for those who had the wisdom to bring them). Yet we did not sweat. The altitude was some 4085 m (13,400 ft) and it was so dry that our perspiration dissipated immediately. Hard work made us breathless, so labour had to be done in short, sharp bursts with a breather in between. Everyone ended up with dirty hands, gradually blackened by the oil and dust that entered the cracks. No amount of washing could remove the discoloration, and we began to see why Tibetans, who rarely washed, were so dark-skinned. We noticed too that sores and cuts took a long time to heal.

We unpacked our tents and erected them. We set up a fuel dump by the river. Base 2 had an orderly, military layout. This was no mistake, as the administrative party that put it together had three ex-army captains on it.

210

Our top priority was the logistic problem of positioning fuel at Tuotuoheyan. If we were unable to do it, then the expedition would be unsuccessful. Gwyn worked out the number of 40 gallon drums we could take on Tang's lorry. It came to 12 diesel and 12 petrol. But the lorry itself would use petrol on its journey, so, just five drums would be left at Tuotuoheyan for *ICI River Rover* to use. Was that all right? I calculated the distance from Tuotuoheyan to the source, added on the distance to fuel dump 'B' and agreed that that was sufficient. We were uncertain what the distance was from Qumerlai to Tuotuoheyan by road, but we estimated 2000 km. Some of the roads we knew were good, but we pessimistically estimated a seven-day journey. If Tang could get there in that time, we would be able to meet him as we came up the river. Who should we send with Tang? Mike decided, in the end, to send two young men: photographer Jeremy and action man Duncan, both of whom would be able to extend their time in China if they needed to. Jeremy Browne was from Northern Ireland, and many in the team enjoyed emulating his accent, which he took remarkably well. He came late into the expedition, Mike having found him in a central London church shortly before the launch. Jeremy found himself inclining towards photography on his art college course, and he eventually majored in it. After graduating, he had decided to take up photography professionally, and was thrilled to get the opportunity to come to China with us, just two years later. A Christian man in his mid-twenties, Jeremy has a capacity for hard work and an ability never to get ruffled, making him much more than a photographer to us. But his professionalism in his specialist field was superb, and we were all very glad he was able to drop his other work to come with us.

Tang's lorry was broken. He came to Mike cap in hand to ask if we could weld the offending bit. Most of the team were unhappy about the principle of that – spares were available in Qumerlai, as was welding equipment, but it would cost Tang to repair it there, and we knew he was pulling a fast one on us. But he was a good man and the only driver (wild though he was) we could trust to drive day and night to get the fuel to Tuotuoheyan on time. So Mike said we would repair the damage – it was to our advantage. He sent it and the TV Landcruiser away two days later, arranging to rendezvous at Tuotuoheyan at 11 a.m. on Friday, 7 June, seven days away. It was an arrangement of faith.

The engineers unpacked and constructed the 'A' frame so that the *ICI River Rover* could be lifted off its lorry. We were delayed by two factors: Neil was ill and feeling definitely off-colour. Then the 'A' frame broke. It very nearly inflicted a serious injury. We had put all the pieces together on the ground, and mustered the whole team to lift it to the vertical. As we were winching it up and had got it to roughly the 30° position there was a terrific crack, and one of the welds snapped. This was followed almost instantaneously by a second crack.

'Jump!' shouted Jim. We all leapt outwards. The frame came crashing to the ground, raising clouds of dust from the powdery sand underneath. Mercifully no one was scratched.

Jim and Steve spent the next few hours honing down the two broken pieces and rewelding them. They had to use the two portable generators in series to develop enough electricity to heat the weld for a good enough bond.

We started to erect the 'A' frame again in the late afternoon. It had cost us almost a day. The 'A' frame holds itself erect by tensioned ropes in a cross from side to side and top to bottom. Peter, who designed it, used one rope for each side. That was fine, providing the ropes were tied at all four corners on each side. When we constructed it this time no one checked to see if this had been done, and the frame, as it stood erect, looked secure enough. We backed *ICI River Rover* on its truck, attached the lifting chain to the shackles, and started to lift it up from the flat-bed. Neil was still feeling groggy, but insisted on helping and, as he had done many times before, climbed on top of *ICI River Rover* to make sure the winch housing did not foul the top horizontal bar of the 'A' frame. We had just got the craft up from the flat-bed when, with a sigh, the whole construction swivelled backwards on its feet to an alarming 45° angle.

'Jump!' came Jim's strangled cry, yet again. We all leapt backwards, and Neil flew off the top of the craft like an Olympic sprinter reacting to a starting pistol.

We stood back and surveyed the scene. For the second time that day we had been graciously saved from injury. The craft had dropped back on the flat-bed, and fortunately was not damaged. The 'A' frame stopped at 45°. It was obvious that the rope on both sides had been merely slipped through the top shackles and not tied securely. We uncoupled the hovercraft and drove it gingerly from underneath. Then we winched up the 'A' fame to its vertical position and tied it securely, testing it thoroughly. It was 9.30 p.m., and we had 20 minutes of declining daylight left. Some wanted to get *ICI River Rover* off at once. But I decided that we would leave it till morning. We had all had enough for one day, and if anything else went wrong, life in the darkness could have been dangerous.

The following day was 'launch day'. Lots of locals were invited to watch the cutting of the rope by the Tibetan Mayor of Yushu, who was travelling 300 km for the ceremony at 3 p.m.

The engineers had much to do. *ICI River Rover* was winched off its flat-bed successfully and Neil and Jim were soon giving her an engine test, needed after the clutch and transmission change at Yushu. Satisfied, they took her out on the river for a test run. All was good.

The rest of us transferred our attention to *Neste Enterprise*. She had to be lifted up on the standby jacks and lowered, nose first, to the ground. The problems began when we tried to lower the tail. The blocks on which the jacks stood sank into the loose Yangtze river sand, and we had enormous trouble stopping her tipping over from an asymmetric loading. How we missed the original jacks! We consoled ourselves with the thought that we would only have to do that exercise twice more on this whole expedition.

Lunch-time came and went. We just went hungry. At 2 p.m. we were still struggling to get the craft down. At 2.30, as *Neste Enterprise* at last sighed on to the sand, it

213

started snowing. We had to get her off the trailer frame. But meanwhile she needed cleaning. The craft was an appalling mess from all the mud, pebbles and stones that had been thrown up from the road on the journey. Most of the filth was at the propeller end, and the whole team ran a chain of buckets from the river to uncake the mud. We also damped the earth around to save the dust blown up by the hovercraft from mixing with the snow, which was still falling steadily. When the cleaners had finished we started her up. It was 3 p.m., and we prayed that all would go well as we attempted to hover her off the frame. It half did. Three times skirt fingers and wires got snagged on trailer protuberances, meaning one of us had to burrow underneath in all the dust and sand that was being blown up to untangle it. Skirt fingers got torn, shackles got broken, and everyone within a ten-metre radius got covered in a thick film of dust.

We manhandled the craft down to the water's edge and switched off the engine, while Mike and the Mayor battled out their speeches in mutually incomprehensible languages against a blustering wind. I gave Rob the privilege of driving *Neste Enterprise* on to the Yangtze this time. As he opened the throttle to drive her on to the slope that had been carved out for us by Colin and Co. a 'ping, ping, ping' was heard by the team. No one took any notice.

Inside the craft the Mayor and his associates enjoyed ten minutes of glorious hovercraft uniqueness. A second sortie of assorted dignitaries was undertaken. Among them were two of our own Chinese team, Mr Zhou the diplomat, and Mr Cheng the policeman. Brave men! I think they were shamed into coming by the enthusiasm and willingness of local Tibetans. This was the one and only nibble at hovercraft experience by our guides, and we were glad to give it to two of the nicest among them. We had to stop after this second ten-minute run because *Neste Enterprise* had developed a rather alarming vibration.

We courteously bade our visitors farewell and turned our attention to the rumble. It was the propeller. To our horror one of the mahogany blades was split right down the middle to about 30 cm. We had no spare propellers. We concluded that a large stone must have been kicked up by the spinning rear wheels of the tow lorry, and had shot at such a velocity that it had broken the prop.

We did not know quite what to do. In the end we bound the top 9 inches of each blade with some of the versatile black tape that Mike has carried with him on expeditions for years to meet a wide variety of contingencies. A quick test run confirmed that the vibration had gone. But whether the tape would stay stuck to a blade tip at 400 mph remained to be seen. We knew we had to mollycoddle the propeller from then on: without it the craft would be useless. Nor was there any way of constructing another. It was quite a blow. We had yet to do any serious travelling on the river from Base 2.

The camp site was excellent for all but two things: hover-craft and water. There was not a really good place to park either craft. The 2 m drop to the water's edge made the slope that Colin had dug very steep. Rob was disenchanted with driving *Neste Enterprise* up it all the time. We had bent the Queen enough at Denke and each attempt at beaching her produced more indentations. There was a flattish spot 100 metres up by the stream, but it was hard work putting her on it. We settled for that as a resting place, but very often *Neste Enterprise* had to sit with her back end in the water. Pulling her up on to the beach was impossible. On that first day we got her nose up, tied it to a stake, and then used as many Tibetans and team as we could gather to try and pull the tail up. No way. In fact the front rope snapped, dangerously, knocking Anne off the hovercraft on to the rocks, and we had to take the craft out and begin again.

Drinking water came from a stream that gushed its semi-frozen turbulent way down the valley some distance from the camp. It was clean enough, but not to drink. We had to have a water run every day, dragging and carrying the very heavy casks some 400 m. Tony Shewell collected a long rod, tied all the containers together, and floated them down the Yangtze to the camp. Transporting water on water; this was an unusual but highly effective piece of army initiative. Tony was a shrewd and very fit young man, who had been

215

recruited for the express purpose of taking *Neste Enterprise* to Papua New Guinea after the expedition had completed its adventures in China. While the heavy negotiations were going on in Chengdu, Tony had been busy in Hong Kong making the necessary arrangements for repair to the craft, container transportation, and facilities for the future. He had arrived with Dr David Langley when the second wave of team members came to Denke. We were glad to have his intellectual, physical and Christian inputs lightening our work load.

We had one more essential task to do before going on our first journey upriver. That was Public Relations photography. We had many commercial sponsors and had to fulfil our obligations to them by taking photographs of both hovercraft on the Yangtze, with all the correct logos in evidence. John Whatmore arranged the whole of the next day for this purpose and it went remarkably well.

That evening Mike briefed the team on our plan to conquer the upper reaches of this river. At the two planned fuel dumps, A and B, we would position four 40-gallon drums of diesel and two of petrol. *Neste Enterprise* could carry internally, at a reasonable maximum, 120 gallons of diesel, but *ICI River Rover* only had 18 gallons internal petrol capacity. We were so far behind schedule that the only way Mike could envisage giving everyone a 'Tibetan wilderness experience' was to take all the early leavers up to dump A in twos and threes, where the apparently simple task of minding fuel would involve a demanding survival exercise in inhospitable wasteland. The following day a new batch of people would come in on *Neste Enterprise*, and a change-over would be effected. It was a complicated logistics exercise, because *Neste Enterprise* could carry only one tonne of weight, and we had to balance the need to give people this survival experience against the necessity to lay down drums of fuel in the time available. Because I was the operations leader, Mike tasked me with the orchestration of it. It harmonised with great difficulty, of course, but I hammered together a detailed plan fully realising that the eventual movements would probably differ

216

considerably. Still it was important to have a baseline from which to work.

The schedule was extremely tight because we wanted to spend as little time as possible servicing fuel dumps, and as much time as possible on the river trying to achieve the source. Our CAS contract was for sixty days, and this would run out at the end of June. A large proportion of the team were committed to returning home to their jobs and were not free to extend their expedition time in China. Mike worked it out that their last day at Qumerlai would have to be 12 June to enable them to start work at home at the beginning of July.

But the plan was also dependent on other things. The serviceability of *Neste Enterprise*, with a damaged propeller, was crucial to the whole exercise: we certainly had all our eggs in one basket. *ICI River Rover* was an unknown quantity. Her serviceability had been variable, and Mike was feeling uncertain about her: she was like the little girl who, when she was good, was very very good, but when she was bad was horrid. Certainly we would not use her in any load-carrying capacity, but in the end her smaller size and better manoeuvrability might get her closer to the source(s). We were pleased, too, that none of the Chinese was coming with us on the river. Although they were delightful company and nice people, most of their contributions thus far had consisted of a very restrictive adherence to rules and regulations, some of which were conjured up on the spur of the moment by fear. We would have enough trouble navigating an unknown river in unpredictable weather at an untested altitude without having to frolic with bureaucratic bits of paper in empty wildernesses.

Mike publicly expressed his disappointment at not being able to use the hovercraft for further medical purposes, or to establish a service between health clinics on this 360-km-plus stretch of river. In fact there were no villages on the river – just Tibetan tents occasionally dotting the landscape and scattered Tibetan yak herdsmen. Our doctors nevertheless carried selected medicines with them wherever they went. Sore eyes, for example, were everywhere.

217

The other worry was how to get 40-gallon drums of fuel into and out of *Neste Enterprise*. We had already cracked the port decking and thereby discovered how potentially weak both sides were. If one drum were to drop accidentally on to the decking, or into the body, or anywhere on the craft, there could be irreparable damage. I challenged a number of people to come up with inventions and many of us applied ourselves to this problem. Most solutions were not sufficiently safe. Mike overrode them all, and said we would just have to hand-pump all the fuel from one drum to another. Hence the need to take up an empty petrol and diesel drum to each dump. It would add time to a tight schedule, but it would not require any heavy or sophisticated equipment, just an efficient pump with a long hose, which, fortunately, we could put together.

We left on our first river adventure at 7.10 a.m. on Friday, 1 June. There was barely enough light to see the river. Rob and I shared the driving. Mike's original concept was to allow as many people as possible to drive each hovercraft, but this became more and more unwise as the days went on. *Neste Enterprise* was our lifeline, and there was no doubt that the driving techniques required for her were different from *ICI River Rover*'s and needed a developing skill and experience. So, initially, Rob and I alone drove her. Then, as *ICI River Rover* became more serviceable, and as the time drew nearer to the main up-river thrust, Mike took me off *Neste Enterprise* and put me in charge of *ICI River Rover*. Thus Rob became the sole driver of the big craft. It was a sensible thing to do, and I was glad to be able to focus my concentration on getting the little craft all the way up to the top with Neil and Steve. The tenacity required for that was as fierce as for the larger one. A mountainous challenge.

The river we drove up was gorgeous for hovercraft. Beyond doubt, no other waterborne vehicle could have tackled it. Rafts could come down, of course. But only a hovercraft could go both up and down. Mostly the river consisted of meandering shallows, divided into multi-choice streams. There were a few gorges, but very few places

218

where there was only one water to ride on. There were multitudinous sandbanks and shale deposits, constantly being built and haphazardly destroyed as the enormous erosive flow tossed them casually aside. At times the river was only a few centimetres deep. Many times the channel of water we had selected to go up ended at a shalebank or contracted into a stream narrower than the width of the craft. Here the delight of being able to hover over land rescued us again and again from trouble. In all these multi-stream areas it was nigh on impossible to determine which stream was the main flow. Water seemed to come down in sufficient quantities and speed to present us with three choices at any one point. And all decisions were last-minute ones. The craft was too low to be able to distinguish a good river, a bad stream or a lake until ten seconds before selection. *Neste Enterprise*'s wide turning circle did not help either. Some good water would turn out to be a cul-de-sac, or be bordered by shale as we came to it. Many times we went wrong. It was by no means relaxed or easy driving. For some reason or other the main flow in these multi-streams was easier to spot going down river than it was going up river. The river flowed light brown with silt, its surface silvered by miniature whirlpools and sudden rapids. Sometimes it was flowing in two or three directions at once, streaming laterally across its own bed or rippling in inexplicable bores backward over the main current. Occasionally it narrowed to less than 50 m across, gushing between multi-coloured rocks.

For the first two hours Rob drove and I navigated. It would seem to be a fairly simple thing to establish one's position on a river, and I had had many years' experience of dead reckoning navigation in single-seat fighter aircraft. I had a stop-watch, and the craft had a compass. The maps we were using were half-million (1:500,000) RAF aviation maps. We had found these to be by far the most accurate maps available, and they had served us well in Nepal and on the Amazon. The one thing we did not have was an assessment of speed, as I have described before. I reckoned to calculate this from pin-points by the side of the river coupled with time. But the actual ground distance

219

covered would be vastly different from the distances shown
on the map because the craft was meandering about across
the river, trying to find the main channel. Our speed assessment, therefore, was as much guesswork as accurate
calculation.

What struck me first was that the huge 'S' bend just
north of Qumerlai did not seem to be there. According
to the map (see Appendix A) we should have started on
a westerly heading, turning just east of south for two and
a half nautical miles (taking some ten minutes), turning
north-west for a further ten minutes, and then, with a south-
westerly wiggle, moved up the river. At no point did we
get through an 'S' bend like that anywhere near Qumerlai.
I shrugged my shoulders. Perhaps the river had changed
course since the map was printed (1973): the fact that it ran
through mountains and could not possibly have done so was
completely baffling. It was like a crossword clue that never
fits. I seriously began to doubt the accuracy of the map.
Some of the other features seemed to tie in reasonably well,
but I could not determine accurately whether we or the map
were right because I had no accurate assessment of speed.

To clarify things we measured our distances and speeds
on the river in nautical miles and knots. Both Rob and I
were used to that through our respective specialisations,
and the RAF map was drawn that way. A nautical mile is
2000 yards, and a statute mile is 1760 yards. The conversion
factor to kilometres, the shortest distance measurement, is
1 nm to 1.82875 km.

We had on board a satellite navigation device called
Satnav. This electronic equipment is used in yachts and
fishing vessels, and is updated every half hour by satellites
whizzing round the earth. However, it needs to have height
in metres installed into its computer to give an accurate
reading. We switched it on at the start of the trip, and I
recorded its position on my map. It read 34 03 69'N, 95
49 95'E. I plotted that on my map, and it put us 38 nm
(69.5 km) down river towards Denke. I checked the height,
13,400 ft, converted it to metres and put it into the Satnav.
There was no appreciable change in position. Just for fun,

I put in zero altitude – mean sea level. There was still no significant change in the position – about 7 nm. So I shrugged my shoulders again, dismissed the equipment as useless and ignored it from then on.

Rob and I swapped driver/navigator after two hours. I gave him our position. But for the next two hours he struggled with the navigation as much as I had.

Mike had asked us to keep a reasonable lookout for a spot to pick for dump A.

'A nice sandy place,' he said, 'by the riverside so that both people and hovercraft can be mutually accessible.'

'And on the northern shore,' I added, 'just in case they have to walk home and can't get across the river.'

'Yes,' Mike replied, 'and, for fresh water, near a stream.'

Life is never ideal. We never found a flowing stream to provide the water. The place we had originally selected on our map was in or near a gorge, and, after four hours of river travel we were getting a twitch that we did not seem to be anywhere near it. Mike was looking at his watch. Eventually he said that we just had to find a place to put fuel dump A, regardless of whether we had reached our planned location or not.

So we did. It looked a nice place. It had a good sandbank to hover on to, and had a little 2 m bank on top of which the tents could sit. We unpacked the tents, and Andrew, Sam and Dr David Johnson clambered out to inspect their new home. We left them with packets of rations and hexamine burners so that they could eat, and we introduced ourselves to the two families of Tibetans who came to examine their new next door neighbours. Their decorated, saddled yak took an instant dislike to us, kicked, mooed and bolted.

Mike had discussed the potential of the hover doctor for Amazonian rivers in Brazil with Dr David Johnson and had invited him to taste operations first hand on the Yangtze. Son of a British missionary father and an outgoing Brazilian mother, David had all the pioneering spirit to be expected with such a background. We look forward to his operating a hover doctor service in his own country. Sam, our genius scientist, mathematician, electronics engineer and negotiator, now had the mundane task of putting together a dome-shaped tent flailing in the wind, after which he searched mindlessly for something constructive to do. Perhaps they could play cards – if anyone had thought of bringing any!

I tried to locate our position. I had noted, some three-quarters of an hour before, that we had flown on a south-easterly heading for about ten minutes. That, I thought, must be significant, for there could hardly be many places that went south-east on a north-westerly river. The only place between us and Qumerlai was where the river crossed the 94 20'E longitude line. So I assumed A to be on or near the 94 10'E line, and settled for that.

The propeller was definitely giving us cause for concern. About every hour and a half we would stop to check a vibration and discover that the black tape strapping had unpeeled and come off one or two of the blades. We tried to think through how we could improve the repair. Certainly we could do something about the duct; the gap between the prop and the duct at the bottom was barely 2 mm wide, and the gap at the top was much greater. When the tape flew off it scored the duct, particularly at the bottom. It was a task for later.

We certainly flew faster down river than we did up river – our assessment touching 40 knots, and averaging 30 knots. It got me into trouble on a couple of occasions, for once *Neste Enterprise* had got wound up she was difficult to slow down, and to turn. I flew over a few sandbanks that I could have avoided. We all tried to remember, from just a few hours before, which was the right bit of river to go on at each point. But it was impossible. The symmetry of the hills, the lack of any distinguishing features in the terrain, the regularity of brown-grey-green on the grassy slopes, all clubbed together to dull the memory. Things became less muddled over the next few days as we drove up and down the river a number of times.

But we knew where the sizeable rapid was. It was not really a rapid, merely a raised wall of water right across the river over a foot high and 30 m across. It caused no problem to *Neste Enterprise*, which glided over it both ways with barely a murmur. But we knew where it was because there was a white Tibetan tent on the southern hillside near it. The white ones were unusual. I knew it could easily be packed up and gone the next time we passed that way. But fortunately it was there throughout our skirmishes on the river, and warned us to be aware of the rapid.

It took us three hours to return, reducing our travelling time by an hour by going downhill, down river, and downwind. Rob and I studied the location of dump A. I was convinced my estimated position was right, but he was not. He was going up river without me the next day to lay down fuel and said he would try and get a sun-shot using the sextant loaned to us by RAF Finningly.

We also debated the propeller modification. When we returned we discovered that Neil had also been thinking about it, and he suggested we cut appropriate lengths of spare rubber-skirt material and glue it on to the props with epoxy resin. We consulted Mel, our materials expert. He agreed that this could be done, but not then. The clouds at 5 p.m. had started to embrace the tops of the hills and, although it was not yet raining, drizzle and high humidity hung in the air. Epoxy resin glue does not like water. Mel said it was better to do it in the dry than to bodge it in the damp and prohibit its curing. So we strapped it up again with black tape and brown sellotape. Then, not to waste time, Steve and I cut out some shims to raise up the propeller in the duct, and soon installed them. The modification helped ease that problem.

We were up early the next day to prepare for the second run to dump A. The craft was refuelled on the hover by the river's edge, using the hand-pump to syphon diesel from the bank. We refuelled three empty diesel drums in the rear cabin in the same way. Rob left for dump A at 9.10 a.m. and the craft looked heavy and sluggish. She had trouble getting over hump initially, but Rob was soon able to put the nose over some shingle and away she went. Steve went up as engineer. Rob took three and a half hours' non-stop driving to get to dump A and 40 minutes to decant the fuel on to the shore. As planned, Tony, Giles and Colin went along with them. This was almost the last time that Giles was to be with the main team. He had proven to be such a masterful interpreter that Mike was reluctant to allow him off to have a bit of adventure, when we would be deprived of our communication with the Chinese. But he got his way, and got his fun. Sam came back with Rob from dump A because he wanted to complete and fit the doppler speed and distance measuring device that he and others had spent so long designing and building in Chengdu. They took two and a half hours to return, averaging over 40 knots, and were back in time for Anne, Neil and Jim to glue the skirt material to the props. It was a dry, sunny evening and the epoxy would be able to cure overnight. We were so much happier that we had been able to repair the props properly.

Meanwhile I was enjoying *ICI River Rover* again, with Neil. We went out to test all her facilities, believing that all her difficult snags had been sorted out. First we took Mike and Sarah along so that they could take afternoon tea with a friendly Tibetan family. Mike gave the small children cuddly toys made by the ladies of Gorsley Baptist Church. To the husband he gave some Lego; he was delighted, and played with it for days on end. Then we took John and his TV cameraman, so that they could get some video of the smaller craft under the overhanging rocks and in front of the massive brown cliffs. Then they wanted to get some video of *ICI River Rover* going through rapids, so we selected a lively section of standing waves under the lee of the cliff. I was driving. Half-way through the rapid and right in the middle of the largest waves, *ICI River Rover*'s engine cut, and we sank into the turmoil. Neil, alert as ever, knew exactly what had happened: we had run out of fuel. The system that had been incorporated into *ICI River Rover* when he and Steve had put the new engine in was that fuel bled off the same tank from which the engine was feeding to go into the other tank, so that fuel transferred across from the in-use tank at double the engine consumption rate. I had not quite switched into this, and neither Neil nor I had noticed the tank contents. John and Mr Lee were appalled, as the waves were breaking

224

over the canopy. Neil banged the fuel transfer cock over, turned the engine starter and pumped the pressurisation tank furiously. For agonising seconds the engine refused to start and we heaved and wallowed our way uselessly through the huge waves, ever closer to the cliff, unable to do anything. At last the engine responded and coughed into life. Well below hump and sensible control speed, we struggled sideways out of the mire, swung drunkenly by the force of the standing waves buffeting our side. I was hyper-sensitive to the fuel situation from that time on.

What I did moan about were the rudder controls. They had been heavy enough on the Peru craft. Now they were ton weights. Neil had done the calculations on the restraining springs, for this craft had twin rudders on either side, where earlier models had only one. Maybe we could remove one rudder? Or lighten the spring tensions? Anyway, something. I suggested that it was ridiculous to flog 500 miles up the Yangtze with controls that wore us out. Neil was convinced that all was fine, so Steve and I, behind his back that night, started to dismantle the rudder system item by item to find out where the restriction was. We eventually discovered that, if we disconnected the bowden cable that joined the two sets of rudders together, the controls became considerably easier. We told Neil. Dubiously, he tried it out. A look of amazement came over his face. Clearly the path that the cable took through the engine bay was too tortuous to allow it free travel. Neil's eyes sparkled. He could remove it. He would fix a couple of brackets on the inboard rudders and connect them with an aluminium rod. That would work. He was very thrilled that his theoretical calculations of spring strength were, in the end, correct. And I was glad for a rudder control that I could wiggle with a couple of fingers. I was so appreciative of the engineers we had. None of them felt any restraint in modifying either craft in any way if performance required it. I recalled that, in Peru, design calculations were considered unalterable, and modifications were pressed through with great reluctance. China was becoming an engineering adventure as well as a driving and logistics challenge.

225

We were forced by the time compression to operate on Sunday. But we all felt that our times of Christian worship should take priority over every other consideration, and Rev Kev ably encouraged us that Whitsunday morning. Straight afterwards, though, Rob headed north again in *Neste Enterprise* on the last of the runs to dump A, carrying one diesel and two petrol drums. He was getting to know the terrain a lot better, and the craft was proving to be a reliable and trustworthy machine. Mike and all of us expressed our delight in her. It turned out to be a dangerous thing to do, for we needed to learn again to 'beware when all men speak well of you'!

Neil, Jim and Fiona were completing preparations on *ICI River Rover*. They slightly decreased the lift fan blade angle and increased the thrust fan angle to transfer more of the power to 'drive'. We were reluctant to reduce the lift fan thrust too much as we had a lot of weight to carry 'up the hill'. It was all trial and error, and depended very much on the feel experienced by the three drivers. Meanwhile I was doing some fuel calculations for *ICI River Rover*. In Chengdu Neil and Jim had put aluminium angle pieces on *ICI River Rover*'s side to support twelve jerry cans of fuel. With the internals, that would give us 78 gallons. At a consumption rate of 6 gallons an hour, it would enable us to travel for 13 hours and, averaging 20 kts, 260 nm. This was close to going from Qumerlai to Tuotuoheyan on our own fuel. But would the craft carry that amount, together with three people, kit, cameras and rations? What effect would the altitude of 4279 m (14,000 ft) have, and would our UK calculations of engine power performance prove correct and adequate? That day Neil and I tried her with ten full jerry cans aboard. She performed superbly, although fore-and-aft trim was a problem. We would have to pack the internal load carefully.

Everyone else – those who had not been transported up to 'survival camp' – were busy paring down their personal equipment or preparing essentials for the up-river thrust. Sam had returned early to install his doppler speed distance device. He had screwed the electronic box of

above Landslips challenge the Chinese road builders and dwarf our convoy in the earthquake region outside Denke.

left Qinghai Province is rightly described as China's Siberia.

above Once away from towns, these Chinese roads tested our initiative to the full.

below left Tibetan costumes at the annual festival brightened our delay at Xiwu.

below 61 roadworks in the space of 70 km nearly caused us to lose *Neste Enterprise* a dozen times.

above Lu Lóng Hú - Green Dragon Lake - must be one of the most beautiful places on earth.

above left Survival practice for many team members was at Fuel Dump A, between Base Camps 2 and 3.

above Mel prepares the test materials for the Loughborough/Chengdu Universities scientific project.

left Which way? Gwyn puzzles out the river from a vantage point above Fuel Dump B. Our map warned: 'Relief data unreliable'.

above Barren hills punctuated our journey up this desolate stretch of the river.

above *ICI River Rover* shows its amphibious capabilities at Qumerlei, Base Camp 2.

tricks on to *Neste Enterprise*'s bulkhead, and had built two antennae on the nose that looked like the eyes of a praying mantis. As he struggled to get the gadget to work properly, he realised that one small segment of the electronics was missing.

No one knew where it was. Perhaps it had accidentally been left in Chengdu. Its absence left the machine useless; all that work for all those weeks only to have it fail at its appointed time. It was a great disappointment to us all. Now we could not get accurate measurements of speed or distance, and, most of all, we would be unable to determine whether the Dam Qu contender was longer or shorter than the Geladandong source.

Rob returned, worn out after so much driving, with Andrew and David Johnson. The next day he was to attempt to locate and establish fuel dump B and the schedule was both demanding and exhausting for one driver. He asked me to refuel *Neste Enterprise*. As I turned the craft on the river to position her at the refuelling point, the engine inexplicably died. The loss of power was a nasty incident: the Deutz diesel engine on *Neste Enterprise* had been the most reliable item of equipment we had. Worse was to follow as we failed to get her going again properly even after refuelling. In the end we had to dump *Neste Enterprise* overnight on the far bank, and get *ICI River Rover* to ferry us across to the camp site in the dark by searchlight.

It snowed all night. On the Monday morning four engineers (including me) gave *Neste Enterprise* a thorough engine run. There seemed to be no problem, so both hovercraft returned to camp to refuel. A few blips on the rpm showed that all was not too well, but Rob decided there wasn't time to do any further investigations, and that he would accept the craft in that condition for the long run up river. If they needed more fuel they could refuel from dump A either on the way up or on return. On board were two drums of diesel and an empty one for dump B, together with Sarah, Mel, Gwyn, Mike, Kevin and Anne. Sarah would drop off at dump A, and the rest would search uncharted river to enjoy the adventure of establishing dump B, where they would pitch their tents overnight.

Anne was the engineer in charge of *Neste Enterprise*. She was very sound and thorough and, although her ICI job was in chemicals, she took to the engineering and maintenance of the large craft with enthusiasm and mounting confidence. No doubt her experience as commander of a Territorial Army Vehicle Recovery Unit helped her considerably in her expedition role. She opened an engineering log for the craft, and got the drivers to record the conditions of each journey coupled with the snags encountered. This log was to prove most valuable as the problems on *Neste Enterprise* were later analysed. Also this journey was to be Anne's swan-song. She and Colin had to return to the UK with the main group, and she had the privilege of going on this first sortie to dump B.

Those of us left at base camp – now a seriously depleted team – tidied up administrative necessities, like washing our filthy clothing and taking photographs. There was still plenty to do. We listened studiously to the radio on the hour every hour for news of *Neste Enterprise* up river.

The radios were a disappointment to us. We had hoped that the H/F wave band would enable the transmissions to get into the valleys and across the mountain tops. But the only success we had at Denke was seven miles contact with base, and less than that between hovercraft. From Base 2 onwards they were all but useless, and we never even had contact between the hovercraft when they were side by side on the river. Every now and then we would catch a very quiet snippet as Mike transmitted hourly. But it was never repeated. Unfortunately we had no radio expert with us who could confront the problem. Apparently earthing through the skirt and producing a radio ground plane was impossible. This was where we missed Chris, the ICI apprentice.

Rob came back in *Neste Enterprise* the next afternoon, bringing with him a bevy of people down from dump A, all of whom really enjoyed their survival exercise. There was, they said, very little to do except climb hills, get invited out by the Tibetan family, and think. The craft had made

228

excellent time down river, averaging 30 knots for three and a half hours. They had established fuel dump B, once again near to a herdsman's black-tented home. They were certain they could find it again, because they knew what the place looked like and had memorised the approaching and surrounding terrain, but they were as uncertain and confused about its exact map position as we all were about dump A. They had left Gwyn and Mel to stand guard and hoped we would be able to find them again. There was no way of communicating with them if *Neste Enterprise* became unserviceable, and the possibility of their having to walk to Tuotuoheyan was reasonably high: tough contingency plans had been established for just such an emergency.

Neste Enterprise was far from serviceable. That purring engine that we had praised so much had developed a sort of mechanical malaria, and the rpm fluctuated unpredictably throughout both the days that Rob was up river. He threw the craft at me and my fellow engineers, told us nicely to get it fixed, and wobbled off exhausted to his tent to sleep.

'What was the river like?' I caught him before he got there.

'Awful,' he replied. 'It's an ideal hovercraft river, but the constant search for the main stream became very difficult when the river was several miles wide. The water is fine, and there are no rapids. But the weaving around we did was both disorientating and disheartening. The multi-stream pattern we have up to dump A gets worse and more testing beyond it. I reckon we must have spent two hours going in a westerly sort of heading and, seemingly, getting nowhere at all. But I know where dump B is and can find it again.'

That seemed like encouraging news.

The engineers went right through the fuel system but found nothing untoward. They replaced each part with a new one anyway, and prayed we would have no more trouble with this engine disease.

The next day was the 'thrust up river'. Both craft were to go together. We would have an early lunch, having refuelled and packed everything we needed. It was difficult saying farewell to our buddies. I was really sad that not everyone

229

was able to share the rest of the adventure with us. I hate goodbyes anyway, but this was one of the hardest.

ICI River Rover set off first at 12.10 a.m. The plan was to get to dump A for the night. She was very heavy, with Steve, Neil and me plus kit and ten jerry cans of fuel on board. She took a little while to get over hump, and we had to use a handy shingle strip over on the other bank before she would accelerate over the critical drag wave. The day was filthy. Low cloud sank half-way down the hills and sleet and snow drizzled intermittently from its dripping base. The temperature was around freezing, and cumbrous clogs of ice visibly grew around the rearview mirrors. The wipers were continually sweeping away the slush, which would accumulate at the edges of the windscreen before dropping off to be sucked with a 'ping' into the whining propellers. We navigated as accurately as we could and Steve and I, who had done the journey to dump A before, pointed out landmarks to Neil as we sped by. We had decided to change over drivers every hour, and Neil kept us to our stint to the minute. All three of us were reluctant to get out of the driving seat, but knew it was good to get a regular break. We were all very excited: this was *ICI River Rover*'s big opportunity. Her earlier unserviceabilities made us (especially Mike) uncertain as to whether she would make the journey, and we were there to make sure she did. For the three hours before we needed to refuel, *ICI River Rover* hummed her way very sweetly up the river, going faster than *Neste Enterprise*, which had started some ten minutes later.

As we waited after refuelling for *Neste Enterprise* to go past us, we were peered at, from 30 cm, by a Tibetan man on a white horse. These rugged people were everywhere. At every place we stopped a Tibetan or two would gather and we often saw little faces under mops of black hair watching us over brows of hills. We came to the conclusion that, even in this vast empty wilderness of green-grey, treeless hills, there was nowhere one could be private.

Neil, the best theoretician among us, was determined to do better at navigating than the rest of us had done. But he fared no better. All of us had set our minds to navigate accurately up this huge river, but all of us singularly failed to do so. There was some key missing and we had no idea what it was.

We passed *Neste Enterprise* on the way to dump A and hunted for the fuel dump in the fog. Because the cloud came down to ground level, the positional parameters – the hills – were all missing and I thought we had reached it a dozen times before we did. I had heard that, to fill time, the 'survivors' had built a large 'A' out of black and white stones on a bank side, visible from the river. We peered through the gloom to find it. What we saw first were two red objects emerging out of the icy mist. They turned out to be red ICI jackets, attached to David Langley and Sarah. They had roughly calculated our arrival (adrift, in fact, by a couple of freezing hours), and were standing by the 'A', waving, hollering and jumping up and down – mobile ICI jackets! We were very glad to see each other. Our 'on river' plan had been to rest at dump A overnight and go on to dump B. But Mike looked at his watch: 3 p.m. Executive decision: we would go on to dump B and spend the night there. *ICI River Rover* OK? Yes! Good! *Neste Enterprise* OK? Yes! Even better!

We dismantled the tents and filled both craft with as much fuel from dump A as possible, then buried the barrels. We bade farewell to the in-house Tibetans, clambered into the craft and set off to locate the people we had deposited in some far-flung corner of nowhere.

Rob was right about the river. We had about ten miles of reasonable stream, and then the valley floor spread out-wards, and the river became more of a lake. But not a lake full of water: a semi-dried up lake that had its bottom showing through. It really was quite impossible to trace the main flow of water, and the river was often 2 km wide. *ICI River Rover* was behind *Neste Enterprise* for this phase, because Rob had been before and knew what he was doing. It was interesting to watch the antics of *Neste Enterprise* from the rear. She would be swinging round to port, then to starboard, and even towards us. She would sometimes stop

231

altogether and we often saw her below hump, with the spray billowing out past the driver's ears. We wondered what Rob was playing at, but, when we got to where he had been, we knew exactly what he had been doing and why. He was merely trying to find water to hover over, and was caught, again and again, in cul-de-sacs and narrow isthmuses and dead water. At this stage of our epic journey the safety and protection of the craft was paramount and neither of us felt inclined to travel over the shale and sandbars. Besides, the water was quite low and some of the land stood out far enough for us to want to avoid it anyway. Had we had the courage to go straight, or had there been more water in the river, we would not have spent so much time dancing tortuously around as we wound up this intriguing waterway.

But in *ICI River Rover* we had another twitch, and it involved navigation again. Just suppose dump A was where we thought it was, round about 94 10'E (see map at Appendix A). We now travelled through this water maze on a heading of 290° to 300°, just north of west, for one and three quarter hours. Taking a mean speed of 22 knots, we would have covered 30-40 nm. From dump A the map was unmistakably clear that, if we were hovering on the Yangtze, we should have been on a south-westerly heading, almost 90° port from the way we were going. The only bit of river that went north-west was the Yangtze tributary Pei-Lu-He, west of the 94'E. If we went on any further we would end up at the Tuotuoheyan road, but some 110 km north of the town we wanted to get to. The lack of an accurate speed measuring device seriously curtailed our ability to know where we were. But now, if in fact we had taken a wrong turning to the north-west, we were adding days on to our journey. Maybe the map was wrong? But I balked against that. I had had twenty years of flying in the RAF using those maps, and their accuracy was a byword and unquestionable. Maybe the river had changed course? Through hills? Hills are even more accurate than RAF maps: it is not a common occurrence for hills to change places. We were stumped. But at least it kept us keyed up and busy through this protracted journey.

When *Neste Enterprise* stopped for a five minute break, I went over to Mike and shared our concern with him. He casually shrugged his shoulders. Regardless of where we thought we were, the way we had come was the way they had gone before, and dump B was on this bit of river, 'just over there'. Mike had been in the RAF, like me. But he had been a physical education officer and not an aviator. I supposed I knew more about navigation than he did, but here he was the boss. We must go his way. I pocketed my anxiety and decided to get peace of mind from God, who is well able to handle what is outside my control and beyond my limitations.

The cloud slowly lifted as we headed north-west, into an observable stratocumulus, based about 2000 ft above us. It remained overcast with frequent snowstorms, and the sun never came through until very late in the evening. The valley was some 10 km wide, the hills forming a frame to our journey 5 km each side of the river.

Mike had said we would recognise the way to dump B by the gap in the hills to the south. These hills were more like a mountain range. Sure enough, the gap appeared intermittently through the snowstorms, and we zigzagged our way towards it, vaguely following *Neste Enterprise*'s duct, sticking out in the distance. It looked as if we were going down a waterfall. The broad band of river disappeared and became the horizon, just as it would do over a cascade. But when we got there, it did another disappearing act over the next hill. It felt as if we were going down river: very odd. Another hour on a south-easterly heading saw *Neste Enterprise* parked on the side, and the team scurrying up and down the hillside above her. At last, fuel dump B. We parked the smaller hovercraft behind her sister, and started to unload our kit for the overnight stay. The time was 9.30 p.m. and we had been on the river some ten and a half hours. We felt we had come hundreds of miles but later calculations indicated that we had travelled just 112 nm (205 km) according to the map. Gwyn and Mel had had a chance to work out where they thought we were and estimated we were around the 93 50'E longitude, or maybe

233

a few miles further on. If so, we had made slow progress. That position would put us some 50 nm (90 km) short of our planned dump B location. Too bad. But we were now half a day ahead of schedule, having progressed past dump A. The snow clouds gradually disappeared to give us a stunning golden sunset, which silhouetted both hovercraft in its reflected glory in the slow-lapping Yangtze water.

The nearly-full moon rose to oversee the pitching of the tents and listen to our companionable laughter over the acrid smell of hexamine cookers. A hot cup of coffee and Oxo-with-rice and curried chicken, both liberally sprinkled with sand, served to bring peace and satisfaction to us all before squeezing three-up into our tents to sleep.

Thursday was another eventful day. Come to think of it, all days on this expedition were eventful, challenging us with new difficulties and stretching us to our limits in order to achieve. The crystal-clear morning shimmered and sparkled as *ICI River Rover* lifted off, fully replenished, at 10 a.m. for Tuotuoheyan. The sun had banished any sign of frost, and all was well. The river snaked its way west through the hills of which dump B was a part. Mel and Gwyn had clambered up to the top of their parent mountain to view the landscape, and had said that, after the gorge, the river opened out again into the Fair Isle knitting pattern with which we had become all too familiar. We soon encountered it. The general direction was south-westerly through the multi-water system, although we did spend some time going west.

It was not long before Steve and Neil's sharp ears, finely attuned to the hum of *ICI River Rover*'s clatter, detected a foreign sound. It was definitely mechanical. We peered round from inside the craft and could see nothing untoward. But, for safety's sake, we decided to pull on to a convenient sandbar and have a closer look. To our amazement the two fan ducts, as well as the grill protecting the two thrust fans, were laden with ice 3 cm thick. The noise we had heard was the 'chink-chink-chink' of one of the blades clipping a piece of ice built up inside the duct.

234

But why was there ice? The day was warm and pleasant. There was no rain, sleet, snow or other precipitation. Where did the ice come from? Why so much? And why had we never had any before? We concluded that the temperature out of the sun was close to freezing, although it certainly did not feel like it. And the water must have come from the spray continually puffed up from under the hovercraft's rubber skirt. Impact with the fan structure would cause the super-cooled water droplets to freeze, much as it does with an aircraft flying through cloud below the freezing level.

In warm sunshine and shirt sleeves we pulled out the black-handled screwdriver and pliers and chipped and walloped the ice from the duct, blades, flow-straighteners and grill. It took some quarter of an hour to do, by which time *Neste Enterprise* had caught us up and sunk on to the same sandbar to offer inquisitive assistance. The well-placed exhausts in front of her propeller prevented a similar problem.

Half an hour's further travel saw us repeat the exercise, having accumulated just as much ice as before. We did this six times, the warning of ice build-up being sounded by a 'clunk-clunk-clunk' of a disconsolate fan blade. It stopped at 4 p.m. when, it seemed, the temperature rose sufficiently for the spray to pass through without freezing.

One of the scientific experiments we were undertaking was the efficiency of the 'Verton' fan blades. Verton was a new ICI product that was supposed to be better than its predecessors, and we were the guinea-pigs to see if this was true. It was. We had no trouble whatsoever with the blades, and none snapped or were broken on this expedition, despite the hammering and the extremes of temperature they were given. Just as good was the noise: the pitch from the blades was lower and the decibels less, making travel in *ICI River Rover* far more comfortable and acceptable than before.

One of our stops to de-ice was with *Neste Enterprise*. The team had brewed up a very welcome cup of coffee for us. Mike suggested that we lead off just in case we needed to stop again.

235

Before us was another mountain range, its snowy peaks and icing-sugar slopes spreading both east and west. There was a gap in one of them in the distance and, as we approached it, it became more and more certain that the river was imperceptibly dragging us in that direction. It was not a big gap. But one by one the stray watercourses wove themselves into one main stream and the river became whole again. As we drew close to the mountain range, we passed, on the rise to our right, a cacophony of Tibetan prayer flags, heralding either an important and holy location or a place where a number of people had died. Ominous.

Neste Enterprise was by now well out of sight behind, because we were in the faster craft. We rounded the bend to be confronted, to our dismay, with a rapid. Though not desperately large, it spread right across the river. I was driving, and all three of us agreed to choose the route to the right. Full power. We hit the waves fast and went up the rapid successfully – until the very end. There we stabilised. *Neste Enterprise* sailed past us, with the crew's looks masterfully expressing 'What's the matter?' I held the throttle fully open and jiggled the controls gingerly. But we fell below hump, and the princess just would not go any further. Sadly I turned her round to try and scoot off down rapid to take her over hump. But no sir! After that she just would not go over hump, and there were no convenient sandbars over which we could accelerate. We pulled in to the side to debate what to do. The shore was sandy but steep. Steve, the heaviest of us, got out to lighten the load. We tried to put the nose higher on the bank and slide off over hump. Steve pulling and pushing for all he was worth. It was no good. We tried and failed with this pattern a dozen times. *Neste Enterprise* had mastered the rapid at her first attempt. Seeing our predicament, Rob stopped her on a nice, flattish sandbar further up. Mike and Gwyn walked down to see us. They helped Steve push and pull the craft, but still without success. Besides, time spent at full throttle and getting nowhere was drinking the petrol alarmingly.

Eventually Mike suggested that we lighten the load. There was no alternative. We took out our rucksacks and untied the full jerry cans from *ICI River Rover*'s sides. We left two on the front to give us correct trim. The team who had walked down to see what was up, carried these loads back to *Neste Enterprise*.

'Do you know there is another rapid further up?' Mike asked.

'No,' was our reply. We were surprised.

'It's worse than this one,' Mike said, 'In fact it's a real challenge. You'll need to come and look at it. As soon as you've got over this one, park on *Neste*'s sandbank and then come and see. There are some very bad rocks and standing waves sticking out on the left-hand side.'

The thought of another rapid was not pleasant, particularly when we could not easily get up this one. Neil and I set off again in our lightened craft, downstream. We stuck the nose on as much of the sandbank as we could, but it did not work. Going out into the main river and finding a patch of bumbly water going downhill, *ICI River Rover* at last struggled over hump. The hump problem really is a very big one for hovercraft, and accentuated here by the extreme altitude. Having got her going, I turned gingerly round in the river, taking as wide an arc as we could to keep her over hump. Rob had gone up the left-hand side, so we decided to do the same. Taking it close to the shore, and going at it fast, we bounced over the big breakers and struggled over the top. We were very relieved. But we were not finished. A few metres beyond, *ICI River Rover* could no longer cope and fell below hump again. I had not given her a long enough run-up, and her momentum was killed by the rapid. But at least we were over the top. We struggled across the river to the team side, where there was no sandbar besides *Neste*'s, 50 m further up. The princess was below hump and straining to go up river. Spray blew over everywhere and everyone. Trim, which was the main cause of her going below hump, was heavily tail down, and more and more water was collecting in the rear skirt as the spray was blown up sideways. We pushed open the cabin, which went forwards, so that it was on its limits and sticking precariously 2 metres over the bow. Neil and

237

I spread-eagled ourselves on the bow, while I steered, with the rudder only, through my knees. That hardly worked. We made progress, but very slowly. All our equipment inside got wetter and wetter with the cabin open, and fuel was getting low. We had half a dozen attempts at this hazardous method of driving and as many rests by the riverside on some aggressive hunk of rock. Mike suggested I came out and viewed the next rapid, while Neil and Steve had a go at getting the craft close to *Neste Enterprise*. I was glad to do so. They, behind me, made progress in the only way possible, at about 2 km an hour, with an enormous struggle, a lot of spray and at maximum fuel consumption.

The next rapid certainly was difficult. It was divided roughly into three sections, and two halves. Our half was certainly the quieter bit of water, but there were many rocks, higher than *ICI River Rover* could accommodate, jutting out from the foam. The other half, where vicious rocks sprang out from the boiling water, was out of the question for *ICI River Rover* at that altitude (4390 m; 14,400 ft). The far half of the river was a total non-starter.

But the near half . . . ?

Mike and I climbed the edge of the gorge that leaned oppressively over the river. It always looks easier from above, and yes, there was a route we could take. Provided we got over hump (a dominant factor), we could skirt on some smoothish water right by the rock edge initially. The rougher water further towards the centre of the river was not, in itself, too difficult, but entering it would slow the craft down and strip away momentum for section 2.

I turned to Mike. 'My driving would need to be very accurate to keep away from the rough and drive on the smooth water, and I will have to hype up to razor sharpness for it. The available gap between roughish water and rocks seems to be only 0.3 m wider than *ICI River Rover* herself. Tricky. Wickedly tricky!'

Mike nodded. I continued: 'Then I will have to cut inside the main flow, fly over a rock 6 inches high (0.15 m), wiggle between two more sets of rocks, and turn back into the mainstream, keeping to the right. That will be section 3.

238

The waves are high there, and it won't be easy – indeed, not possible – to judge from here the best path to take to the top of the rapid. I will have to judge that as I come to it. Section 3 is a long, difficult climb through rough water. It will only be possible if I am able to maintain speed and momentum over sections 1 and 2.'

Mike went further up river to see if there were any more rapids and returned to report that there was nothing visible, but that there was a sandbank on the other side on to which we could rest if we got through the rapid.

I was subdued as I went back to Rob and Steve, and asked if we could pray together about it. The alternative prospects were unmentionable – that the Yangtze had conquered us instead of us conquering her, that we would fail altogether in our task, that we would have to retrace our steps back to Qumerlai, or that *ICI River Rover* would be left and *Neste Enterprise* plough on alone to Tuotuoheyan and then to the source. *ICI River Rover* and crew's adventure would be over. I would need all the dexterity in the world to get up this one impossible rapid and for that I required supernatural skill, collected concentration and perfect peace: all beyond my natural gifting. We put full jerry cans of fuel on *ICI River Rover*'s nose to keep her in trim. We asked Rob to move *Neste Enterprise* further down river on our runway of sand; we needed the maximum take-off distance to get over hump and go straight for the rapid. There was no place to get out into the river to accelerate any faster.

Mercifully the sandbank was shelved at a small angle, and we should be able to continue to poke the nose up it as we moved off, keeping the front of the craft over sand for as long as possible to get her over hump. (Hovercraft always fall downhill, so it is a bit of a trick to stop it happening on a slope.)

All was ready. Neil and I clambered into the craft. Although I was driving (my privilege) we were both in this together – a kind of welded partnership that thinks, feels, talks and acts as one person. It was unique.

Our journey up that rapid ran exactly according to plan. All the detailed thinking and preparation for an adventure of this sort is over in one short minute. The craft accelerated sweetly to over-hump speed on the sand, and we entered the river going well. Going round the bend was very tricky: too much speed and not enough elevon would crash us into the rocks to the right. Too little speed would stop us getting up the hill. Too vicious an elevon control would kill the speed as well. All hovercraft driving is 'seat of the pants' – a knowledge of what the craft can and cannot do, born out of experience in the machine itself. Speed assessment is purely instinctive, and the turning circle and speed combination entirely a matter of time in the driver's seat getting hands-on know-how. The first section was passed without incident, and the calmer water enabled *ICI River Rover* at least to maintain her forward momentum, if not actually increase it. I jabbed the right elevon to steer her through the narrow channel between the rocks. The 6 inch rock, over which we flew, mercifully presented no problems.

Then we hit the rougher water at the top. It is very difficult to assess which is the better path to take in a rapid. I selected a pathway that was just right of centre: it looked by far the smoothest I could see.

'To the right, to the right,' shouted Neil. I glanced right and could not see anywhere where the waves were lower and could give us any greater chance of success.

'No, no!' I responded, 'we'll go up there,' and I pointed to the bit I saw was best.

Waves in a rapid are sometimes a bit like the Loch Ness Monster's coils: there one moment and gone the next. And then appearing again from nowhere. It was like that in this rapid. Big waves started to kill our speed, and the incline began to pull us back. I struggled to steer the craft through the nicest of the water, but it was extremely hard: troughs in the water would suddenly appear, followed by a huge wave up which we had to climb. I glanced left and right to see if there was a way out; *ICI River Rover* was getting close to hump speed and to go below that would be disaster. I realised, in my glance, that the path to the right would certainly have been the best, as Neil had suggested. Just as quickly I realised that it had been hidden from my sight

240

by the rearview mirror when Neil pointed it out. Too late: we were in the middle and struggling.

To this day I do not know just how *ICI River Rover* reached the top of that rapid. One moment we were fighting for every knot of speed and losing it. The next moment we were over the top, into gentler water, and the little princess was beginning to accelerate away. Neil and I looked at one another in relief and burst out laughing. We'd made it! But only by the skin of our teeth. We certainly didn't want to have to give that one another bash. We continued up river and rounded the bend to the left. There was, indeed, no other sandbank but the one Mike had told us about earlier. It was on the wrong side, but we flew gladly up its little hump, leaving room for *Neste Enterprise* behind, and sighed to a standstill.

It was gone 2.30 p.m. and Neil and I pulled out a hidden packet of compo rations and chomped dried biscuits and chicken pâté to await the arrival of the larger craft. We were both desperately thirsty, and I tried to filter some of the brackish, frothy, muddy sand-water. It looked quite disgusting, and we just hoped that the filter system was man enough to handle such pollution.

The gorge was squeezed by steep edges of barren rock, grey-black and brown in the afternoon sunlight. Barely a blade of grass could force its pathetic way through the granite and past the boulders. It was a severe and forbidding area uninhabited and uninhabitable. Sparse snow covered the round or jagged tops as we looked back down river, but a great deal more snow lay on the crags that stuck up behind the immediate mountainside. The river had forced its way through this narrow pass in this range of hills, and had eroded what little soil had once been there. Endless showers of rain or snow throughout the long winter months had done the same to the rest of the hills, and now only stark, barren rock painted the landscape with its austere colours and threatening appearance.

Neil and I waited patiently for *Neste Enterprise* to come up behind us. I had been hoping to get some photographs of her in the rapid, but there was no way on our side of

241

the river to walk past the granite cliffs that bit straight into the water.

Rob, meanwhile, had unloaded as much equipment as the team could carry and asked them to walk by the riverside to a location beyond the rough water, where he hoped to pick them up later. *Neste Enterprise*, with her greater length and power, was able to mount higher waves than *ICI River Rover*. This was vital because her lack of manoeuvrability and greater width precluded her going up the path we had taken. But Rob had to stick to the same side of the river – the right-hand – because the left was appallingly dangerous. So *Neste Enterprise* had to travel up the rapid through heavy water all the way.

He lifted off, just as we had done, using the sand runway, which enabled him to crank up a respectable speed before hitting the cascade. The craft motored sweetly up section 1, and then hit section 2 where the water frothed and boiled in a cauldron of spray and waves. It came as a relief to Neil and me that even *Neste Enterprise* struggled over that one. In fact we had done better than Rob because as *Neste Enterprise* topped the hill she fell below hump. Rob, pressurising the throbbing craft at full power, managed to force her through the heavy, turbulent waves into the more moderate waters beyond. But from then on, well below the critical hump speed, she strained her way at 3 knots, blowing spray out from her billowing sides to where we were resting *ICI River Rover*, taking 20 minutes to do this. At least we were all up, and no damage had been done. Yet the rapids had eaten away precious time and fuel. We must have taken some three hours to negotiate the white water, and *ICI River Rover*, particularly, had swigged two hours' extra fuel trying to make way below hump at full throttle.

The balance of the team made their way slowly up the far bank, picking their path carefully and breathlessly through the boulders strewn haphazardly at the foot of the cliff. Neil and I transferred all our kit and jerry cans back from the queen to the princess and released *Neste Enterprise* to go across the river to fetch the hikers.

At 3.30 p.m. we were on our way again, *ICI River Rover* leading. We sat in trepidation as we waited for another rapid round each bend. But we waited in vain. We were blessed by their absence. The mountainsides by the river, however, grew in ugliness. Giant outcrops of rock, poking up like gargantuan fingers from the landslide beds on the hillside, leered menacingly over the edge of the river, threatening at any time to collapse upon us in an avalanche of rock. Whole hands of fingers, silhouetted criss-cross against the blue sky as we looked up at them, were black and blue with age and rusted with brown strands of iron, forming a formidable, and in its own way, beautiful intrusion into our safety and peace.

Two tributaries came down from the snow-capped peaks into the muddy waters of the Chang Jiang as glaciers. Solid ice clasped the slopes from the silty river-edge up the little valleys, clawing its way round the bends and out of sight.

The hills gradually fell back as the two craft twisted and turned through the gorge, taking away their fears and threats and gradually accumulating mossy grass. The darkness was over; we were moving out into fresh air again, into the light. The gorge was about 11 nm (20 km) long, but we only knew that in retrospect when we later discovered where we were. At the time I thought our position was around 93′E; only a couple of hours away from Tuotuoheyan.

The terrain into which we emerged was flat and broad, a sort of endless plain terminating in the shimmering, misty distance in fierce, jagged, snow-covered mountain peaks. Getting good photographs of either craft from the other was difficult: there were few outstanding features and no back-drop by which distance or size could be demonstrated. Oh, for a helicopter! A vertical view, showing the intertwining hieroglyphics of the complex pattern of river paths, as inde-cipherable and enigmatic as the ancient Chinese script itself, would have been magnificent. The river seldom skirted the base of any hills, but mostly took its vagrant path out in the plain. We saw no yaks and no other animals. The only things we saw were pairs or flocks of swan geese, bean geese and bar-headed geese, dolled up for courtship in this

243

June springtime. I later discovered that the swan goose is a very rare bird, and it was a privilege to have seen it.

The river went west. That tied up with our map, all right. But then it went on. And on. Not just one hour of wriggling through tangled knitting, not two. Four hours later we were still going west, and no nearer Tuotuoheyan. *Neste Enterprise* was taking the southerly portion of the river and we were to the north, out of sight. The evening started to close in, and in *ICI River Rover* we found ourselves virtually on a lake, stretching as far as the eye could see. We could not identify it on the map, particularly as it was part of the river, unless it was the patch just to the east of Tuotuoheyan. If so, then a river direction north of north-west (which was what the map demanded) was just not there. We looked west where the river/lake continued into the distance with no hills, and thought it could well be Tuotuoheyan.

But we pointed south to join up with *Neste Enterprise*, running over spits of land and many sandbanks. Going up and down the river was difficult enough. Going across it was formidable. The top of *Neste*'s duct soon became visible, lit up by the gold of the setting sun. She had stopped. Mike had decided to camp by the riverside. They had actually found an island of land, about 6 cm above the racing river's edge, covered with grass. I remembered when, in Peru in 1982, we had found a similar flat of sand to camp for the night, only to be swamped by midnight. A very small rise in water level would do the same for us here and I wondered if it was quite wise. Anyway, it was beautiful. Both hovercraft could travel to it with ease, and we had no trouble pitching our tents on flat ground. The only trouble we did have was getting our matches to light the hexistoves in the gentle evening breeze that fell down from the hill behind us.

To the west was a solo round-topped hill, and just north of that was open ground (our lake) into which the golden sun sank with yellow, orange and green scene changes. A single cloud, daintily shedding snow, was silhouetted like a black powder puff in the sky. And high above it was a wild streak of curly-tipped cirrus, mirroring the magic of changing colour orchestrated by the sinking sun. As the

244

sun went down in front of us, the full moon, silver and regal, rose over the pointed rim of the hill behind us. We all felt like staying round the campfire and telling stories; the night had that kind of feel about it. But we retired to our little red or yellow mushrooms by 10.30 p.m., exhausted.

It was Friday morning, day 3 of our momentous journey to the source of the Yangtze. We had not found Tuotuoheyan yet. When we eventually did, we would then have to try for the source, 160 nm further beyond. We still had a long way to go and a lot of travelling to do.

My guess was that the river would go beyond the lake. So I anticipated our moving to the north of our round-topped hill, now green in the rising red of dawn and sparkling with the hard frost that condensed our breath as we broke camp. Then we would go across the lake and on to Tuotuoheyan, which I thought to be 'just there'.

Alas no. The river that ran past our island was deep and fast-flowing – obviously the main stream. We followed it. To my amazement it started to flow left, to the south, and we went round the corner of the hill that had backed on to our camp. The water remained one, and it was taking us through an open gorge. The hillsides were grassy and fell away, giving a light sunny aspect to the water, which burbled delightfully as it turned slowly through the hills. Behind the river, on both sides, the odd snowy peak poked up, but not nearly as many as in the 'rapid gorge'. We did not expect a rapid in this confine; it did not have that feel about it. And we were right. Some 5 nm (9 km) later we came out into a plain.

In the far distance to the south some lowish hills, 150-300 m high (500-1000 ft) butted against the skyline. There was nothing significant about them, but their lower slopes would probably have stopped the river going their way. The river, given the freedom of space, chose to drift in a capricious and unpredictable manner, hindering any decent progress by hiding its main flow in a conjuring trick of confluences. Still perplexed and bewildered by our uncertain position, Rob took a sun-shot with the sextant while waiting for us. He had to choose a position from which to

245

start, and he guessed a latitude and longitude. The shot was 5.5 nm from his guess. It was the first time we had any idea of where we actually were. It put us on the river at 92 58′E. It could, of course, be anything up to 10 nm out; but it was at least better than anything we had had since leaving Base 2 at Qumerlai.

We started to go west. That was good. We were itching to go north-north-west because we knew we had to cover at least 12 map nm (18 km) in that direction before reaching our Base 3, Tuotuoheyan. I was still believing the map, although every indication was nonsensical. The map could not be that stupid: it had never been before. We still did not know what the missing key was. From a westerly direction we went south-west. Through the meandering river, we just flogged on and on going west or south-west and even south for a total of three hours. Wouldn't we ever go north? Where was this place Tuotuoheyan anyway? Perhaps that did not exist either, despite the assurances of all the other Yangtze source adventurers. Ah, well . . . !

I started to twitch over another issue. The continuous operation of *ICI River Rover* at full throttle at the rapid had burnt a lot of precious petrol. We were definitely down. How much longer to go? I took out my calculator. At 6 gallons an hour, how many more hours could we travel before the craft packed up and we had to abandon it by the waterside and walk, who knows where, in who knows what direction for who knows how long? It was a question of survival.

I worked out that we had travelled about seven hours on the river from dump B. It would take us about five and a half hours to return, bearing in mind our earlier experience of travelling faster down river. That would need 35.75 gallons of petrol: dump B was our only known source of fuel, and if we needed some that was where we needed to go. After all, Tuotuoheyan seemed as mythical as the Chinese dragon itself. Had Jeremy and Duncan arrived there at all? To be sure, *ICI River Rover*'s highly-tuned Renault 21 turbo engine could no more run on the 70 octane Chinese petrol than water. She had to run on our 95 octane leaded fuel or she just would not operate. We were nearing a sticky place.

We reached it. In aviation circles it is called the 'point of no return'. It is the place where you are committed to go on when there is not enough fuel to get back to the place of departure. We carried on. We watched a grey wolf swimming across the river; he gave us some light relief.

Shortly afterwards, *Neste Enterprise* stopped by the water's edge. There was not an increase of hills but an increase of bank and the water was restrained into single flow. Mike had stopped because he had spotted a Tibetan tent about 50 m inland. We had a Chinese speaker with us, Mr Lee, the TV cameraman. He was the only one. His English was dreadful but he had become pretty slick at sign language. *ICI River Rover* stopped too, and a group of us accompanied Mike, John and Mr Lee to the tent.

Along the ground between them and the river were ropes of plaited yak hair. We had learnt that they were for tethering the yaks overnight. The Tibetans wove other ropes round the yak necks, put rings on them, then attached the rings to these dozen or so lengths of rope for night-time security. At this time of the day, of course, the yaks were out grazing the hills under the watchful eye of the man of the house. A fierce sheep dog, prettily decorated with colourful strands of wool, was racing round a stake firmly fixed into the ground, and attached by a substantial chain. The hound was leathering and lathering the atmosphere with non-stop barks, snarls and growls.

Mamma and junior came out to see what all the palaver was about. I sensed she felt fairly vulnerable on seeing one Chinese and umpteen white foreigners advancing on her, bizarrely dressed to the throat in red and blue Gortex jackets, salopettes and dark glasses. It must have seemed like an invasion from Mars, particularly as we were accompanied by noisy vehicles that drove over land as well as water. The contrast in cultures could not have been greater nor, for her, more threatening. Her husband was up in the hills somewhere and could offer her no protection if we turned out to be hostile or extra-terrestrial.

247

'Yangtze?' John waved his arms at Mr Lee, trying to indicate he wanted him to ask Mamma whether we were on the right river or not. It was a basic parameter to verify, crucial, as much as anything else, to our peace of mind.

It really did take quite a long time to establish even this simple bit of information. We were not quite sure if John's semaphore was unwholesome or whether Mr Lee had actually attended the same semaphore course. Moreover it seemed that Mamma's Chinese was not the same as Mr Lee's. Anyway it was dubious, certainly pidgin.

It eventually came back to us that, yes, this was the Yangtze. 'Tuotuoheyan?' We were really quite concerned to know whether our destination was up river or down.

The lady pointed in a vague direction up river. That was a real relief. It *seemed* to be reliable information at the time, not least because what she told us brought the peace of mind we were so eagerly seeking.

We thanked her for her assistance, helped ourselves to a liberal quantity of video on and in her home, and bribed junior with a handful of boiled sweets. We departed, leaving junior struggling with the sweet papers, and not quite understanding why the goodies didn't taste as great as they looked. I contemplated telling him how to unwrap them, but by then we had exhausted our communication reserves.

I said to Mike, 'I'm not particularly bothered by it, but *ICI River Rover* has passed the point of no return.'

'What do you mean?' he asked.

'We do not have enough fuel to get us back to dump B. We are committed to going on, wherever it takes us.'

'It sounds like another step of faith,' he replied, grinning. 'Just like the whole of this project. Come to think of it, faith and persistence have been the hallmark of all three hovercraft expeditions. Let's go!'

We went.

The single flow continued for a while and *ICI River Rover* led the way. Bewildered by a T junction in the river, we went left. The section we went up was brilliant hovering for *ICI River Rover* and great fun for Steve, who was driving. It turned and twisted like a butterfly trying to escape from a thrush, with many glistening cascades increasing our delight. We wondered how *Neste Enterprise* was coping. It was quite a wide river, but had a very different pattern from the river we had been on. I started to get a gut feeling that we had made a mistake. It increased when the river turned south and stayed south. After 20 minutes we stopped. I asked Steve to switch off the engine and see if we could hear *Neste Enterprise*. All was silent. I said we would wait for five minutes to see if the queen came our way, but after two minutes we agreed to go back down again.

We reached the T junction and turned left. The water here was like the old river so we persevered and went up it. It too went south-west. But, gut-wise, it felt better. There was no sign of *Neste Enterprise*. They had seen us go up the tributary and decided that it would cost too much in fuel and time to go after us. If they pressed on to Tuotuoheyan, they could (hopefully) refuel there and come back and look for us, stranded in the wilderness, out of petrol and ideas.

The terrain changed again. The hills that stood around the Tibetan family had long gone and we were in a wide, horizonless plain. We were amazed to see a metre of ice sitting, unmelted, on the sandbanks skidding by. The waterways, of course, were not frozen. But we found ourselves manoeuvring through banks of ice, being very careful not to let it touch the skirt. A tear or rip in the skirt, killing the hover cushion, was an ugly thought.

Other signs of life appeared. A herd of horses pawed and snorted by the riverside, some drinking. They swished their tails and headed off at a gallop at the sound of the hovercraft. None of us could see a herdsman or any human life at all. We presumed that the horses were wild. Pairs and flocks of nesting geese continued to accompany our passage, augmented by the odd tern and black-headed gull. But nothing that might encourage us to believe we could be approaching a human settlement.

At 3.45 p.m. as we were screwing through the ice fields, we saw on the horizon a black square object. Yaks look like that sometimes and we had seen others that turned out to be a tent or even nothing. We kept our eye on it, interested but not impressed.

'There's another,' called Neil.

'Isn't that something else too?' Steve pointed over the rudder control. No one could quite identify what we had spotted for a while.

'Lorries,' suddenly Neil spoke up.

'How do you know?' I queried from the back seat.

'They're moving.'

They certainly were. Our hearts rose within us. Tuotuo-heyan at last? We drew closer, straining to see what could be seen through the reflection off the water and refraction through the shimmering haze. A line with spikes underneath. Could this be the bridge? Lorries, certainly. What a relief! What a welcome sight!

As we gradually drew nearer and items could be better identified, we saw *Neste Enterprise* parked by a raised roadside near the northern end of what was now obviously a bridge. We were three-quarters of an hour behind her. She was surrounded by people. If this was Tuotuoheyan, it was much smaller than I had imagined it to be. There were about four housetops over the raised road on the other side. Otherwise there was a bridge, and that seemed to be all.

We skidded through the water and over the last remaining sand dunes to park behind *Neste Enterprise*. We clambered out, glad to walk and have a stretch. We were even more pleased to have arrived at Base 3. The time was 4.30 p.m.

9

Achievement!

He is no fool
Who gives what he cannot keep
To gain what he cannot lose.
                              (Jim Elliott)

'We're in trouble,' Mike said, as I strolled smilingly up to
him. He had been there for some while and had got the
situation well under control.

'What trouble?' I asked, dismayed.

'This is not Tuotuoheyan,' he said.

'Not Tuotuoheyan . . . ? But the bridge. The lorries.' My
voice trailed off unbelievingly, my mind totally confused.

'No. It seems that we are some 40 km south of Tuotuoheyan. We've obviously missed the river junction to the
north, and come down here.'

'What are we going to do?' I had trouble catching up with
all the information that Mike had been able to assimilate
while awaiting our arrival.

'The good news is that this is the main arterial highway
from Xining to Lhasa through Golmud. The Chinese have
tarred it and it's beautiful. In fact we've hit the only other
bridge on this road in 2000 km. There's just this one and
the one at Tuotuoheyan.'

'Wow!' I rejoined, 'If that isn't the grace of God . . . We
could have gone on to any bit of river, never found this road,
and never got near either bridge. When our fuel ran out, we
could have been left anywhere in this empty wilderness,
with no one to help and not knowing where to go.'

251

'Too right,' Mike said. 'It's quite incredible. I don't know how we missed the river to the north, but having missed it, we couldn't possibly have arrived at a better place.'

'What have you been able to fix up?'

'Well, you can see the lorries. Chinese curiosity is too fierce for any driver to miss an incident like this. They've all stopped to look. And what we did was simply go round the drivers and hire an available lorry to go into Tuotuoheyan for us to pick up some fuel. Two drums of diesel and one of petrol.'

'Brilliant,' I said. 'Who's going and what fuel?'

'Gwyn and John Whatmore and Mr Lee. Mr Lee will take film of it all and will act as their interpreter. I've asked Gwyn to find Duncan and Jeremy, provided they've arrived, and to get our own fuel down to us. Now that we know where we are, we should be able to make Tuotuoheyan tomorrow. In fact they're just about off now.'

I looked up to see our three stalwarts climbing on to the back of a lorry, and cheerily waving at the rest of us as they shot off on their own personal adventures. The driver, delighted to help out in a crisis, all the more for the unexpected cash it brought, waved enthusiastically from his cab, covered us all in black diesel smoke, and zoomed up the road into the northern distance. We wished them godspeed.

I looked at the road and then at the bridge. The road was beautifully made and tarred to the very edges. It was clearly an important route. Marks on the surface showed that tanks passed that way. The bridge was well constructed and the stonework professionally pointed. It was somewhat low for *Neste Enterprise* to pass underneath, but it was a credit to the Chinese civil engineers. This 2100 km stretch of road from Xining to Lhasa was opened on 25 December 1954 and was still in very good condition. We assumed that it was an important military necessity.

I went back to *ICI River Rover* and told Steve and Neil the situation. There was little to do but wait. It seemed a good time to relax and get some food down. We set up the hexi burners by the side of the hovercraft. There was

252

no 'downwind' side to afford shelter as the wind motored horizontally across the plain, totally unimpeded, and the stoves took perseverance to light. While the water was boiling I checked my map, which was now in pieces and nearing extinction. This bridge was indeed marked on it. I measured 42 km to Tuotuoheyan. At last we knew exactly where we were, a feature that had been manifestly absent since we began this epic journey three days earlier.

The fuel took longer to come than we wished. But many of the team took the opportunity to eat, rest and wash; Mel even had a strip-down bath, difficult because the river banks were not at all high and there was no other cover. Some dozed. Some chatted untranslatably to Chinese and Tibetan onlookers. We just waited. Rob decided not to waste time, and took a sun shot with the sextant. It came out 2.25 nm from the bridge. That was a good confirmation that the sextant was AOK.

At around 8 p.m. an army (PLA) truck arrived, turned off the road, and started to come down the sandy bank towards the hovercraft. Out of it stepped Tang, our young Chinese scientific student. It was so good to see him. He explained that, yes, this was our fuel. Yes, Jeremy and Duncan were in Tuotuoheyan and had been there three days. Certainly, this was a PLA truck: it had been loaned to us free to get us out of our crisis, in contrast to our expensive encounters with vehicles nearer Chengdu. And yes, it was now very definitely stuck in the sand and unable to move.

We moved in to help with all our western know-how, and did no better than the Chinese lad who was driving. Shortly after a few skidded slides down the incline, a squad of soldiers turned up. The senior man was a four-star general and, it was said, the PLA commander for Qinghai. Heavy stuff. A number of three-pip and two-pip officers accompanied him, most of whom spoke English. Some of the young officers were very sharp indeed. These men were from one of the top tank regiments in China. We wondered what restraints they might impose on us. But none appeared. They had clearly not been privy to any of the tortuous negotiations that had taken place prior to our departure from Chengdu, so they came to us gladly, delightedly and with absorbing interest. One of the clever young officers was able to tell us in beautiful English all about our British Centurion and Challenger tanks – their performance, speed, capacity and fire control system. The latter was classified information. It was quite alarming.

We decided to roll the barrels of fuel down to the hovercraft, and thankfully replenished both. Then we went back to the stuck truck, which had now become the centre of attention for the PLA. It was even more important to the general than the five-minute ride in the hovercraft that we offered him.

Numerous suggestions from different people produced more skidding and zero success. My proposal was to use a bevy of onlooking lorries to tow the distressed one out. This was rejected as a viable solution because it entailed loss of face: first, by admitting that the PLA had made a 'horlicks' at all; second because they were unable to solve the problem using their own vast resources. You will probably never guess what their eventual solution was: they decided to send a jeep back to the PLA base at Tuotuoheyan, and dispatch a tank to pull it out! We left them to it.

At 8.45 p.m. we departed. We needed to go as far back down river as we could to find the place where the Yangtze went north. The river we were on was, according to my map, the Mu-Lu-Wu-Su-He, and would be the route we could have taken to find the Dam Qu source of the Yangtze. We fancied coming back to that spot, but did not know whether we could; time was our biggest enemy. This diversion did not help at all. We were prepared to travel by night. That was to be a new experience for all of us, and we anticipated it, in the queer river knitting, with trepidation.

ICI River Rover led, and both craft made excellent progress. The princess stopped at 9.45 p.m. allowing Mike to take the lead and make all executive decisions. We switched on the searchlights in both craft, trying to pick our way between the sandbanks and wiggle randomly down the vague patches of water as they reflected the starlight above. We hoped for a moon, and knew one was around. But at

254

10.30 p.m. it became obvious that progress was dangerous to the safety of both craft and Mike found a grassy bank under a long rockface on which to rest the team for the night. The moon came up with the tents, but it was too low and too late for us to make use of it that night. We fell asleep, exhausted, under its silver glimmer.

The geese woke us in the morning, flying on and off the cliff behind the camp. A very hard frost had coated craft, grass and tents with ice. Mike got us up at 7.30 and had lit a fire before our water bottles had managed to filter through to full. I had forgotten by now how many days late we were, but this was now Saturday, 9 June.

ICI River Rover's engine boiled very quickly after starting. The temperature was −10°C. Why it should boil was yet another puzzle, as the coolant was filled with antifreeze. The sun's heat seemed to clear the blockage, and we were off at 9.17 a.m.

The Satnav in *Neste Enterprise* confirmed our position – very close to the place where the Yangtze came in to the Dam Qu from the north. Was the equipment working again? None of us could understand how we had missed the location on the way up. Even though we did not know where we had been, we had stuck to the northern edge of the river like glue. There just hadn't been a waterway that we could see.

Neste Enterprise went to the left (north) of all the water we were in. Rob was most unhappy as he had to drive through gaps no wider than the craft itself, and round bends that were impossible for him to negotiate. They often went up the bank, below hump and over the land. *ICI River Rover* did better, but it was still pretty difficult for her. Mike was determined to find this waterway that led to Tuotuoheyan, however difficult it was.

Neste Enterprise went left round the corner and stopped. We caught her up. There was a stream coming from the west, just behind the hill that had backed on to our overnight camp. What did we think?

It could not be the Yangtze: its width and lack of water convinced us that, at best, it was a little rivulet that ran into the main flow. But Mike was determined to give it a go. Everyone else disagreed with him, thought it was a waste of time, and said so. He made a unilateral decision. *Neste Enterprise* would go up the channel and, if the water did not peter out, then he would signal with a flare for *ICI River Rover* to follow.

They set off, and disappeared round a bend going south. We all knew it was wrong. The river we wanted needed to go west then north-west. We waited for some 20 minutes. There was no sign of a flare. But suddenly *Neste Enterprise* came into sight. She appeared round the bend, with Jim on her deck. We looked through the monocular: he was definitely beckoning us to follow. We started the engine and followed. All of us were convinced that it was stupidity.

The river wound slowly south, then broke up into the same sort of fragments we had been well used to. But it was so shallow and contained such little water that there was no such thing as a main flow. It was impossible to stop going over spits of land and, after a while, we gave up trying. All we could do was avoid those bits of land that had a bank higher than 15 cm. Surely this was all another terrible waste of precious time?

To give Mike some credit, the water did continue to flow. For much of the way there was hardly any. But it still came down the hill, which rose quite steeply before us. And, after the first hour went by, the direction turned north-west, which was exactly where we wanted to go. We gave Mike more credit.

It was beautiful hovercraft country and great fun to drive. It was, however, a laborious task of twisting and turning every ten seconds, and took both time and fuel.

We eventually gave in, and handed Mike total credit. It led to Tuotuoheyan. Three hours later blocks of houses appeared on the horizon, and we were soon alongside the bank just below the PLA depot. We named the place where we had turned off on to the Yangtze 'Cole's Creek', after our erstwhile unilateral but right leader. We had averaged 9 knots, a very low speed.

Tuotuoheyan was mainly a large PLA establishment with

huge radio aerials and mobile radar, five large fuel storage tanks, and houses. It was clearly an 'overseas posting' for the Chinese army, and some new recruits were soon discussing with us their symptoms of altitude sickness. We, of course, had been fully acclimatised by our slow ascent to 4420 m (14,500 ft). Army establishments all over the world accrue a civilian support population round them like moths. So there was a fair amount of decent trade in the main street, by now fully investigated by Duncan, Jeremy, Gwyn and John. They had booked a room in the government hostel, which was run entirely by and for the PLA. Nice it was too. It had carpets on the floor and double glazing on the windows. It also sported a western-style loo, which we looked at with glee. Further investigation confirmed that this loo was, like some human beings, more beautiful on the outside than inside. And, by golly, was the outside filthy! Perhaps next year . . .

We set up our tents by the waterside, just down river of the PLA compound, which was empty of all vehicles. Mike determined to waste as little of our valuable time as possible, so decided to try and establish fuel dump C that afternoon. We would take a drum each of diesel and petrol and set it up river past Tuotuoheyan as far as we could go in *Neste Enterprise*. On the craft would be Rob, Mike, Jim (engineer) and me.

We set off at 1.30 p.m. The first obstacle we had to negotiate was the bridge. Like its sister on the down river cul-de-sac, this was a low concrete bridge supported by masonry pillars. But there was not just one bridge. There were two of the beasts running parallel to each other, some 5 m apart. The second was lower than the first. Would *Neste Enterprise*'s duct get under it?

We set Jim on top of the craft to report the duct distance from the base of the bridge, and Rob chose the northernmost span to go through. It looked the highest. He reduced power so that the cushion would be lower.

'Two feet,' called Jim. There was a terrible scraping noise inside the cabin. What was that?

'Only the radio aerial scraping on the underside of the

257

bridge,' I called out.

'One foot,' came Jim's voice through the half-open hatch-way. Rob reduced the power.

'Six inches.' Rob reduced it further, praying that it would not get any less. It was very close indeed and the hovercraft duct was no match for the bridge if it came to a battle. It didn't. It stayed like that until we were well clear.

We fared little better beyond Tuotuoheyan than we had reaching it. A strong gusty head wind added trouble to the meandering river which went strictly according to the map. On this source side of Base 3 the map seemed to be very accurate, the position and shape of the hills coming out in beautiful relief in just the right places. From then on the map was an excellent and helpful companion. We gave up trying to decipher the down river navigation problem.

The head wind balked our advance, and after two hours we had made only 25.5 nm (46.6 km). There Mike decided it was far enough. The position was just on the 92′E longi-tude line and was where the river turned from south-west to north-west. A substantial hill lay to the south of the sandbank we chose and would, we hoped, shield the fuel drums from prying eyes. Across the water to the north, a line of hills running north-south was a good landmark, its base ending at the river itself. Further to the south-west stood a range of snow-capped mountain peaks, rising some 305-460 m (1000-1500 ft) above us. We could relocate them easily.

We unloaded both spare drums and bedded them in the sand. Then we laboriously pumped diesel into one and petrol into the other. We took photographs from the vantage point above dump C, climbed back into *Neste Enterprise*, and Rob allowed me to drive back while he slept in the back.

It was good to get my hands back on the queen. But it was not so good to drive under those conditions. The wind speed had gradually increased as the afternoon wore on, and, although the sky was clear and the sun bright, the wind speed now averaged 30 knots and gusted 40 knots. It had been easier to drive into wind. The straightening effect of the duct had constantly swung us back into wind. Although that was a nuisance, it was safe. But now, with the wind behind, the whole craft was appallingly unstable. I took her over a spit of land to get her over hump. Once there, she shot forward like greased lightning. *Neste Enterprise* has no braking system like *ICI River Rover*. The only thing one can do is de-clutch. That cuts off the main propellor, but also cuts off the control surfaces. Moreover once the craft had started turning, the wind swung her round frighteningly. Five and half tons of sliding hovercraft going sideways out of control was pretty exciting, or rather, extremely alarming. And there was little I could do except go up banks sideways or stay below hump. I fought the situation for some ten minutes. We covered a lot of ground in that time, but it was very hairy! Not by any stretch of the imagination could I say I was fully in control. The last critical time came at a point where I turned left to stay in the main flow. The craft swung left and then continued sideways, moving heavily and fast across the water to the highish bank on the right. I knew exactly what to do. De-clutch, full power and let her ride up over the little hillock. At that point the engine surged, and the rpm dropped from 2100 to 1200.

I am not prone to panic. But I confess that I ran out of ideas very fast. The craft was travelling sideways towards this bank, and needed full skirt pressure to get over it. To close the throttle would be to hit the bank with a wallop and do severe damage: we were far too close to the obstruction for that. The skirt pressure was dying anyway as the rpm fell. In fact I didn't do anything. I just held the controls where they were, bent the throttle into the Full position and prayed that the engine would recover enough to get us over. It half did. The revs were rising as we hit the bank and the only thing that happened was that the hull scraped badly on the sand.

Once over the top and off the water I had to straighten the craft and then plough across sand dunes and over culverts until we reached the water again. I knew I had to keep the craft going. We fell down a bank by the water's edge, the engine having recovered, but only after we had scratched, grazed and scuffed our way over the rocky shingle and sand dunes. I had had enough.

'It's no good,' I said, 'This craft is really uncontrollable in these conditions.'

We glanced at the wind indicator now that we were stationary. It was holding at 40 knots. I switched off the engine, got out of the seat and ate a diesel-contaminated chocolate bar while we sat out the storm. By this time in the expedition Rob had developed a driving technique on this river in *Neste Enterprise* that had given him greater experience than I had, and I was glad to let him have it back.

After an hour the wind abated slightly and Rob set off. He fared little better than I and the engine surges increased in frequency. So he brought the craft down on a decent sandbar and suggested Jim did something about it. Again we drained the collector tank and the water filter. And again we waited for the wind to drop. When it was down to 20-25 knots we set off once more, gingerly and carefully. The engine responded satisfactorily and took us back to Tuotuoheyan by degrees, and we arrived back as the sun was setting behind the huge snow showers at 9.30 p.m.

Rob and I were offered, by the team, the privilege of hostel accommodation, which we took with gladness and gratitude.

The others had been working hard. All the kit that was unnecessary for the source run was stored in a spare room in the hostel and had been lugged there by hand. I thought we had sieved out as much as was possible already, but there was still more weight to disgorge, including the generator. We had to leave the remainder of our fuel barrels unattended at the camp site and asked the PLA to keep a watchful eye on them. To hire guards would cost money and we were not about to enter that arena again.

We woke up early on another Sunday morning. Time was too short for us to contemplate having a service, and no one had been asked to put one together. We prayed together later, as was our practice. Sleep had been very comfortable in the hostel, and very cold in the tents. The ground was covered by a layer of snow, and it was still falling in minute flakes from a black, oppressive and dismal sky. At times like this we reaped the benefits of the superb clothing we had been given by ICI and Neste. Different team members chose either the ICI or the Neste kit, but all were very pleased. We were warm, waterproof, windproof, and all had far too much clothing to carry with us. Not knowing how cold the source might be, most of us opted for taking extra and carrying it if necessary. No precipitation penetrated; that was the most important factor.

We were surprised, as we left the warm hostel building and sauntered out through the compound gates, to see that the PLA parking lot was packed with 200-300 lorries. Duncan told us that they left full and returned empty every day. Where they went was anyone's guess, but we knew the area was a training ground for tanks. Indeed they even had one of the new French AFVs (Armoured Fighting Vehicles) here that they were putting through its paces. Young PLA soldiers were walking in and out of the gates and sitting near the lorries smoking their cigarettes. We guessed that lung cancer was not such a burning issue there as it was in the UK.

We packed up the camp, burned or buried the rubbish, and set both craft ready for travel. But we could not leave yet. John Whatmore was having trouble with his TV crew. Mr Lee had accompanied us up from Qumerlai, and the rest had climbed into their Landcruiser and driven the 2000-plus km to Tuotuoheyan, carrying Duncan and Jeremy, and accompanying the fuel lorry. Now they wanted two to go. Two or nothing – as opposed to the one person we had previously agreed. John Whatmore was very unhappy and brooded in his tent. Mike spoke to Jim and this eventually broke the deadlock. He talked to the TV crew and told them that they were jeopardising the whole expedition. Using Jim rather than John saved some face. If they insisted on two of them going to the source, then no TV coverage would be taken, and we would head west without a cameraman. Mike told Rob to start engines. They gave in and Mr Lee stepped into *Neste Enterprise*.

261

The contretemps took one and a half hours off our departure time. But in fact it did not matter. The snow was still
gently but obliteratingly falling from the blackening heavens
and, with the arrival of dawn, fog had set in. We could not
see more than 100 m and we prayed that it would lift. At
about 10.00 a.m. the snow stopped. At 10.45 the fog had
turned to mist, and by bending down we could see it forming
a base off the water surface prior to lifting.

We left at 11 a.m., *ICI River Rover* leading and *Neste
Enterprise* being held up by the low arch of the bridge.
Ahead of us, some 15 nm (27 km) to the west, was a hill
on the northern side of the river. It was a good landmark
and it stuck out in isolation. A range of hills to the south
accompanied us most of the way from Tuotuoheyan, but
this one on the right was higher and parallel to the river
direction. Near it there was another water flow that came
in from a lake further west, and we needed to avoid that. The
hill was not visible when we started, but gradually emerged
as we swayed to and fro in the all-too-familiar watercourses.
Having travelled that way the previous afternoon I was able
to guide Neil and Steve into most of the main channels of
water, and we made good progress. After the hill, when the
river bent left towards south-west, I took over driving and
immediately got the craft into awful trouble. I thought the
main water was to the left, and it certainly looked that way
to begin with. But all the channels emptied out into micro
streams and became, in the end, nothing. I found myself
travelling mostly up culverts in the sand dunes, not all of
which had water in them. It eventually became ridiculous.
We did not know whether to go on or go back, or try and
run over the land to get to the right side of the river bed
to find the better water. The area was 1-1.5 km wide. The
situation was disturbing.

It was even more distressing when I grounded *ICI River
Rover* completely. I had been travelling up this culvert and
reached a fork. Between the fork was a high bank of sand
that was much too tall for the hovercraft to go over. The
greater water was coming from the right, so I jammed on
elevon to go that way. It was too tight for *ICI River Rover*

262

to take, and she started skidding sideways towards the sand hill. I knew what to do: present the belly of the craft to the side of the hill, put on full throttle to increase the cushion pressure and she should just bounce off, slide down and carry on. She didn't. She rode up the hill, the cushion pressure disappeared, and she sat perched on the top at a rakish angle. No amount of throttle would help. Rocking her did not help either. She was too heavy to lift or push. We were stuck. *Neste Enterprise* was nowhere in sight – we had been thinking of a tow.

After 10 minutes of pushing, shoving and thinking, Steve came up with an answer: dig it out. Steve is a remarkable man, the ever hardworking, practical, reliable, faithful engineer. He was competent and gracious with it. He preferred to play second fiddle, and did not push himself forward. He was an enormous asset on this expedition. At the same time he greatly missed his wife Rachel at home.

We had no shovel. Steve got down on his backside, lifted the rubber skirt and started to kick the loose sand and shale away. We joined in. It was the only thing we could do. It might take an hour, and it was very dangerous: a tonne of hovercraft might fall on us at any time as the sand was scraped away from underneath. We moved a lot of sand on the uphill side, and then got out to see if we had done anything. The craft now rocked on the starboard edge of the underbox. The other two suggested I get in and start the engine, while they pushed and shoved. They rocked the craft side to side and then shoved like mad. *ICI River Rover* scraped off her perch, and that small movement was enough to create a tiny cushion pressure, which enabled her to go a bit further downhill. More shove. More pressure. She was off! Relieved, the other two got in and waggled a disenchanted finger at me for getting us into difficulty. It was thoroughly deserved.

But I was certainly enjoying the driving. It was the ultimate test of *ICI River Rover*'s manoeuvrability and my own ability. What a challenge. It felt a bit like Formula One Grand Prix motor racing. I was glad that, at different times, all three of us were given the opportunity of having a go at these extremes of driving.

We had to travel a fair bit across land to get to the real water. That was first because the little waterways petered out altogether. Secondly we decided to abandon caution and just flog overland in a straight line. We had been reluctant to do this before to preserve the integrity of the fingers, but we now gave up. From then on we travelled much more over land than before: we'd had our baptism of negligence and irresponsibility. It was not that we were careless now: we were more carefree.

Neste Enterprise had caught us up as a result of our mishap, but we were able to pass her again and head for fuel dump C. A long range of hills to the right was dotted with many herds of yak, while the hills to the east were far more distant and snow-capped. Dump C was easy to find, and we filled our jerry cans and internals with what fuel we needed. From now on we were on our own. What we carried was all we had. This amounted to ten full jerry cans and full internals. That should take us 200 nm, depending on what progress we were able to make on this bifurcated river. It was 99 map miles to the source. We could just make it to the source and back to C if we handled the craft and the throttle for maximum range. We discussed it together, and determined to set the rpm at 4000 and try to leave it there. Then, as fuel reduced, to inch it backwards for maximum economic cruise. *Neste Enterprise* also refuelled. The craft log recorded '20 hours fuel on board'. We addressed the fuel problem to Mike, and asked if he could take the remainder of the petrol drum – half – in *Neste Enterprise*. It was the only way we could guarantee to get *ICI River Rover* to the source and back in safety. He reluctantly agreed. Taking on further weight at this altitude was a hard decision to have to make; we had already refused an extra TV crewman.

The river turned the bend to the right at the base of the hills, and went north-westerly. From the map it was obvious that there were some large subsidiary river ingresses that we could wrongly divert up, all coming from lakes. The first one to the left was easily avoided as we stuck to the right-hand side of the river. The second was at a right-angled bend to the left. Neil was far from certain that we were correct here, so we put *ICI River Rover* on to a thin sandbar and closed down to listen for the larger craft. We waited ten minutes and heard her approach. The area we were in was, again, full of multi-rivers, and had a high cliff (6 m; 20 ft) to the south. The area, in a wet season, could easily turn into a lake. Pressing onwards, it was far from easy to see where the main river flowed into the area. If the map was right it should scoot off to the left round the cliff end. It did exactly that, but was impossible to see until we were right on top of it.

We went west. An open plain to the left sported many yak herds and a number of Tibetan tents. To the north was a long hill about 300 m (1000 ft) above us. It was a useful landmark and stood out from both directions. There was a tributary near its western end that led off to a large lake to the north. This tributary was very difficult to find, and we never saw it on the way up. We even had to search for it on the way down, and I believe I spotted it.

All was well. Both craft were performing smoothly. Some light cumulus cloud dotted the blue sky. A stretch of white cloud indicating 'weather' covered the horizon to the north, but it was a long way away. We had travelled some four hours from fuel dump C. We knew where we were and the terrain tied up with the map. What a relief (if you'll excuse the pun). We were not, technically, on the Yangtze, and had not been since Cole's Creek. That was the place below which the Yangtze started. Above that we had actually been flying over the Tuotuohe. We were now in it and heading peacefully for the source.

I smelled an odd odour. I mentioned it to Neil, who was driving *ICI River Rover*. He did not make much of it. Three minutes later Neil shouted, 'Water temperature – I'll dump her.'

He headed for a sandbar at once, threw *ICI River Rover* on it, and banged the engine shut. Too late. The temperature had rocketed off the clock. Smoke and steam poured from the starboard fuel filler trap, unseen until we were stationary. That had been the smell I had caught, for the 'air conditioning' system (that is, holes) came into the cabin through the side, fed by cushion air.

Neil knew what it was. It was a break in the subsidiary water system. Tim Longley at Fleet had introduced this secondary system, first to take some of the temperature off the main system and keep it cooler; secondly to provide demisting and cabin heating in the anticipated cold climate of China. It was a good system, but now very broken. We presumed something had chafed the pipe or a stone had bounced up and caught it. We did not bother to investigate the cause.

Neil stepped up on the back and opened up the engine hatch to allow her to cool down. At the time, Gwyn was riding with us, having changed places with Steve for a bit of light relief.

We could not put water in for at least half an hour. Everything in the engine bay was red hot. Neil explained that he was going to cut the hoses to the secondary system and reposition them so that it was by-passed. When he had done this we then tentatively poured Yangtze water in, and heard it gurgle and boil around the system. Very dodgy.

Neste Enterprise soldiered back down the hill to see what was up. Everything seemed to be fine as we filled up with brackish water. We made a note that there was now no antifreeze in the system, and we would be obliged, in this sort of weather, to drain the radiator each night and refill it each morning. There was no more antifreeze left in the spares pack.

After 70 minutes we could set off again, hoping that no damage was done, but eyeing the gauges regularly. Sure enough, half an hour later, the water temperature started to rise again.

'Dump her,' we shouted. This time it was better and the temperature at least remained registered on the clock. But we were puzzled. Why would this happen? Had we run short of water again? Another leak? We all got out to see. Neil was in the process of unbuttoning the engine cover again when something in the engine exploded with a deafening

266

bang, and a cloud of steam leapt in the air right into his face. He sprang backwards off the craft: it was a miracle his face wasn't burnt to a cinder.

'It's the turbo,' he said a few minutes later as he clambered back up warily. The engine was still steaming copiously. 'I expect the turbo has blown up.'

We had anticipated such an occurrence, given the extremes to which we were pushing this engine. We had a spare turbo in *Neste Enterprise*. We lifted the cover carefully, and started to unbolt the mechanism that held the turbo on to its housing. There is only a certain number of spares one can carry and we prayed that we had everything we needed. All now was self-help. We were 70 nm (128 km) from Tuotuoheyan, in one of the remotest places on earth. We could expect no help from anyone else in the world. The area was totally inaccessible, like the last place in the universe.

Neste Enterprise came up. Gwyn had signalled to her by holding up the engine cowling like a flag. Steve came in, and soon spotted that the large hose just beneath the turbo had split throughout its length. That was the explosion. He rotated the turbo – it was free. It seemed that all was not lost. We bolted up the parts we had undone and someone found the spare hose in *Neste Enterprise*. This we changed and then refilled the steaming engine with more river water.

But why had it boiled? The engineers discussed it together. They came to the conclusion that the first time the engine had boiled, the aluminium cylinder head had been warped by the intense heat. If so, it was very bad news. From now on we could expect air to enter the water system, create an air block, and cause the engine to overheat again. We had had the foresight to bring a new cylinder head on the expedition but it would have taken three or four days to put all the valves and other fittings on it: anyhow it was in Qumerlai, too heavy to carry up the river with us.

What were we to do? I was not yet convinced that this had happened. We would give it another bash. We refilled the water system and set off up river. Ten minutes later the engine temperature rose again. We dumped her on the

267

southerly bank – the nearest, and switched off. Her days, or rather hours, were numbered. This craft could never reach the source. *ICI River Rover*'s expedition to the source of the Yangtze was finished. She had died before reaching her destination. It was impossible to express the depth of our disappointment.

Mike came up in *Neste Enterprise* and we shook our heads sadly. The three of us were very despondent as we climbed wearily up to the back again, removed the engine hatch and began the routine of sorting out a boiling engine.

The time was ten to eight in the evening. That swathe of cloud that we had seen above the horizon to the north now overshadowed us. From it snow started to dribble down. There were big decisions to be made about *ICI River Rover*'s future. Mike decided we would pack up for the day and camp on the other side of the river. Rob drove *Neste Enterprise* there with all the rest of the team, leaving us to sort out the princess's power problem. We would call him to come and fetch us when we had sorted it out.

It was very good to have space. We drained the water system completely, once it had cooled, to stop it freezing overnight. Then we climbed back into the cabin to talk over a plan of action. We all felt it was better to present Mike with a solution that was acceptable to us than to force him into a difficult position.

Neil, above all, was most distressed. *ICI River Rover* was his baby and he had lived with her, as I mentioned, for over two years. The fact that she failed some 60 nm (109 km) from the source was a great disappointment which he took as a personal failure. We knew how he felt, for we loved the little thoroughbred too. Mentally we made a note to do our best from now on to take only air-cooled diesel engines in our hovercraft. The electrics of a petrol engine are a potential hazard, for they are most sensitive to water. And a water-cooled system was the point of failure on this, the most challenging and dangerous of all our expeditions.

So what could we do? All three of us wanted to reach the source ourselves. Perhaps we should abandon *ICI River Rover*, sell her to the Chinese and say 'Go and fetch her –

268

she's all yours.' Neil was unhappy with that solution. If it was possible to recover her, then we should try. But this would mean we would have to abandon our desire to reach the source – a personal ambition that we had all cherished for three or four years.

If we were to recover *ICI River Rover*, how could we do it? The engine was virtually kaput, and we were some 71 nm (130 km) from Tuotuoheyan by map: it had taken us seven and a half hours to get up there. We would travel faster down river, certainly, but how long would it take us? And how would we achieve it? What could we do when we reached Tuotuoheyan? She certainly wouldn't travel back down to Qumerlai.

We discussed the possibility of using the engine to get her to Tuotuoheyan. To do it we would have to keep her cool: to allow her to boil once more could almost certainly force us to abandon her completely by the river's edge. We could reverse the engine hatch which would cause the air to be thrust down over the engine bay. We could take off both 'elephant ears' by the side of the engine, allowing cooler air to blow through and round the compartment. We could remove the thermostat, forcing the engine to run cool. After that, we would just have to stop and let her cool down if she got hot. We selected a temperature indication on the gauge beyond which we would not allow it to go. The only other thing we could do was to keep the rpm as low as possible and try to maintain hover on a floppy skirt.

As we discussed it we started to warm to the idea. To get the craft down the 130 km to Tuotuoheyan in one piece was a greater challenge than we had yet encountered, and an exclusive adventure all on its own. It would be a test of initiative over adversity, the vaguely possible over the inconceivable, faith over failure. Yes, we were definitely warming to the trial that began to open up before us.

After Tuotuoheyan? We filed that. Let's get the princess down there first. Perhaps we could hire a lorry to Xining and Chengdu, as we had hired one to transport our fuel two days earlier? We would have to see.

The snow had been steadily falling, and as we talked we

brought a condensation fog into the princess's cabin. We emerged to a light dusting of snow all over the local country-side, and a distinct drop in environmental temperature. Our view of the other side of the river was being swallowed up as visibility deteriorated into a blackout end to the day. We called to Mike and Rob and asked them to come and fetch us in *Neste Enterprise*.

The camp site was set on a hill about 50 m from the large hovercraft, and about 5 m above the river. There was a flat patch before the ground rose beyond and disappeared into the grey of the snow-heavy sky. Neil, Steve and I pitched our tent among the others and put on some water to boil for a much-needed supper. Mike and the others called us together to discuss the best course of action. Our location was only about 4 nm (5 km) from the right-angled turn south to Geladandong – the source of this mighty river. We held our 'confab' in *Neste Enterprise*, to get out of the snow.

We put our suggestion to Mike – that we three set off at our own time and pace in *ICI River Rover* while *Neste Enterprise* pressed on to find the source. It saved a lot of unnecessary discussion. Everyone agreed that this was the most sensible, logical and practical thing to do. If we failed, then we would just have to survive on our own until *Neste Enterprise* came to pick us up. It was decided.

ICI River Rover had conquered 430 miles of the greatest test as yet given to a hovercraft. She had reached 4802 m (15,750 ft), an altitude record for a petrol-engined hover-craft. This was no disgrace.

We brewed up with steak and kidney pudding and finished with diesel-sweetened chocolate before turning in. The dark and dismal snow forbade any further activity, except to admire three Tibetan horsemen who stopped on the hillside behind us and threw together a large white tent in ten minutes flat.

We were rudely awakened at 7 a.m. by Mike. 'Wake up,' he called. 'It's a beautiful crisp morning. The moon is up and looking wonderful.'

We prised ourselves from our sleeping bags and put on our trousers and jackets (Mike never took his off). No one

270

carried pyjamas or anything sophisticated like that. We just climbed back into what we had been wearing for the last month, sleeping in our thermal underwear under the downy folds of Mountain Equipment Himalayan elasticated sleeping bags. The outer cover of our mushroom-shaped tent was pressing down on the inner in many places. Snow? Never mind. Mike said it was a lovely morning. We unzipped the tent flap and peered out. Mike had lied.

The ground was a good 15 cm deep in snow. The visibility was down to 10 m (30 ft), and we could not see the hovercraft by the riverside. We searched frantically to find the moon, and caught occasional glimpses of it through a high overcast. The one addition to the previous night was that it was freezing hard, and had been for a good few hours.

We brewed up, using melted snow. It was somewhat inefficient until a reasonable quantity of water had been accumulated. Rolled oats and apricot flakes, liberally mixed with a whole sachet of sugar, tasted as good as a royal banquet, giving us nerve for the next onslaught on the mighty Yangtze.

I had one last task to do before we parted company from the rest of the team. I had a word with Gwyn. 'Do you think you could write a record of what happens to you all between here and the source? For the book?' He agreed. He had nothing more essential to occupy his time.

Mike briefed around a hexi-fire brewing mid-morning coffee. *Neste Enterprise* was about 1 tonne heavier than she ought to have been, and we worked to clear all the snow and ice off her decking and top. When that was over, Rob drove Neil, Steve and me, with our kit, to the other side of the river, where our princess was heavily covered in camouflage.

Neste Enterprise poddled back to the north side of the river, and everything happened slowly. The visibility was so poor that there was no expectation of either hovercraft going in either direction until it had cleared. As the sun rose – somewhere – the fog thickened. It was a well-known meteorological occurrence, and encouraging. Sure enough at 10.50 a.m. the fog base started to lift in one long line, like an enormous giant slowly raising his hat. At eleven *Neste Enterprise* launched on to the water for her attempt to reach the top of the river.

Gwyn takes over the story from here.

*   *   *

We certainly benefited in those conditions from having a pre-heater to help start the engine, but Jim was less than happy to find one of the two alternator belts broken on his morning inspection. There was no further spare and there would now be extra strain on the remaining one.

We aimed to reach the source that day. That morning, while reading of the prophet Nehemiah's successful efforts to rebuild the walls of the Temple in Jerusalem, I echoed his words: 'All nations round about us perceived that this work had been accomplished with the help of our God' (Neh. 6:16). My prayer then was that it would be God, not team members, who would receive any glory for whatever our achievement might be. We still had seventy miles to go, so I was perhaps a little premature in thinking yet about reaching our goal.

By midday we found the river much more defined. It was now only 30 metres wide in places. Everything was going well. The sun was shining in a clear sky and we were on target within the limitations of time and fuel. Jeremy was cleaning his camera lenses in preparation for being at the source. John and his cameraman Mr Lee were on the decks of the craft filming the low hills streaked in snow, through which the water flowed its first few miles towards the sea. As the river narrowed once again the suitability of hovercraft became evident. Despite its size it could cut tight corners by sliding over the shale banks, thus retaining its momentum. It was on one of these that there was a thump, as if we had hit a large rock. At the same time Rob noticed that all his instruments had returned to zero and he was losing control as the hovercraft skidded round to face downstream. We slid across to the other side of the river, over another small sandbank towards the rocky river's

272

edge. Fortunately the throttle was still responsive. By giving a burst of power and inflating the skirt to full pressure, Rob was able to provide a cushion which protected the decking structure. In the accident down river from Base 1, some had seen a rip and gaping hole in the skirt which they now feared again. Thankfully this never reappeared. If it had, we would have faced a long walk out.

Some sort of damage had apparently occurred when we had hit a rock, but when we looked back at the sandbank there was nothing to be seen. On closer inspection clearly two things had happened at once. A vital cable in the steering system had sheared and at the same time the last alternator belt had broken. Both were pretty serious. From now on there was no skirt shift mechanism. This was the device controlled by two buttons on the steering wheel that 'banked' the hovercraft in a turn. My mind recalled the first time that Dick, Rob and I had had a detailed inspection of the mechanics of the Griffon in Southampton, the previous autumn. We had looked at the vital skirt shift steel cable in the nose of the vessel with the designer, John Gifford. Dick had asked how regularly it needed replacing and John's answer had been that up to that time he had never known one to break. However, never up to this point on the Yangtze river had *Neste Enterprise* been turning so often. It was yet another example of how we were stretching our facilities to the limit. We could never sit comfortably and assume we would reach the source without a hitch.

There was no replacement for the steel hawser. If a 1¼in steel cable had snapped, no cord would suffice in its place. The best that Rob could do was to secure the skirt shift in a central position and then order the rest of us to move from side to side to achieve the lean required at each bend. Similarly, underneath the engine cover at the back of the hovercraft, Jim had nothing with which to replace the broken belt. Various suggestions were made on materials. Ray, as our sole lady, was asked for her 'proverbial' tights. She didn't have any. The best idea came from Jeremy, which was to use the nylon web straps from the life jackets. Jim was sceptical. They were neither strong enough nor

273

had the same grip, but it was worth giving anything a try. Without an alternator the batteries would quickly die.

If these problems seemed to be coming so late in our time on this mighty river, they did not dampen our spirits at all. Time remained to reach the source that day, and the weather was glorious. As Duncan prepared lunch on the sandbank while the repairs continued, a single marmot watched this strange invasion, sitting up on its hind legs in the begging position, issuing its high-pitched, birdlike call. A wander to the top of the nearest hill revealed a large herd of yaks grazing along the next bend of the river. Presumably there would be a shepherd with it. Would he be the first human to be alive down from the source of the Yangtze? If he was, I am certain that he would have been oblivious to the significance of the spot in which he had chanced to be.

By 2.45 we were able to start again. The great advantage of the diesel engine over petrol for us at this time was that it did not require constant electrical power from batteries to keep going. Those batteries were not now being charged. From now on it was no afternoon jaunt riding in the back of the hovercraft. Duncan, sitting immediately behind Rob's seat, conveyed instructions, 'Right a touch' or 'Hard left', as everyone in the back moved from side to side to turn the craft towards the bends. The lack of battery power also affected Rob's ability to accelerate the craft over hump, because there was now no longitudinal trim available. When we started, or when the course of the river caused us to slow right down, it was necessary to dispatch people forward through the gull wing doors to sit on the nose. Fore and aft trim was normally achieved by pumping fuel between the nose and tail tanks. The electrical pump was a high-capacity one, and used a lot of electricity. Now we had to use team members.

Continuing on through the vast wilderness in this way we covered a further 18 nm as storm clouds gathered ahead of us to the south. At 3.45 p.m. Mike estimated that there would then be no more than one hour's worth of navigable river remaining. By 4.15 p.m. thick ice was narrowing the river all the time, so that the flow was less than 15 m wide, and much less on a sharp bend. As we entered the snowstorm, hemmed in by ice, Rob decided that he had to beach the hovercraft in order to tighten the temporary skirt shift repair. He had problems hovering on to the land. Led by Duncan, one by one all jumped ashore through the spray to heave on the rope and pull the bow of the hovercraft to land. Most of the river bed was now ice with large chunks breaking away from the ice walls.

With the skirt fixed, everybody took shelter back inside. Mike, half turning round from the navigator's seat, addressed us with his decision. We had reached the navigable source of the river for hovercraft. Our map position put us 15 nm short of where the water issued from the glacier, but most of that distance was too narrow for *Neste Enterprise*. One hard strike of the rubber skirt on protruding ice in the narrow channel would rip it to shreds. That would heavily damage the hovercraft, and place the team in a dangerous situation. The safety of the team and the integrity of the hovercraft prevented us from going hover ice-climbing. A hovercraft can move over smooth ice, but not on a glacier pitted with holes.

Melting glacial ice on the south-western slopes of Mt Geladandong (6621 m; 21,518 ft), the main peak in the Tangquea mountains, provides the water to start the Tuotuohe river, which is the source tributary of the Yangtze. The glacier is called the Glacier of Wolves. The air is rarefied, with an extremely cold, arid, continental climate and a large area of permafrost. The melting waters of the Tuotuohe start the great journey of the mighty Yangtze as an ice stream in a canyon 9.5 miles (17.37 km) long. Numerous rivulets reinforce the infant river, but then disperse across a labyrinth of stone banks and frozen snow fields gummed up by substantial chunks of ice. This continues for a further distance of 14 nm (25.6 km). We penetrated 8.5 nm (15.54 km) through this area.

There was only one start of the engine left available from the batteries. This had to be reserved for a resumption after a night stop. More than that and the drained batteries would fail us. Future operations of a hover doctor service in Papua

New Guinea demanded that we get back home to prove our viability.

With this decision firmly and sensibly taken, we all went back out into the snowstorm to take photographs and savour the wilderness. John wished to manoeuvre the hovercraft into a better position for his cameraman, and while doing this, as if on cue, the sky, like studio lights, cleared to produce bright sunlight. This time we could jump out and really savour a moment that most of us would remember for the rest of our lives. Before we left England our doctors had warned us that one of the symptoms of acute mountain sickness was euphoria. Despite being at 4893 m (16,050 ft), none of us had this disease. But perhaps we were excused for showing a little of the symptoms. What a triumph it was for Mike Cole. He had called the Yangtze 'the Everest of rivers' and this project 'the team's toughest challenge yet'. He had been navigating up the many channels to this point, but more importantly he had guided the whole project from the beginning ten years before. More than anyone else he had pioneered the use of hovercraft in remote parts of the world to the benefit of isolated people. Now he was standing on a frozen river bed on 'the roof of the world' accepting congratulations from fellow team members, and waving the flags of the UK, China and Finland (the last in honour of Neste Oy, our principal sponsor).

Looking around I saw Mel Richardson, so responsible for obtaining sponsorship and fostering the vital Leicestershire–Sichuan twinning link, waving his Union Jack purchased for this moment from Carnaby Street. Jim Mudie, the quiet engineer, was pondering the damaged state of the craft. John Whatmore was directing his Chinese cameraman towards Duncan Hanton, the team's youngest member, who was delivering a report which would be whisked as soon as possible to the studios of BBC *Blue Peter*. Dr Ray Pinniger, the most familiar of all of us with this part of the world, was kneeling down to test a trickle of water which dripped off the bed of ice we were all standing on. She then inflated her Gammow bag, a new life-saving device for one person that reduces the ambient pressure in cases of

276

altitude sickness. The bag is blown up using a foot pump. Fortunately, we never needed this device for real. Dr Ray, interested in the psychological effects of altitude, mentioned that a long march out from the source, taking several weeks, would constitute an ideal behavioural study!

The only person not on the ice was Rob Watson, who stood anxiously on the nose of *Neste Enterprise*. He was using his sextant and the welcome sunshine to establish and confirm our position. He was refusing to bathe in the glory of coaxing the hovercraft to a new altitude record so far up the river. This he had done with most of his steering removed, no electrical power and a cracked propeller. Furthermore he had been driving almost continually for ten days. Now he was looking at a new set of black clouds bearing down from the mountain of Geladandong, and urging that we begin the second half of our journey – 500 nm back to Base 2.

Indeed I felt most privileged to be included in the nine team members at this spot. We were among a very small and élite group of people who had been to that remote corner of the world. Others, who could not share this moment of triumph with us, but who had contributed in important ways, were either now on their way back to UK to meet the deadlines of their employers, guarding fuel dumps, or minding the base camp. Below us at this place ran a water course of 5989 km (3720 miles), providing water for the most populated nation on earth.

*   *   *

We had successfully fulfilled the medical, scientific and adventure objectives of the expedition and navigated over 500 miles of the headwaters of this magnificent river.

10

Another Tomorrow to Conquer

Great things are done when men and mountains meet,
This is not done by jostling in the street.

(William Blake)

Finding, following, cleaving, trusting,
Is He sure to bless?
Saints, Apostles, Prophets, Martyrs,
Answer: Yes!

(8th cent. Tr. J. M. Neale)

Back with our injured *ICI River Rover*, Steve, Neil and I had watched *Neste Enterprise* hum off into the gloom. After that it somehow felt a lot lonelier. That was not because we were without expertise: Steve and Neil were half the engineering team and magnificently qualified. Nor was it because the *Neste Enterprise* crew could have assisted us in any way. It was just that we missed one another's company – the jokes, the cheerfulness, the wisdom, the sympathy, the appreciation. We were now on our own.

We turned slowly back to our crippled craft and made her ready for travel. We refilled the water system, removed both elephant ears and jammed them into the rear cabin compartment. We turned the top engine hatch upside down; mercifully it fitted.

We had half a ton of ice and snow to clear off her decks first. Worryingly, the engine took a little time to start. She always did in the cold mornings, but this morning, with no back-up battery and no other means of starting, it was a crucial time. At least we had alternator power. At last she

278

coughed into life. We did not want to warm the engine up too much prior to lift off, or the journey would be curtailed because of the temperature limitation. But we let her idle long enough to scrape the rest of the ice off the hull and clean the frost off the windows. The craft no longer had any cabin heating or windscreen demisting.

We left at 11.12 a.m. Neil drove, keeping the rpm down to 3600. *ICI River Rover* was sluggish at those revs, but it was the only thing we could do to keep the water temperature down. After a few minutes we realised that we had packed the craft badly, and she was waddling down the river nose-high, like a water-skier sitting back on his skis. After 20 minutes Neil gave up and put her on to a nearby bank, shutting the engine down. We rearranged the jerry cans on the decking, so that we would always have two full ones at the forward position. We then used another internally for trim, sitting it with the person in the centre seat and moving it from side to side to help the craft to turn. Normally, with a full cushion, the rear passenger only has to move to one side occasionally.

We left again 33 minutes later, watching the temperature like a hawk. It stabilised between marks two and three on the gauge. Neil tried to hold the rpm at 3500, but had to increase it to turn corners, and there were hundreds of them. After half an hour the temperature rose and we had to pull in and close down to allow it to cool. There was nothing we could do but wait. This second stop lasted for 57 minutes.

Steve drove next, and we took off at 1.34 p.m., trying to use the same techniques that Neil had formulated earlier. Exactly 20 minutes later the temperature started to rise dramatically and we put her down again. This time we decided to use our camping tins to throw water into the radiator. We did this from the engine side down through the top, because, with the engine going, the lift fan cooling air would blow the water through the radiator grill. It had a good effect on the temperature, which went down fast. We were learning. Keeping the engine ticking over while we did it was an experiment and we had to be fast in getting the first two or three tins in before the temperature rose too high.

279

Our down time was reduced to 13 minutes and we were able to drive for 38 minutes before stopping. This time Neil tried to splash water on the radiator from the back end of the craft. It was a bit messy because the fan would blow all the spray out at us. But the temperature drop was dramatic and by far the finest method of reducing it. Cold water through the radiator grill was a far more effective cooling device than cold air.

I was able to drive away after only a few minutes' stop. A while later the temperature, which had levelled at about the second mark on the gauge, suddenly rose sharply to go off the clock.

'Dump her!' both the others shouted in unison.

Swiftly I chopped the throttle, engaged the clutch, which cut off all the fans, and switched off the engine. We were in the middle of the river, and sank into the water, which rose outside the craft to the level of our waists. I thought the craft would float like a boat, and that we would be able to continue our journey by drifting downstream. But, with a crunch, we settled on the bottom and stayed there; the water was just too shallow. We looked at each other in dismay. We did not know what had happened to the engine, but it was obviously something serious.

There was no point in getting out to look at the problem because a snowstorm had started. We had been watching this enormous battery of cumulo-nimbus cloud creep up on us from the rear. Beautiful and wild, it had first of all wisped over the sun, blotting out the crisp blue of the sky, and then erased the tops of the surrounding hills with white. I had known these clouds of old, and anticipated one of their side effects, a gusting wind. Preceding the snow were erratic gusts coming from all directions, making driving in the hovercraft very difficult and, at times, dangerous. I had to use full throttle on numerous occasions, and the craft fell below hump on as many others. My heavy use of the throttle would account for a rise in temperature, but not for one that went off the clock.

Now the snow was on us. It was stupid to go out into it: we had to wait for the temperature to cool anyway, and we would combine our waiting period with lunch. We cracked open a tin of steak and kidney pudding and ate it cold. 'Biscuits Brown' and liver pâté followed. I wish they would put more jam in those compo rations! The snow flakes flurried past us, the wind swirling them round the craft, and whipping the water into splashes and bangs on the side of the hull.

When it stopped an hour later we clambered out to see what the problem was. Another burst water hose would have been the end: we carried no more spares on us. That was not the problem. What a relief! The jubilee clip on the main hose had somehow loosened and fallen off, spraying boiling water over the engine. It had cooled by the time we found it, and we were soon able to fix it and refill the system. In 40 minutes we were off again. The snow had passed and only small gusts of wind followed the 'grumbly', which went on flashing and battering its way eastwards.

Between these gigantic showers the sun shone brilliantly, and the rarefied atmosphere, cleansed by the enormous vacuuming of the thunderstorms, accentuated the greens, browns and reds in the hills and the virgin, gleaming white of the billowing clouds. Dainty yellow irises sparkled in the sunshine on the river banks, the whole barren scenery dancing to the disco of the afternoon floodlight: there was always something in China to gladden our hearts in the midst of every disaster or disappointment.

Had *ICI River Rover* broken another water hose we would have been stranded in the middle of the water, bottomed on a bed of shale in the centre of a river pattern a kilometre wide. And China would have abandoned us. We foolish foreigners, risking our lives for who knows what purpose, would be confronted by 'a Great Wall of lethargy, helplessness and double-dealing' (Paul Theroux in *Riding the Iron Rooster*) and left to our own devices. On the river we were free to do as we pleased. If it pleased us to die, or to walk 150 km back to civilisation, that was no concern to most Chinese.

Through this tedious and tortuous day of adventure to bring the crippled hovercraft back home, we stopped ten times: seven times for temperature reasons, and once each to refuel, retrim, and ditch for the snowstorm. The collective time hovercrafting was 4 hours 15 minutes. It took us 8 hours 24 minutes to achieve it. We passed fuel dump C at 6.18 p.m. and skimmed laboriously up the multi-channel to the north-east. We reached the hill that marked the direction change of the river to easterly at 7.36 p.m., just 15 nm (27.4 km) short of Tuotuoheyan, as the sun was painting a new pattern of gold, orange and pink to close the day's account. We debated whether to spend the night on the river or, as Neil put it, 'in the hassle of the camp area'. We opted for the wilderness.

It was a glorious evening, the clear atmosphere granting us still reflections of the giant thunderstorms in the little lagoons formed by a falling river height. We had time to cook ourselves our favourite chicken curry (there wasn't anything else), fully flavoured with oxtail soup. We pitched our tent on the sandy shale, listened to a pair of sky-larks warbling their way down-sky and examined the hardy shrubs, clinging on to life after being overturned and up-rooted by some past flood. It was an evening of peace and solitude, beautifully complemented by the golden-red sunset: an occasion to be savoured and recalled for ever.

We had a leisurely start in the morning. There was no sign of *Neste Enterprise* and we presumed that the crew were camped for the night. So we stretched and yawned and had a relaxed breakfast of delicious rolled oats and apricot flakes (again). We packed up the tent, buried our rubbish, refilled the radiator, and set off finally for Tuotuoheyan at 9.56 a.m., Steve in control. He kept the revs down to 3500, and the craft bit into the sand banks, scraped along the shale and waddled reluctantly in the water, now 4 inches lower than the previous day. There was hardly enough skirt pressure to keep her afloat. But the low revs did at least keep the engine temperature down, and we drove for the longest time we had done since the engine had broken. We reached Tuotuoheyan and parked, gratefully, by the campsite.

Our partnership with *ICI River Rover* in this adventure expedition was over. *ICI River Rover*'s private tussle with the mighty Yangtze was also over. From now on *Neste Enterprise* was the sole survivor and source of transport south; her greatest battle, though, was yet to come.

*   *   *

Neste Enterprise struggled in at 2 p.m. The three of us awaiting their arrival were so glad they had made it back successfully. We knew little of what had befallen them at the source, and were itching to find out. *Neste Enterprise*'s struggle from the source had been less traumatic than *ICI River Rover*'s, but it had been difficult enough with the loss of both electrical power and skirt shift.

Now there was much to do. The craft itself needed repairing, and Jim set off at once to the PLA maintenance yard to locate an alternator belt and a huge Allen key to install it.

ICI River Rover needed a truck. Mike was thrilled and relieved that we had been able to get her to Tuotuoheyan in one piece. The only course of action now was to carry her down to Chengdu by road. He appointed Gwyn and Neil for that task. They were to negotiate with a suitable lorry driver and chaperon *ICI River Rover* all the way to Sichuan's capital. We would see them 3000 km later.

Jim took the strands of fractured alternator belt with him to the PLA. It took three hours to find just one of the same size. Our craft needed two. It took him another hour to undo the powder coupling, which attached the engine to the lift fan, and put on the new belt. Having finished it, he ran the engine. It looked satisfactory, and the alternator was charging. We restarted the engine to move the craft closer to the camp site for packing and refuelling, and within 30 seconds the new PLA belt broke with a bang, shedding bits of rubber all over the engine bay. So much for that! From then on we definitely had no alternator for our long journey back to Qumerlai. Difficulty, if not disaster, loomed ahead.

Meanwhile Steve, Rob and I tried to sort out the skirt shift problem. The main cable had sheared. We set off to the PLA compound to see if we could find another piece of hawser long enough. Surprisingly we discovered one that would do. Unfortunately it was attached to a broken aerial lying between an abandoned radio lorry and a hut in the dishevelled PLA yard. We asked, foolishly, if we could unscrew it from the aerial mast. It would have been better not to have asked. A man in civilian clothes shook his head. We thought he did not understand. So we trudged off to find an officer who could speak English. We eventually rooted out an administrative type with two pips on his shoulder and dragged him through the rubble to our bit of wire. He eventually cottoned on to our requirements, and asked the civilian, who shook his head as firmly as he had done to us, now more than a little hacked off at being dragged from his warm cup of tea in his fug-laden office out into the cold a second time. No way! This time we had to abandon the quest, disappointed. We returned to *Neste Enterprise* and tried to make a hawser out of strong nylon rope bought in Chengdu. But it too was unsuccessful.

We packed the craft quickly as the evening was being hastened on by heavy overcast and drizzly snow. The batteries in *Neste Enterprise* were being charged by the Honda generator, which roared noisily on the port decking. That was something positive at least.

The night was cold, snowy and very windy. Mike woke us at 6.00 a.m., his normal time. We needed to leave as soon as possible. He was trying for a record, to see just how fast we could get down to Qumerlai. In a crippled hovercraft, of course. *Neste Enterprise* roared off into the expanding light at 8.30 watched by Gwyn and Neil who were relishing the challenge of trucking the broken-down *ICI River Rover* back to Chengdu.

Neil takes up the account of *ICI River Rover*'s recovery.

*　　*　　*

The previous night Gwyn had visited the local Tuotuoheyan noodle house, where most of the truckers travelling to and from Lhasa stop for food and tea. He had found a driver

284

willing, at the drop of a hat, to take on the job of transporting our machine to Chengdu. It was at a steep price, 7000 yuan, as far as Chinese standards go, but the value of getting the craft back made the sum seem insignificant. An additional 500 yuan was offered if the trucker would get rid of four petrol drums and the personal belongings that were taking up space on the truck bed. *ICI River Rover* required the whole bed. The deal was agreed with 1000 yuan in advance. This money was scraped together from the team members, and the driver was instructed through one of the Chinese TV crew to return the following morning at nine. In fact he turned up at 10 p.m. that evening.

He arrived again next day, this time an hour late. I positioned both truck and hovercraft for loading, trying to explain in sign language to our driver that we did not have a crane and so would be lifting our machine on to his truck by hand. Gwyn and I then headed off to the PLA camp to muster up some labour for the job. A price of 100 yuan had been agreed the previous night with a three-star officer for the use of his men. At a blast on an out-of-tune whistle, two dozen half-asleep men dressed in creased green PLA uniforms appeared in the corridor. They were nothing like the real army we had met a week earlier at the road bridge 43 km south of Tuotuoheyan. The shabby crew were trooped to the hovercraft and it did not take very long for pandemonium to break out. We watched as each soldier attempted to impress his superiors, thinking that he had the solution to the loading problem. There was a complete lack of discipline such as I had never seen before: men were rolling empty petrol drums into each other, digging holes and even trying to lift the craft on their own! Eventually, with the help of the officers, we regained some semblance of order and I hovered *ICI River Rover* to just in front of a deep crater, stern at the lip. Two young privates dug two holes into the floor of the crater for the rear wheels of the lorry to sit, thus lowering the back end to form a ramp. By lifting the hovercraft at the heavy stern end, using the lifting rail added specially for this purpose, and dragging it slowly backwards, we inched it on to the lorry bed. The whole operation went surprisingly smoothly and after the craft was completely loaded we were treated to a lesson in 'how to tie down a load PLA style'! Each knot required re-tying and every rope re-tensioned before all was in order. Our driver had watched the carry-on with astonishment, but now joined in the laughter.

Negotiations were started with the PLA for the selling of our excess fuel, and a ridiculously low price of 150 yuan a barrel was offered and refused. Without success, Gwyn set off to the truck stop on the main road to find a better deal. It was approaching midday and our driver was becoming impatient for our departure. Sensing this and also knowing that our first leg would take at least eight hours, we reluctantly decided to settle for the PLA offer for the fuel. As always in China nothing was that simple. Having relocated the officer who had originally done the negotiating, he insisted on Gwyn seeing his superior, and this man spent half an hour finding enough money for the deal, then at the last moment wanted to examine the drums for himself!

At close to 2 p.m. we finally headed for Golmud, much to the relief of all concerned. An early attempt to establish the name of our driver proved a demanding task as he did not speak a word of English and seemed incapable of understanding our sign language. A name of Mad Max was hit upon because he drove like a snail!

The first stage of our journey was a steep climb through a partially snow-covered mountain pass close to 5000 m above sea level. The only building we spotted was a meteorological testing station that appeared deserted. I imagined how this place might look in winter and wondered how anybody could survive in such a desolate landscape.

As we travelled, a constant flow of army convoys streamed past us on their way to Lhasa, truck after truck, all new diesel Isuzus, painted in matt army green and, no doubt, loaded with military hardware.

After four hours we came to an abrupt and unexpected halt. Our driver had buried his head in the steering column as if to sleep. Obviously too much rice wine the previous night! I jokingly offered to continue, and much to our surprise Max agreed. Every gear crunched until it was apparent that a double de-clutch technique was required. The slop travel in the steering wheel was greater than 20 degrees. A quarter of an hour passed before both Max and I had had enough. He had suddenly become very awake!

Duncan had told Gwyn that the journey from Golmud to Tuotuoheyan had taken them approximately eight hours. So after a while we began looking out for the city of Golmud. This proved to be a big mistake. At 10.30 p.m. we pulled into a small PLA refuelling settlement to eat noodles and neck a bottle of Pijiu (local lager). The chef had a small English vocabulary and so Gwyn produced his pocket road atlas to ascertain our location. At first we misunderstood the position he gave us, thinking we were only 13.8 km away, but we soon realised he had meant 138 km – three hours driving!

On departure from our supper stop we noticed a change in our driver's technique, from a snail's pace to that of his namesake. At first we were convinced he would crash, but soon we were accustomed to it and encouraged Max to drive faster!

In the early hours of the morning the glow of Golmud appeared on the horizon and thoughts of bed and deep sleep entered our minds, ideas quickly quashed as a police checkpoint loomed in the distance. Max jumped from the cab to show his licences, but due to the unique load on his vehicle the police were more than slightly inquisitive. Eventually one peered into the cab to find us pretending to sleep under our jackets.

We were instructed to get out of the vehicle. In expedition fashion we attempted to explain to the policeman with the most stripes, in sign language, the nature of this strange machine we were carrying. Initially it seemed all was in order when the policeman, smiling, indicated we should climb back into the cab. No sooner had Max restarted the Jiefang engine (meaning Liberation) when he was summoned to the police buildings. On returning to the lorry his face had turned a whiter shade of yellow and he was waving a collection of licences frantically in front of us, counting them 'y, er, san' (one, two, three). It was obvious something was wrong but we did not understand what at this point.

The remainder of the night was spent at a trucker's hotel in town. The beds were flea-infested and I was eaten alive. In the morning Max attempted to leave on his own, still waving his licences at us and counting them. He looked very frightened, but we insisted he took us with him wherever he went. We left the hotel lorry park and drove at a walking pace through the town. Max began acting more peculiarly than ever, looking in every trucker's compound that we passed. I joked, saying that he had had enough, so was looking for some other outfit on which to dump us since we were a 'hot commodity'! Eventually we picked up speed and headed back down the Lhasa road to the police checkpoint.

In typical Chinese manner Max, believing foreigners were incapable of doing anything for themselves, indicated that we were to remain in the cab, but being *weibin* we strolled casually behind him into the police office. Armed with our passports, an Aliens Permit for Sichuan Province, and a Chinese translation of the contract signed between the expedition team and the Sichuan Academy of Science, we attempted to bluff our way out of not having the correct travel permit. The policeman with the stripes studied our documents carefully. We pointed to the clause in the contract that mentioned travelling through Golmud and after much deliberation he opened, with a smile, a drawer in his tatty desk and produced a licence. Now we could understand Max's terrified behaviour the night before.

Max quickly ushered us back to the Jiefang truck and we wondered tentatively whether we were out of the heat. He returned several minutes later indicating that money was required. A bribe or a fine – we knew not which. Acting as though we hadn't the foggiest notion what they meant, we once again produced our meagre documents. The policeman either got bored or realised we had no intention of lining his pockets with cash, and returned the licence and waved us out of his office.

With a beaming smile on Max's face we rolled back towards Golmud. Gwyn shouted 'Xining' at him and pointed in the general direction of the next major city on our route. A reply of 'Xining whoosh!' indicated that he understood. On arrival back at Golmud, Max again began to survey the vehicle yards, stopping at several to investigate on foot. Eventually having stocked up with biscuits and drinks for the journey, we turned back into the hotel yard where we had spent the previous night. Gwyn recognised a scruffy man pacing across the yard, eating dumplings. He was Max's mate who had been with him originally in the trucker's stop at Tuotuoheyan. Max pulled the Jiefang alongside a tarpaulin-covered pile; these were the things we had supposedly paid the boys to dispose of. Using our expedition fuel pump we swiftly refuelled the truck from uncovered petrol drums, and then to our annoyance the two truckers began strapping their junk on to and into *ICI River Rover*. To accelerate our time of departure we agreed to allow their personal possessions to be carried, but insisted they sold the remaining fuel drums.

Having completed the loading we left the hotel compound with anticipation of a long, gruelling day of travelling ahead, only to stop for lunch a few hundred yards down the road. We finally hit the road to Xining at close to 1.30 p.m. and entered the great Qinghai desert, 800 km of sand-covered wilderness.

*   *   *

Meanwhile *Neste Enterprise* had swerved and slithered down river and reached Cole's Creek at 10.40 a.m. We had travelled for 2.10 hours, comparing well with the 3.30 hours it had taken to come up the same stretch. I was navigating dogmatically, determined to plot our position moment by moment, not just occasionally. I had been pretty conscientious coming uphill and had got lost almost as soon as we left Qumerlai. But now we had started from a known pin-point and I was going to keep accurate track of our whereabouts. The map had been very good once we had

289

hit the bridge 42 km south of Tuotuoheyan and had been excellent all the way to the source and back. The Satnav had also proved excellent from then on. It was a pity we ignored it on the way up. But now the Satnav was useless – there was no electricity in the craft.

Cole's Creek looked bigger than when we had battled up only a few days earlier. Clearly there was now a lot more water in the river after the enormous thunderstorms, and the major waterways between Tuotuoheyan and Cole's Creek seemed so much easier to find and negotiate than they had been previously.

Balance on the craft was achieved in the way that the team had found suitable down from the source. Rob would shout, 'Left a little' or 'Right a bit', and the crew would wake up, rush over to the other side of the craft and sit huddled together until the turn was over. Then Rob would shout, 'Centre', and we would resume our normal positions. It kept us on our toes. Those who wanted to be on the outside had to pair up, so that there was one on each side of the craft. At this stage, balance was not too critical.

An hour or so later we turned left through the laid-back gorge, and entered the wide open tract of river that flowed east–west. All was going well. At 1.08 p.m. we entered the 'rapid gorge'. Rob's plan had been to let some people off to lighten the load before hitting the rapid, in case the craft was difficult to control in the heavy waters. He changed his mind. He now had enough confidence just to go for it, and there certainly seemed to be much more water. He called all the external people inside, turned round the corner, and went for the rough water. He knew that he had to aim for the left-hand side, for that was the least problematical. We thumped and heaved our way down, everyone poised to move in case Rob wanted to turn left or right in a hurry. We emerged without incident after the second of the two rapids, ready to continue our journey. The time was 2.06 p.m. and we had averaged 15.6 knots down the gorge. What had proved to be a monumental obstacle on the way up was sweetly conquered on the way down. We stopped for a convenience break and more diesel-flavoured chocolate bars.

above *ICI River Rover* tackles the severe rapid between Qumerlei and Tuotoheyan.

above *Neste Enterprise* fights through heavy water above 4,400 m (14,500 ft).

left *Neste Enterprise,* dominated by overbearing mountains, emerges triumphant through the great rapid gorge.

above
Dr David Langley makes a house call - a far cry from his Devon practice.

above Of the two bridges at Tuotoheyan, the second was almost too low for *Neste Enterprise* to pass underneath.

above Fuel Dump C: the last chance for refuelling before the source.

above Our overnight stop before the source covered both craft in ice and snow. From here, disabled *ICI River Rover* limps back to Tuotoheyan; *Neste Enterprise* powers on.

above Nearly at the navigable source, we lose our alternator and skirt-shift hawser. We go on!

above Ray Pinniger demonstrates the Gammow Bag at the source.

Ice-floes, brooding thunderstorms, wind and snow blessed us at the source at over 4,800 km (16,000 ft) - a world height record for hovercraft.

above The navigable source of the Yangtze. The first upriver journey is completed.

The mega-channel of river that we had had so much difficulty going up was easier going down. We entered this multi-way just after the Tibetan prayer flags, and soldiered down the next 20 nm trying to find the main flow, which was much simpler now the water was higher.

Two hours later at 4.05 p.m. we passed the entry of a tributary that we had noted on the way up, and we were therefore just about where I had originally estimated fuel dump A to be. Half an hour later, as we turned to the north and the river narrowed into a recognisable flow, we chanced upon fuel dump B! As we approached the high hills, we started to recognise the surrounding area, and, right opposite the dry river bed that came down from the hill in front of the camp, we saw the symbol that the team had erected for us. A cairn of rocks had been constructed, mounted by a dry yak's head. Just below it in bold white stones was an enormous 'B'. Gladly we drove round the edge of the promontory and put the craft on the sand bank that she had last occupied one week earlier. There was an urgency to get there that day, Thursday. Mike had arranged with David Langley that, if the hovercraft had not returned by Thursday, they were to make arrangements to walk or ride out. We had initially said to them that they should go to Tuotuoheyan, because we thought that it was the nearest point of civilisation. The actual distances now turned out to be: Tuotuoheyan 110 map nm (201 km); Qumerlai 60 map nm (109 km). David had casually asked the local Tibetan family in the nicest possible form of pidgin language which town they would go to. They said Qumerlai, and it would take four or five days to get there. They did not seem to have heard of Tuotuoheyan.

*   *   *

The desert road from Golmud to Xining was uncharacteristically good, as Chinese roads go, and stretched in a laser-straight line over the hazy horizon. A dramatic orange mountain range ran parallel on our right, and disappeared beyond the extent of our vision to the left in flat grey sand. The only features to break up this barren landscape were small fertile oasis settlements – a tribute to Chinese irrigation mechanisms.

The relatively smooth road allowed the second driver, dubbed Wheels by us for the sake of argument, to make good progress while Max slept on a bed of clothes made up in the cabin of the *River Rover*. He was lying directly over the rear axles of the truck and must have felt every bump on the road. It was about this time that Ronnie, one of the Chinese guides, went by on the local bus; he recognised the hovercraft going the other way. He had been sent up to Tuotuoheyan by Xie Jinkang to *stop* us going any further past that town, because we did not have written permission. He was far too late!

By early evening we had reached a spectacular mountain range of jagged brown crystal rock structure and proceeded to climb through it, travelling over a winding pass and back down into the desert once more. During our descent Gwyn began to study his pocket China Airlines atlas for a possible overnight stop. We had travelled an average of 50 km per hour and by 9 p.m. were nearly half-way to Xining. We pulled into a town of around 200 dwellings, stopping for noodles and compo coffee.

On departure from this oasis town Max took a stint at the wheel of Jiefang, leaving Wheels to settle down in *ICI River Rover*. He smiled and shouted, 'Xining whoosh.' As midnight came and went it was clear that Max's words meant we were going non-stop to Xining!

As we travelled through the night the road gradually deteriorated and slowed our progress. It had gone 2 a.m. when a group of red lights was seen in the distance apparently waving at us to stop. We had come across a police road block in the middle of nowhere! From what I could gather they were checking all vehicles to and from Golmud. I could not tell why. As before, our passports and insignificant documents were presented for inspection. The desert police were puzzled how two foreigners, with a military-looking machine, came to be travelling through a sensitive province without a permit or official Chinese guide. The Golmud–Xining travel clause (even though it stated planes and trains as the means of transport) was pointed out, and by giving an impression that we believed we were breaking no laws and finally explaining about our weird contraption, we persuaded the policeman to move us on. Max grinned again as we sped away.

The vast Qinghai lake, the largest in China and supposedly of outstanding beauty, was sadly passed before the sun had a chance to make an appearance. All I could make out were brilliant silver reflections of the full moon on the rippling water.

Dawn broke as we headed down a tree-flanked road towards the city of Xining and we had only a fleeting glimpse of the town as it awoke. I took a snap of the impressive railway station that Max pointed out with some pride. The police barracks were situated on the other side of town. I think our driver drove purposely through the city to avoid having to pass them. As we left Xining Max broke out into a kind of laughter, knowing as we did that the Qinghai–Gansu border was less than 100 km away.

As the sun rose our Jiefang motored past misty, water-logged paddy fields, just like a picture postcard view of China. There were groups of tiny emperors and empresses dressed in brilliant coloured outfits on their way to school with large abacuses strapped to their satchels. Field workers were being gathered in the roadside villages for their work assignments, women washed clothes in the brooks and old wrinkled men dressed in blue Chairman Mao uniforms sat lazily watching the world pass by. The air was fresh and although I was lacking a few hours sleep I felt wide awake, being soothed by these idyllic scenes.

It became obvious we were travelling straight on to Lanzhou by the words 'Lanzhou whoosh!' being delivered in actor's style by our smiling driver. Our route to Lanzhou took us over and along the famous Yellow River. It looked more muddy-brown than yellow but was still spectacular. The river appeared wide as we travelled close to its banks. However, much of its water was being drawn off for the irrigation of the surrounding paddy fields.

293

Lanzhou is famous in China for its smog and choking air. It has a large industrial base supported by a population in the millions and has the Yellow River at its centre. As we drove along its 5 kilometre promenade the sun was shining and there was no sign of pollution. The local girls were wearing fashionable summer dresses as they cycled along. This city could have been like any in the West, with its fun fairs and recreation gardens crowded with people making the most of the good weather. Gwyn informed me that all the expedition fuel had been refined here in Lanzhou.

Max indicated that the truck was low on petrol and began looking out for a refuelling stop. In Lanzhou this was an easy task. Having driven through the centre of town we pulled into a petrol station of typical western appearance, the only one of its kind I had seen in China. It had a trade name of Guzzy on the forecourt, very appropriate to the fuel consumption of Chinese trucks. Leaving the two drivers to organise the filling up, Gwyn and I wandered off to purchase snacks for the continuing journey. Back at the station we were introduced to a cashier who spoke a little English. He had been asked to explain that our truck required repairs and so we had to spend two days in a place called Baoji to do them.

'Why Baoji and not Lanzhou?' was our reply. We were tired because we had spent twenty-four hours in the truck cab and so a night in Lanzhou was inviting. The cashier shrugged his shoulders and repeated that our drivers insisted we go to Baoji.

Gwyn, determined to make a stand, wrote clearly down in his mileage booklet, for our friend to read, that if we did not make Chengdu by the 17th the drivers would incur financial penalties. We were seeing how far we could push our luck. The cashier had a friend who was willing to continue the journey for us if our drivers proved uncompromising and this gave us greater leverage. After much deliberation and commotion, Max promised they would work harder and get us to Chengdu by the 18th, but we would still be going to Baoji. We did not understand at this stage why we had to go to this place, Baoji, but we had our suspicions.

On departure from Lanzhou both Max and Wheels were acting weirdly, stopping the Jiefang in every small settlement, changing over roles, exchanging a tatty piece of paper, and talking to locals. During our supper stop, the two truckers, unusually, sat at a different table in the restaurant, examining receipt-type pieces of paper and scribbling on the back of an empty compo coffee sachet. The discussion was intense and heated and I thought perhaps there was a disagreement over their cuts for the job. The disco throbbed out a mixture of the London Boys, Village People and Euro-music.

Upon leaving Max drove at crawling pace, looking nervously at groups of locals congregated along the roadside. A quarter of a kilometre later we came to a halt, Max jumped from the cab leaving the engine running and summoned a crowd over to the street corner. He produced two paper articles stamped with official-looking red emblems, and a dubious looking character dressed in a black leather jacket and wearing dark shades barged forward to examine the documents and quickly dragged our driver away.

Wheels had climbed into the cab, a cigarette dangling from his mouth. A semi-grin gave us a hint that they were up to no good. A police siren could be heard coming our way, and the crowd swiftly dispersed as it raced by, totally uninterested in what was happening, much to the relief of all! Wheels rolled the truck away from where the crowd had re-formed. Where was Max? He had been escorted to one of the neighbouring buildings, we thought, to complete 'the business'.

Max came jogging across the street and mounted the already moving vehicle. Wheels then put the pedal to the metal and we sped out of town. I was shaking my head in disbelief as Gwyn pointed his finger at our grinning driver as if to say 'we know what you've been up to!' Wheels drove even more like a maniac for several hours, constantly viewing his mirror and I half expected a police road block to

295

appear in front of us to take us all off to the clink. How on earth could we explain this black market exchange as well as everything else?

We began to ascend a terraced mountain range in Ningxia Province. The road was fair but wound around the hilltops making actual progress slow. This was a region of cave dwellings dug into the mountainside. Many Chinese live in such caves and as night fell the area was full of glowing holes from the candles lighting up these homes.

On descent from the range Max began his stint at driving like a lunatic, half-asleep, giving us little confidence as we skidded and screeched round the bends. My hand often reached out for the steering wheel as we appeared to be heading off the road; no chance for us to sleep.

A driver change was a relief at eleven. I asked Wheels how long to Baoji; he indicated on his watch, moving his finger from the hour to ten to; 50 minutes to a good night's sleep! Twelve passed and we began looking eagerly for Baoji; each time a glow of lights appeared in the distance our anticipation of sleep grew, only to be dashed as we sped through. By 2 a.m. it was clear that Wheels had meant ten hours – another uncomfortable night on the road. We settled down using the Gwyn-patented technique for sleeping in a Jiefang truck – bums on the dashboard, heads on the seats and knees on the floor. Gwyn had it worst as his long legs were a distinct disadvantage in a cab designed for an oriental.

Dawn broke as we entered the wheat fields of Shaanxi Province. Labourers brought in from other provinces from the north were being gathered for the harvest. These men looked very interbred and were probably suffering from cretinism. It was difficult to comprehend how this vast expanse of yellow sea could be reaped in a week, but seeing the number of hands it became believable.

The driver stopped our truck down a back street in a smallish town called Fengxiang, an hour or so from Baoji. We were outside the gates of a mini truck yard and our truckers were greeted by a red-faced woman. Obviously they had met before. They wanted all their gear off *ICI*

River Rover to leave in this yard. I took a great gulp of the remaining water from my army water bottle and was pounced upon by a second woman wishing to refill it. Reluctantly I agreed. A full understanding of why Max and Wheels insisted on a stay in Baoji was crystal clear. They had arrived home!

The much-awaited Baoji was first viewed from a hilltop around late morning, a gloomy industrial town sprawled on the banks of the Huang He (Yellow River). A hostel in the centre of town was to be our home for the night. Having parked the truck in the hostel compound our drivers were greeted by several scruffily dressed men wearing identical green jackets. We had arrived at their work unit. All their friends, and no doubt their relatives, lived in or around this town. We were dragged into the reception of the hostel, the usual ritual of filling in foreigner movement cards and producing passports was required even though the cards were in Chinese. Max left us and vanished up a flight of stairs. An hour passed before he returned with an extremely attractive but moody girl who showed us to our rooms. She was later to barge into the washroom as I took a strip wash!

To clean our few clothes and our festering bodies with hot water was bliss. It must have been at least two weeks since I last had a full hot wash, back at Base 2 (Qumerlai) the day before we set off in our hovercraft to fly to the source of the Yangtze. I smelt awful!

All cleaned and freshened, Gwyn and I headed for a noodle house down the street from the hostel. Max was not around so sign language was necessary to order, much to the amusement of the young chef!

Back at our room two official-looking men in brown suits waited for our return. The elder of the two showed his identity, Foreign Affairs, and requested our documents. The usual pieces of paper and our passports were collected. The travelling clause in the expedition contract was carefully studied as we offered them compo tea, refused, of course. Sitting on the sofa directly in front of us, the two officials, muttering to each other, deliberated over the documents,

297

then they suddenly nodded, got up and left. We did not see or hear from them again.

The arduous 49 hour stint in the Jiefang had sapped my last ounce of energy, so having switched on the television to see Scotland scrape a draw in the World Cup and to watch scenes of the crash of *Neste Enterprise* on the news, I climbed under my mosquito net and into bed. Gwyn did likewise.

*   *   *

As *Neste Enterprise* parked at dump B, we were delighted to see that they had carved a huge text into the sand by the side of the river: SARAH, DAVID & FEE LIVE 'ERE. NO 10 YANGTZE MANSIONS. We giggled. Clearly they hadn't had enough to do for a week, and were inventing ideas! Fee rushed down the hill towards us, and hugged us all. She looked bronzed and very healthy.

'Where are David and Sarah?' we asked.

'They went up the hill there,' she replied. 'We all try to get up there every day, just for fun. I expect they heard the hovercraft coming, so they will be down soon.'

'Good,' said Mike. 'We want to get on. Can we pack up the tents and clear the site rubbish away?'

While Rob, Jim and Steve refuelled *Neste Enterprise* from the half-full drum of diesel that was left at dump B, the rest of us broke camp and carted the packages down to load her up. It was not long before we saw David and Sarah running down the hill towards us. Both were as fit and sprightly as Fiona, tanned by spending a lot of time out of doors and up in the hills.

'This is the thirteenth consecutive day I've spent chaperoning fuel drums,' David said. 'We are pretty familiar with each other now.' We laughed.

David was full of questions about what we had done and where we had got to. He was expedition conditioned, having been on the one in Peru and nearly been lost in the Amazon forest. Astute, energetic and a superb doctor, he was an asset to any expedition. His wiry and very fit frame

298

enabled him to compete with the logistics people on equal terms, and he brought with him a vast grasp of medical and Christian knowledge. He was the senior doctor in the GP practice at Brixham, from which we had acquired so many of our medical staff on all three hovercraft expeditions.

'What's this?' someone asked. It was Fiona's turn to laugh. 'It's a yak's head. I thought I'd take it back to Edinburgh for examination and let it rest there as a trophy.'

David broke in, 'We found the place where the Tibetans slaughtered their yaks, and we called it the Valley of Dry Bones. There were enough bones there to satisfy any vet!'

'Come on, let's go!' came Mike's voice as we chuckled and joked our way down the slope to the craft, which was still ticking over. We did not dare stop the engine, for we had no means of starting it again. We handed the remaining fuel to our Tibetan friends, not knowing quite what they might do with it so far from civilisation, but we had no more use for it.

We clambered aboard. Rob applied full power, and *Neste Enterprise* slid sluggishly off the sand bank and over the water.

'Left a bit,' Rob's voice came from the front. I was sitting right behind him, and trying to control the balance. I repeated the call. Three people rushed over to the other side of the craft, as we had been used to doing, and the whole craft tilted alarmingly over to the left.

'Right!' This time Rob's voice was urgent and a bit desperate. They went back again. The craft wheeled drunkenly over to the right. 'Balance!' shouted Rob, and we strove to balance her.

Suddenly this craft had become hypersensitive to the position of people inside. I tried to control the situation as much as I could, and we gradually got it sorted out. David was still so keen to hear what we had done in our week of absence that he was plying me with questions one after another like a machine-gun. I was trying to answer them as best I could, not realising quite how difficult driving the hovercraft had become. Rob was getting desperate in the front. He still had no skirt shift and no electricity.

He was driving even more 'by the seat of his pants' and the craft was both sluggish and sensitive. It was not very long before we had to ask David to stop firing questions. We all had to concentrate now on banking the craft where Rob needed her to go. David was standing or kneeling in the centre of the aisle, glad to do something other than look at mountains and yak's bones. He was quite amazed that he could actually bank the craft by standing in the middle and merely leaning to one side or the other. No longer did we have to move two or three people across when we wanted to bank, because the balance was exceedingly delicate. I was able to direct David, and he tilted the craft by shifting his weight a centimetre or two. We soon got the hang of it. But initially it caused Rob a lot of trouble. I stayed behind Rob from then on. Being a driver and knowing what was needed to turn, and how much was required for each turn, I was able, if nothing else, to give Rob the extra confidence he needed to concentrate on steering and speed. It was very tiring for all of us. At no time could any of us relax.

Why had the driving suddenly become so difficult? There did not seem to be more wind, although that certainly gusted as the afternoon drew into evening, and made our progress even more hazardous. John was sitting down puzzling the thing out, and started to calculate – as much as he could – the weight of everyone's kit and accoutrements. Licking his pencil, scratching his ear, and changing his headgear yet again (the river ate up three beautiful hats of his), he arrived at a figure. We were carrying 2005 kilos.

'What is the normal maximum weight we can carry?' he asked. I had forgotten. But Rob, over his shoulder, replied, '1800 kilos maximum sea level capacity.'

We were at about 14,000 feet. And we were 205 kilos overweight. No wonder the craft was so sensitive; it was like a tight-rope walker balancing on a skinny bit of string. Every move and the craft swayed from the upright, making Rob fight to control the beast.

This precarious down-river journey was certainly the greatest test this craft had undergone. It was probably the most gruelling task to which any hovercraft has ever been subjected. It was also incredibly tiring for the whole team. Even now, on the penultimate day of the river journey, there was no peace from the hassle that had dogged us throughout the expedition.

But our determination was such that no circumstance, be it mechanical, human, cultural or spiritual, would break us or deter us from our goals. We were in good heart, locked in together to conquer, as one man, this new trouble that had confronted us. We were going to win, come what may.

Leaving dump B at 5.17 p.m., we followed the map as carefully as possible. This was far more feasible than it had been going up river. The area between 94 30'E and 95'E was the trickiest. The river water had definitely increased since we had come up a week earlier. Much of the area was like a lake, which made hovercrafting far easier, more enjoyable and faster. But again it was very difficult to measure speed and distance. There were few topographical features to help us. The odd dry stream bed which came down through the steep winding valleys was sometimes so narrow and ancient that it was hardly there at all. We often wondered whether we were fitting the terrain to suit the map, or fitting the map to suit the terrain – a common problem with all orienteering. I inveigled Sarah, with her experience as a ski instructor and orienteering genius, to help with the navigation. We felt we were doing OK. At 95'E the river direction went from just south of east to south-east. This should have been easy to spot, but the river twisted through east and south-west before it stabilised into other wiggles averaging south-east.

Evening was drawing in and the visibility was deteriorating by the time we came to fuel dump A. Of course, we had no clue where it was going to be. But, as we sped past, we spotted the huge lines of stones that the team survivors had moved together into a massive 'A' on the river bank. The time was 8.06 p.m. I marked the location very carefully on our map. It was 18 nm (32.9 km) from Qumerlai. It was also shortly before the one rapid we had found on this side of the river – where the Tibetans had put their white tent on the nearby hill.

We scratched our heads in growing bewilderment. We knew that fuel dump A was a minimum of three hours away from Base 2. Yet here we were, 80 per cent certain of our position, only 18 nm from Base 2. That should take us only 50 minutes. We watched carefully during the remaining hour of daylight to try to establish our position firmly. The streams that came in from the hills tied up. The river that we previously thought was to the north of the hill, now came out in the correct place, to the south. So we knew we had been wrong before, for now the topography and the map correlated exactly. At 9.50 p.m. we went through a series of chicanes south-east, north-west, south-east. The map was right. That was the place where the river did an 'S' bend just before Qumerlai.

I said to Mike, 'According to the map, Base 2 should be just round the corner here.' We turned. No Qumerlai. The terrain was nothing like the area with which we were familiar near our base camp. I threw the map on to the seat beside me, and gave up. Sarah did the same. We had not yet found the cause of our navigational problems, and at ten o'clock at night we were unlikely to find the solution to the difficulty.

Indeed other things had become more important, and very critical. The weather had gradually been deteriorating, and it had started to drizzle at about 7 p.m. Both Mike and Rob used the wipers very sparingly, but the blades gradually moved across the windscreen slower and slower. In the end they gave up altogether; the batteries had died.

Maintaining the fore and aft trim was becoming more acute as fuel was used up, so we decided to put more people on the outside decking. We now had four. The wind whistled round them and the spray and drizzle blinded their eyes. It was very cold, and most of them stayed outside far longer than they should have done. Those inside passed chocolate and other food through the windows to them. We called for them to come forward or to go back to get the trim right. When the wipers packed in, two of those outside moved forward (causing the other two to move back), in order to wipe the windshield for us. The paper cloths got wet very quickly as the rain increased, and the resulting smear was often worse than the rain itself.

By 10 p.m. our hover time was 10 hours 50 minutes. Mike had wanted to do the journey in twelve hours if he could. We were adrift from this schedule. Perhaps we could still do it in one day?

The sun had set ten minutes earlier, but the moon was lagging behind the dusk, so there was no possibility of it appearing until midnight, and the cloud cover still obscured most of the stars. Now our task was to get a hovercraft crippled by total lack of electricity, exceptionally delicately balanced, unable to trim either side to side or fore and aft, through a dangerous river bordered by rocks. At night. In the rain. We had no spot lamp to help us see the edge of the river. All we could do was to try and see the reflection of the water in what little light was coming from the dying sky.

We were all very tired, Rob most of all. Mike had asked him if he wanted to continue driving, and he said he would have a go. I was very happy with that – I was the spare driver! He had now been working since 8.30 a.m. with hardly a break. The job he did was absolutely magnificent.

We could not see the bit of river we were on. We knew that the direction went round to the left. But as Rob started to turn, there was a crunch and scraping noise from under our feet. We shouted to those on top to tell us if they could see anything. They could see very little. It seemed as if we had turned into a side water that ended in nothing. The patch we were on was a shale bed by the river side, and the main flow was 'somewhere over there to the right'. Rob turned the craft with full power on (we were immensely thankful that the engine was behaving itself at this time), and we scratched and scuffed our way off the shingle rise and back on to water again. From then on we were much more vigilant. The craft wandered from one side of the river to the other, as much from the steering and balance difficulties as from the inability to see anything at all. Still no one complained; not even those frozen on the outside, not even Rob. We just went on as best we could, making a little headway, and often having to fall below hump because we just had to keep going slowly.

Mike eventually surrendered. It was 10.30 p.m. He suggested we pull in to the side when we could find anything near a reasonable spot. We were not going to hit Qumerlai that night. We were far more likely to hit something definitely less encouraging. Rob found somewhere to land. It was shingle, but no one minded. The craft 'boinged' as he cut the engine to rest on whatever was there; clearly a 'sticky-up' protrusion of masonry. Who cared about another hole in the hull anyway?

Rob's tenacity and concentration were superb throughout. We were all dependent on his skill and his ability as he drove carefully and arduously down the great Chang Jiang. No praise could be too great for the exceptional job he was doing.

We emerged stiffly from inside the craft. Those outside jumped down, frozen and sore-bodied. Still we had not finished for the day. We now needed to find a place to sleep. Between us and the shore was a static lake of water. This we had to wade through, carrying the tents; there was no way that we could sleep on the shingle. Someone lit a hexi stove to give us light and warmth, and we placed our tents as carefully as we could in the dark, trying to avoid little tufts of prickly vegetation which smelled very strongly of mint, and which prised their sharp little way through the waterproof bottoms of our tents to spike us viciously.

Rob and Mike were to sleep in the hovercraft. Before they closed the engine down we all helped to lift the Honda generator on to the port decking. Once there, it was started up and connected to the batteries to give them some sort of charge prior to restarting in the morning.

Most of us settled down by 11.30 p.m. All was well for a quarter of an hour. Then Rob made his way up to the rudimentary camp site, struggling to pick his path through the water and the dark. He was trying to find Steve, who was fitfully sleeping in my tent. Of course he had no idea which tent Steve was in, so he woke everybody up.

304

'Wazzermarrer?' Steve tried to speak. It was nearly midnight.

'I think there's something wrong with the generator,' Rob said desperately.

Steve struggled out of his sleeping bag, silently gracious, and dragged his trousers on. They went back to the craft. Sure enough, there was something wrong: the charging device, which had been trouble-free for the whole expedition, now selected this time to pack up. It was not reparable; certainly not at this time of night. There was no way that we were going to get any more electricity into those batteries.

'Quick,' said Steve. 'Start the engine.'

Rob leapt into the driver's seat, and turned the starter motor. Incredibly, the dead batteries, which could not even sweep a wiper across the windscreen, turned the 2000 cc, eight cylinder diesel motor over one revolution. Because the engine was still hot, it fired just once. That was enough. It burst into life, and sat there purring contentedly. Again, we were so thankful that diesel engines do not require electricity to keep going. Rob, Mike and Steve breathed a sigh of relief, and thanked God for this thrilling miracle. Rob and Mike threw their sleeping bags on to the seats of the hovercraft, and were rocked to sleep by the rhythm of the engine. Steve crawled back into my tent with a sigh of relief. I was asleep. The time was near 1.30 a.m.

Mike woke us all at 6.15 a.m. Barely a night's sleep. He wanted to leave at 6.45, even before it was light. His aim now was to get to Base 2 inside the twenty-four hours, which meant we had to be there before 8.30 a.m. and we were not quite sure just how much further we had to go. Rob was driving cautiously, which everyone approved of, but it meant that we could not calculate the time left.

The morning came upon us as a threat. Low cloud had gathered overnight and covered the tops of the surrounding hills. From it streamed a heavy drizzle, which massacred our movements at every point. However, 6.45 was too ambitious a programme for lift off, and it was not until 7.15, after prayer together, that we were ready to give the mighty Yangtze our last shot.

The journey was horrendous, even more difficult than the previous evening. The only redeeming feature was that there was gradually emerging daylight to ease the driving situation. The decks were slippery with the rain, and the four outsiders had to hold on tightly as the craft weaved and wobbled round the corners of the river. Banking was still very critical, and David Langley again swayed delicately across the aisle in the centre of the craft. The rain on the windshield was worse than before, and we ran quickly out of mopping-up rags, Ray and John smearing the glass once every two minutes in an attempt to prolong its transparency.

We wallowed twice, when the craft tipped into the water through overbalance on one side. We hit rocks underneath a couple of times, for the skirt pressure was not man enough to lift the overweight craft clear of the shingle banks. We hit a little island, and stopped for a short time, trying to get her off. We lost hump on numerous occasions, as the confluences of the river and the difficulty of finding the main flow continued to handicap us.

The terrain started to become more familiar, and soon we recognised hills and flows that were close to home. That road on the hill to the right, warning us of the heavy river flow that had nearly drowned *ICI River Rover* when her engine stopped, came towards us. Just one more bend. We watched the monument to the 1986 rafting expedition go by, and there in front of us was the abattoir on the top of the hill, and the green and yellow tents of Base 2 below it! We roared past it and turned to land upstream. The time? 8.15 a.m. We had done it within the twenty-four hours! Considering the condition of the hovercraft itself, it was a substantial and remarkable achievement. I calculated the exact on-river time: 12 hours 43 minutes. Next time we'll knock a couple of hours off that!

Andrew and Tony Shewell rushed out of their tents to see our arrival, and welcomed us with open arms. They had received no news of us for eight days and had been fearing for our safety.

Ever since both the craft had become crippled at the top of the river, the possibility of trying for the Dam Qu

306

source had been eliminated. Besides, our attempt to con-
struct a distance-measuring device had failed, so we would
not have been able to tell, any more accurately than a
map, whether the Dam Qu source was longer than the
Geladandong source. We could neither substantiate nor
deny How Man Wong's conviction that the Dam Qu was
some 60 km longer than the traditional source: a pity. Perhaps next time . . . . ?

We unloaded all the kit while food was cooking, and
then hauled *Neste Enterprise* up the ramp between the fuel
barrels that remained. It was far too difficult for us, but with
heaving and groaning, and Rob running her at full power, we
gradually pulled her up, covering everybody with a liberal
sprinkling of dust and filth. We then left her there while we
ate 'brunch' before transferring her to the trailer base in the
afternoon. Again, with considerable difficulty, we were able
to place her accurately on the trailer for the long journey
home. Only then were we free to close the engine down.
We had been running it virtually non-stop for three days.

Remarkably, the date was only 14 June. It was extraordinary because, all of a sudden, we had caught up with
our original schedule, and were now on time – for the first
time since we had arrived in Chengdu at the beginning of
March. Those of us who were not particularly needed to
stay in China could use their air tickets, and travel from
Hong Kong as originally planned. Cathay Pacific had been
enormously helpful to us, giving us 'flexi-tickets'. Now we
would not inconvenience them too much. And we were
only two days behind the majority of the team who had
been forced to leave early.

The Chinese guides had heard that we had arrived back,
and came to see us that same afternoon. Mike expressed
his desire to leave in three days time – Saturday. The
Chinese were already thoroughly disgruntled with staying
in Qumerlai for the length of time they had, and were as
delighted as we were to go. John, Duncan, Sarah and David
needed to leave as soon as possible, to try and get back for
the *Blue Peter* TV programme at the end of June. They were
to go the next day, Friday, in the red Landcruiser.

The afternoon proved to be too much for all of us. The sun beat down upon us, and the sweltering heat made life so uncomfortable that we decided to pack in for the rest of the day. Many slept. Some washed and shaved.

Just about 10 p.m., when most of us had bedded down for the night, a mother and father of a thunderstorm hit us. The flashes of lightning went on for one and a half hours, and averaged one and a half seconds between each. The rain was lost among the hail, and, what with the continuous roar of thunder and the beating of the hailstones on the tent tops, it was like trying to sleep in the wake of Concorde in full reheat. We poked our heads out of the tents every now and then to enjoy the fireworks. When the monster had passed over at long last, it left behind 9 cm of hailstones on the ground. The whole area was covered in white, and the tent tops were bent down under the weight.

In the morning there was a lake right in the middle of the camp. Those brilliant guys who had initially set up the camp had located the personal tents on the ridge near the river. They were clear of water. But the other tents – mess, rations, engineering and medical – were in the dip in the ground right where this lake now sat. During the night Dr Ray had to evacuate the medical tent. She was the only person who was sleeping in any of the main tents, and some of the team were called out of bed during the storm to dig trenches around it to enable her to get some vestige of sleep. Now we needed to dig more trenches to get rid of as much of the lake as possible. When we eventually channelled the water past *Neste Enterprise* and down the ramp to the water, we were astonished to see that the rain had already cut a groove in the ramp nearly a metre deep. It suddenly came to me: if we had waited till that day to draw *Neste Enterprise* up the ramp, we would have been completely unable to do it. The hole in the ramp would have dissipated the cushion air from underneath her, and she would have been unable to hover.

The wet ground stopped us from putting the wheels on the trailer bed: it would have been too dangerous to have attempted to raise the 5.5 tonne machine on the secondary

308

jacks, with the base in a quagmire. So we all helped to dismantle the main tents. I felt very strongly that we did not need any more rain. It hung in the air like a balloon ready to burst, and everybody expected it to happen. But I felt that God would not have it, so prayed against rain that day. It was hard work because the sight of the rain clouds threatened to kill my faith. But we made it; the other thunderstorms passed us by, and no rain actually fell on the camp, although it was hammering down in the surrounding area. The freedom from rain enabled us to pack up the camp satisfactorily, and some watery sunshine poked through now and again to help dry the soaked canvas. Before lifting the trailer, we felt it prudent to drain the fuel from the back tank. We had sold 15 empty fuel drums to Mr Qumerlai 'Plod', and he went quite berserk as we shovelled earth for two hours to dam up and bury the diesel and stop it polluting the Yangtze. We were unable to provide sufficiently small or enough containers to catch any of it; he cried at the waste of 80 precious gallons that he could make a killing on. We were then able to raise *Neste Enterprise* and her trailer bed on to her wheels during the afternoon, and were more than grateful that this was the final go at this exercise, until we came to a place where better equipment would be available.

We asked Steve to see if he could put new alternator belts on. He searched through the engineering spares and found the two that we should have taken with us up river. He disconnected the joint between the engine and the lift fan, and discovered that the new belts we had brought with us all the way from the UK were too small. We had been given the ones that fitted the 1500, not the new 2000 TDX!

While he was there, he decided to investigate why we often felt a vibration from the engine. Of course, we had the propeller problem. But we felt that there was something else. He had noticed that the powder clutch, positioned between the engine and the lift fan, wobbled as it rotated. He took it off. To his astonishment, he uncovered yet another near disaster. The shaft on which the clutch sat was normally held in place by a key and two grub screws.

309

The grub screws had sheared and the ends welded into the spline, some quarter of an inch around the shaft, and it was only the key that had stopped the whole affair bursting. If it had broken, then the craft would have been without a lift fan, and totally inoperable. No hover – no hovercraft. No hovercraft – no expedition. No expedition . . . we had been saved again.

It took us until 10.30 p.m. to get *Neste Enterprise* tidy for the long journey home. The sides had to come up, the covers put on, the kit had to be put into the cabin, and the whole affair roped safely together. The rest of the team pulled down the mess tent and all the other tents, loaded as many of the fuel drums as were left into the back of one of the trucks, and filled up the stores lorries. It was grinding work for us all. We missed the rest of the team, as much for their labour as their presence, and that morning Duncan, Sarah, John and David had sped away in the Landcruiser, depleting our forces even more.

The road journey home to Chengdu was to be via Xining and Lanzhou. Mike knew that it had taken sixteen gruelling days in all to get to Qumerlai from Chengdu, and we certainly did not want to repeat that exercise along those roads any more times than we were forced to. It was reported that the road to Xining was good – Xie Jinkang had recently gone there and returned. The distance to Chengdu via those two capitals was twice as long as the distance we had come via Sichuan. But it could take us a fraction of the time because the roads were so much better. Besides, most of the team were hungry to see more of China now that we were here, and two new capitals of two other provinces smelt good to us all. It did not take long for the Chinese to agree to it. They all wanted to get home as fast as they could. Andrew pointed out that the team had arrived at Qumerlai on 16 May, and finally left on 16 June. Exactly one month.

Day 1 took us to Qingshuihe where, this time, we were accommodated in PLA barrack rooms, rather than in the multi-sex stall. In a most extraordinary way, we were able to divest ourselves of all our Tibetan Christian literature there. It came about by mistake. One of us tentatively offered a

310

one-page tract to one Tibetan, and within five minutes the whole town wanted one. Even a Buddhist monk came to us for any kind of Christian literature, pleading and pleading until he got something. I think we gave him a Chinese New Testament, feeling that, out of most of those there, he could probably read Chinese best. It was remarkable, because the next day we left old Tibet and had no further opportunity for distributing Christian literature. Doing this was very much peripheral to our main expedition aims, but we had brought literature into China openly in our rucksacks, and did not hide it at all. But what we had, we gave away.

On the second day the drivers worked harder than on any previous occasion. We travelled for fourteen hours, stopping only at Ma'do for lunch. At the end of 530 km we reached Gong He, a Han Chinese town of no little significance. It was quite extraordinary to return from Tibetan to Chinese areas, the latter in the last 5 km. It was all so quick. We had become used to the Tibetan way of things, their countryside, their colourful costumes, the wide open spaces. China was tight, cosmopolitan, sophisticated, green and civilised. The return to civilisation was very sudden and unexpected, and quite a shock. I tried to catch the reaction of some of the team to this instant return. Tony felt depressed – back to restrictions and Chinese oppression. Jeremy had been there before (on his way to Tuotuoheyan via Golmud), and was not impressed with the place, especially for the second time. Rob was reminded of home, which, for almost the first time in the expedition, he was longing to reach. I warmed to the atmosphere. I had been very thrilled to be out in the sticks for any length of time, but I thought to myself that I *am* a westerner, and I belonged in a western style of culture. For the first time in what seemed living memory, we came below 3000 m. Our bodies started to sweat once more and the dirt rolled off our grimy hands. I had not realised how much I had missed the simple things like washing, shaving and shampooing. And real loos. Well, semi-real ones anyway.

The greatest discovery of all on that day's journey was the solution to our navigational problems on the river itself. I

311

happened to saunter back on the coach to chat to Tony, who was wielding a map. He knew where he was, and had been following the road throughout the weary kilometres. We got talking, and I expressed my perplexity at the difficulty we had in determining our position at practically any time on the river. Coming down was much better, but we had given up when we arrived at Qumerlai, because we found we still had another hour and a half to go. I discovered that he was as baffled. He had stayed behind at Qumerlai, and had climbed all available hills, even taking photographs of the whole sweep of terrain through 360°. He said he could not see how Qumerlai could possibly be in the place the maps said it was. He came to that conclusion because, on the journey in, he had been following his map as assiduously as he was now doing. But, towards the end of his journey, his driver had asked him to drive, and there was some 70-100 km that he did not follow on the map. But he was convinced that Qumerlai was far further south than the map said it was. Some 70 km or so. All of a sudden it went 'clunk' with me. Of course! I took out my photocopied line-drawn map on which I had written the details of the trips up and down river, and looked at the Satnav position that I had casually jotted down for Qumerlai: it was on the river, exactly 48 nm (87.8 km) further south. In fact, right opposite Z'do, to which we very nearly went when we discovered the road between Yushu and Qingshuihe was so appalling. The key to understanding why our navigation was invariably wrong on the way up was that we started our navigation 48 nm too far up river! I retraced our steps on the map, and it all fell into place. The map position of Qumerlai was badly wrong. Extraordinarily, all the maps we had, Chinese as well as British, were exactly the same, showing the town 87 km out of position. I made a mental note to write a detailed (and probably brusque) letter to the RAF mapping authorities.

At Gong He we left old Tibet – which is now carved up into five Chinese provinces – and I thought about what we had seen and heard. The Tibetans put up with the Chinese because they are a peace-loving people. They shrug and grumble, but do nothing. The Chinese despise the Tibetans, because their peacefulness makes them seem weak, and the Chinese sneer at any weakness, real or apparent. The Chinese approach to the Tibetan is a reaction of culture, not a reaction of intellect or understanding. If they only thought for a moment, they would see that they have in no way conquered or even dented the way of life of the Tibetan, who makes money in a way that no Chinese could, owns and herds his yaks unmolested, worships in the way he has always done, and is utterly untouched by the attempts of China to annexe him or train him into Chinese ways. I have been continually baffled as to why China took over Tibet in the first place. They were no threat, and they were not a buffer to any other threat, and the result is an uncomfortable arrangement. Besides, the land is practically useless for anything. All it has cost China is a lot of hassle and a lot of money.

Day 3's route pointed to Xining, the capital of Qinghai Province. Flat plains, tarmac roads, rounded hills, market garden plots, straw hats, hand carts, trees, grid pylons, large irises, road distances going from 200 to 100, then suddenly and inexplicably changing to 2100 to 2050, bicycles, women and children in pretty clothes, factories belching blue, smoky effluent, railway lines, and traffic lights. We had not realised just how much junk civilisation accrues to itself. But here it all was again, and back in our court.

Xining was a city not much different from Chengdu – dry, characterless streets, dirty with constant rubbish and constant sweeping. Paul Theroux's comment in *Riding the Iron Rooster*, that 'The Chinese are not scrubbers, but inexhaustible sweepers', applied so well. I thought the city would be barren and fairly empty, because it was so far north. But it was a fair metropolis, bustling with life and buildings and people. The hotel was certainly the best we had yet met. It was modern, with a strong western, almost colonial flavour. Outside were fountains in a garden of peonies under shady, overhanging trees. The front door squeaked and they had not realised the UK was on British Summer Time. We sat on a very comfortable settee and were entertained by the antics of the staff trying to alter

313

the time in London (at my suggestion). It was good to know the time in Tokyo, Moscow and New York, if even for fun. The hotel staff felt they knew us; they had been watching the epic happenings on the river on National TV.

The hotel was also very comfortable for the Chinese drivers. They were in fact somewhat out of their depth in such luxury. But they wanted more of it. The following day was absolutely typical of the misunderstandings and frustrations we had with them. We arranged to leave at 10 a.m. Come eleven, there was no sign of anyone except Tang, the student, and Ronnie, who knew nothing. No Madam Zhou, no Xie Jinkang, no Mr Zhou, no Plod, no Lili, no drivers, no one. Just us foreign fools predictably being taken for another ride by the inscrutable Chinese. The bus driver had taken the bus away to buy a new windscreen wiper motor. True, it needed one, and Xining was the first location for purchase. But there was no communication: not even the Chinese guides knew where they were or what they were doing. They too were missing. In the end – around 12.30 – we discovered that the guides were trying to arrange a party for an official who had helped them (us too, apparently) in some of their difficult negotiations to get permits for us for Qinghai. Why hadn't they told us? It never occurred to them! We were the foreign 'devils', they were in charge, we should do what they said. Although we were now outside the closed area and there was no longer any need for us to be chaperoned, we were imprisoned. Mike was furious. He threatened to ring the British Embassy in Beijing, and increased his threats until he actually did. They were thrown by that, and worried. We did not tell them that Norman Willimot was out and had not received the call. But it had the desired effect on the guides. The guides decided to release the convoy to go, regularly calling us the *Lao wai*, a derogatory term. But not so fast! It was time for the drivers to stop for lunch. And lunch they had. They had us over a barrel. No driver, no travel. They all walked off and ate. Why had they been quite happy to travel the day before for fourteen hours and hardly stop? Mike was determined, from then on, to get out of their clutches as soon as he could. He set his mind to go by train from Lanzhou onwards.

The trouble with the Chinese drivers was that they were accountable to no one. When they decide they are going to delay for a day, they cannot get the sack or lose pay; the iron rice bowl remains unbreakable. On return, no one will question them or challenge them or do anything. We achieved on the river itself because, in the final analysis, we were not dependent on Chinese – drivers, regulations, guides – for anything. Just us and our own expertise, our engineering skills and flexibility. The Chinese rationale was to do their own thing or do the 'official' thing in such a way that the westerners are incapable of doing theirs because the two happen to be diametrically opposed. Praise God for the exceptions like Sophie, who was a lady with a very different spirit.

Lanzhou was the next stop. A good road and easy travel, marred by the bus driver stopping just out of Xining to install the new windscreen-wiper motor. It was hilarious watching the wipers wipe the grill first, the lights second, and then fly asymmetrically and alternately around the glass. Three quarters of an hour later they settled it, and we set off in the light drizzle for the capital of Gansu Province.

Just outside Lanzhou we met the red Landcruiser that had taken Andrew into the city ahead of us to try and start the search for railway tickets. We stopped by a railway line, where the steam engines fascinated us for the next 50 minutes or so. The two Chinese drivers in the vehicle said we ought to wait for the rest of the convoy. No amount of persuasion could convince them that it would simply be better for us to go to the hotel and await them there; after all they were destined for it too. It was Rob who eventually broke the deadlock. He merely asked them just how long they were planning to wait for the convoy. One hour? Two? Three? A day, maybe? We left. It took us one and a half hours from the outskirts of Lanzhou to get to the government hotel, which was as posh as the Savoy.

The city was hemmed in from expanding by stark, arid hills that soared vertically upwards not far from the river's edge. It was therefore stretched out, hugging the shores of the mighty Yellow River. Here at Lanzhou the river was some 200 m across, limpid brown and glugging sedately through the centre of the city. The houses were set back from the river's edge by boulevards and avenues of trees and parks. The other side was the old city; we were in the new. The road to the hotel end of town was a dual carriageway, lined with pagoda trees (*Sophora japonica*), whose feather-shaped leaves draped down over the pavements in delightful swathes, shading the pedestrians from the strong summer sun. These trees formed avenues throughout the city, bringing delight to us weary travellers. It was one of the most beautiful cities that I have seen, and it even had signposts on the dual carriageway forbidding the use of horns and klaxons! The streets were tidily laid out. This city was clean. At 1700 m high, it was more tropical than temperate, and the humidity, catching the industrial smog, lay obscurely over the valley until the sun finished the day in glorious gold, yellow, green and orange.

The Chinese decided to take us out to a restaurant for dinner (Peking Duck), but forgot actually to invite us, or inform us in advance. The restaurant was clean but basic, and the food, according to those who enjoy Chinese, good. Tony finished off a plateful of snake. I stuck to the egg–tomato combination, and slid out into the kitchen every now and then to get a first glimpse of World Cup football – our first re-association with TV for what seemed a lifetime.

Andrew had been unable to purchase railway tickets. They have a peculiar system in China. You have to get them three days before your train goes, or pay on the black market. Four days is too early, two days too late. One day is impossible. Mike went to the CITS (the China travel service) to try for tickets. He got there just about 10.45 a.m. Sorry. Lunch is at eleven, come back at two. He went back at two. Sorry, not open – not back from lunch yet. He returned at three. Sorry, the guy who does it is out. (He had been there before lunch, and could easily have done it for us.) I use it as an example of the total lack of interest that shop assistants have in relation to customers. Requests are intrusions. They had their wages: it did not

316

matter to them if we went without tickets, or if they lost the job. They would never lose theirs. So who cares? The iron rice bowl is unbreakable.

We got our tickets. How we managed it is a trade secret. Andrew Sneller was the undercover agent. All I know was that Andrew was about to pay someone something when Ronnie (Mr Xie's ADC) found out and cut Andrew's braces; apparently we foreigners have to pay in FEC (Foreign Exchange Certificate), not in Renminbi (Chinese people's money). Andrew found another avenue for tickets that we said nothing about to any Chinese. These were for the train leaving the next day.

We arranged for Steve, Jim and Tony to go with the convoy and escort the precious hovercraft down to Chengdu, while the rest of us went back on the train. We planned for them to leave at 8.30 a.m., but at nine the drivers were still changing their tyres. The cabin of Big Mac stank with no sanitary provision for the two puppies, Pang and Pong, which we had befriended at Base 2 and which the driver was determined to take back to Chengdu. Moreover the windows had to be kept shut (temp. 25°C), because the police would butcher any dog they found in the city precincts. We discussed breaking the windows before the animals suffered asphyxiation. But we thought better of it: there was little value in creating more hassle. Poor pups. We hurt for them.

We were due to leave on the 1.25 train. Taxis, grossly overladen with kit, carted us to the station, and the train left on time. Mr Xie, Mr Zhou and Lili (in tears) came to see us off, and we were touched by that. Mr Xie had sent Ronnie on to the train to chaperon us, and to make sure we did not get into trouble: he really did not trust us at all. Any more, I suppose, than we trusted him.

*   *   *

Gwyn and I (Neil) were woken by a banging on our door in the early evening. It was Max. He had scrubbed up well and wore a pressed white shirt, brown trousers and polished black shoes. He had arrived for supper, us paying of course, and, yes, noodles again, but in a restaurant quite obviously run by his friends or relatives!

It was Saturday evening and the town of Baoji was alive. The populace were kitted out in their best outfits, walking carefree up and down the main street. After supper Max ushered us to a photographic studio. In fact he owned it. Inside was a pretty girl of around four or five years old. We had been taken to see his family.

Back at the hostel I took another strip wash and on returning to our room found Gwyn, Max and a large family group of local factory workers, one of them speaking good English, conversing on the sofas. At last the real name of our driver was ascertained: Mr Lee. Wheels was Mr Wang.

Mr Lee had invited his friends along to explain that, because the journey from Baoji to Chengdu passed through an area forbidden to foreigners, we must complete our travels by train while he and Mr Wang transported the hovercraft by road. We broke into forced laughter and said under no circumstances would *ICI River Rover* travel without us. Lee replied, via his friend, that the only other possibility was to travel through the forbidden region at night, and so this would mean leaving at three o'clock on the Sunday afternoon. We understood. He was trying to extend the length of their stay in Baoji a few more hours. But since we also would be grateful for the extra time to recover, we agreed.

Now that all parties were relatively happy, sleep was the priority, for us anyway, and so Gwyn and I shifted the Chinese out of the room and climbed into our beds with the thought of another gruelling two days non-stop travelling to look forward to.

On the Sunday morning I had breakfast in the canteen of a workhouse along with all the harvest hands. The previous night a rainstorm had closed in and was still beating down enhancing the disgusting smells floating in the polluted air. The harvest for today had been cancelled and the labourers from out of town, with no home to go to, lined the pavements, sitting and staring into space.

Having packed and taken lunch in the hostel kitchen (the sign Can-Tin – dining room – above the entrance), it was time to fuel up the truck. Mr Lee chugged off on his rotavator tractor to fetch the necessary petrol. I took the time to examine the truck while he was away. No repairs had been made: we had been completely conned!

Lee returned with two drums at the agreed time of three o'clock. We siphoned the fuel into the two truck tanks and also the jerry cans strapped to the *ICI River Rover* deck. Where was Mr Wang? He had not turned up! Having waited an hour Mr Lee was forced to go to his home to fetch him. Lee was not happy with his mate, showing distinct annoyance as he rapidly left the yard. At ten to five Wang arrived sitting on the trailer of a mini-tractor. He was all smiles, and from the look of things had had an eventful Saturday night/Sunday morning!

When Lee returned, his machine, driven by a friend, screeched to a grinding halt outside the compound and the real fun then began! Max (alias Lee) jumped from the rotavator, shouting at the top of his voice and viciously waving a black umbrella. He stormed at ramming speed towards Wang, being prevented from collision by a trucker with stripes on his work unit jacket. A face to face slanging match followed with the two respective labourer stooges who drove their tractors trying to cool things down. We stood and watched. One thing the Chinese people cannot abide is losing face in front of a foreigner.

Mr Lee stormed out of the yard after the intervention of their comrades and Wang stomped back and forth mumbling under his breath. Max returned with a spare front leafspring. This was supposed to have been fitted to the truck already, but he climbed into the cab and rolled out of the compound.

The rain was still pouring down as we left Baoji, adding to the gloomy scene. Jiefang wipers are air-propelled, requiring a fine art in setting the pressure levels for initial start and continuous running, an art which Mr Lee had not mastered. On each attempt to activate them too much air would be supplied and the wipers would shoot off the windscreen. On one occasion when Mr Wang was driving, Gwyn jumped from

319

the cab to reposition the wipers after Wang had shot them off the screen. From that point on they never worked again and Wang was reprimanded by Lee, adding to the tension between the two.

By nightfall the drivers had changed roles many times, hardly a word spoken between them. Due to the rain and no wipers, progress was slow and everyone's tolerance was about to break. Wang, still feeling uncomfortable, took over for a longer stint, driving only on instinct as his eyes were close to being shut. At two in the morning he suddenly brought the truck to an abrupt halt, indicating his watch to say it was Mr Lee's shift. He got out and called up at the *ICI River Rover* cabin. There was not a sign of Mr Lee stirring. After several attempts we took over, climbed on to the hovercraft and dragged the sleeping driver to the cab. Lee, wearing his usual 'What's happening?' smile, reluctantly drove for an hour and then began sleeping on the steering column.

The drivers were supposed to have used our stay in Baoji to recuperate, but instead they had spent their time on other things. Gwyn had seriously lost his patience and dragged Mr Lee from the driver's seat to take his place at the wheel. The truck had been driven by Gwyn a few hundred yards when Max miraculously awoke, a touch perturbed. He insisted Gwyn stop and he take over. A masterful stroke by Gwyn and we were off again not caring that our driver was half-asleep.

We did eventually stop for a few hours rest, till dawn, at around 4 a.m. on a military looking road near a town called Hanzhong in Shaanxi Province. On awakening our driver realised he had taken a wrong turning and we headed back the way we had come the previous night. Breakfast of noodles, hot bread and pancake sticks was taken in the first settlement we passed through; it was the best breakfast I had had in my entire stay in China.

The Sichuan border was no more than one hundred km away. For the entire journey we had only had in our possession a travel permit for this province, and we had travelled through four others. The road began to climb into

320

luscious, tree-covered hills and ran parallel to an extra-ordinary railway line that cut its way through the hillsides and traversed streams on viaducts, a tribute to the engineering of the Chinese people.

It rained persistently, but the damp added to the mystic splendour of this rich green landscape. The top of our climb signified we had reached the corner and the noticeable deterioration of the road surface confirmed we had entered Sichuan. Sichuan Province has a bad reputation for the quality of its roads in mountainous regions; we had experienced them before on the difficult journey to Base 1 at Denke.

The estimated time of arrival in Chengdu was being continually revised as the rutted roads persisted, when to our horror the boys dropped another bombshell. The town I assumed we had stopped at for lunch, was actually where they intended getting the new leafspring fitted. Frustrated, we forcibly indicated they had no more than an hour and a half in which to do the job, and walked off to find a place to eat.

Quite a crowd gathered to watch us eat our noodles, the old lady who ran the restaurant going out of her way to make us comfortable as if she was privileged in having us there. A young boy appeared wearing a large Chinese peasant hat made from banana leaves: I have always fancied one of these traditional coolie hats and offered the lad five yuan for it. The older folk in the crowd quickly made him accept even though he didn't want to sell and the deal was made. I had a feeling I had given much over the odds for this tatty article, but to me, at 50 pence, it was a bargain! The boy returned just as we were finishing our noodles, a torrent of tears streaming from his eyes and holding out the 5 yuan note. I sympathetically gave back the hat, but to my astonishment the old lady produced her own from out back. The same deal applied and so everyone was happy.

When the repairs to the truck were complete we drove onwards to the Jialing river. The rains had swollen the river to almost bursting point and thoughts of hovercraft operation on this swirling, muddy water went through my mind; it was

321

ideal. At Guangyuan we stopped for an early supper, not noodles this time. The rain had enhanced the cesspit stench of this river town to an almost unbearable level. Hexi was the next town *en route* and here we crossed the Jialing, entering a region of paddy fields cut into the hillsides.

Having settled down as comfortably as possible for the remaining 200 km to Chengdu, we encountered a traffic jam of twenty or so vehicles. A Dong Feng truck (meaning East Wind) and a bus had collided, and no vehicles were allowed to pass until the police had arrived. The waiting drivers and passengers had congregated around the accident, so Gwyn and I decided to investigate, much to the annoyance of Mr Wang. He still had not forgiven Gwyn over the wiper incident. The bus was lodged in a ditch and on the brink of overturning. Fortunately none of its occupants had been injured.

The locals, having lost interest in the accident, turned their attention to Gwyn and myself. I opened a tin of compo sweets and began offering the boiled ones to the children, eating the chocolate ourselves. Gwyn offered 2 yuan to an elderly man for his coolie hat, who with a face of astonishment swiftly took the cash. Again it appeared we had offered too much!

Two police cars arrived. They cleared up the situation with lightning speed and just before nightfall we were rolling again. By midnight our drivers settled into their usual half-asleep, half-awake driving routine. To be honest I did not care that the truck was wandering from one side of the road to the other as our driver drifted in and out of sleep. A hot bath at the Medical University was all I was interested in.

In the early hours the rain returned, giving additional perils, and our inoperative wipers meant we were almost driving blind. Our driver leant forward with his nose on the windscreen to see the road ahead. At dawn we had arrived at the Deyang–Chengdu toll road. It was dual carriageway for the majority of the remaining kilometres, enabling constant speeds of over 50 km per hour to be achieved. By nine we were skimming the outskirts of Chengdu itself and Mr Lee was lost! We offered to assist with directions to the university, but he did not believe that foreigners could possibly be capable of knowing their way around. We directed him anyway, using hand signals, sometimes in his face, and arrived at the campus having avoided the rush-hour bicycle traffic.

We had driven close on 3000 km in the most appalling fashion imaginable. All in all, the expedition had travelled 6183 km of Chinese roads; an endurance test of vast proportions.

At this stage we did not have the money to pay the two truckers and were banking on John Whatmore being already at the university with money received from Andrew at Qumerlai. We left Lee and Wang with truck and hovercraft to get a few hours sleep while we organised the cash and labour for unloading. At the residence for foreigners we found John and Rob. They had arrived the previous day by train from Lanzhou. We now had the necessary money and were delighted to learn that *Neste Enterprise* had successfully reached Qumerlai, and was now on the road to Chengdu.

Two o'clock was the agreed time for unloading. Our driver friends were asleep in their cab, but quickly awoke when they got a whiff of money: 7000 yuan was the price agreed at Tuotuoheyan, but we held back the extra 500 yuan because we had ended up carrying all their extra equipment from Golmud to Baoji. Mr Wang shook his head and indicated they wanted the extra 500 yuan. We walked off to the playing field where our containers were situated and beckoned them to follow.

Having positioned the truck in line with the *ICI River Rover* trailer I began unfastening the ropes and straps while Gwyn continued the negotiating. I was soon spotted and Mr Lee tried physically to prevent me continuing, but with the assistance of Ken, an American teacher, we carried on regardless. Two of Ken's female students were helping Gwyn with the interpretation. The argument had reached a level that required the Foreign Affairs Office intervention when the drivers threatened to take us to court. Gwyn jogged off to the office while Ken and I attempted to retrieve

323

the cash, saying they could keep the hovercraft but they must give back the money. Wang switched on the engine as if to drive away, so in response I wedged a railway sleeper between his rear wheels. Revving his engine to full power he dropped the clutch and ploughed off with the sleeper close to ripping the rear axle away. They had both the cash and the hovercraft and were heading towards the university entrance. Sprinting flat out, hurdling over small conifer bushes, I also headed to the gates shouting at the gate police to close them.

An English-speaking student explained the situation to the gate police and they agreed to keep the gates shut. Gwyn had arrived back with an official from the FAO, and a long drawn out discussion ensued for an hour. By this time our student labour had disappeared. A compromise on our part was made, appreciating they may have been out of pocket when selling their fuel. We offered an extra 250 yuan to cover this loss. This was instantly refused. We sensed they were tired and they did not really want to keep *ICI River Rover* and so were determined to compromise no further.

Mr Wang spat at our feet as though we were scum and at last swiped the extra 250 from Gwyn's hand. Smiling, we guided the truck back to the trailer, but our manpower had gone! We set about recruiting others with the help of an unusually muscular basketball player and before long had thirty hands. Unloading proved awkward with the bed of the Jiefang being damaged in the process. It was sad to fall out with the truckers in this manner as our epic journey half-way across China was an experience that all four of us would remember. Finally, with *ICI River Rover* securely on its own trailer, I could have the bath I had dreamed of for two and a half months!

*   *   *

The twenty-five hour train journey from Lanzhou to Chengdu was sweet refreshment for the rest of the team – freedom from the hassle of the tormenting and challenging Yangtze, and freedom from the harassment and tussle of Chinese restrictions.

We were travelling in soft seat luxury, our compartment fringed with lace antimacassars, which were always getting in front of the camera lens. We were in carriage 11 of an eighteen-carriage diesel electric train. Mike and I managed to prise open our window, which ruined the air conditioning system.

The beautiful Lanzhou valley continued as we headed east, following the course of the Yellow River down its green-bottomed valley. Desert hills gradually turned greener, and then layered like Lego on the gigantic Chinese terraced land-recovery scheme. Near Lanzhou the oil seed rape was being harvested. We paralleled the Yellow River for some while, and then turned off on to a tributary. After another 4 hours of descent the barley and wheat had ripened, and, an hour later into the journey, was being harvested. Many workers, including children, shared in scything, collecting, stacking, stooking or carrying bundles into a central collection area. These were of concrete, where threshing, winnowing and separating seed were being done by whole communities. The whole world was busy, and hand-carts, peci-pecis and mini-tractors pulling cart-loads of harvested grain were beetling across the landscape.

The hills and lush green fields were a magnificent sight, stretching across the valley floor, and green and yellow harvest grain caught the evening sunlight in rows of golden lines tiered up to the hilltops. Many rivers or waterways accompanied the train, some parallel, some crossing, some full, some empty. The green parts of the fields, planted with vegetables and crops other than cereal were littered with bamboo greenhouse frames from which polythene had been removed to reveal tomatoes, beans and other vegetables, now enjoying the full health of the sun's 25°C temperature and high humidity.

The villages we passed through were affluent, clean, rural and busy. The homes were of a different style from others we had seen in China. Tidily built in brown-grey brick and roofed with neat red-brown tiles, they were enclosed by

325

a mud wall compound to the front. All the houses were exactly the same. The village roads were avenued with shady trees, as people ate their tea, relaxing for a few moments, sheltering from the hot work of harvesting.

The train stopped at Tanshui to change the engine, and we watched a huge 'grumbly' gather momentum and over-shadow us as we stopped. The wind was warm, balmy and pleasant as we started off again. Raindrops soon began to spatter the inside of the carriage as the flashes of light-ning and rumble of thunder announced that the 'heavy' had caught us up. The delicious scent of wet, scorched earth, singing out a thirsty satisfaction of much-needed water, penetrated the confines of the compartment. We soon had to choose between being delighted or soaked, so we closed the window. The lightning shot across the grey heavens, and the tops of the hills disappeared in the thirst-quenching deluge. The thunderstorm and the night drew on together, closing down the harvesters' labours and initiating the twinkle of lights from the homes, as the evening meals led to well-earned rest. As we clickety-clacked down the track, we seemed to be the only living things in a world going to sleep.

The night was hot, sultry and sweaty, and ventilation was encouraged through the open window. After Mike had woken us up at 6 a.m. to view a spectacular sunrise – bless him – we found ourselves passing through a beauti-ful gorge, going south. A university professor told us in perfect English that the river was the Cha Li, which joined the Yangtze at Chongqing. Houses, farm fields, trees and tracks perched precariously on the steep hillsides, terraces glimpsing the river through their toes. Pagodas poked out of the rock face, and hills squeezed up to green tips in the pink morning, verdant and lush in their tropical abundance. Tight farming and habitation forced the railway to descend to the bottom of the hills and to circumscribe the river, forcing the corresponding road to be on the other side of the water. Little hillocks had brown walled homes capped with dark brown tiles perched on top with their own private copse. A few sampans occasionally graced the riversides, and one pretty red one was ferrying schoolchildren across at 7.30 a.m.

The gorge fell back and the visibility fell in as we moved towards Chun Yuan, where we stopped at 9 a.m. to let dainty white-clad women tap the train wheels with long handled, tiny-headed hammers. The increased humidity stuck our T-shirts to our backs as we poked our cameras into Chinese privacy: we must have learnt that style from the Tibetans! The railway line both into and out of Chun Yuan was bordered by beautiful pink azaleas and bushy rhododendrons, which characterised the quality and scope of the local horticulture and agriculture. Soon, however, the line bent right on to a tributary of the Cha Li, which, exceptionally, was green and clear. Most rivers we had met in China, and all main rivers, were initiators and carriers of erosion; brown and sandy, the water deposited its soil wherever its level diminished. This river, like the Cha Li, was terrific for hovercraft – shallow, sand-banked, and taking broad sweeps round wheat and maize fields on which buffaloes heaved and steamed. Where the river narrowed, leafy domineering hills with rocky outcrops produced wonderful and colourful reflections in the green-mirror water. Fuzzy topped trees on spiky trunks altered the profile of the hills, contrasting with the sparkling white water as it tumbled over tinkling rapids.

By 11 a.m. the narrow confines of the hills, shrugging over the crystal stream, had fallen back, giving way to the Sichuan landscape with which we were most familiar – a wide, flat plain, overhung by grey, depthless cloud, and framed by a fathomless visibility which ended all features in mist. The same intensive sterilised farming that the Han Chinese had perfected over the centuries covered the land, now enhanced by luxuriant growth of trees of all descriptions. Summer was here. It felt and smelt like it. Bare-backed men and thin-bloused women worked in far greater abundance than when we had left in April. Wherever we looked the fields bobbed with straw hats.

We arrived in Chengdu at 1.45 p.m., on time. We taxied to Waxi, and, at last Ronnie came good. He waved our

PLA contract at a policeman and got clearance to allow our minibus through the city to the university. There we found that Gwyn and Neil had arrived, unpacked *ICI River Rover*, put her into the container, and sorted out the problems.

Mopping up the expedition took the now familiar route of prevarication, complication, impediment and opposition. While many of the team went back to the UK, Andrew, Gwyn, Mel and Mike remained to clear up the loose ends. Steve and Jim stayed on to bed the hovercraft into their containers for shipment back to England. Andrew decided to play the Chinese at their own game. When the negotiators arrived for the finalising of the financial side of the contract, he took as long as he possibly could arguing out the details. The bills, for instance, that Madam Zhou had collected from the various hotels and hostels we had slept in, were in total disarray. Andrew went through them one by one, and scrutinised each in turn. After three days he suggested a fair total if they wished to consider it, and then went on patiently picking up one bit of paper at a time. At the start of the expedition it was we who were short of time; now it was the Chinese, and they were getting some of their own medicine back. The next morning they agreed his total! Andrew's final figure for money spent in China was £97,000.

Gwyn stuck doggedly to his task of getting clearance for the containers to get to Hong Kong, and stayed on a further fortnight to do so. He then arranged with Ben Line to transport them back to the UK. Plans are now being made to ship *Neste Enterprise* out to Papua New Guinea to join the hospital patrol team in the Fly River Delta. There, an Australian mission hospital is serving the isolated tribe of the Gogodala people. *Neste Enterprise* would be at home in such company.

Tucked into my mind was the future of Mike's expeditions. He left the RAF in September 1987, and has since been working as Short Term Experience Project (STEP) Director for Latin Link (formerly EUSA). He arranges many aid projects in shanty towns and lonely Andean villages throughout the South American sub-continent annually and encourages young people to go for a few months to tackle these tasks. He was taken on by Latin Link on the understanding that the China expedition was still an outstanding commitment. Now he is too involved in the expanding STEP work to allow himself much time to arrange and lead many further hovercraft expeditions. So what would happen when Mike bowed gracefully out at the end of this one to China? He recruited nine young men and women under thirty years of age to pass on the concept of 'adventure with a purpose', and took them with him to China.

Nigel Pool also had ideas for the future. He suggested we form a UK charity and call it 'Hoveraid'. This would be the umbrella organisation for future expeditions. Within that system Nigel dreamed of short-term, as well as long-term, expeditions. He envisaged retaining one or two hovercraft in the UK on a hire or rent basis. For any water-type disaster anywhere in the world, there would be a craft that could be hired by a nation or an aid agency, flown out on a jumbo-jet, and be available for immediate relief. These hovercraft would be the workhorses and the money-raisers for Hoveraid, providing a much-needed financial footplate from which the Christian expeditions could be launched indefinitely.

Nigel's men have not been idle. Tim's fertile mind had been working for many years on a brand new hovercraft, utilising the patented and extremely effective control system developed in *ICI River Rover*. They call it Hover Lorry. They are designing it to carry three tonnes and to fold up into a ship or aircraft container for instant transportation. This craft could revolutionise isolated areas of the Third World, to bring prosperity, medicine or emergency aid to those who live on or near those parts of the world's rivers that are unnavigable by boat.

Bridges of friendship had been built. A Governor's reception and banquet appropriately preceded the departure of the team from Chengdu. It was chaired by the Vice-Governor responsible for science and technology. Mike was both surprised and pleased when the Vice-Governor apologised for the self-centred attitudes of the truck drivers.

'Next time we will do better,' he said. He expects us to return.

The test programme on materials on the hovercraft carried out by Mel and Sam had proved most productive. Scientific links with Sichuan and with Loughborough and Leicestershire could now be expanded.

In September the University of Loughborough awarded the project an honorary degree in technology. Partnered by Magdi Yacoub, the heart surgeon, Mike received the degree on behalf of the expedition. Their expertise was very much at opposite ends of the medical/scientific spectrum, but equally valid to exploration in the 1990s.

Early in 1991 the expedition received two further accolades. The *Guinness Book of Records* accepted the altitude record for hovercraft of 16,050ft. And we were awarded the Sir Christopher Cockrell Award for advances in the use of hovercraft. This was only the second time it had ever been granted.

The real success of the project would be if the Chinese would now take hovercraft permanently to their remote areas. We had shown it could be done. We had encouraged peoples living in remote areas. We had participated in the global UNICEF programme by vaccinating children. Our medical staff have been invited back to China to serve in different capacities – an invaluable spin-off from the expedition itself.

Some people question whether such expeditions, using sophisticated western technology and money much needed elsewhere, should ever go ahead. Others question whether the Christian Church should have any part in such enterprises, and whether such technology is appropriate hardware for the proclamation of the cross of Christ. We feel that it is the West itself that has bled the developing world, starved them of their own food, ignored their plight, and failed to cancel their financial debts to enable them to start again. In such circumstances we western Christians have an obligation to apologise for the sins of our own countrymen by taking the highest technology and the very best we can find to those we have wronged, and delivering it free of charge. That should ever be the commission of the Church to the poor. Our Commanding Officer has not yet rescinded his orders to get up and go to those in need. A member of the Chinese TV crew wrote a series of reports in a Sichuan newspaper about our expedition. He was so impressed with our approach and attitude to those to whom we went that he called his articles 'Yangtze love'.

The first-ever journey to the source of the Yangtze had been completed.

We had been given a priceless and unrepeatable privilege.

Epilogue

Thank you for joining us, for your companionship, for your prayer, for your support. I hope that you have been renewed, as we were, by your experience of China. Life can never be the same again.

Please don't go back into a dull routine.

I want to invite you, now, to seek out a mountain of your own to conquer; to find something new for you that will brighten your life, challenge your initiative, stretch your boundaries, test your faith.

There's a new world beyond your road that is very beautiful, but often laden with grief, full of heavy hearts, desperate for a helping hand to support and comfort: people in need.

What about extending your skills – languages, music, art, poetry, technology? Travel? Creativity? Prayer?

Choose your mountain.
Set your will.
Share your vision.
Collect your companions.
Arrange your facilities.
GO!

APPENDIX A

Map of the upper 700 miles of the river Yangtze

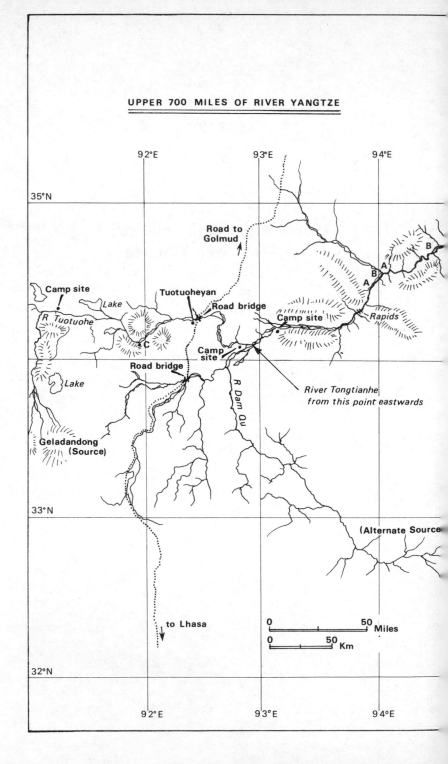

UPPER 700 MILES OF RIVER YANGTZE

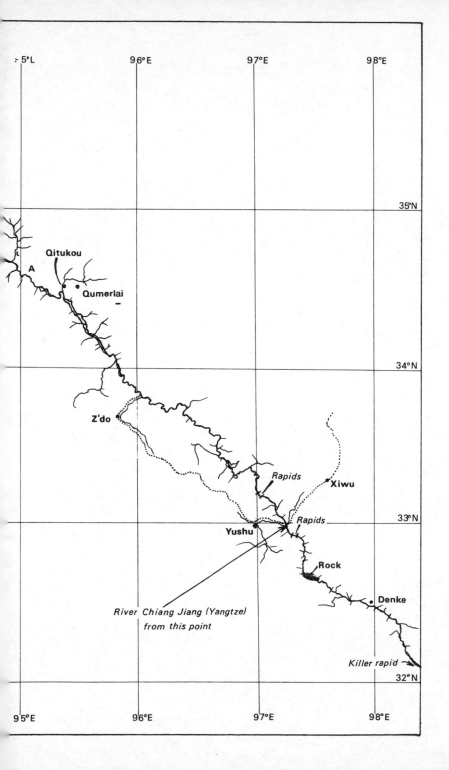

APPENDIX B

Abbreviations and Chinese words

AMS	Acute Mountain Sickness
BSC	Beijing Sports Commission
CAAC	Civil Aviation Authority of China
CAC	Chengdu Aircraft Corporation
CAD	Computer Aid Design
CAS	Chinese Academy of Science
CITS	China Inland Travel Service
CSS	China Sport Service Company
CUST	Chengdu University of Science and Technology
EPI	Expanded Programme of Immunisation
EUSA	Evangelical Union of South America
FAO	Foreign Affairs Office(s)
FEC	Foreign Exchange Certificate
FOC	Friends of China
H/F	High Frequency
MCH	Mother and Child Health Unit
NAPS	Neste Advanced Power Systems
OCU	Officers' Christian Union
OMF	Overseas Missionary Fellowship
PLA	People's Liberation Army
PRC	People's Republic of China
PRI	Polymer Research Institute
RARDE	Royal Armament Research and Development Establishment
RBMU	Regions Beyond Missionary Union
REME	Royal Electrical and Mechanical Engineers
SMA	Sichuan Mountaineering Association
STEP	Short Term Experience Project
UNICEF	United Nations International Children's Emergency Fund
UNIDO	United Nations Industrial Development Organisation

337

danwei	work unit
guanxi	who you know; your connections
Lao wai	'old foreigner'. A derogatory name for foreigners.
Pinyin	Chinese script
Putonghua	Mandarin language
taohua	peach blossom
waibin	foreigner
xinghua	apricot blossom
Yinggua	English language
yuan	Chinese currency: approximately 10 yuan to the pound
zixingche	bicycle

APPENDIX C

The hump problem on hovercraft

Many people believe, quite mistakenly, that a hovercraft hovering stationary over water needs very little thrust from its propellers in order to move forward. 'Surely,' they say, 'isn't it riding on a cushion of air?' The answer is, 'Yes it is,' but that cushion of air is actually creating a trough or depression in the water beneath the hovercraft's skirt. The water so displaced is actually equal to the weight of the hovercraft, in just the same way as a boat or any floating object displaces its own weight of water.

Just as a boat produces a bow wave as soon as it starts moving forward, so does a hovercraft. Then, as speed increases, so does the size of the bow wave. If there is sufficient thrust from the propellers there will come a point where the craft will literally climb up over its own bow wave and begin skimming or 'hydroplaning' over the water. It is this phenomenon which is known as 'getting over hump'. Having once succeeded in doing this (at between 10 and 15 mph – known as 'hump speed'), the craft will quickly accelerate to its cruising speed (between 30 and 40 mph). At this speed it is usually possible to reduce power, and the amount of fuel used per mile travelled could be less than one-fifth of that used by a craft struggling 'below hump'.

Where a short length of beach or flat land is available, a heavily loaded hovercraft can use it to accelerate to a speed faster than hump speed, so that when the craft reaches the water it will continue in a hydroplaning condition.

Tim Longley
Hovercraft designer

339

APPENDIX D

Expedition scientific report

Introduction

A primary objective of the expedition was to study and field test the effectiveness of new innovative hovercraft materials and structures under extreme environmental conditions. Also of interest were the Permafrost characteristics in the source area of the Yangtze river. In the former case particularly, it was entirely appropriate that the project was carried out in association with several international companies and institutions, especially the Finnish State Oil Company (Neste) who were the principal sponsors. Other major supporters included ICI plc, Cathay Pacific, Exxon (Esso) plc, Chengdu Aircraft Corporation, Loughborough University of Technology (IPTME), KHD (Deutz) UK, Renault UK and Herbert Pool Ltd. (A full list of sponsors, including those who supported the scientific programme, is in Appendix F.)

A prominent Chinese university with an international reputation in polymer science and composite materials, Chengdu University of Science and Technology, was involved as part of the Leicestershire–Sichuan Province friendship 'twinning' scheme along with seconded scientists from the Chinese Academy of Sciences. The expedition also helped to consolidate the 'twinning' links that exist between Leicester City and Chongqing City.

Two hovercraft were eventually taken on the expedition, the six-seater *ICI River Rover* and the 18-seater Griffon 2000 TDX *Neste Enterprise*. These formed the basis of the scientific study.

Structures and materials

Of particular structural interest on the hovercraft were low-weight composites, with sections of the craft suitably instrumented to allow 'in-flight' monitoring of temperature, heat flux, fatigue,

341

vibration, environmental and corrosion effects and so on. A key area of the Loughborough University research input was in the development of ICI 'Verton' glass fibre/nylon propulsion and lift fans. Here the enhanced mechanical properties provided by the relatively long 'short-fibre' reinforcement were utilised without precluding their fabrication by an injection moulding route.

Similarly, new composites with a Neste blister resistant gel coat were developed for propeller ducts.

In the case of the decking area, ICI 'Plytron' fibre reinforced thermoplastic composites were formulated into a unique geometry and cut to shape using advanced, high-powered, computer-controlled laser guns. Performance, lightness and cost were optimised using special fibre treatments and monitored by strain gauging, ultrasonic NDT and electronic speckle pattern interferometry as appropriate.

Frames carried beneath the craft allowed the impact, abrasion and environmental resistance of a series of small, pre-conditioned composite panels supplied by PERA, Melton Mowbray, to be tested in live hazardous conditions. Similarly, frames on the deck carried Neste and LUT 'blister resistant' GRP panels for exposure-testing in the extreme environmental conditions. In the latter case the field testing confirmed the breakthrough currently being made at Loughborough in formulating weather resistant composites.

Where possible, the special insulation materials used to keep vaccines at controlled temperatures were also monitored. Of particular interest were solar-powered refrigerated (NAPS) containers and metallised plastic pouches.

Hybrids

Prior to the expedition, laboratory experiments indicated that it was possible to produce cost-effective, high-performance polymer composite materials by judicious reinforcement and mixing (hybridisation) of both high- and low-performance fibres in the same matrix system. A typical example of this was the combination of carbon (high-performance) fibre and glass (low-performance) fibres in a polypropylene thermoplastic matrix. Such a hybrid composite was proposed as a decking material for experimental hovercraft for use in Third World contexts where low cost is as important as good performance. It is significant therefore that (high cost) carbon-fibre laminated structures in which 50 per

342

cent of the fibres are replaced or 'diluted' by (low cost) E-glass fibres have been shown to produce hybrid composites in which 90 per cent of the original flexural strength can be retained at an approximate 50 per cent cost reduction. This assumes that the carbon fibre content is the predominant cost parameter.

In preparing to study the performance of the hovercraft decking material and the propulsion fans, three stages were identified.

- Pre-expedition characterisation of materials and structures.
- Field recording and assessment of environmental and applied operational conditions.
- Post-expedition characterisation of materials and structures with particular reference to degraded performance.

Initially several different polypropylene-based decking materials were evaluated including quasi-isotropic 8-ply glass/carbon fibre lay-ups based on $0°/90°/0°/90°/90°/0°/90°/0°$ and $-45°/0°/+45°/90°/90°/+45°/0°/-45°$ geometries. Finally, however, the most promising system was found to be based on a solid polypropylene core, stiffened by polypropylene skins reinforced with $0°/90°$ carbon fibre. Similarly the fan blades were based on long 'short' glass fibre reinforced Nylon 66 injection mouldings.

A full programme of mechanical property characterisation was carried out using ESH hydraulic test methods and following CRAG recommendations, which established tensile/compressive strength and modulus, flexural strength and modulus, and the interlaminar shear strength of the materials under investigation. Falling weight impact tests were carried out using a Rosand IFWIT system. Polymer matrices were characterised using infra-red spectro-photometric and differential scanning calorimetric techniques, and fibre orientation was studied using X-radiographic and ultrasonic C-scan techniques. Matrix water content was established gravimetrically.

Field assessment

A detailed record was kept throughout the expedition of both the environmental conditions and the response of the materials exposed. Figure 1 lists the various transducers used and Figure 2 their location on the two hovercraft. The specific experiments that were attempted are detailed in Figure 3. A full, post-expedition, examination of the composite structures on the hovercraft is still currently taking place, including ultrasonic

343

C-scan assessment and mechanical testing so that the effect of environment on property changes can be established.

Additional testing will eventually include full scanning electron microscopic examination and a limited number of tension-tension fatigue tests on post-expedition samples for comparison with unconditioned control samples.

Permafrost characteristics

A study of the Permafrost (permanently frozen subsoil) and debris flow conditions in the Upper Yangtze region were carried out by Wang Yuzhang and Tang Zhongshi of the Chinese Academy of Sciences. Their general conclusions may be summarised as follows although their detailed findings will be published later in a full report.

First, permafrost is horizontally distributed both widely and discontinuously.

Second, the horizontal distribution is affected and limited by the warming effect of rivers, lakes and geological structures such as fault zones.

Third, the vertical distribution is affected and limited by both latitude and altitude resulting in complex patterns.

Preliminary conclusions

Initial results indicated some interesting trends after the two months' exposure to extreme weather conditions (such as high intensity UV sunlight, surface temperature variations between −10°C and +50°C, rain, hail and dust storms all capable of occurring within the same twenty-four hour period; see Figure 4).

First, the Plytron deck performed well without any evidence of cracking, delamination or fibre pull-out. Difficulties of paint adhesion were tackled using acid etch pretreatments to provide better 'keying'.

Second, Neste and LUT gel coats were found to perform well without blistering particularly those derived from poly(propylene glycol maleate) and isophthalic systems.

Third, Verton fan blades optimised at 35 per cent volume glass fibre reinforcement proved particularly effective with sufficient stiffness to be aerodynamically efficient and yet with sufficient flexibility and toughness to facilitate water passage without fracture (when passing through rapids).

344

A full scientific report in support of this article is available from the author on request.

M. O. W. Richardson
Scientific leader

Figure 1. The data recorded on the hovercraft

Temperature
  external air
  cabin surface
  deck surface upper
  deck surface lower
  engine exhaust gas
  engine cooling water
  river water
  solar fridge

Vibration
  rear deck
Strain
  duct
Heat Flow
  rear deck
Windspeed
  external

Humidity
  external

Figure 2. Transducer locations

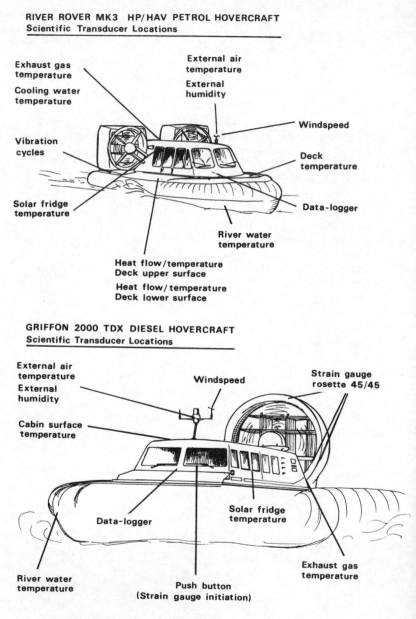

RIVER ROVER MK3 HP/HAV PETROL HOVERCRAFT
Scientific Transducer Locations

Exhaust gas temperature
Cooling water temperature
External air temperature
External humidity
Windspeed
Vibration cycles
Deck temperature
Solar fridge temperature
Data-logger
River water temperature
Heat flow/temperature Deck upper surface
Heat flow/temperature Deck lower surface

GRIFFON 2000 TDX DIESEL HOVERCRAFT
Scientific Transducer Locations

External air temperature
External humidity
Windspeed
Strain gauge rosette 45/45
Cabin surface temperature
Data-logger
Solar fridge temperature
River water temperature
Push button (Strain gauge initiation)
Exhaust gas temperature

Figure 3. Specific experiments on board the hovercraft.

1 Plytron CFRP Deck Performance
  degradation evaluation, eg fibre pull-out
  coating evaluation, eg paint delamination
  (additional samples in exposure frame)
2 Neste GRP Duct Performance
  stress/strain evaluation
  gel coat blister resistance
  (additional samples in exposure frame)
3 Verton Propulsion Fan Performance
  impact resistance
  strength and modulus
4 Neste Solar Fridge Efficiency
  internal temperature maintenance
5 PERA GRP Performance
  pre-impacted exposure panels

Figure 4. Some examples of environmental conditions

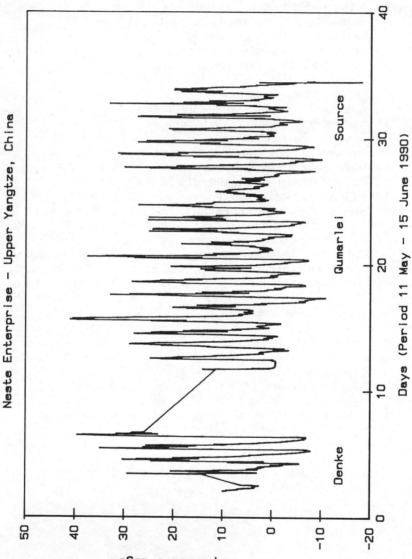

APPENDIX E

Expedition medical report

Introduction

The prospect of reaching the source of the Yangtze river in a hovercraft excited all of us who were in the planning stages of the expedition from the beginning. The adventure aspects of the expedition were evident and the scientists were enthusiastic about the experiments they wanted to perform. It was obvious that the medical team would have quite a responsibility in looking after the health of the expedition team but we hoped that we might also be able to contribute something of value to the Chinese during the time of the expedition. We discussed with the Chinese health authorities how best we might contribute, realising that unless we could respond to their felt and perceived needs we would be wasting their time and ours. The initial discussions highlighted the possibility of our expanding their immunisation campaign in the remote areas and amongst the minority groups where the logistics of getting the vaccines delivered in good condition and at the right temperature was proving something of an obstacle for them. It was also clear from our discussions that any teaching in the form of exchange of ideas would be useful and acceptable. We hoped to learn about the Chinese system of medicine and to see some of their traditional medical practices, and the concept of 'experience exchange encounters' with our Chinese colleagues and counterparts was an exciting one.

The medical programme of the expedition was led by Dr Rachel Pinniger, a paediatrician with extensive experience in the Third World. She was assisted by Miss Bridget McClune, a nursing sister from St Thomas' Hospital in London. In addition, four other doctors who had been involved since the planning stages spent approximately two months each (that is, half the total time) at different times on the expedition. They were Dr Arne

349

Brantsaeter, a microbiologist and physician from Norway, Dr Bill Gould, a surgeon and general practitioner, Dr David Langley, a general practitioner, and Mr Padman Ratnesar, an ENT surgeon, all from England.

Miss Fiona Rhodes left her veterinary practice and lecturing post at Edinburgh University to join the team as a vet. Mr Ton Schreuders, a physiotherapist from Holland working in Thailand in a leprosy programme, was also a valuable member of the team for a short time as an adviser and lecturer in leprosy, and Dr David Johnson, a surgeon working in Brazil, came on the latter part of the expedition as an observer, but proved to be a great help to the medical team also.

Context

Over the past thirty years China has made enormous improve-ments in many areas, including health. The policy of the one child family, though not without its social implications and ramifica-tions, has improved the health of that one child greatly. Now such states as frank malnutrition are rarely seen. Campaigns for the control of a number of diseases through immunisation have also been very successful, for example in Sichuan Province in 1985 the authorities set a goal to be reached in 1990 of 85 per cent vaccination coverage in children in their first year of life against six diseases (diphtheria, whooping cough, tetanus, polio, tuberculosis and measles). Not only did they reach their goal, they actually achieved a 92 per cent rate of fully-vaccinated infants and saw a dramatic decline in the morbidity and mortality of four of these diseases. (Childhood TB and neonatal tetanus are not reportable diseases.) Nevertheless the logistical problems of reaching all the children are considerable in a province such as Sichuan, which contains one-tenth of China's population: 43 per cent of the province's land area is on the plateau to the north-west but only 1.5 per cent of the population reside there. Consequently there are less than four people for each square kilometre. The vaccination coverage among this group is considerably less than that among the people in the more densely populated areas because of the vast distances involved and the problems of transport. Consequently when the medical programme for the expedition was discussed with UNICEF staff in Beijing on one of the early preparation trips, the idea of the expedition's team assisting in the immunisation programme in the remote areas to be visited was suggested. This was later approved by the Chengdu Health Authorities.

Background of medical programme

For three years prior to the expedition, the medical programme was under discussion. During that time there were five reconnaissance visits when we were exploring how best we might assist and contribute medically while in China. We drew up a 12-point medical plan, the cornerstones of which were the immunisation programme and a teaching programme. Through a series of seminars in the city hospitals and Medical School of Sichuan, we would teach but also learn from our Chinese counterparts. Ultimately our 12-point plan was condensed to a 4 point plan because this was more acceptable to the Chinese Health officials.

Team health – pre-expedition

Numbers on the expedition varied at different times and were dependent on availability as well as the specific tasks that had to be performed at different times. However an average number was thirty members of which six were women. Ages ranged from nineteen to sixty-nine years. We were travelling to one of the remotest areas of the world and the health risks were not inconsiderable. Consequently a very detailed protocol of pre-expedition health care was drawn up which included:

(a) 10 months ahead of departure a letter to each expedition member's general practitioner asking if they would give the member a full medical assessment, supervise the vaccination schedule (tetanus, hepatitis B, rabies, typhoid, polio, BCG, meningococcal meningitis, Japanese B encephalitis and immunoglobulin) and carry out the following tests – full blood count, urinalysis, blood pressure, chest X-ray and blood grouping.

(b) A letter with (a) above to each team member outlining the vaccinations and tests which their GP was being asked to carry out.

(c) A detailed questionnaire to each member similar to the questionnaire insurance companies send to people who apply for insurance policies. Obviously past medical, surgical and psychiatric histories were investigated. We felt there was

351

also much value in the information we gleaned about spouse, children and parents in giving background to a member's situation.

(d) A training weekend three months ahead of the expedition's departure in the YMCA National Centre Lakeside in the Lake District National Park. Lakeside specialises in running development training programmes and they put on an excellent weekend for us. We planned the programme together and the staff at Lakeside were so cooperative and understanding of our needs. The value of spending time together pre-expedition was very clear and our only regrets were that it was a once-only opportunity and all too short. During that weekend we outlined a fitness programme spanning the next three months so that members of the expedition would be at peak fitness by the time the expedition started.

(e) Two months before departure each member was issued with a six-page document called a Health Brief, where general advice on diarrhoea and oral rehydration therapy, malaria prevention, insect and snake bites, exposure etc. was given. In addition a fairly detailed account of the possible effects of high altitude and the prevention, recognition and treatment of acute mountain sickness were detailed, in view of the fact that we were going to be travelling to altitudes around 16,000 ft (5000 m) above sea level.

Medico-legal aspects

The medical team were well aware that they were involved in a potentially dangerous expedition, considering the possibilities of acute mountain sickness, the hazards of temperature extremes from $-10°C$ to $+50°C$, the difficulties of transportation over narrow mountain passes and the dangers on the river once the hovercraft were in operation. Consequently we discussed the wisdom of warning each team member of the potential hazards of joining the team and also of requesting each team member to sign a disclaimer to the effect that neither they nor their relatives would institute legal proceedings against any member of the medical team should there be any complication following medical advice or treatment. The discussion came out of news from a previous expedition on the Yangtze river in which the youngest American member of a Sino–American rafting expedition died of altitude sickness and was buried alongside the upper reaches of the river.

A court case was held, and the verdict of the court was that the expedition officials could not be blamed because the man had been aware of the potential dangers in such a hazardous expedition. However, when we took legal advice to see if we might persuade expedition members to sign a disclaimer absolving us from blame, we were told that such a document would not be worth the paper on which it was written.

Politico-medical aspects

Originally we discussed a 12-point medical plan of campaign with the Public Health Bureau in Chengdu. Detailed plans were jointly formulated for some aspects. Others we anticipated would require a little further discussion and clarification when we arrived. However, just before we left for China the original immunisation programme was reduced and upon our arrival in China various other objections were raised. Exactly what these were was not always easy to ascertain, but over the period of weeks when we were experiencing delay after delay it became apparent that the mechanism was not yet in place to support a larger immunisation programme in such a remote area, and politically the areas through which we would be passing were too sensitive to allow us much contact with local people. They did not want us to treat their people except in an emergency and we agreed not to do this except in consultation with the local practitioner.

Careful negotiation was the order of the day, and a précis of our original 12 points became a 4-point plan which proved to be acceptable to the People's Liberation Army in Beijing. We also signed a contract with the Public Health Bureau of Sichuan Province in which we agreed to cooperate together in the planning and implementation of an immunisation programme. We agreed to donate four solar refrigerators for use in their expanded programme of immunisation (EPI), two to be located in Chengdu for training and evaluation and two in Dege County Epidemic Prevention Station. We would also assist in their vaccination programme, supply the syringes and needles, hold a training course on the installation, operation and maintenance of the refrigerators, conduct medical seminars and donate the finance for these programmes.

Teaching programme

During any visit to another country to give assistance an important question to address is 'What can I contribute to this country that is going to be of value after I leave?' Our discussions with the Public Health Bureau officials on previous visits had left us in no doubt that teaching, lectures and demonstrations would be welcomed. Consequently a series of twenty seminars for doctors, nurses, medical students and paramedics was arranged in the university and city hospitals in Sichuan's capital Chengdu. The response to these lectures was both encouraging and overwhelming. In addition, as the expedition proceeded up the river, further teaching was done in the small towns alongside the river. In Dege following the training programme on solar refrigerators, Ray Pinniger took eight seminars on primary child care. At Denke the doctors from the local hospital came out to the camp to see a slide presentation on the management of diarrhoea and entered into discussions on treatment with locally made rehydration fluids. It was obvious that such teaching and involvement was much appreciated, whether in the academic environment of a university city or the grass roots environment of a remote township.

We were fortunate to be able to strengthen our medical team for the seminar programme in Chengdu by the addition of Professor Garth Hastings, a UNIDO adviser and consultant on artificial limbs and braces. His contribution was invaluable as was that of our leprosy expert from Thailand, Ton Schreuders, as he spoke on the prevention of disability in leprosy.

Following on from the seminars we received invitations individually to visit our counterparts in various specialties, and in a number of instances to return and give help at a later date. Mr Padman Ratnesar was welcomed into the ENT unit. Professor Hastings was able to visit the Artificial Limb Centre and advise. He is already planning to return there in 1991. Bridget was shown around an intensive care unit. Ton and Bill spent time with the orthopaedic surgeon and leprosy specialist and were later invited to visit one of the four leprosaria in Sichuan Province, an overnight train journey further to the south. They were asked to advise on some thirty patients who had various deformities as a result of their leprosy infection, and Ton gave two further lectures following on from his teaching in Chengdu. Their visit was especially appreciated and the thanks they received were very warm. A further by-product of our being delayed in Chengdu was that of being able to visit the Sichuan Research Academy of Traditional Chinese Medicine, where we saw acupuncture and moxibustion being performed, a Mother and Child Health Unit and an exhibition at the Family Planning Unit. After the end of the expedition, Ton received an invitation to return to China to give further advice on leprosy, and Ray was invited back to give a series of seminars in Chengdu on paediatrics. This was a sure indication that the medical programme had been well received and the team were leaving behind something of lasting value.

Disappointment

Having been involved in so much hard work in the planning and negotiation stages, in the seminar programme and the post seminar spin-offs, it was with real sadness that because of the lengthy delays in Chengdu, Arne, Bill and Padman had to return to their homes and other commitments without having been on the river. None the less their hard work in Chengdu most certainly facilitated the rest of the team's journey to the mighty river.

Mountain sickness

Much has been written about mountain sickness in recent years. There are two main types – acute mountain sickness (AMS), which may affect anyone within three weeks of ascending rapidly to altitudes over 3000 m (10,000 ft); and chronic mountain sickness. This is much rarer than AMS and was originally thought to occur only in South America. Recently, however, it has been described by Dr Pei of Lhasa in Tibet and others as occurring in the Han Chinese who have lived many years in Tibet.

Bill and Ray tried to make contact with Dr Pei by letter, and during the waiting period in Chengdu were able to travel to Lhasa to discuss the whole problem of altitude sickness with him.

We were responsible for an expedition team travelling up to altitudes of 5000 m and the possibility of at least one member suffering from severe AMS was quite likely: we needed to be well prepared. We had already taken certain steps:

(a) Team members were taught the importance of prevention and slow ascent, and to recognise the signs and symptoms of AMS.
(b) This teaching was reinforced by a printed handout.

355

(c) We had adequate supplies of drugs used in AMS, including diuretics and oxygen, and had also a treatment protocol to be followed in case of emergency.

(d) We carried with us a Gamow bag which we had been able to hire. This is the very latest and apparently the most effective weapon in combating the effects of severe AMS by simulating an altitude descent of nearly 3000 m (9000 ft).

(e) At altitude each team member would fill out a questionnaire daily which could pick out prodromal symptoms or highlight possible dangers.

Nevertheless we thought it would be beneficial to meet a local expert who had first-hand experience of altitude sickness, and who might be able to suggest a joint research project. Dr Pei kindly showed us round his unit and expressed interest in the expedition. We would not be allowed to take blood samples from local people alongside the Yangtze river, so we could not investigate chronic altitude sickness in this area as we had hoped, but Dr Pei affirmed our ideas of monitoring expedition members at certain altitudes by looking at their blood pressures, pulse rate, haemoglobin, haematocrit, urea and cholesterol.

Dege medical programme

Dege is internationally famous for its Buddhist monastery and for its Tibetan scripture publishing press (where every process is done by hand). It lies in close proximity to the river and was the centre chosen for us for the immunisation programme. We had realised that Dege is a politically sensitive area and restrictions were placed on our movements and activities. We wanted to visit the local Tibetan and Chinese hospitals, but that privilege was withheld. However, the local inhabitants gave us a real welcome, as did the staff members of the Anti-Epidemic Station and the Mother and Child Health (MCH) Unit.

It is worth tracing the background to China's Immunisation Programme:

14 per cent of China's 1.2 billion people are children up to seven years old.

1972 – Immunisation started.
1982 – Cold chain strengthened and coordinated by UNICEF and WHO through the EPI programme (the Expanded Programme of Immunisation).

356

1986 – Goal set of 85 per cent vaccination coverage in children under twelve months (age limit extended to eighteen months for remote areas).
– Goal set for eradication of polio nationally by 1995.

Achievements
1989 – In a sampling survey 92 per cent of children under one year were fully vaccinated against the six EPI diseases.
– Vaccine quality is improved.
– Morbidity and mortality rates of the target diseases were reduced between 1987 and 1988 with a decline of 15-50 per cent in four of the six diseases (figures for TB and tetanus are not known).

Our input at Dege was:

1. Training programme on solar refrigerators
Participants came from the local MCH Unit and from the Anti-Epidemic Stations of Dege and as far afield as two and a half days' drive away. Dr Fang Gang from the Provincial Anti-Epidemic Station in Chengdu coordinated events and the team appreciated this cooperation.

Fiona Rhodes (our vet) and Duncan Hanton (logistics team) spent the first three days teaching and giving practical training on the two solar refrigerators which we were donating to Dege. They proved to be both popular and expert communicators. Immunisation coverage can only be extended by extending the cold chain, that is by refrigeration, and the solar refrigerator is an excellent addition to this process. However it is essential for the people using the refrigerators at the local level to understand the working and upkeep of such machines so that efficiency is maintained all the time. Otherwise the vaccines will lose their potency.

We used presterilised disposable syringes and needles for the immunisations and were able to donate a supply to the EPI team.

The participants on the course made a frame for the solar panels out of local materials and fixed it to the roof of the building where the refrigerator was located. The other refrigerator was put in the unit's jeep for transporting vaccines. Originally these mobile fridges had been christened Camel fridges because they had been loaded on to camels in Africa. In these high mountains of China and Tibet the yak is the only animal capable of carrying such heavy loads. We now have a Yak fridge. During our time in Dege we demonstrated that the yak can carry the vaccines

357

in the fridge, the batteries and the solar panels, all 120 kg, to remote settlements, so extending the cold chain and thus removing one of the greatest hindrances to total immunisation for children in China.

These solar-powered refrigerators were donated by Neste/NAPS for use in the EPI programme along the river bank in the remote areas through which we passed. We left two in the Provincial Anti-Epidemic Station in Chengdu for training and evaluation purposes and two remained with the expedition. All of these continued to function very well under extremely rigorous conditions. A report received from Dege five months later stated their two refrigerators were continuing to function satisfactorily in the cold chain. The assessment made by the provincial immunisation programme managers on these units is that they are extremely valuable in such remote areas where there is no electricity and transport relies on porterage by man or animals, but that at the present time in a country the size of China the cost is prohibitive.

2. Immunisation programme
Immediately following the demonstrations, the immunisation programme began and the six vaccines were given to the children of this area. Vaccines administered were BCG, diphtheria, pertussis, tetanus, measles and polio. Many of the children we saw had already had some of their immunisations, but in general the uptake in the area is low and the authorities felt that there was great value in using the expedition team to publicise and popularise the immunisation programme. The local media carried news of the event.

3. Seminar programme
In the last two days Ray gave a series of illustrated lectures on topics in primary child care of particular interest to the participants.

Team health during expedition

1. Medical cover and equipment
The journey from Chengdu to the upper third of the Yangtze proved to be a major logistical exercise and also a test of our medical planning. The team was split into three groups, each group travelling independently of the others. At least one medic was assigned to each group and each group had an emergency medical

kit carried in Leisuremed cases. Depending on the vehicles in the convoys and on road conditions – snow, ice, mud, landslides – the journey took from three to eight days. During the journey passes up to 4917 m (15,755 ft) were crossed. The potential for acute mountain sickness (AMS) was there so we were fortunate that the only symptoms encountered were headache, insomnia, shortness of breath on exertion and loss of appetite. We had issued a clear guideline to the team that nights should be spent at a lower altitude than the highest point reached that day by road (the important point being that descent is the best antidote to AMS) and generally this was observed but on occasion, having been caught in snow and difficult road conditions, the team had no option.

Once operational on the river, emergency kits were carried in each hovercraft as well as in the support road vehicles. Each medic carried a more comprehensive kit. There were instructions in the emergency kits on the treatment of the more common and likely medical problems.

Very strict rules and regulations were in force concerning the wearing of life jackets while on the hovercraft.

Specialised equipment included a Gamow bag (see AMS), a Laerdal resuscitation kit and a comprehensive collection of surgical equipment which meant we were ready to carry out major surgery should the need arise. After all we were several days from Chengdu by road, even allowing for good road conditions, and evacuation by air or helicopter was not an option.

2. Camp logistics
(a) Water. A safe water supply is an absolute essential for an expedition team. We carried a stellameta filter and a large katadyne filter for camp use, and a small katadyne and PWP personal filters for use away from camp. We also had with us a Paqualab portable laboratory with which we could check all our water sources for bacteriology, turbidity, conductivity, pH, and hardness. In addition we could also carry out fifteen biochemical estimations. We found that all samples, with the exception of those taken near the source of the Yangtze, were heavily contaminated with E.coli, a sure sign of faecal contamination. Ammonia levels and conductivity also indicative of faecal contamination were high in several samples and copper, boron, silica and fluoride levels likewise were raised. The increased turbidity in the main river is a direct risk to health as the suspended particles

359

offer ideal sites for bacteria, offering them protection against disinfection. However, we were pleased to find that all the filters produced clear, bacteria-free drinking water.

The Paqualab, though heavy to carry, is an extremely impressive and useful piece of kit for water testing in the field.

(b) Food. Supplies in these remote, mountainous areas are difficult to obtain, so we carried sufficient army rations and other tinned and packet food for the entire expedition. Fresh vegetables and fruit are scarce, and those available are transported out from the Chengdu basin, China's fertile 'rice basket'. 'On the road' meals were often taken in local hotels avoiding unboiled water and uncooked vegetables. The almost complete absence of flies undoubtedly helped to limit the amount of gastro-intestinal upsets.

(c) Latrines. Deep pit latrines were dug in each camp and surrounded by hessian. Apart from providing interesting spectator value to the locals and the mishap of one member who fell in, these arrangements were adequate.

(d) Sleeping arrangements. Our two-man tents generally slept one, two or on occasion three people. Most were fitted with mosquito nets but at those altitudes, mosquitos and other insects were not much trouble. The wind and dust storms produced the most discomfort.

3. Monitoring team health
This was done by:

(a) carrying the records of the doctor's check from home
(b) recording various parameters at each new altitude reached, at approximately two-week intervals. We found the following:
   – blood pressure and pulse rates rose but after a varying number of weeks began to fall again.
   – haemoglobin and haematocrit levels rose as expected.
   – body weights fell during the source attempt but otherwise generally remained fairly stable.
   – urea and cholesterol estimations were unfortunately either insufficient or not accurate enough to draw conclusions.

For the haematocrit recordings we used an Ames mini-centrifuge which is small, light and very easy to use. The other blood tests were done using the companion Ames minilab, a small photometer. We had a number of problems using this under expedition conditions, but the main draw-back was that the bulky reagents needed to be maintained within a certain temperature range.

(c) Altitude adaptation assessment forms filled in by each member (see AMS).

(d) The expedition nurse, who treated minor ailments, checked out problems and recorded them on personal history forms.

4. Actual medical problems seen

(a) A few viral infections and gastrointestinal problems emerged during our stay in Chengdu.

(b) Sunburn. This was mainly a problem on the journey out to the river when many people suffered superficial burns following a day on a high pass digging vehicles out of the snow.

(c) Mild diarrhoea and vomiting.

(d) Dry cracked skin.

(e) Minor injuries.

5. Drugs used

We carried a large and comprehensive stock of drugs, considering our isolated situation. However, though the potential for accidents and illness with fifty people (including the Chinese team) on a dangerous expedition for four months was considerable, the team kept remarkably healthy.

The drugs we actually used were:

antibiotics – 3 courses

analgesics (aspirin, paracetamol) – small quantity

oral rehydration solution – 10

lomotil – small quantity

eye ointment or drops – 2

Tetanus research

Many observers have noted that tetanus is not common at altitude. The theory was propounded many years ago that this is related to the calcium content of the soil, and that in regions where calcium is washed out of the soil tetanus is rarely seen. We measured soil pH which is related to the calcium content, and found that calcium is present in moderate amounts. However, there were conflicting reports of the incidence of tetanus and so at present no firm conclusions can be drawn.

Visits to local hospitals

Besides hospitals visited in Chengdu and Lhasa, we were also able to visit those in Denke, Yushu and Qumerlai. The staff were warm in their welcome, showed us around their hospital and provided us with some interesting discussions on patient management. Yushu has 150 beds and a number of specialised departments; the other two were much smaller. We were particularly interested to see the mix of Chinese, Tibetan and western medicine and the way in which they are used to complement each other. Also the staffing structure of the health services in China where the term 'doctor' applies to many levels of health worker with varying lengths of training and expertise but who between them provide health care from the primary level up to specialist care.

The commonest conditions said to occur are respiratory, gastrointestinal, eye and ear infections.

In each hospital we were able to make donations of dressings and syringes and in Qumerlai, which has no electricity, we gifted solar lights.

Local health problems

Our impressions of medical needs were gleaned from patients we saw in hospital and from those who sought us out. We had hoped to be able to ascertain more from the villages near to our camps, but this proved impossible because of constraints of language and restrictions imposed upon us. Once it was known that we had a particular type of medicine, however, that disease suddenly became very popular. Nevertheless we saw and were able to help a number of people.

(a) Problems seen. The most common were:
    1. mild abdominal pain
    2. cataract
       corneal scars – both presenting with reduced vision
       conjunctivitis
    3. leprosy – obvious because of the deformities
    4. respiratory infections
       There were occasional cases of goitre, but China now has programmes for the iodination of salt.
(b) We distributed:
    1. glasses. Appreciated not only for the correction of visual defects but also for their appearance.
    2. blankets – of value in the severe cold of winter
(c) Of particular interest to us was the couple who brought their moribund newborn infant to the camp. We learnt so

much from the father who seemed naturally to know the importance of keeping the baby warm, of intimate contact with him and of resuscitation techniques. His appreciation of what we could do was quite genuine.

Veterinary involvement

The economy in these mountainous areas is based entirely on yaks, horses and sheep. During the Cultural Revolution each family was allowed only a certain number of animals, but recently these restrictions have been lifted. Obviously the health of their animals is extremely important to these people and it was in the expectation of being able to see something of the problems and perhaps of being able to contribute that the expedition had a vet.

In Chengdu Fiona visited the Vet School, and in Yushu the local vet hospital. In Qumerlai she made contact with the local officials and was taken around to see some of the sick animals. In fact there were no sick animals, but she was able to have some interesting discussions. Besides this she was an extremely adaptable member of the expedition and could turn her hand to almost any task.

Team health – post-expedition medical check

At a six-month check no expedition member reported any illness which could have been connected with the expedition. A further check will be conducted at twelve months.

Hover Doctor potential for the future

There are exciting prospects in the pipeline with new craft being developed at economical prices and low maintenance and repair costs. Workers in countries like Papua New Guinea and Bangladesh are expressing interest in the concept of the Hover Doctor service and both of these countries would be excellent locations for the hovercraft. In the same way that the Flying Doctor service makes a significant contribution to medical care in various parts of the world, we believe that the Hover Doctor service has a great potential for the future.

W. M. Gould MB, ChB, FRCS, DTM&H
R. G. Pinniger MB, ChB,
MRCP, DTM&H, DRCOG, DCH

APPENDIX F

Supporting sponsors

Principal sponsor

Neste Chemicals International (Finland)

Major sponsors

Ben Line
Cathay Pacific
Herbert Pool Ltd
ICI Chemicals and Polymers (C&P)
KHD Deutz
Loughborough University of Technology
PARAMINS Division of Exxon
   Chemical Company
Renault (UK)

Supporting sponsors

Alpha Courier Services
The April Trust
Army Catering Corps
Astral Post/Link Ltd
Autodesk
Barret-Howe Agency
Bayer China Co. Ltd (of Hong Kong)
Bayer UK Ltd (Baypharm)
Cyril Black Trust
BOC Ltd, Newport
Bowring Insurance
Bristol Royal Hospital Nurses' League
Bristow Helicopters

British Aerospace plc
British Council
British Telecom International
Britool Ltd
Brixham Baptist Church
Robert and Liz Brockbank
Brook Bond Foods
Bury & Hopwood Ltd
Calcomp Ltd
Campbell Scientific Ltd
Carbonflo
Card Protection Plan
Casio Electronics Co. Ltd
Charterhouse Textiles
Chiddingly Parish Church
Clark's Shoes
The Coldor Trust
Dr and Mrs R. F. J. Cole
Cyanamid
Dams Hall Wildfowl Trust
Dista Products Ltd
R. M. Douglas PLC
Dudley Stationery Ltd
Duphar Laboratories Ltd
ELE International Ltd
Ensors (Chartered Accountants)
ERL Systems
Eurotherm Ltd
Ewevale Ltd
Exxon (Esso) International Oil
Flectalon Ltd
Ford-Iveco Ltd
Foxprint
Marie France, Newberry
Francis Searchlights Ltd
Friends of St Luke's House, Brixham
Fuji Film
GB Britton
GEC-Plessey Telecommunications
Glaxo Allied Division
Gold Cross Pharmaceuticals
The Good News Trust

Gorsley Baptist Church
Granby Plastics (Nyloil)
Griffon Hovercraft Ltd
Mr Peter Gunner
Charles W. Hall (Hosiery) Ltd
Mrs Harvey
Harwell Research Establishment
Hawker-Siddeley Rail Projects
Viscountess Head
Hedley Trust
Hendersons
Mr Walter Hill
Hoechst UK Ltd
Horiba Instruments Ltd
Eric and Francis How
Lady Agnes Humphrey
Husky Computers Ltd
ICI China Ltd
ICL (International Computers Ltd)
Lillian James
Jones Lang Wootton (Hong Kong)
JVC (UK) Ltd
K Shoes
Karrimor Rucksacks
Keswick Pencils
Kimberley-Clarke
Kodak Films (Hong Kong)
Ladybird Books Ltd
Laerdal
Laing Properties
Major Nick Launders
Lederle Laboratories
Leicester City Council
Leicestershire Chambers of
    Commerce and Industry
Leicestershire County Council
LeisureMed Ltd
Lex Systems Leasing
Eli Lilley & Co. Ltd
Lilley Industries Ltd
Linguaphone UK
Lisbon University

Lloyds Bank plc
London Fan Co.
Lonely Planet (Roger Lascelles)
Lorex Pharmaceuticals
Loughborough Consultants Ltd
Mainair Sports
Maxell UK
May & Baker Ltd
MEDIA SVS
E. Merck Ltd
Merck Sharp & Doehme Ltd
Merieux UK
Monmouth Baptist Church
Mott MacDonald Consulting Engineers
Multifabs Ltd
NAP Engineering Microsoftware Ltd
Norris Hamilton Associates
Northern Engineering Industries
Nycomed
Nyloil Bearings
Overseas Development Administration
  (Embassy Fund, Beijing)
P & O
Mrs Sybil Payne
PERA
Pittard Garner plc
PLC Communications Ltd
Popeye's Gym
Mark Priest
Production Engineering Research Establishment
Quiggins Kendal Mint Cake
Racal
RADA
Mr and Mrs Randall
RARDE
Reckitt & Coleman
REME
Roche Products Ltd
The Royal Bank of Scotland (Holts, Farnborough Branch) –
  Expedition Bankers
Neville Russell Trust
St Peter's Church, Ditton

Safe-Breaker
Schering Health Care Ltd
Sentra Microfax
Silicon Express Ltd
Sleland SL
Smith & Nephew Pharmaceuticals Ltd
Smith Kline & French Laboratories
Sonomatic Ltd
South Cambridge Rotary
Span-Lok
Spanset
Spice of Life Restaurant
Stella-Meta Filters Ltd
Sterling Research Laboratories
Stuart Pharmaceuticals Ltd
Syntex Pharmaceuticals Ltd
Tarmac
Tear Fund
Trebor
TV-AM
Ullswater Cumbria Ltd
UNICEF
United Biscuits
Vector Instruments
Walker Charitable Trust
Waysun Communications HK Ltd
Mrs Beatrice Wilde
Wilfred Chan Management Consultants
Wilsons Kendal Mint Cake
Winchmore Hill Baptist Church
Winthrop Laboratories
Zenith Data Systems Ltd

APPENDIX G

The Expedition Team

Sqn Ldr Bob Abbott, MBE	UK liaison
Wg Cdr Stan Baldock, DFM, MBE	Artist
Sqn Ldr Dick Bell	Operations leader (Author)
Dr Arne Brantsaeter, Norway	Team doctor; interpreter
Sam Brooks	Scientist; negotiator
Jeremy Browne	Photographer
Tony Burgess	Engineer; planner; negotiator
Gareth Clegg	Medical
Sqn Ldr Mike Cole, OBE	Team leader
Capt. Gwyn Davies-Scourfield	Logistics leader
Chris Fox	Engineer
Dr Bill Gould	Team doctor
Peter Gunner	Engineer
Duncan Hanton	Logistics
Anne Hart	Engineer
Colin Hart	Logistics
Sqn Ldr Mike Holdsworth	UK liaison leader
Dr David Johnson, Brazil	Team doctor
Dr David Langley	Team doctor
Dee Larcombe	Logistics
Tim Longley	Hovercraft designer
Sarah Mather	Logistics
Bridget McClune	Medical
Revd Kevin Mentzel	Rations
Stephen Moody	Engineer
Sgt Jim Mudie	Engineer
Jim Newberry, USA	Engineer
Dr Rachel Pinniger	Medical leader

Mr Padman Ratnesar	Surgeon; negotiator
Fiona Rhodes	Veterinary surgeon
Keith Richardson	Negotiator
Dr Mel Richardson	Scientific leader
Ton Schreuders, Netherlands	Medical
Capt. Tony Shewell	Logistics
Neil Smith	Engineer
Andrew Sneller	Treasurer; negotiator
Giles Wadsworth	Logistics; interpreter
Capt. Rob Watson	Hovercraft driver; navigation leader
John Milton Whatmore	Publicity, PR and media

APPENDIX H

Contract between the expedition and the Chinese Academy of Science

CONTRACT

I. THIS DOCUMENT DESCRIBES THE FORMAL CONTRACT BETWEEN TWO PARTIES –

   1. CHENGDU DIVN OF MOUNTAIN DISASTER &
       ENVIRONMENTAL RESEARCH INSTITUTE,
           CHINESE ACADEMY OF SCIENCES . . . . (PARTY A)

   2. HOVERCRAFT SCIENTIFIC TEAM . . . . (PARTY B)

IN RELATION TO A SCIENTIFIC PROJECT INVOLVING THE OPERATION OF TWO HOVERCRAFT BELONGING TO PARTY B ON THE UPPER REACHES OF THE CHANG JIANG.

II. THE TERMS OF THE CONTRACT BETWEEN THE TWO PARTIES REFLECT THE SPECIAL RELATIONSHIPS WHICH EXIST AND THE SPECIAL NATURE OF PARTY B'S ACTIVITY, INCLUDING –

   1. THE FRIENDSHIP-LINK BETWEEN THE PROVINCE OF SICHUAN, PRC AND THE COUNTY OF LEICESTERSHIRE, UK

   2. THE SPECIAL RELATIONSHIP BETWEEN CHENGDU UNIVERSITY OF SCIENCE & TECHNOLOGY (POLYMER RESEARCH INSTITUTE) AND LOUGHBOROUGH UNIVERSITY (IPTME), AND THE MATERIALS EVALUATION PROPOSED WITHIN THE PROJECT

   3. THE CO-OPERATIVE SCIENTIFIC RESEARCH BETWEEN PARTIES A & B ON THE UPPER REACHES OF THE CHANG JIANG

4. THE CO-OPERATION BETWEEN PARTY B AND THE SICHUAN PROVINCIAL PUBLIC HEALTH BUREAU IN A PROGRAMME OF SEMINARS, VISITS, AND OTHER JOINT MEDICAL INITIATIVES AS MAY BE AGREED

III. THE CONTRACT BETWEEN THE TWO PARTIES RELATES DIRECTLY TO THOSE SERVICES PROVIDED BY PARTY A TO PARTY B IN RESPECT OF PARTY B'S OBJECTIVES OF REACHING THE RIVER, OPERATING ON IT, AND RETURNING FROM IT. WITH THE EXCEPTION OF AN ESTIMATED TWO OR THREE DAYS BEFORE LEAVING CHENGDU (FOR LOADING) AND TWO OR THREE DAYS AFTER RETURNING TO CHENGDU (FOR UNLOADING), THE CONTRACT RELATES ONLY TO ACTIVITY OUTSIDE CHENGDU.

IV. PARTY B WILL PAY THEIR OWN TRAIN AND AIR TICKETS FOR THEIR ANTICIPATED JOURNEY FROM GE'ERMO (GOLMUD) TO CHENGDU VIA XINING AND LANZHOU, AND FOR ANY OTHER TRAVEL BETWEEN CITIES IN CHINA. IT IS FURTHER PROPOSED THAT PARTY B WILL PAY THEIR OWN RAIL FREIGHT CHARGES FOR TRANSPORTING GOODS IN CHINA.

V. ANY SERVICES PROVIDED BY PARTY A TO PARTY B WHILST PARTY B IS IN THE PROVINCE OF SICHUAN APART FROM THOSE DESCRIBED IN CLAUSE IV ABOVE WILL BE THE SUBJECT OF A SEPARATE CONTRACT OR CONTRACTS.

VI. ALL PAYMENTS BY PARTY B TO PARTY A WILL BE IN FOREIGN EXCHANGE CERTIFICATE CURRENCY.

VII. REGISTRATION AND SCIENTIFIC PROGRAMME FEE

REGISTRATION: THE NUMBER OF PEOPLE INVOLVED IN THE PROJECT FROM PARTY B WILL BE 38 PERSONS. PARTY B WILL PAY PARTY A FEES FOR REGISTRATION AND PERMITS AMOUNTING TO 500 YUAN PER PARTY B PERSON, EFFECTIVE FOR THE WHOLE DURATION OF THE PROJECT.

SCIENTIFIC PROGRAMME FEE. PARTY B WILL PAY PARTY A THE SUM OF 20000 YUAN AS A SCIENTIFIC PROGRAMME FEE.

VIII. GUIDES

> GUIDES ARE THOSE CHINESE TEAM MEMBERS WHO ARE NOT
> CLASSIFIED AS DRIVERS OF VEHICLES. THIS CONTRACT RELATES
> TO THE PARTICIPATION OF 8 GUIDES –
>
> 5 ACADEMY OF SCIENCES
> 1 SMA
> 1 SCFAO
> 1 PSB
>
> PARTY B AGREES TO PAY FOR THE GUIDES AT THE FOLLOWING
> RATES –
>
> 1. EQUIPMENT COSTS: 700 YUAN PER GUIDE – THIS COST IS FOR
>   THE WHOLE DURATION OF THE PROJECT, IRRESPECTIVE OF
>   PROJECT DURATION. (MAKING A TOTAL OF 5600 YUAN)
>
> 2. SALARY: 37 YUAN PER GUIDE PER DAY, FROM THE DAY
>   THE PROJECT TEAM LEAVES CHENGDU TO THE DAY OF ITS
>   RETURN TO CHENGDU. (ASSUME 60 DAYS PROJECT DURATION
>   MAKING A TOTAL OF 17760 YUAN)
>
> 3. FOOD ALLOWANCE WHILST PROJECT TEAM AT CAMPS. AN
>   ALLOWANCE FOR FOOD NOT EXCEEDING 30 YUAN PER
>   GUIDE PER DAY DEPENDING ON THE EXTENT TO WHICH
>   THE GUIDES SHARE FOOD PROVIDED BY PARTY B WHILST
>   IN CAMP. WHEN PARTY B PROVIDES MEALS FOR GUIDES,
>   THIS ALLOWANCE WILL BE REDUCED BY 10 YUAN PER MEAL
>   PER GUIDE. (ASSUME 35 DAYS IN CAMP MAKING A TOTAL
>   OF 8400 YUAN)
>
> 4. INSURANCE: 300 YUAN PER GUIDE FOR THE WHOLE
>   DURATION OF THE PROJECT. (MAKING A TOTAL OF 2400)
>
> 5. 'HOTEL' ACCOMMODATION WHILST PROJECT TEAM AT CAMPS:
>   ON THOSE OCCASIONS WHEN GUIDES DO NOT USE THE
>   PROJECT TENTS PARTY B WILL PAY PARTY A AT THE RATE
>   OF 25 YUAN PER GUIDE PER NIGHT. (ASSUME 35 DAYS IN
>   CAMP MAKING A TOTAL OF 7000 YUAN)

IX. VEHICLES AND THEIR DRIVERS

> WHERE PARTY A PROVIDES VEHICLES FOR USE BY PARTY B,
> PARTY B WILL PAY PARTY A ACCORDING TO TYPE OF VEHICLE

AND ACTUAL DISTANCE TRAVELLED. THE CHARGES WILL BE
REDUCED IF PARTY B SUPPLIES FUEL.

THE TRUCKS FOR MOVING THE HOVERCRAFT TOGETHER WITH
THEIR DRIVERS ARE CHARGED ON A DIFFERENT BASIS TO THE
OTHER VEHICLES AND THEIR DRIVERS.

TRUCKS FOR THE HOVERCRAFT
   THE TWO TRUCKS FOR THE HOVERCRAFT ARE:
   ONE TO TOW THE LARGE HOVERCRAFT ON ITS TRAILER
   ONE TO CARRY THE SMALL HOVERCRAFT ON ITS LOAD BED

THE FOLLOWING IS AGREED:

   THAT THE FIXED PRICE OF 65000 YUAN WILL BE PAID FOR BOTH
      TRUCKS FOR UP TO 11500KM TOTAL DISTANCE TRAVELLED
   THAT IN ADDITION THE DRIVERS WILL BE PAID 40 YUAN PER
      DRIVER PER DAY. (ASSUME 60 DAYS PROJECT DURATION
      MAKING A TOTAL OF 2400 YUAN PER DRIVER)
   THAT IF ADDITIONAL DISTANCE IS TRAVELLED, AN
      ADDITIONAL PAYMENT OF 3.70 YUAN/KM WILL BE PAID
   THAT THE TRUCKS WILL BE FITTED WITH AIR BRAKES AND
      CARRY ICE-CHAINS
   THAT PARTY B WILL SUPPLY FUEL AS AVAILABLE, AND THAT
      PARTY A WILL PAY OR CREDIT PARTY B FOR SUCH FUEL
      ON THE SAME TERMS AS AGREED FOR THE OTHER TRUCKS
   THAT THE TRUCKS MAY BE ALLOCATED TO DUTIES OTHER
      THAN TOWING OR TRANSPORTING THE HOVERCRAFT

OTHER VEHICLES
THE BASIC PAYMENT FOR THE OTHER VEHICLES USED
(INCLUSIVE OF FUEL) IS AGREED AS FOLLOWS –

   1. SMALL BUS .... 4.00 YUAN/KM
   2. TRUCK .... 3.70 YUAN/KM
   3. PASSENGER VEHICLE FOR ROUGH ROADS .... 2.20 YUAN/KM

ON THESE DAYS OF VEHICLE USE, THE MINIMUM DISTANCES
CHARGED WILL BE AS FOLLOWS –

   1. SMALL BUS .... 120 KM
   2. TRUCK .... 100 KM
   3. PASSENGER VEHICLE FOR ROUGH ROADS .... 100 KM

ON SOME DAYS ONE OR MORE VEHICLES MAY NOT BE USED. ON
THESE DAYS A WAITING RATE WILL BE CHARGED AS FOLLOWS –

APPENDIX H

1. SMALL BUS . . . . 240 YUAN/DAY WAITING
2. TRUCK . . . . 150 YUAN/DAY WAITING
3. PASSENGER VEHICLE FOR ROUGH ROADS . . . . 100 YUAN/DAY
WAITING

PARTY B FUEL: IT IS AGREED THAT PARTY A WILL ACCEPT FUEL
FOR THEIR VEHICLES WHEN IT IS OFFERED BY PARTY B. IF
PARTY B SUPPLIES FUEL FOR PARTY A VEHICLES, PARTY
A WILL CREDIT THE TOTAL COST BY 0.91 YUAN PER KG OF
FUEL SUPPLIED.

DISTANCES TRAVELLED: THE ODOMETER OF EACH VEHICLE WILL
PROVIDE THE NORMAL BASIS OF CALCULATING DISTANCES
TRAVELLED.

DRIVERS. PARTY B WILL PAY PARTY A AN ALL-INCLUSIVE
ALLOWANCE OF 60 YUAN PER DRIVER PER DAY FOR THE
DRIVERS OF ALL VEHICLES PROVIDED BY PARTY A OTHER THAN
THOSE MOVING THE HOVERCRAFT.

X. 'ON THE ROAD' EXPENSES
THIS CLAUSE DOES NOT APPLY TO DRIVERS.

FOR FOOD AND ACCOMMODATION IN THE COUNTIES AND
DISTRICTS (THIS HAVING BEEN EARLIER DESCRIBED AS 'ON THE
ROAD' EXPENSES BETWEEN PROJECT CAMPS WHILST AWAY FROM
CHENGDU), PARTY B WILL PAY FOR THE FOOD AND
ACCOMMODATION FOR BOTH THEMSELVES AND PARTY A
MEMBERS. PARTY A WILL ASSIST WITH THE ARRANGEMENTS,
AND IN ADDITION TO THE COSTS PARTY B WILL PAY PARTY
A AN ADDITIONAL 10% AS A HANDLING CHARGE. (ASSUME AN
AVERAGE DAILY COST OF 45 YUAN PER GUIDE AND 25 DAYS
ON THE ROAD MAKING 9000 YUAN FOR THE GUIDES. ASSUME
30 PARTY B PERSONS, WITH AN AVERAGE 20 DAYS ON THE
ROAD MAKING 27000 YUAN. ASSUMED HANDLING CHARGE
OF 2700 YUAN)

SHOULD IT BE ABSOLUTELY ESSENTIAL FOR GUIDES TO RETURN
FROM THE PROJECT OTHER THAN IN THE VEHICLES CONTRACTED
TO PARTY B, PARTY B WILL PAY FOR THEIR TRAVEL, FOOD, AND
ACCOMMODATION EXPENSES AT THE RATE OF 60 YUAN PER
PERSON PER DAY UP TO THE FOLLOWING MAXIMUM VALUES –

FROM DEGE/DENGKE – 180 YUAN
FROM SHIQU/YUSHU – 240 YUAN

377

FROM QUMERLEI/QIDUKOU
OR TUOTUOHEYAN – 300 YUAN

XI.   OVERALL SERVICE CHARGE. AT THE CONCLUSION OF THE
PROJECT, IN ADDITION TO PAYING PARTY A IN ACCORDANCE
WITH CLAUSES VII-X ABOVE, AND CLAUSE XIII WHERE
APPROPRIATE, PARTY B WILL PAY TO PARTY A AN ADDITIONAL
15% OF THE TOTAL COST AS AN OVERALL SERVICE CHARGE.

XII.   PREMATURE CURTAILMENT

IF A DECISION IS TAKEN BY EITHER PARTY TO CURTAIL THE
PROJECT ACTIVITY, A COMPENSATION OF 10% OF THE COSTS
ALREADY INCURRED SHALL BE PAID BY THE PARTY MAKING
THE DECISION TO THE OTHER PARTY. SHOULD PREMATURE
CURTAILMENT ARISE FROM NATURAL CAUSES, ANY OF THE
EXPECTED REMAINING COSTS WOULD NOT BE PAYABLE, AND
ANY RESULTING PROBLEMS WOULD BE PROPERLY DISCUSSED.

XIII.   UNANTICIPATED COSTS. ANY COSTS INCURRED WHICH ARE NOT
THE SUBJECT OF THIS CONTRACT WILL BE MET BY THE PARTY
INCURRING THE CHARGE.

THE FOLLOWING ARE GIVEN AS EXAMPLES –

PARTY A WOULD PAY FOR THE REPAIR OR REPLACEMENT OF
A TRUCK TYRE SHOULD IT BE DAMAGED.
PARTY B WOULD PAY FOR THE HIRE OF LOCAL LABOUR IF
REQUIRED TO UNLOAD OR LOAD THE TRUCKS.
PARTY B WOULD PAY FOR THE EXTRA COSTS ARISING DUE TO
DELAYS FROM TRAFFIC CONGESTION.

XIV.   CONDITIONS OF CONTRACT

IT IS A CONDITION OF CONTRACT THAT

1. AN ADVANCE PARTY SHOULD LEAVE CHENGDU FOR THE
RIVER WITHIN TWO DAYS OF SIGNING THE CONTRACT
AND
2. THE MAIN GROUP OF PROJECT TEAM AND GUIDES SHOULD
LEAVE CHENGDU FOR THE RIVER WITHIN FIVE DAYS OF
SIGNING THE CONTRACT.
AND
3. THE REAR GROUP OF PROJECT TEAM AND A GUIDE SHOULD
LEAVE CHENGDU FOR THE RIVER WITHIN TWO OR THREE

DAYS OF THIS GROUP'S ARRIVAL IN CHENGDU. THEIR
ARRIVAL IS EXPECTED TO BE ON THE 2 MAY 1990.

XV. ADDITIONAL TAX

IN RESPECT OF BOTH THIS CONTRACT AND THAT FOR
THE FUEL MOVEMENT ARRANGED BETWEEN PARTY B AND
REPRESENTATIVES FROM CHENGDU AIRCRAFT CORPORATION
(CAC), PARTY B AGREES TO PAY PARTY A AN ADDITIONAL
10% OF THE TOTAL VALUE. THIS BEING UNDERSTOOD TO BE
A GOVERNMENT TAX TO BE CALCULATED AND PAID AT THE
CONCLUSION OF THE PROJECT.

XVI. TERMS OF PAYMENT –

1. PARTY A AND PARTY B AGREE THAT IMMEDIATELY
   FOLLOWING THE SIGNING OF THE FORMAL CONTRACT
   PARTY B WILL PAY PARTY A THE FOLLOWING AS AN
   INITIAL PAYMENT –

   20000 YUAN TO COVER INITIAL COSTS THE COST OF
   REGISTRATION DESCRIBED IN CLAUSE VII

   MAKING A TOTAL INITIAL PAYMENT OF 39000 YUAN.
   IF PARTY B DECIDES TO WITHDRAW FROM THE CONTRACT,
   THIS PAYMENT IS NOT REFUNDABLE. IF THE CONTRACT
   CONTINUES, THE PAYMENT BECOMES PART OF THE
   EVENTUAL TOTAL COST.

2. BEFORE LEAVING CHENGDU AT THE START OF THE PROJECT,
   PARTY B WILL PAY PARTY A AN ADDITIONAL SUM OF
   211000 YUAN TO MAKE A TOTAL ADVANCE PAYMENT OF
   250000 YUAN. PARTY B WILL PLACE A FURTHER 150000
   YUAN ON DEPOSIT WITH THE FOREIGN AFFAIRS OFFICE
   OF THE SICHUAN PROVINCIAL GOVERNMENT, AND THE
   FOREIGN AFFAIRS OFFICE WILL MONITOR THE PROGRESS
   OF THE PROJECT. ON RETURNING TO CHENGDU AT THE
   END OF THE PROJECT, BOTH PARTIES WILL CALCULATE
   THE COST ACCORDING TO THE CONTRACT TERMS, AND
   THE NECESSARY BALANCING PAYMENTS WILL BE MADE.

3. PARTY B GUARANTEES TO PAY IN FULL THE EVENTUAL
   TOTAL COST OF THE PROJECT ACCORDING TO CONTRACT
   TERMS. THE RIVER ROVER HOVERCRAFT WILL BE

> HELD AS SECURITY BY THE SICHUAN PROVINCIAL
> GOVERNMENT FOREIGN AFFAIRS OFFICE UNTIL THE
> FINAL PAYMENT IS MADE.
> ONCE FINAL PAYMENT IS MADE, THE SICHUAN PROVINCIAL
> GOVERNMENT FOREIGN AFFAIRS OFFICE WILL
> GUARANTEE THAT THE HOVERCRAFT CAN BE EXPORTED
> FROM CHINA WITHIN A MONTH.
> 50000 YUAN OF THE SCFAO DEPOSIT MAY BE PAID IN US
> DOLLARS AT AN EXCHANGE RATE OF 4.75 USD/YUAN FEC
> LESS BANK COMMISSION CHARGES.

XVII. BUDGETARY COSTS

> FOR THE PURPOSE OF CALCULATING AN ANTICIPATED CONTRACT
> VALUE THIS CONTRACT HAS ESTIMATED COSTS WRITTEN
> IN TO IT. THESE FIGURES, AND RELEVANT ASSUMPTIONS
> ARE CONTAINED WITH CURLY BRACKETS {}. BEFORE THE
> COMPLETION OF THIS PROJECT PARTY A AND PARTY B CANNOT
> CONFIRM THE ACTUAL COST.

– – – –

BOTH ENGLISH AND CHINESE VERSIONS OF THIS CONTRACT ARE OF
EQUAL EFFECT.

SIGNED FOR PARTY A: SIGNED FOR PARTY B:

Mr Xie Jinkang   Michael E. Cole

. . . .
Date: Date:

[Drafted 25 April 1990]

380

Map of Sichuan, Qinghai and Tibet

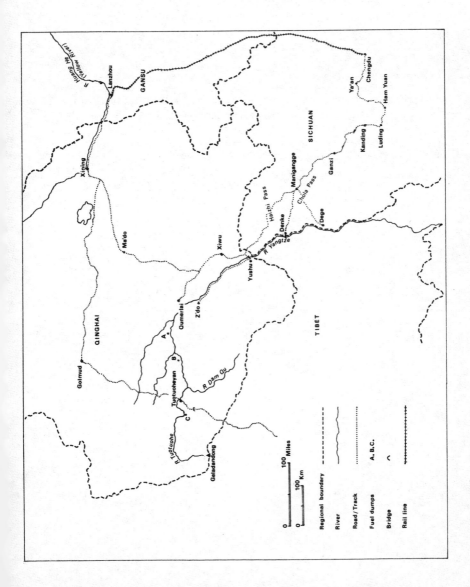